D1879695

IGNORED CLAIMS : A FOCUS ON TRIBAL EDUCATION IN INDIA

IGNORED CLAIMS

A Focus on Tribal Education in India

Editors

Dr. Nanjunda D.C.
Dr. Anjali Kurane
Dr. Steven Wind
Dr. Annapurna. M
Jyothi Lakshmi S.

PUBLICATIONS

KALPAZ PUBLICATIONS

Ignored Claims : A Focus on Tribal Education in India

Rs. 1250

© Editors

ISBN: 81-7835-679-1

All rights reserved.

Published in 2008 in India by
Kalpaz Publications
C-30, Satyawati Nagar,
Delhi-110052
E-mail: kalpaz@hotmail.com
Phone : 9212729499

Lasser Type Setting by: Quick Media, Delhi
Printed at : Singal Print Media, Delhi

Dedication

To the Tribal Children

Contents

Foreword

Empowerment means taking control over lives; becoming conscious of their own situation and position, setting their own agendas, creating space for themselves, gaining skills, building self-confidence, solving problems, and developing self-reliance. It is not only a social and political process, but an individual one as well - and it is not only a process but an outcome too. Realizing that Natives or Scheduled Tribes are one of the most deprived and marginalized groups with respect to education, most of the programmes and measures were initiated ever since the Independence. The issues and challenges in tribal's education can be categorized as external, internal, socio-economic and psychological. The external constraints are related to issues at levels of policy, planning and implementation while internal constraints are with respect to school system, content, curriculum, pedagogy, medium of instruction etc. The third set of problems relates to social economic and cultural background of tribals and psychological aspects of first generation learners. The literacy level of Scheduled Castes and Scheduled Tribes is very low compared to the general literacy rate. Recognizing that education provides opportunities for a permanent change in the socio-economic status of these people, this Government gives top priority to education.

The extent of education among tribal women is lamentably low. In most tribal societies, men and women enjoy equal status and work shoulder in home, the field and the forest. Women are not segregated or confined behind the *pardah*. If men alone are educated it creates an imbalance among couples with the husband educated and the wife unlettered. There is emotional mal adjustment. Educational young men long for educated wives and if they are even prepared to change their faith. It should also be remembered that the education of a girl has a more lasting impact on society than that of a boy. When the educated tribal girl becomes a mother and the mistress of a house, she will see to it that her children receive education even though it may mean some sacrifice and inconvenience for the family. Education of tribal girls would also provide a large number of women teachers for the primary schools. Nurses and women social welfare workers would also be available in large numbers. In many tribal areas, Ashram and Residential schools have proved very useful. Tribal's education planning should enable the tribals to learn the way of cooperation, acquire a sense of self-reliance and meet the new challenges of life. If the tribal's education programmers were sincerely worked out it would definitely bring tremendous change in the economic structure of tribal's areas also. Special vocational education is to be imparted to tribal girls in crafts like tailoring, cutting, typewriting, embroidery, and other non-traditional skills like computer education. Tribal's economic development is closely related to their educational development. Programmers of economic development and the spread of education should go side by side if both are to succeed. The approach to education should be flexible. Ashram schools , Vikaswadis and Non-formal education programs are well suited to tribal's cultural fabrication. Finnaly I would like to congratulate Dr. Nanjunda D C my friend and a good academician and other authors for their voluminous effort in bringing this volume. I wish all the success in their endeavor.

Dr. Iyyer Rhithelen Martin
Toronto-Canada

Introduction

Realizing that Scheduled Tribes are one of the most deprived and marginalized groups with respect to education, most of the programmes and measures have been initiated ever since the Independence. Elementary education was a priority area in the Tribal sub-plans from the 5th Five Year Plan. Education of ST children is considered important, not only because of the Constitutional obligation but also as a crucial input for total development of tribal communities. One of the super goals of SSA (serva shikshan abiyan) is to "bridge all gender and social category gaps at primary stage by 2007 and at elementary stage by 2010".

The issues and challenges in tribal education can be categorized as external, internal, socio-economic and psychological. The external constraints are related to issues at levels of policy, planning and implementation while internal constraints are with respect to school system, content, curriculum, pedagogy, medium of instruction etc. The third set of problems relates to social economic and cultural background of tribals and psychological aspects of first generation learners. The literacy level of Scheduled Castes and Scheduled Tribes is very low compared to the general literacy rate. Recognizing that education provides opportunities for a permanent change in the socio-economic status of these people, this Government gives top priority to education. Hence out of a sum of Rs. 548.91 crores provided in the Budget Estimate for 2006-2007 to this Department, more than70% is earmarked for schemes related to education. There is a need to evolve sensitive model of tribal education rooted in the psychological strengths of tribal children.

Implementing of Tribal Education in India

The strength of a society lies in the role of education in training, development and allocation of its manpower resources. Education has been conceived as training for better life and better social adjustment in a community or group. It is a phase of the social process which is fostered by society for life in-group. It can be said that education is the complete development of individuality so that one can make an original contribution to human life according to one's best capacity.

It is clear that in an under developed tribal community, where the poor people form the majority, owing to sheer poverty, they could not avail of the educational opportunities. Thus, the educational development of the marginalized people is inter linked with their socio economic condition. Hence prior to solving the problems associated with the educational backwardness of the tribals the problem of bread must be satisfied. Among the these people who hardly get meal twice a day, education is a tall talk, taking into account the predominant role played by socio economic factors in determining the utilization of facilities by the ST and SCs.

Education cannot change in any fundamental way unless we change our basic patterns of thinking and interacting so that learning can become a way of life. Teachers, parents, administrators, district resource and community people are coming together throughout hundreds of school communities to learn how to revitalize their schools with a process known as "Tribes." Evaluation of Tribes Learning Community Schools (TLC) has examined the impact of the Tribes process on student behavior, academic performance, school culture, and teacher collegiality. Studies have shown that; Tribes TLC has a positive impact on classroom environment, teachers report spending less time managing student behavior, students are significantly less likely to be referred for disciplinary problems, the Tribes process helps teachers address performance and content standards, students in well-implemented classrooms score significantly higher on standardized tests than students from comparison groups, teachers report increased staff collegiality and planning. "Responsive Education" is an essential pedagogy for academic achievement and school reform. It is the synthesis of artful teaching practices. It is based on understanding the critical developmental needs of a student age and cultural group. The Goal is to engage all teachers, administrators, students and families in working together as a learning community that is dedicated to caring and support, active participation and positive expectations for all students.

In spite of sixty years of independence and more than fifty five years of planned development and social provision for accelerated socio economic development of weaker sections, the gap in literacy levels among the general population and the socially disadvantaged sections is persisting and in some cases this gap is further widening. There were 16 million ST children (13.87 million of 6-11 years and 6.12 million of 11-14 years) as of March 2007, out of the total child population in India of about 198 million in the age group of 6 to 14 years. [Selected Educational Statistics – 2006 Government of India] – Education of ST children to considered important, not only because of the constitutional obligation but also as a crucial input for total development of tribal communities. Most tribal children do not understand the textbooks, which are generally in the regional language. The appointment of non-tribal teachers in tribal children's schools is another problem. The teachers do not know the language the children speak and children do not understand the teacher's language.

First of all I would like to Solute *Shri Shirdi Sai Baba* for his blessings. I owe a special debt to all the contributors for this edition. Further, I would like to thank University Grants Commission (UGC-) for providing fellowship to work on Tribal Education Project. I would like to thank all the Editors of various Journals, Books and Magazines. I am very thankful to my friend, guide and philospeher Dr. Steven wind (USA). Next, I am most grateful to Dr. Midatala Rani M, Prof. Annapurna M, DR. Anjali Kurane, Dr. Lancy D Souza for their vital role. I am also thnakful to Dr. Hari Mohan Mathur, Prof. P R G Mathur, Dr. B R Ghosh, Prof. Fleming Just, Dr. Jakka Partha Sarathy, Dr. Shiva Prasad, Dr. R S Reddy, Venu Gopal P N (Ph.D.) Jyothi Lakshmi S. Dr. Srivatsa, Dr. Manjula, Smt.Nandini, and Raji for their logistic help. I owe a deep sense of gratitude to Nagesha D, Linga Raju, Suresh Kumar M, Dr. Sneha, Raji and Asha, H for there role. Somehow I could not contact few authors to acknowledge their contributions. Hence, I am hereby greatly acknowledging their articles. More imporetenlty I am very thankful to the proprietor of Kalpaz Publication. Heartful thanks to my parents also. Further, I extend my acknowledgement to the research staff Editorial Committee of my NGO sharing their knowledge.

Dr. Nanjunda DC

1

Tribals and Human Development : A Policy Analysis

—*Naresh C. Saxena*

Tribals are at the bottom of social and political ladder in India. Development projects have not only bypassed them, but have often harmed them by taking away their lands and other resources on which their livelihood was based. Unless the processes which result in their proletararianization are identified and corrective action taken to prevent it, chances are that new programmes will continue to ignore their interests as in the past. Articulation of such processes will not only lead to appropriate solutions but it also helps in sensitizing field officers who in the past often held a negative stereotype about tribals. From the viewpoint of policy, it is important to understand that tribal communities are vulnerable not only because they are poor, asset less and illiterate compared to the general population; often their distinct vulnerability arises from their inability to negotiate and cope with the consequences of their forced integration with the mainstream economy, society, cultural and political system, from which they were historically protected as the result of their relative isolation. Post-independence, the requirements of planned development brought with them the specter of dams, mines, industries and roads on tribal lands. With these came the concomitant processes of displacement, both literal and metaphorical—as tribal institutions and practices were forced into uneasy existence with or gave way to market or formal state institutions (most significantly, in the legal sphere), tribal people found themselves at a profound disadvantage with respect to the influx of better-equipped outsiders into tribal areas. The repercussions for the already fragile socio-economic livelihood base of the tribals were devastating—ranging from loss of livelihoods, land alienation on a vast scale, to hereditary bondage. As tribal people in India perilously, sometimes hopelessly, grapple with these tragic consequences, the small clutch of bureaucratic programmes have done little to assist the precipitous pauperisation, exploitation and disintegration of tribal communities. Tribal people respond occasionally with anger and assertion, but often also in anomie and despair. However that too is branded as a typical 'law and order' problem, ignoring its socio-economic dimensions. Briefly speaking, the following persistent problems have by and large remained unattended, and need immediate redressal: Relation with forests, and government monopoly over Non Timber Forest Products-NTFPs Land alienation and indebtedness Involuntary displacement due to development projects and lack of proper rehabilitation Ineffective implementation of Panchayats (Extension to the Scheduled Areas) Act of 1996 (PESA, 1996) for Schedule V areas Shifting Cultivation Weak governance, and poor programme delivery, especially in health and education, and Insensitive reaction to upsurge of tribal anger against the exploitative system. These are discussed below.

There is much evidence to show that tribals' access to NTFPs for meeting their basic subsistence needs has deteriorated, and that this is fairly widespread. Some of the processes which have caused this are; deforestation, preference for man-made plantations in place of mixed forests, regulatory framework, diversion of NTFPs and forests to industries, nationalization of NTFPs, and exploitation by government agencies and contractors in marketing of NTFPs. The nationalization of the NTFP commodities, done in different states in various years from1960s to the end of 1970s, presumably with the intention of helping the poor, has affected their interests adversely. Nationalization reduces the number of legal buyers, chokes the free flow of goods, and delays payment to the gatherers, as government agencies find it difficult to make prompt payment. This results in contractors entering from the back door, but they must now operate with higher margins required to cover uncertain and delayed payments by government agencies, as well as to make the police and other authorities ignore their illegal activities. This all reduces tribals' collection and incomes. Initially, this right was acquired ostensibly to protect the interest of the poor against exploitation by private traders and middlemen. Since the state could generate revenue (royalty) through exercising this monopoly right, it has been steadily extended to cover myriad of NTFPs. On paper the state agencies have worked with multiple objectives - to collect revenue; to protect the interests of the tribals as sellers; and to satisfy the conflicting demands by industry and other end users. In practice, a hierarchy of objectives developed: industry and other large end-users had the first charge on the product at low and subsidized rates; revenue was maximized subject to the first objective which implied that there was no consistent policy to encourage value addition at lower levels; tribal and the interest of the poor was relegated to the third level. A close scrutiny of the political economy of institutions involved in marketing is essential. The Corporations set up by the state (KFDC in Kerala, GCC in AP, LAMPS in Jharkhand) are confronted with growing liabilities. They have a huge and redundant capital and man-power base. Even on variable cost basis, they need huge mark-ups to break-even. Faced with this situation, they wish to pursue a completely risk-averse policy. In the commodities that the Corporations trade, purchase transactions are first finalized; these selling prices are down-marked to fix the procurement prices for the tribals; because of the middlemen involved, the actual prices received by the tribals could be lower still. More generally, under the current policy of the day, the institutions have opted to extend their role by becoming reenters. Beginning with bamboo and sal seeds, collection rights of a large number of NTFPs have been given to paper mills, owners of oil extraction plants, and auction bidders (Tamil Nadu and Karnataka). State monopoly has provided room for private monopoly, and is aiding and abetting market imperfections. In order to ensure that tribals' livelihoods are supported by NTFPs, one would have to address three inter-related issues; how to increase NTFP production, how to improve access of the poor to NTFPs, and how to maximize their incomes through marketing. Norms for silvicultural practices were developed in times prior to the current scenario of high human and cattle pressures, and must now be adjusted accordingly. If the national objectives have changed to prioritize people's needs, there must be an accompanying change in silvicultural practices and technology. One requires a complete reversal of the old policies, which favored commercial plantations on forest lands, and trees for consumption and subsistence on private land. "Scientific" forestry should therefore mean that environmental functions, wild fruits, nuts, NTFPs, grasses, leaves and twigs become the main intended products from forest lands and timber a by-product from large trees like mahua and sal. The reverse has been the policy for the last 100 years. Although after the advent of the new forest policy in 1988 there has been great efforts to involve forest communities in management, more thought should be given to make necessary changes in the technology which will be suitable to the changed objectives. Secondly, a government agency like the Forest or the Tribal Development Department assisted by civil society should be involved in informing tribals and gatherers about the prices prevailing in different markets, improve marketing practices, and act as a watch-dog. It maybe worthwhile to examine if promotional Marketing Boards, as distinct from commercial corporations (which are inefficient, and hence demand monopoly), should be set up with responsibility for dissemination of information about markets and prices to the gatherers. Government should encourage bulk buyers and consumers such as exporters of herbal medicines establish direct links with the villagers. Government should also address issues like creating proper marketing yard, market information system, storage space and minimum processing facilities at the local level. Simple processing activities such as broom making, leaf plate making, tamarind processing, mat and rope making should be encouraged in the household/ cottage sector. It has often been suggested that there should be price-based aggressive buying of NTFPs by state agencies, as has been done for wheat and rice. This alone can break the dominance of the wholesale traders and their linkages with the village level market. The nature of produce and actors involved makes it obvious that without government support there can be no justice to forest gatherers. While assigning a bigger role to government institutions, which were earlier accused of inefficiency, collusion with traders, and callous attitudes towards forest gatherers, care needs to taken that there is all round improvement in governance and in efficiency of the States' organisations. Price support combined with aggressive buying from government can certainly improve gatherers' incomes, but it becomes difficult to sustain it over a long period. Government corporations make huge losses, and therefore the entire operation requires continuous subsidy from the government. While such subsidies can be justified easily as a part of the poverty alleviation programmes, continued subsidies can result in subsidizing inefficiency and corruption of government organisations. Therefore such organisations should compete with private trade, and not ask for monopoly. Collaboration with socially committed private sector/exporters should also be considered. Clearly laissez faire is not going to help the poor in all cases. Where government alone does marketing it is inefficient; and where it is left to private trade, it may still not provide sufficient returns to the gatherer on his labour. Thus de-nationalization per se may not remove all market constraints which inhibit a gatherer in realizing the full value of his labour. To conclude, rather than be a monopoly buyer of NTFPs or try to regulate price through panchayats, government should adopt market friendly policies, facilitate private trade, and act as a watchdog rather than eliminate the trade. It should encourage local bulking, storage and processing, and bring large buyers in touch with the gatherers, so as to reduce the number of layers of intermediaries. 1.2 Specific suggestions for tendu Tendu (Diospyros melanoxylon) leaves play a vital role in the economic life of central India. The tree is called Blackwood (Indian ebony), and is of less significance than its shrub, whose leaves are used for making bidis (an indigenous cigarette, which uses the tendu leaf instead of paper). Tendu (called Kendu in Orissa) fruit, which is sweet, is also eaten but has little marketing value, rarely even making it to the local weekly markets in tribal areas. For the poor, plucking of tendu leaves represents a major source of income and employment especially since it coincides with the slack period of the agricultural cycle. Tendu leaf generates 150 million person days of employment during the agricultural lean season in Orissa including labour involved in making bidis. Jharkhand, Madhya Pradesh and AP should also be generating similar numbers for employment through tendu.

The massive sums of money involved in the tendu business offer opportunities for patronage to both big and petty politicians and forest department officials. In the former case, the money is to be made in the process of negotiating tenders in the disposal of tendu leaves, while in the latter case, power and influence is exercised in selecting the agents who handle the purchasing centers. These agents get advances from the forest department to purchase tendu leaves or sal seeds and get a commission on the final amount. The purchasing agents are experts at under weighing, wrong entries and sheer blustering, and for them tendu and sal seed purchasing contract can be very rewarding. At the local level then, there is a great deal of jockeying to get the contracts. For the field level forest staff, such as Rangers and Forest Guards, collection of tendu is a highly lucrative business. There are several sources through which they are able to enrich themselves. First, in the appointment of fictitious seasonal staff that is appointed for carrying out government work. The FD in Orissa alone engages about 40,000 seasonal workers and labourers, some of them are non-existent. This is in addition to about 8 to 12 lakh pluckers who are to be paid according to the fixed government rates. However, the usual practices of under-counting, rejection, under-payment, over-invoicing, etc. help the government staff in pocketing a significant amount of government funds, at the cost of peoples' livelihoods and extra revenues to government. Given the enormity of scale of operation, tendu has to continue under State nationalization. Private trade would not be able to arrange for 15 to 20 billion Rs. in just 40 to 50 days that is required during the season every year in central India for the entire operation. Although revenue generation has a higher priority for government, the entire operation has several elements of welfare and poverty alleviation too, because of its significance for local employment in the agriculturally slack season. Pluckers are lately getting organised, and part of the explanation for increase in their wages must be the pressure they are able to generate on the political system. Both these objectives – revenue and employment – would suffer under private regime. Further, bringing in private traders would again encourage political patronage and corruption, as was the experience before tendu was nationalized in the seventies. The present system, however, has a large number of infirmities. The following suggestions would improve benefits to the pluckers. States should pass on the enormous profits made in the tendu leaf trade as bonus to the tendu pluckers. Even if 50 per cent of the royalty (surplus) generated from the tendu leaves as of now is shared with the pluckers, it would, on an average lead to an additional income of Rs. 1000 to Rs. 1500/- per annum per household (HH). A detailed analysis for the Bolangir tendu division shows that sharing of 50 per cent of royalty would increase the total earnings of an average HH from tendu plucking upto Rs. 3000/- per annum, more than what most of these HHs earn from agriculture (Vasundhara 1998). Considering that almost all the families involved in tendu collection are below the poverty line, this additional income assumes great importance for their livelihood. The importance of this additional direct income (over Rs. 200 crores a year) for the rural poor can be understood by the fact that to generate the same amount of income through IRDP investment, an amount of approximately Rs. 1000 crores will have to be invested (assuming that all the investments are successful and there are no leakages of funds).The collection prices should be hiked so that returns from plucking are at least equivalent to the minimum wages fixed for unskilled agricultural work by the states. Even in Andhra Pradesh, where wages are higher by about 15 per cent than in Orissa, despite Orissa's leaves being superior in quality, a study (IAMR, 1998) showed that returns from leaf collection were only 55 per cent of the minimum wages, and 87 per cent of what they would get elsewhere in the market. Pluckers in MP get slightly less than in Orissa, but are compensated because the government does not keep any profit with itself, and the entire profit is ploughed back to the pluckers. In Madhya Pradesh, gatherers share in profits through a bonus plan at the end of each season, whereas in Orissa, the gatherers get only wages for collection. Village level tendu pluckers' SHGs and cooperatives should be gradually given the responsibility of managing collection centers, and their maintenance etc. At present these are managed by petty contractors, with long experience in this line. Mechanisms for linking quality of tendu leaves with purchase prices should be explored. Possible local institutional arrangements to improve the quality of tendu produced through various arrangements such as contracting out bush cutting to tendu pluckers associations, forest committees etc., linking bonus to Phad wise realisation of sales etc. should be explored.

Uniform pricing of tendu leaves, irrespective of their quality. does not inspire the pluckers to procure leaves of better quality. Therefore payment should be related to the quality of leaves. Delayed payments should carry an interest of 15 per cent per annum. All records pertaining to names of people employed and their period together with date of payment should be displayed on the district website for anyone to verify. The Group Insurance for tendu pluckers as followed in MP should be adopted in Jharkhand and Orissa. Part of the income from tendu plucking can be saved by the pluckers through forming SHGs - this would help them in avoiding credit from moneylenders at a high interest. The payments to pluckers should be made weekly with no delay. This will require procedural changes in the way funds flow to the phad. The entire tendu trade is the exclusive responsibility of the Forest Department or its agencies, and there is no internal review of its limitations and failures by other sister departments of government. The Department of Rural Development, which is incharge of poverty alleviation and the Department of Social (or Tribal) Welfare which is supposed to look after the interest of tribals and scheduled castes take no interest in the tendu operation, although millions of the supposedly target group who are the responsibility of these departments are affected by the poor implementation of the tendu procurement. Had these departments been more vigilant, there would have been pressure on the Forest Department to improve its performance. It is unfortunate that there are no effective administrative mechanisms in the states for inter-departmental coordination for achieving the broader goal of welfare of the poor. The Indian administrative culture does not encourage one department critically appraising and reviewing schemes of the other department. We suggest that an inter-departmental Study Team/Commission should be set up to look into our suggestions as well as the systems being followed by other States (especially MP). The Commission could also suggest ways to achieve the objective of welfare maximization for the tendu pluckers. The Commission/Committee should include members from tendu Union, representatives of tendu pluckers and from NGOs and academic institutions. This independent Commission should study the purchase operations every year and give its assessment on the extent it has furthered peoples' livelihoods and how the operations have improved as compared to previous years' campaign. It should also suggest practical measures to improve transparency and reduce corruption in the purchase operations. Its suggestions should be considered by the Cabinet. The states have to give primacy to the welfare aspects of tendu production and trade, and relegate revenue objectives to the secondary position. Tendu trade is one opportunity where Self-Help Groups - self-selected groups which start savings and credit using group-devised savings and credit modalities, and may move on to take up other joint income generating activities.

Several NGOs working on JFM have preferred JFM committees over panchayats as the organisational unit for managing the resource and sharing benefits. It is undoubtedly easier for them (and also for Forest Department) to deal with new and informal organisations that they3Secretary to the Ministry of E & F tried to reconcile the differences in a circular issued in 1998, but it had little effect in the field.

In Andhra Pradesh there is a clear contradiction between PESA and GOM 173 dt. 7/12/96 of the Environment, Forest, Science and Technology Department. The Usufructory Rights of Vana Samrakshana Samitis prescribed therein include, '(a) All Non-Timber Forest Produce except those for which GCC holds monopoly rights. However the right to collection shall remain with the VSS members, if they so desire. The members shall be paid the collection charges upon delivery of the produce as per the rates fixed by the Government'. It can also be seen that there is a contradiction between the `ownership' vesting in Gram Panchayats/Sabhas clause and the monopoly rights vested in GCC. Whether bamboo constitutes major or minor forest produce is also an unsettled question. Another problem with the Orissa legislation is that instead of giving clear rights to Gram Sabha, space has been kept in the state law for involvement of higher order Panchayati Raj institutions instead. This has been done because it is easier for local politicians and bureaucracy to manipulate Chairperson of district or block level panchayats, but not that easyto do so with the Gram Sabha. Thus the spirit of the GoI Act with focus on empowerment of the Gram Sabha has not been followed in Orissa. This is again a violation of the Central Act 4 Many other states have also diluted the GoI Act.

Both the Gujarat and Maharashtra Acts make ownership subject to the relevant state acts on NTFPs. The Maharashtra state Act leaves bamboo and cane out of the list of NTFPs over which ownership is granted to the panchayats. which explicitly forbids usurpation of powers of a lower level panchayat by a higher level panchayat. Such indifference to PESA can be seen in many other states too. The irony is that while PESA remains unimplemented, Ministry of Mines in GoI has proposed amending Schedule V of the Constitution itself to open up tribal areas for commercial exploitation by national and multi-national corporate interests. The afforestation schemes in AP often ignore tribal customary tights over podu (shifting cultivation) lands. A recent report on Andhra Pradesh by OXFAM shows that although FD does not evict podu cultivators, it includes old podu lands within the scope of JFM, which increases the fears of the tribals that after wage earning programs are withdrawn, their food security would be jeopardized. The report goes on to conclude that JFM has failed to give fair attention to the forest dependent communities, such as tribal artisans, headloaders and podu cultivators. The MTR and other reports of the AP Mission do not discuss the impact of JFM on shifting cultivators, who are all tribals. 1.4 Tribal eviction from forest lands It is clearly stated in the Common Minimum Program that "Eviction of tribal communities and other forest dwelling communities from forest will be discontinued.' However, notwithstanding the assurance given to the adivasis, they continue to be evicted, threatened with eviction or assaulted by armed police brought to evict them. The threat of eviction, which confronts about 1.5 million adivasi families in the country is a result of the failure of the respective Forest Departments to implement the Guidelines issued by the Government of India on 18thSeptember 1990. In view of the large scale threat confronting 1.5 million tribal families, the Inspector General of Forests issued a letter on 30thOctober 2003 assuring that no eviction drive will be undertaken without implementing the Guidelines of 18thSeptember 1990 mentioned above. The Government of Maharashtra laid down a procedure to ensure implementation in a transparent and participatory manner with the concurrence of the Gram Sabha through an Order dated 10thOctober 2002. This is the only example of a procedure being adopted by any state government. GoI should make certain that a transparent and participatory procedure as laid down by the Government of Maharashtra is uniformly adopted across the country. This should ensure that (*a*) All concerned are informed, (*b*) All encroachers have the opportunity to make their claims in their language, (*c*) The weaker sections of the community are spared the time and expense of travel, and (*d*) An assembly of the village should be held to ensure participation of the community. Lastly, Ministry of E & F should approach the Court with a pro-tribal stance. In the past, the Supreme Court has not hesitated to defend the interests of the tribals in a responsive and responsible manner. In the Banwasi Sewa Ashram cases (1985-1994), the Court made available special courts and legal aid to ensure that adivasis were restored the lands to which they were entitled and which were under threat of acquisition for afforestation. This was one of the massive and impressive actions undertaken by the Supreme Court, which reconciled ecological needs with tribal needs. Such an exercise is necessary now. In Pradip Prabhu's case (1995), the Supreme Court remanded matters back to Maharashtra to determine the rights of landless adivasis who had land entitlements under the Government's own plans. Similar orders were passed for Madhya Pradesh. In the Samata case (1997), a majority decision took a comprehensive view of the entitlement of tribals to the land and its rich resources to direct that benefits from those areas must secure the uplift and socio-economic empowerment of the adivasis. Even after the Balco case (2001), the Samata judgment is unscathed as a fitting testimony to how an equitable justice can reach the most disadvantaged. Now comes the Forest case. I am certain that the Supreme Court did not intend a volte face on previous commitments to social justice for tribals. But much depends on Government of India's petition before the Court. Rather than take a narrow view, MOEF should consult the Ministry of Tribal Affairs, and other stakeholders and not misuse the Supreme Court's order to terrorise the tribals. On the other hand enthused by the huge influx of arbitrary power, the MEF — in furtherance of the Court's orders — created the Jaykrishnan Committee with no tribal representation and with lay members more concerned with animals than the ecology as a whole. Past policies and commitments appear to have been forgotten and swept under the carpet.The Ministry of E & F has recently (21st December, 2004) issued a circular, the relevant portion is being quoted below: 'After a critical examination of the issue of settlement of claims over forest lands and eviction of ineligible encroachers of forest lands, what emerges is that the State/UT Governments were not able to distinguish between the encroachers, and the original tribals and other forest dwellers living on forest lands since time immemorial. The Central Government is convinced that the difficulty in distinguishing between genuine tribals/ forests dwellers and ineligible encroachers by the State Governments/UT Administrations is the main cause of the problems of tribals. Therefore, some kind of interim measures are necessary to safeguard the interests of the tribals and forest dwellers who have been living in forests since long, and whose disputed claims are yet to be settled. In view of the above, and without prejudice to Supreme Court's order dated 23-11-2001 and 23-2-2004, it has been found appropriate to request the State/UT Governments, that as an interim measure, they should not resort to eviction of tribal people and forest dwellers other than ineligible encroachers, till the complete survey is done for the recognition of such people and their rights, after setting up of District level Committees involving a Deputy Collector, a Sub-Divisional Forest Officer, and a representative of Tribal Welfare Department, by the State/UT Governments as reiterated in guidelines dated 18-09-1990 and 30-10-2002 of the Central Government. The State/UT Governments are advised to exclude such tribals/ forest dwellers, other than ineligible encroachers, from the eviction drives. Simultaneously, it is also clarified here that this interim measure does not stop State/UT Governments from evicting the ineligible encroachers from forest lands. Suitable instructions may be issued to forest functionaries at all levels to keep the aforesaid in view while dealing with eviction of ineligible encroachments from forest lands.' It is hoped that the state governments will stop tribal eviction after this order, and hasten the process of regularisation of their occupation over forest lands, as has been suggested in the circular issued in September 1990. 2 Land alienation and indebtedness: Tribal land alienation is the most important cause of the pauperisation of tribal people, rendering their economic situation, which is extremely vulnerable even at the best of times, even more precarious. We have already noted how the access of tribals to forests for their livelihoods has shrunk both because forests themselves have shrunk, and because the regulatory regime continues to restrict tribals from collecting and processing non-timber forest produce for their livelihoods. Shifting cultivation has also been severely restricted. The most important livelihood option of the tribal today is settled agriculture. However, as tribals are systematically deprived of their cultivable holdings, by non-tribals and even by government itself, they are reduced to asset less destitution. The Department of Rural Development, Government of India commissioned in 1997-98 a number of state-specific studies of the problem, and reports were then received from Bihar, Andhra Pradesh, Madhya Pradesh, Gujarat, Rajasthan and Maharashtra.

The reports paint a grim and disturbing picture, which confirm that massive alienation of tribal lands continues in tribal regions in all parts of the country. The magnitude of the problem can be assessed in the Andhra Pradesh report for instance, from the fact that today non-tribals own more than half the land in Scheduled Areas of the state. The figure is 52 per cent in Khamman district, 60 per cent in Adilabad district and 71 per cent in Warangal district. It may be noted that these are official figures based on land records, and would not include 'benami' holdings in the name of tribals but held by non-tribals. Situation in Andhra Pradesh The lush green jungles of the Eastern Ghats, spread over nine districts of Andhra Pradesh and comprising 11,595 sq. miles of the State, are no longer a secure haven for nearly 33 tribal communities, including seven primitive groups, inhabiting these highlands. In the four decades since Independence, the tribals have steadily lost their hold on much of this area. While many have lost their sources of livelihood, others have sought refuge in deep forests. According to the 1991 census, the region's tribal-non-tribal ratio had dropped to 2:1 from the 1950 proportion of 6:1. And this demographic change has been largely brought about by official policies. Thanks to amendments made to the land transfer regulations in the tribal belt by the government, the non-tribals are holding almost 55 per cent of tribal lands either benami or through clandestine means. The setting up of minor and medium irrigation projects in areas meant for tribals has been another way to dispossess the locals. Although such projects came under tribal sub-plans, the emphasis was on cultivating crops alien to the Adivasis. For example, the tribal sub-plan for Warangal district is aimed at bringing 1.56 lakh hectares under cultivation, though tribals hold only 24,000 hectares. Apparently, the government has been sanctioning too many reservoirs, minor irrigation schemes, lift irrigation and medium canals in the tribal belt only to facilitate the cultivation of land occupied by people from the plains. While the non-tribal is holding the rich lands, the tribal has to depend on podu (hill slope) cultivation. The continuing gravity of the problem in Madhya Pradesh has been assessed by the Census which reveals that the percentage of Scheduled Tribe cultivators to total Scheduled Tribe workers fell from 76.45 per cent in 1961 to 68.09 per cent in 1991. Correspondingly the percentage of Scheduled Tribe agricultural labourers to total Scheduled Tribe workers rose from17.73 per cent to 25.52 per cent. Similar empirical evidence is available from other states as well. The studies commissioned by the Government of India have revealed the causal chain that leads to this state of affairs and confirmed that the fundamental reason for tribal land alienation is the fragile, constantly shrinking economic base of the tribals. Their traditional skills in the gathering of forest produce lost significance with the introduction of state ownership of forests, so that from food-gatherers they were reduced to wage-earners or encroachers. Private property in land extinguished the erstwhile right of tribal communities to free access to land in consonance with their needs. Settled agriculture brought with it its inevitable linkages with credit, inputs and markets, rendering the tribal even more dependent and vulnerable. As the tribals have an innate fear based on bitter past experience of banks, cooperative institutions and other government sources of credit; they prefer the predictability of the moneylender despite his usurious interest rates. In any case, most banks and cooperative institutions are unwilling to provide consumption loans, and moneylenders are the only sources of consumption credit. A combination of these factors leads to an extreme dependence on moneylenders on the part of the tribal, keeping him in perpetual debt and resulting in the mortgage and ultimate loss of his land. Though this phenomenon is common enough, another particularly tragic outcome of this indebtedness is the phenomenon of bondage, wherein people pledge their person and sometimes even that of their families against a loan. Repayments are computed in such terms that it is not unusual for bondage to persist until death, and to be passed on as a burdensome inheritance to subsequent generations. The practice of bonded labour is known by different names in different regions. In Rajasthan, it is called Sagri; in Andhra, Vetti; in Orissa, Gothi; in Karnataka, Jethaand in Madhya Pradesh, Naukri Nama. The studies also establish the sad fact that government policy itself has, directly or indirectly, contributed to the phenomenon of tribal land alienation. It has been noted in several states that tribal land is being legally auctioned by co-operative credit societies and banks to recover dues. Auctioned land is purchased by non-tribals as well as rich tribals. Authorities responsible for regulating sale of tribal lands to non-tribals have been found to frequently collude with non-tribals to defraud the tribal landowners. The same collusion has deprived tribals of their rights to land in times of land settlement, or implementation of laws giving ownership rights to occupancy tenants. A study by the Tribal Research Institute, Madhya Pradesh concluded that 'while on the one hand section 165(6) of the M.P. Land Revenue Code prohibits transfer of land fromaboriginals, the later part of the same section permits it under certain conditions. All other clauses in the interest of the aboriginals seem to be overshadowed by this and transfer of the land from the tribal to the non-tribal is a regular feature'.

The study notes that 46.3 per cent of cases in which the Collector gave permission to the tribal landowner to sell land was for the repayment of government loans. The reports states 'Indebtedness is the main cause of land alienation. Actually what happens in the area is that tribals mortgage their land to non-tribals and take loans...... They would then take loan from Government and use it for repayment of the private debts. Having failed to pay the loan due to Government, they apply for permission to sell land which is granted. In fact the sale is to the mortagagee, while on paper it assumes the shape of innocent transfer for repayment of Government loans'. The study further notes that 'the quantum of illegal (benami) land alienation from tribals to non-tribals is like that part of the iceberg that remains under the surface of water. Seemingly though the quantum of legal transfers is not very much, the incidence of illegal transfers not easily detectable is very high'. In order to secure redressal and reversal of such systematic subversion of these protective laws, the Madhya Pradesh legislature in 1976, and then in 1980, introduced highly significant amendments in the Land Revenue Code, 1959 to secure belated justice to the dispossessed tribal landowners, particularly through the section 170(B) of the Code. There were many powerful elements in this Section 170(B), some without parallel in any other state. It instituted *suomoto* responsibility of the revenue court to enquire into all transactions from tribal to non-tribal, even without an application from the tribal. The burden of proof was shifted to the non-tribal to prove that fraud did not take place, and the presumption of the court supported the legal rights of the original tribal landowner. Appearance of advocates without permission has also been debarred in these proceedings. There is provision for a single appeal to the Collector. Despite the existence of such a radical piece of legislation for social justice for tribals, its implementation has been in most districts of the state not in consonance with both the letter and the spirit of the law. Land of which possession has been officially restored to the original tribal landowners forms only 12.65 per cent of the total land under dispute. But given the socio-economic realities facing tribals and their powerful non-tribal opponents, it is unlikely that even after receiving formal legal possession of even this small proportion of their erstwhile lands, tribals would have the local administrative and political muscle to ensure that they would retain possession. 2.1 Leasing of cashew plantations in Orissa: In Orissa, cashew plantation has been raised by Soil Conservation Department on 120,000 hectares of "Government Wastelands" in Schedule V areas. In many cases such lands in the past were under cultivation by tribals but their rights were not recorded. In many regions of Central India land records were generally in a bad shape where land was of poor quality, as such lands did not have the potential of giving revenue income to the state. When settlement took place, tribals because of their ignorance were not in a position to get their possessions recorded, and thus land under their possession got recorded as government land and sometimes transferred to the Forest

Department. Thus the poor tribals got described as encroachers even on lands which were cultivated by their ancestors. In such cases, no compensation was given to the poor farmers, because their land rights were not recorded. These cashew plantations, raised on land that was supporting livelihood needs of tribals, were handed over to the Orissa State Cashew Development Corporation for management. As the Corporation could not run profitably, it started giving annual leases for harvesting of cashew crops to private parties through open auctions. Often such plantations are in a degraded condition because of lack of maintenance. Two years back Orissa government even contemplated giving long term leases to private parties for managing cashew plantations. One such advertisement appeared in the Economic Times dated 20/4/99. The leases would be given for a period of 35 years for a minimum area of 2000 ha. This is land reforms in reverse! Thus lands that were once with tribals would now be with private corporations, with the tribals getting no compensation, or rehabilitation. Many of them shifted to the hill slopes, and that resulted in more soil erosion, the prevention of which was the objective of the scheme. It is ironical that these plantations that deprived the tribals of their possession were funded by a scheme called, 'Economic Rehabilitation of the Rural Poor (ERRP). It is understood that in addition to cashew, there are similar plantations of coffee and other commercial crops, the exact details are not known. Orissa government should give these lands back to the tribals, or to palli sabha, rather than to commercial houses. The Palli Sabha should be encouraged to take up the management and upgradation of these plantations. Financial resources for this could be made available under various Government schemes through the DRDA.

Summing up: The studies commissioned by the Government of India with regard to other states, referred to earlier, also establish that transfers of land from tribal landowners to non-tribals continued despite the various enactment's, for a variety of reasons. Collectors or other agencies responsible for protecting the interests of tribals while regulating such transfers, in most cases did not apply their minds to issues of vital importance to the tribals. These include whether or not, the tribal had any other alter tribal livelihood, or sufficient land for viable cultivation even after sale, whether sufficient price was being paid, whether the sale was actually to enable repayment for usurious loans from a moneylenders etc. Legal transfers also took place by actions for recovery of dues and mortgages, by decrees of civil courts, misuse of provisions for settlement of occupancy tenants, settlement operations etc. The persistent problem of indebtedness amongst the tribals is one of the manifestations of their poverty. Despite the existence of legal/protective measures to curb the business of money-lending in tribal areas and provisions for debt-relief, their enforcement has been weak and ineffective. Also, the non-recognition of the tribal needs for their day-to-day consumption purposes by various credit extension programmes makes the otherwise vulnerable tribals fall as easy victims into debt-traps. Although the practice of bonded-labour stands abolished in the country through an Act of Parliament viz., the Bonded Labour System (Abolition) Act 1976, yet a total number of 2.52 lakh bonded labourers (including STs) were identified in March 1993 in 12 States i.e., Andhra Pradesh, Bihar, Karnataka, Madhya Pradesh, Orissa, Rajasthan, Tamil Nadu, Maharashtra, Uttar Pradesh, Kerala, Haryana and Gujarat. Immediate action is needed to review bothe laws and their implementation to resote alienated lands to tribals.

Displacement: It is estimated that some 50 million persons have been displaced since 1950 on account of various development projects, of which more that 40 per cent are tribals. These projects include large irrigation dams, hydroelectric projects, open cast and underground coal mines, super thermal power plants and mineral-based industrial units. In the name of development, tribals are displaced from their traditional habitats and livelihoods with little or no rehabilitation, and are rendered destitute, bewildered and pauperised by the development process. They are pushed into a vortex of increasing assetlessness, unemployment, debt bondage and hunger due to loss of access to traditional sources of livelihood viz., land, forests, rivers, pastures, cattle etc. In these large development projects, tribals lose their land not only to the project authorities, but even to non-tribal outsiders who converge into these areas and corner both the land and the new economic opportunities in commerce and petty industry. Even wage employment to local tribals is rare. In Chotanagpur area, though the tribals constitute more than 50 per cent of the total population, there are not more than 5 per cent of them in the industrial working force. In some of the large firms like TISCO, Jamshedpur and Bharat Coking Coal Ltd., Dhanbad, the tribals employed are less than 5 per cent. Development for the nation has meant displacement, pauperisation, or, at its very best, peonage for the tribals. A National Policy for Rehabilitation for the Displaced Persons was drafted during 1998-99. when I was posted as Secretary, Rural Development in GoI. The draft not only ensured that no deterioration takes place in the living conditions of the tribals prior to their displacement, but also provided for betterment. The suggestions given in the draft if adopted would have achieved the following:- (a) It will minimise displacement and prevent state-induced impoverishment of people on account of compulsory acquisition of land, and will search for non-displacing or least displacing altertribals to people displacing projects; (b) It will ensure that displaced and adversely affected families have a standard of living superior to the one before their displacement and, in any case, have an income above that prescribed as the poverty line; (c) It will compulsorily provide agricultural land to all agricultural families in irrigation projects and for tribals in all projects; (d) It will ensure justice to women by adopting a gender neutral definition of family, and recognising full rights of unmarried, widowed and separated adult women. (e) It will address the special needs of the poorest, especially tribals, in the rehabilitation and resettlement measures by improving their skills and knowledge and thus their incomes on a sustainable basis; and(f) It will ensure quick but peaceful acquisition and faster access to land required by large projects for faster economic development. (g) The draft aimed at the empowerment of the displaced, so that they are able to influence and share control over priority setting, policy making, resource allocations and access to public goods and services at the new site. A final decision on the draft was taken by Government of India only in 2004 and a National Rehabilitation Policy has now been promulgated on 17thFebruary 2004. This has unfortunately none of the progressive clauses that were put in the earlier drafts after consultation with the civil society during 1998-99. It is ironic that the Policy recognizes the limitations of compensation through cash and states that the 'system of extending cash compensation does not by itself, in most cases, enable the affected families to obtain cultivable agricultural land, homestead and other resources which they have to surrender to the State'. However, all that the Policy gives to the displaced people is some extra cash, but no support for livelihoods. We summarise below the main clauses of the new Policy, and how it has ignored earlier proposals (referred to hereinafter as draft), many of which were concurred by the Committee of the Secretaries too. 1. Comparing the new government policy with what was proposed earlier As decided in the R & R Policy 2004 by Government What was proposed earlier Objective. 2. To provide better standard of living to PAFs To ensure that displaced families have a standard of living superior to the one before their displacement and, have a sustainable income above the poverty line. 3. Gains to the displaced should be of the same scale as to the project beneficiaries. 4. Definition of family Includes spouse, minor sons, unmarried daughters, minor brothers or unmarried sisters, father, mother and other members residing with him and dependent on him for their livelihood Every major adult member, her (his) spouse, along with minor children below the age of 18 years. 5. For a single adult without spouse or children, all benefits of this policy would become half. Adulthood to be determined by the date of displacement or date of payment of compensation, whichever is later. 6. Minimize displacement Administrator to identify non-displacing or least displacing alter tribals in consultation with the requiring body, and hold consultation with the project affected families only for preparing a resettlement and rehabilitation scheme/plan. 7. Project to form a high level committee with NGOs, PRIs and representatives of PAFs before section for full consultation with PAFs in options for the project and resettlement site selection so as to minimise displacement. 8. Procedure laid down by the Ministry of Rural Development for consultation for Scheduled Areas under PESA to be followed for all cases of acquisition in tribal areas. 9. Land Only if government land is available, and only to those who lose their entire land Mandatory allotment of land for all in irrigation/hydro-electric projects, and for tribals in all projects. Land to be acquired from rich farmers in the command area. 10. Housing site Only for those who owned house Housing site for all (at least 50 sq m per adult); whether they owned house or not, constructed houses for BPL families Job opportunities Commits itself to providing training only, silent on wage employment Each PAP must be made literate and trained for semiskilled or skilled jobs. All unskilled new jobs and semi-skilled direct employment created in the project would go to the PAPs only. Even those private enterprises (such as ancillary industries and contractors) that benefit from the project would be charged in the same manner with responsibility for providing skills and jobs to such people. The displaced people should be resettled as near as possible to the developmental project sites so that they get multiple access and facilities as well as economic benefits generated out of the developmental projects. Links with LAN link Make Policy justiciable by linking it with LA Act. Amend LA Act suitably to make it people-oriented and consensual. Include land for land principle in LA Act. Basic amenities Government would decide what amenities are to be provided. It is desirable that drinking water, electricity, schools, and dispensaries are provided at the new site. Twenty six basic amenities were identified in the draft that had to be mandatory provided at the new site. These included roads, safe drinking water, plantation of inhabited areas, educational facilities, community hall, and basic irrigation facilities at project cost. Some new ideas will be Nil. If land acquired for a commercial undertaking, 10 per cent shares to be given to PAFs free and equitably. Enable projects to take land on 99 year lease, by paying an annual lease rent of twice the gross annual produce. Whenever land acquired for a public purpose is transferred to an individual or a company for a consideration, 25 per cent of the difference between such consideration and the compensation will be given to the original land owners. All benefits to persons/ families, if further displaced within a period of 20 years, shall be doubled. Special provisions for tribals in scheduled areas For the predominantly tribal Scheduled V area of Central India, Government had passed an Act 'The Provisions of the Panchayats (Extension to the Scheduled Areas) Act, 1996'(popularly known as PESA Act), which inter-alia provides under sub-section (i), section 4 that 'the Gram Sabha or the Panchayats at the appropriate level, shall be consulted before making the acquisition of land in the Scheduled Areas for development projects'. Detailed executive instructions were issued by Government under my signatures as Secretary Rural Development sometime in 1998 to describe the modalities of consultation with the GramSabhas or with the Panchayats where more than one Gram Sabha is involved. The procedure to be followed for acquisition of land in Schedule V areas was deliberately made difficult so as to discourage projects to displace tribals. For instance, it provided that the companyrequiring land must produce a letter of consent from each of the concerned Gram Panchayat, in favour of the proposed acquisition of land (see annexure for the complete order, which fortunately is still operative, though almost forgotten by the state governments). I was also contemplating incorporating a suitable sub-section in the amended Land Acquisition Act, 1894, which would reflect the spirit of this notification. It is very unfortunate that the new Policy makes no reference to this government notification issued in 1998 to make the spirit of section 4(I) of the PESA Act a reality. It is feared that the states may in due course of time ignore the provisions of the executive instructions issued, as just now neither the Policy nor the Land Acquisition Act remind the acquiring authorities of their responsibilities about tribals in the V Schedule area. Panchayats in Scheduled V areas: The PESA which came into force on the 24th December 1996 extends Panchayats to the tribal areas of now nine States; namely, Andhra Pradesh, Jharkhand, Gujarat, Himachal Pradesh, Maharashtra, Madhya Pradesh, Chattisgarh, Orissa and Rajasthan. The Act intends to enable tribal society to assume control over their own destiny to preserve and conserve their traditional rights over natural resources. All States barring Jharkhand have enacted State

Legislation to give effect to the provisions contained in Act 40, 1996 as mandated under the Central Act. PESA is unprecedented in that it gives radical self-governance powers to the tribal community and recognises its traditional community rights over natural resources. Prior to the passage of this Act, laws passed by central and state governments were applied mechanicallyto tribal areas, even when these contravened traditional tribal practices and institutions. For instance, the Gram Sabha, which is locus of political power under the PESA, may be in other states no more than a convenient administrative label for the relevant assembly. However, under PESA the law focuses on settlements which the tribal people themselves perceive to be traditional and organic entities. In fact this is the first law that empowers people to redefine their own administrative boundaries. PESA provides that the tribal Gram Sabha so defined would be empowered to approve all development plans, control all functionaries and institutions of all social sectors, as well as control all minor water bodies, minor minerals and non-timber forest resources. It would also have the authority to control land alienation, impose prohibition, manage village markets and resolve internal conflicts by traditional modes. In one stroke, the Act creates a space for people's empowerment, genuine popular political participation, convergent community action, sustainable people oriented development and auto-generated emancipation. In reality, however, since its passage it has almost been forgotten and has not become part of mainstream political or policy discourse. Many state governments have passed laws not fully in conformity with the central law. Academics, administrators, policy makers and even parliamentarians remain unaware of it. The tribal communities informed about the provisions of the law greeted it with enthusiasm but found themselves progressively handicapped by the lack of actual preparedness to negotiate development and democratization in the manner envisaged by the law. Minimalists interpretation: The implementation of the law has been severely hampered by the reluctance of most state governments to make laws and rules that conform to the spirit of the law. Weak-kneed political will has usually led to bureaucratic creativity in minimalistic interpretations of the law. Bureaucratic subversion of the letter and spirit of the law has been most visible in the interpretation of that provision of PESA by which panchayats at appropriate levels and the Gram Sabha have been vested with the ownership of minor forest produce (MFP). For tribal forest dwellers, the forest department has been the most visible oppression (One piece of anecdotal evidence, recounted by Verrier Elwin, is particularly revealing. When queried about his idea of paradise, a tribal described it as miles and miles of forest, but without a forest guard!). Enforcement of PESA is perceived as weakening the stranglehold of the forest bureaucracy, and it is instructive to study the interpretation of PESA favoured by the state governments for its attempts to minimise the bureaucratic loss of control. Firstly, the state governments have argued that the power of Gram Sabhas can extend only to forest located within the revenue boundaries of a village. This one provision, if accepted, would nullify the law because often reserved forest in most states is not located within a revenue village. The spirit of the law is clearly to extend ownership to the Gram Sabha to MFP from forests located in the vicinity of the village which they traditionally access. In fact, in the case of Joint Forest Management (JFM), the Madhya Pradesh government vested the village forest committees with authority to manage forest falling within a radius of five kilometres of the boundaries of the village. A similar dispensation would be eminently suitable in the case of PESA. Secondly, MFP has been defined to exclude cane and bamboo. This is contrary to the commonsense definition of MFP which is 'that part of a tree that can be sustainably harvested without damage to the survival of the tree'. MFP is a product of the living tree, as opposed to timber which is product of the dead tree. More significantly, the state governments deny access to poor tribal artisans to two types of MFP, bamboo and cane, on which their livelihoods are most critically dependent. On the other hand, many state policies have subsidised bamboo for private industry. Another controversy is in the interpretation of the concept of `ownership' of MFP by the Gram Sabha. The status quoist view is that ownership does not provide Gram Sabha the right to take any decisions related to stewardship, management or sustainable harvesting of MFPs. Contrary to a whole body of empirical evidence from the national and international experience of JFM and community control of forests, it is claimed that the exercise of `ownership' of MFPs by Gram Sabhas in this sense, would inevitably lead to a destruction of forests. Therefore, `ownership as provided for in PESA is reinterpreted to mean the right to net revenues from MFP, after retaining administrative expenses of the forest department. These interpretations have almost killed the concept of ownership and control of local resources by Gram Sabha. The status of the operationalisation of other powers envisaged in PESA by the State Governments are given in the following:

Definition of Village: A village consists of a habitation or a group of habitations or a hamlet or a group of hamlets comprising a community and managing its affairs in accordance with traditions and customs All States adopted this definition except Maharashtra, which is silent on this subject. Status and Functions of Gram Sabha Every village will have a Gram Sabha which will be competent to safeguard and preserve the traditions and customs of the people, their cultural identity. All State Acts follow the Central Act. However, regarding customary mode of disputes resolution Andhra Pradesh Act puts a condition that it will be subject to without detriment to any law for the time being in force'. The Orissa Act adds that it should be consistent with the relevant laws in force and in harmony with the tenets of the Constitution and Human Rights. Constitution of Panchayat Panchayats will be constituted at village level with reservations for Scheduled Tribes in the manner prescribed in Part IX of the Constitution. Andhra Pradesh and Himachal Pradesh Acts have extended the reservation of elective seats and Chairpersons to both Gram Panchayats and Mandal/ intermediate Panchayats. The Maharashtra Act does not mention it. Acquisition of land for development projects and resettlement of displacedpersons Prior consultation with Gram Sabha or Panchayats at the appropriate level shall be made mandatory In Andhra Pradesh, Gram Sabhas have no role. Gujarat assigned this power to Taluka Panchayat, however, no provision relating to coordination of such projects at state level. Orissa assigned the power to Zilla Panchayat with no role for the Gram Sabha/Gram Panchayat Planning and Management of Entrusted to Panchayats at the appropriate level: Maharashtra Act does not make any mention of it. Orissa assigned power to Minor Water Bodies appropriate level Zilla Parishad instead of Gram Sabha/Gram Panchayat Grant of Prospecting licence or mining lease for minor minerals Prior recommendations of Gram Sabha or the Panchayats at the appropriate level shall be made mandatory. Andhra Pradesh- gives primacy to Gram Panchayat in place of Gram Sabha. Gujarat-does not make mention of it. Himachal Pradesh- retained primacy of Gram Sabha but term 'shall be made mandatory' has been replaced by 'shall be taken into consideration'. Madhya Pradesh – No mention in the Madhya Pradesh Panchayat Act but the relevant Subject Act Mines and Minerals (Regulation and Development Act) 1957 amended to assign powers to Gram Sabha and Panchayats at appropriate level. Maharashtra assigns powers to GramPanchayat. Gram Sabha has no role in the matter. Orissa gives powers to Zilla Parishad. Grant: of concession for exploitation of minor minerals by auction. Prior recommendation of Gram Sabha or Panchayats at appropriate level shall be made mandatory. Andhra Pradesh and Maharashtra assigned the function to GramPanchayat in place of Gram Sabha, Gujarat - No mention of it. Madhya Pradesh – Madhya Pradesh Panchayat Act does not make mention of it but the Subject Act Mines and Minerals (Regulation and Development) Act, 1987 amended to assign the power to Panchayat at appropriate level. Orissa- assigned the power to Zilla Parishad. Enforceprohibition/regulate or restrict sale and consumption of any intoxicant.

Panchayats at the appropriate level and the Gram Sabha to be endowed with the powers All State Acts followed the Central Act except Madhya Pradesh which does not make provision for it in its PR Amendment Act. However, the Subject Act Madhya Pradesh Excise Act 1915 has been amended to give powers to Gram Sabha. Ownership of Minor Forest Produce (MFP) Panchayats at the appropriate level and the Gram Sabha endowed with the powers of ownership All State Acts follow central Act by assigning this power either to GramSabha or to the Gram Panchayats Prevention and Restoration of Tribal Alienated Land: Panchayats at appropriate level and the Gram Sabha to be endowed with this power. Gujarat, Himachal Pradesh, Madhya Pradesh Panchayati Raj Amendment Act do not make provision for this. However, in case of Madhya Pradesh, the Madhya Pradesh Land Revenue Code, 1959 has been amended to givepower to Gram Sabha. Manage Village Markets: Panchayats at appropriate level and the Gram Sabha to be endowed with this power. Gujarat and Maharashtra Amendment Acts are silent on this matter. Money lending to the Scheduled Tribes Panchayats at appropriate level and the Gram Sabha to be endowed with this power: Madhya Pradesh Amendment Act does not make a mention of this subject.

13 Exercisecontrol over institutions and functionaries in all social sectors. Panchayats at appropriate level of the Gram Sabha to be endowed with this power. All States Acts except Madhya Pradesh assign this power either to Gram Panchayat or Panchayat Samiti/Mandal Parishad. The Madhya Pradesh Amendment Act has given this power to the Gram Sabha and the Janpad Panchayat or the Zilla Parishad. Control over Local Plans: and Resources including Tribal Sub Plans Panchayats at appropriate level and the Gram Sabha to be endowed with this power. State Acts of Andhra Pradesh, Gujarat, Himachal Pradesh, Orissa have assigned the power to Panchayat Samiti/ Taluka Panchayat/Mandal Parishad while the Madhya Pradesh and Maharashtra Acts assign this power to Gram Sabha. In order to make the Central Act effective, it is necessary for the State Governments to make appropriate amendments in their State Laws/Acts which impinge on specific provisions contained in the Central Act namely (i) Land Acquisition Act; (ii) Excise Act; (iii) State Irrigation Act; (iv) Minor Forest Produce Act; (v) Mines and Minerals Acts; (vi) Land Revenue Code / Act; (vii) SC/ ST Land Alienation Act; (viii) Money Lenders Act; and (ix) Regulated Market Act. No doubt, some State Governments (MP) have already amended some of the relevant Acts, others are yet to follow suit. The above review of the Central Act 40 reveals that most State Acts and especially Orissa have assigned a less prominent role to Gram Sabha / Gram Panchayat in Schedule Areas than envisaged in the Central Act. The State of Orissa has made complete departure from the Central Act by assigning the powers to be consulted to the Zilla Parishad in place of Gram Sabha / Gram Panchayat in respect of (a) acquistion of land and resettling and rehabilitation of the persons affected by the acquisition of land; (b) grant of prospective license or mining lease for minor minerals; (c) grant of concession for the exploitation of minor minerals by auction; and (d) planning and management of minor water bodies. It is pertinent to highlight the fact that the spirit behind the provision regarding mandatory consultation with Gram Sabha or Panchayat at the appropriate levels in respect to subjects like acquisition of land, grant of mineral lease, etc. is that the tribals may own land but they have no control over it and are not able to put it to productive use, they have generally been out-maneuvered and are losing control

over natural resources. In view of this, to safeguard their interests, the consent of the local tribals at village level has been made obligatory. Further, the land to be acquired, mineral resources, water bodies etc. may fall within the jurisdiction of more than one village/block/district. Therefore, to cover this aspect, the phrase 'Panchayats at the appropriate levels' has been used in the Central Act. The real danger thus is that the far-reaching changes introduced in the law will remain a dead letter unless they are translated into action and sustained by a process of awareness and capacity building among the tribal communities. There are a number of grave problems that must be overcome if the law is genuinely to transform tribal reality, but it is important to stress that none of these barriers to tribal self-government are insurmountable. Shifting Cultivation Shifting cultivation is both a labour intensive and land extensive form of cultivation, but requires little capital. The Task Force on Shifting Cultivation (1983) has pointed out that approximately 0.64 million families, mostly tribals, of which 95 percent live in the northeast, Orissa and Andhra Pradesh, are engaged in shifting cultivation over an area of 4.36 m ha, which is about 6.5 per cent of the recorded forest area. Since then this area must have come down, because this form of cultivation requires extensive land per unit of labour. As the availability of land declines and population increases, shifting cultivation gives way to settled agriculture. It has shown the comparative use of land, labour, and capital in different forms of landuse. Shifting cultivation is considered by many experts to be ecologically destructive and its practice is looked upon as a major cause of deforestation and soil erosion. It is also held responsible for causing floods in the plains since soil erosion results in sedimentation or river beds. Daman Singh (Last Frontier: People and Forests in Mizoram, TERI, 1996) has argued that average loss due to jhuming in Mizoram has been 12 mT/ha/yr. It has converted multi-tier forests into secondary bamboo forests, and in the process has displaced both plant and animal species. There is also a contrary position. According to this view, shifting cultivation is the only practical way out from the inherent difficulties confronted in preparing a proper seedbed in steep slopes. In interior areas where communications are not developed and where sufficient land suitable for terracing is not available, shifting cultivation is the only system of cultivation which can be operated at the present stage of development. Alarming Problem in Orissa. In Orissa 0.53 m ha is under active shifting cultivation on which 150 thousand households belonging to different tribal groups are dependent. In Phulbani, Kalahandi and in Koraput the forest dwellers have gone on the top of the hills to do cultivation. Even in Phulbani and Kalahandi the damage done to ecology by cultivating such steep slopes is very serious but the situation in Koraput is alarming. The innumerable muddy rivers flowing in this region tell the story of heavy soil erosion that is going on in the region. It is very clear that they must not have been cultivating those high hills in the past. It is definitely a case of their being pushed up and up by a combine of government policy, rich farmers and traders. The energy input to cultivate such areas is very high and returns are too low. As they find difficult to make twoends meet, they try to bring more areas under shifting cultivation. Shifting cultivation is legally prohibited inside RFs and PFs of Orissa but it may be allowed in other categories of forests such as unclassed forests with the permission from Revenue Department. However, the practice is quite prevalent even inside the RFs and PFs despite punitive action against the offenders taken by the Forest Department. Unfortunately the FD is not involved either in tribal development or resolving the problems arising out of shifting cultivation excepting the routing work and taking punitive action against the 'offenders'. So the question of the image of FD in the eyes of the tribal people is negative. It has to becorrected. However, while jhum/podu cycles were long, regeneration of land affected by shifting cultivation was possible. But the scenario has changed. Its negative aspects, therefore, far outweigh its positive points now. The drastic shortening of the podu cycle has resulted in distortions both in ecological and economic terms. Shortening of cycle has taken place for a variety of reasons such as population pressure, desertification, tribal land being taken over bydominant peasantry as a result of which tribal are pushed or they themselves withdraw to more interior/higher (altitudes) areas which are generally more inhospitable. Shifting cultivators have been universally denounced. The official view has been that shifting cultivation "seriously" interferes with the eco-system in the region of its incidence and brings about permanent and cumulative degradation of the Quality of Environment (QOE). Therefore the official effort has been to contain shifting cultivation. There have been any number of programmes such as eviction of shifting cultivators, soil conservation, afforestation etc., to contain the problems created by shifting cultivators. As can be seen these programmes are directed to improve the QOE and not the Quality of Life of the shifting cultivators. ITDA is directly related with tribal affairs. Sporadically they have taken measures to tackle the problems arising out of shifting cultivation. In certain places in Kalahandi. I T D A has taken up SALT model of experimental basis to arrest soil erosion and provide livelihood alter tribals to tribal people. Incidentally these measures have been taken without involving the forest department formally or informally. Therefore, efforts need to be made to expand agricultural extension programmes in the tribal areas to wean the tribals away from the practice of shifting cultivation besides rehabilitating them with permanent alter tribal cultivation. Efforts should also be made to accelerate the pace of progress of the on-going programme for control and transformation of shifting cultivation, especially in the North-Eastern States, where this practice is very much in vogue. 6 Governance Apart from policy failures listed above, tribals have also suffered because of the poor quality of governance. Programme delivery has deteriorated everywhere in India, but more so in tribal areas, where government servants are reluctant to work, and are mostly absent from their official duties. Government seems to have surrendered to political pressures from the staff, as many of their posts have now been officially transferred from tribal regions to non-tribal regions, where they can draw their salaries without doing any work! It is a pity that massive vacancies exist in tribal regions in the face of acute educated unemployment in the country. Poor implementation of existing schemes in the tribal regions has meant that not only poverty continues at an exceptionally high levels in these regions, but the decline in poverty has been much slower here than in the entire country, as shown below. We discuss below the failure of government programmes in certain key sectors in tribal regions. Education The continuing gap between literacy levels of STs and the general population is shown below.

Thus the gap in literacy levels, both for tribal men and women, is increasing despite the fact that the largest proportion of centrally sponsored programmes for tribal development are related to the single sector of education. This sector tends to dominate budgetary allocations in state governments too. In states like Madhya Pradesh, tribal education is administered directly by the tribal welfare department and separate from the education department on the premise that the educational needs of tribal communities are at variance from the needs of the rest of the population. The strategy of special tribal hostels and residential schools makes eminent sense, because tribals reside traditionally in extremely small and dispersed settlements in difficult and remote areas. Therefore, the logistics of serving each of these settlements with day schools are unmanageable. The solution has been found in locating residential tribal schools and hostels even in the deep forest interiors, although quality and basic amenities remain a problem. The amounts paid as scholarship and stipends to tribal students, have enabled resource-strapped tribal families to invest in education, even though there is evidence that part of the money is diverted by some families for non-educational purposes. A recent evaluation carried out by the Ministry on the scheme reveals that the performance of certain States in providing matching grant, maintenance of services and management of hostels is not encouraging and the pace of construction of hostels has also been very slow and the basic amenities provided therein are of substandard. A review of the scheme of Ashram Schools revealed that some of the schools are very badly maintained and deprived of even basic facilities. Also, no separate sections exist in the hostels for primary school children which is a pre-requisite. Tribal hostels and residential schools in remote interiors are notoriously poorly managed, plagued by badly maintained buildings and leakages and delays in payments to students and purchases. Teachers, if they teach at all, are often poorly motivated and sometimes display prejudices against tribal children. The greatest failing has been in the context of education in tribal schools. The sensitive rhetoric of stated tribal policy of 'integration' and enabling tribal communities to 'develop according to their own genius' is entirely forgotten, as mainstream school curricula are imposed wholesale on tribal schools. The problem is not merely the medium of instruction; again, contrary to stated national policy of enabling children at the primary level to study in their mother- tongue, there are almost no tribal schools in which teaching is in tribal languages. Even more serious is the cultural bias of school curricula, which tends to be urban, upper-caste Hindu in content. Studies have also established patriarchal and communal trends. Even the dedicated Ramakrishna Mission schools in remote regions of Bastar and Arunachal Pradesh, which have been actively promoted by the Indian state, provide high-quality education but of a kind that is exclusively and unapologetically Sankritized Hindu in terms of its cultural moorings, values and idioms. The Christian missionary schools in tribal regions country-wide have been equally aimed at assimilation, although into a different cultural ethos. However, despite all these limitations, education is a growing and powerfully felt need of tribal communities. The most visible evolution in tribal aspirations even in remote tribal hinterlands and among so-called primitive tribes, has been for education. The attraction is partly for eligibility for employment, particularly in government. However, the major impetus is to acquire skills to negotiate the complex, exploitative external world. The challenge remains of meeting these aspirations without alienating tribal communities from the roots that sustain them. Nutrition. A diet and nutrition survey of the tribal populations living in the Integrated Tribal Development project (ITDP) areas, in the States of Kerala, Tamil Nadu, Karnataka, Andhra Pradesh, Maharashtra, Gujarat, Orissa and West Bengal was done during 1985-87. A repeat survey was carried out during 1998-99 among tribal population living in the same ITDP areas to assess time trends in food and nutrient intake, nutritional status as assessed by anthropometric indices of nutritional status and prevalence of nutritional deficiency signs. Comparison of data between the two surveys in tribal population showed that over time there has not been any improvement in the food and nutrient intake. The tribal population is more under nourished than their rural counterparts. in South-Eastern

UP With a view to discern the working of TPDS in a remote backward region, Duddhi block in Sonbhadra district of south-eastern UP was selected for study (Shankar 2004). Duddhi block is predominantly tribal as they constitute 57 per cent of the block population. Forest cover is still 60 per cent and only 6 per cent of the cultivated area is irrigated. Roughly 10 per cent of all those having a BPL card, Antyodaya card or Annapurna card were randomly selected from 21 villages. In all 593 households were surveyed out of which 463 had a BPL card, 119 had Antyodaya card and 11 had Annapurna card. It will be seen that per household per annum purchase of food grain by those who purchased was 8.5 kg per month, as against a quota of 35 kg per month. Antyodaya households - 119 households who were getting foodgrains under Antyodaya scheme were surveyed. They were entitled to get 35 kgs of foodgrains. Wheat would be given at a highly subsidised rate of Rs. 2 per kg and rice at Rs. 3 per kg. It was found that not all the households could draw the entire quota every month and the shopkeepers invariably charged Rs. 2.50 per kg for wheat and Rs. 3.50 per rice on the plea that they had to meet transportation and other charges. Table 7 shows the number of times the households could purchase foodgrains during the 12 month period as also the quantity purchased each month.

Thus only 28 per cent of the households succeeded in getting foodgrains every month of the year. The respondents who purchased less than three times complained that, by and large, the shopkeeper would tell them that supply has not come as yet and on another occasion would say that it has been finished. They were tired of frequenting the shop every now and then and some reported that they were disgusted. It appears that those who maintained good relation with the shopkeepers succeeded in getting the foodgrains on a more regular basis. 6.4 Wrong classification.

Another example of anti-poor tribal policies can be cited from the Chakrata Block of Dehradun district in Uttaranchal where a comprehensive study has been conducted by the LBS National Academy of Administration. The whole of 'Jaunsar-Bawar area' of Dehradun district has been notified as 'tribal area' in 1968 but maximum benefit of 'tribal schemes' has been taken away by the richer sections of the society. In the Jaunsar-Bawar area land holding inequalities are very high wherein the lowest stratum of 40 per cent of cultivators control only less than 9 per cent of the cultivated land. Thus the poorest sections i.e. Kolta, Das and Bajgi communities (20 per cent of the total tribal population) within the tribal area have been constantly living under deprivation and not getting the benefits of government schemes. These communities have remained under serfdom or bonded labour to the rich Brahmin and Thakur 'tribals' in that area. On account of 'tribal' status given to the whole area, these communities (Koltas, Bajgis and Das) are not even getting any benefit from SC development schemes. Due to acute poverty the women in some pockets in this area have been forced to do prostitution. There is urgent need to denotify the tribal status given to the Jaunsar-Bawar area and only the Koltas, Das and Bajgi communities should be given tribal status (or at least the scheduled caste status) along with distributing some of the surplus land among these households. Movements: The long history of penetration and profound disruption of tribal communities, the sustained and frequently brutal expropriation of tribal wealth, and the resultant anger and despair, have resulted in a situation in which many regions of tribal concentration are immersed in an unending cycle of violence. All states in the Indian northeast have been ripped apart byseparatist, and sometimes sectarian, violence. In many stretches of forested Central India, it is the People's War Group and an array of other Naxalite Marxist-Leninist outfits, which continue to channelise tribal anger into violent resistance to state power. These regions are caught in a hopeless cycle of mutually retaliatorystate and Naxalite violence: so-called police 'encounters' in which Naxalites are killed in cold blood by police personnel, and the regular killing by Naxalites groups of alleged 'police informers' and police personnel often through powerful land mines. In some pockets, state authority and control have shown signs of near-collapse, and Naxalites have described these as 'liberated areas'. There is evidence that in areas of Naxalite influence, petty exploitation especially by government functionaries has been contained. However, it is still unlikely that there is a clear and wide mandate within the local tribal communities for the perpetuation of violence either of the Naxalites or the state. Meanwhile, as violence from both sides nonetheless continues unabated, there seems no light at the end of the tunnel for local tribal communities condemned to survive in the crossfire. Role of the Ministry. It is unfortunate that the Ministry of Tribal Affairs created in 2000 (or even the Ministry of SJAE before that) does not give sufficient attention to these issues on the plea that many of these subjects have not been allotted to them. Even then they should play a more activist role in addressing these issues by pursuing with the concerned Ministries, where these subjects get a low importance, as the Ministries' excuse is that they are concerned with 'bigger' and more 'general' issues. At least, the new Ministry can set up a monitoring mechanism to bring out the dismal picture of tribal areas that would put pressure on the sectoral Ministries to improve their policies and implementation. When a new Ministry is set up to help the marginalized people, it is expected that it would take a holistic view of their problems, and coordinate the activities of all other Ministries that deal with the subjects impinging on the work of the newly created Ministry. It would develop systems that inform GoI how and why tribals are denied justice. On the other hand, it has been observed that the new Ministry takes a minimalist view of its responsibility, and reduces itself to dealing with only such schemes (such as distribution of scholarships) that are totally outside the purview of the existing Ministries. Such ostrich like attitude defeats the purpose for which the Ministry is created.

It is rather sad that the Ministry of Tribal Affairs is more concerned with spending its budget (and with controlling institutions such as Trifed that create opportunities for distribution of patronage), and less with the impact of overall policies on tribals. This attitude under-plays the role of non-monetary policies and the impact they have on the lives of the people. As has been shown in the first six sections of this paper, certain government policies harm the poor much more than any benefit that accrues to them through money-oriented schemes of the Ministry of Tribal Affairs. Even the Planning Commission does not monitor the impact of existing policies on the tribal population and pull up the concerned sectoral Ministries. Policies and budgetary provisions, despite the rhetoric, have not been integrated so far. Changes in policy or laws, are not seen as an integral part of the development process because these have no direct financial implications. One lesser known reason for this isolation is that development and planning in India are associated with spending of money. That Planning = Expenditure = Development is the mindset behind such beliefs. The Indian planner unfortunately has still to understand the difference between planning and budgeting.

2

Education Among the Scheduled Tribes in India : Some Observations

—*Sujatha K.*

This paper examines the educational progress among tribals with reference to primary education. The first section deals with the literacy status of tribal population in the country focusing on spatial and gender disparities. The next section examines the issue of provision of schooling facilities followed by an analysis of enrollment, retention and attainment levels of students. The last part is devoted to a discussion of innovations and special initiatives implemented in tribal areas in recent years as well as issues confronting the planners in ensuring education for all tribal children.

Indian Constitution identifies for special consideration certain ethnic minority groups, traditionally referred to as tribes or tribals, as Scheduled Tribes who constitute around 8 per cent of the total population of the country. There are 573 Scheduled Tribes living in different parts of the country. Most of the tribal communities have their own languages different from what is spoken in the State where they are located. There are more than 270 such languages. The tribal languages in India belong to all major language families among which the Austric, the Dravidian, Tibeto-Chinese, Indo European families are the dominant ones.

One of the distinguishing features is that majority of them live in scattered habitations located in interior, remote and inaccessible, hilly and forest areas of the country. Nearly 22 per cent of tribal habitations have less than one hundred population and more than 40 per cent have 100 to less than 300 population, while others have less than 500 people. Though tribals constitute only eight per cent of Indian population, they constitute a majority in several States and Union Territories and substantial numbers in others. In particular, they constitute an overwhelming majority in Mizoram (94.75 per cent), Lakshadweep (93.15 per cent), Nagaland (87.70 per cent) and Meghalaya (85.53 per cent). However, the states of Madhaya Pradesh, Orissa, Bihar, Maharashtra, Gujarat, Rajasthan, Andhra Pradesh and West Bangal account for 83 per cent of the total tribal population, even though the non-tribals constitute the majority in these states.

Policies and Programmes

Recognising that the Scheduled Tribes constitute the most deprived and marginalised sections of Indian society, a host of welfare and developmental measures have been initiated for their social and economic development. In this regard, particular reference has to be made to the tribal sub-plan approach which came into existence as the main strategy from the fifth five-year plan. Along with core economic sectors elementary education has been accorded priority in tribal-plan approach. Elementary education was considered important not only because Constitutional obligation but as a crucial input for total development of tribal communities particularly to build confidence among the tribes to deal with outsiders in equal terms. Since primacy was accorded to elementary education, a broad policy frame for education was adopted in tribal sub-plan emphasizing equal importance for quantitative and qualitative aspects of education.

A second important development in the policy towards education of the tribals came with recommendations of the National Policy on Education in 1986 which specified among other things that:

- Priority will be accorded to opening primary schools in tribal areas.
- There is need to develop curricula and devise instructional material in tribal language at the initial stages with the arrangements for switchover to regional languages.
- Promising ST youths will be encouraged to take up teaching in tribal areas.

- Ashram schools/residential schools on a large scale in tribal areas will be established.
- Incentive schemes will be formulated for the STs, keeping in view, their special needs and lifestyle.

The unique feature of the policy is its recognition of the heterogeneity and diversity of tribal areas. The policy also proposed the transformation of the structure of primary education with special emphasis on improving the access in tribal areas. The policy has also underlined the importance of instruction through the mother tongue for effective teaching and encouraged incorporating locally relevant content and curriculum besides emphasized on the localized production of textbooks in local dialects. Based on these considerations, the norms for establishing primary schools were relaxed to suit the tribal areas in order to improve access to education. For instance, Andhra Pradesh has gone to the extent of establishing schools in habitations where there are even twenty school age children; Madhya Pradesh has steadily decreased population size norms in order to open schools in habitations with 200 population. However, in spite of such relaxation of norms many tribal localities are still without school, as they do not meet even the relaxed criteria.

Progress in Literacy

Literacy is an important and primary index of educational development. The present section provides data on the actual position of literacy among the tribals in terms of decadal growth of tribal literacy, gap between tribal and non-tribal population in terms of literacy, and inter-tribal variation etc. It will also highlight inter-state, inter-group and gender variation in tribal literacy in the country.

The data on literacy since 1971-91 shows that literacy rate has gone up from a low of 11.30 in 1971 to 29.50 in 1991 for Scheduled Tribes. But the increase in literacy percentage does not express the over all growth of educational standard. In fact, even though in absolute numbers the number of illiterates has increased over the years, the gap between ST and non-ST population has also increased from 22.50 to 33.05 between 1971 and 1991. Even today the tribal literacy falls well below the national average and shows the abysmal rate of educational growth among the tribals. In fact, data reveal that Scheduled Tribes even have lagged behind the Scheduled Castes in their educational progress.

It is found that the degree and level of educational development has been quite uneven among different States and among different segments of population within any given State. The data indicates that some of the States with higher tribal concentration in relation to their total population have done exceedingly well in terms of higher literacy rate. States in the northeastern region of India like Mizoram, Nagaland and Meghalaya fall in this category. But in the States of Madhya Pradesh, Orissa, Rajasthan and Andhra Pradesh that are inhabited by much larger number of tribals than the northeastern States tribal literacy continues to be very low. In 1971 tribal literacy in Madhya Pradesh was at 7.62 per cent which increased marginally to 10.68 per cent during 1981 and stands at 21.54 per cent as per the 1991 census figures. The figures are similar for Bihar, Orissa and Andhra Pradesh. In fact, Andhra Pradesh has the lowest tribal literacy rate in the country at 17.16 in 1991.

But what is important is the growth of literacy rate between 1981-91. The growth rate was steady between 1971-81, but increased significantly during 1981-1991. The trend is visible even in relatively backward States like Bihar and Madhya Pradesh. Another factor that needs mention is that though educationally developed States like Kerala, Tamil Nadu and Karnataka have higher general literacy rate they are way behind the smaller and tribal concentrated States in terms of tribal literacy rate. On the whole, disparity among various States in terms of literacy rate is pretty high ranging between 82.27 per cent in Mizoram to 17.16 per cent in Andhra Pradesh.

Further, the States where the literacy among tribes is lower than the national average tend to lag behind the national average even in general literacy rate. The States of Bihar, Madhya Pradesh, and Rajasthan are of this category. This shows that educational development of the State is possible only when its disadvantageous sections are properly taken care of. Disparity in educational level is not only between States but it also exists at district level. Out of the total 414 districts with tribal population 13 districts have a tribal literacy rate of 0-10 per cent and in as many as 86 districts, it is only 20-30 per cent. A substantial number of districts (240) have a tribal literacy rate of 10-40 per cent. And only three districts among all the districts of India have 90-100 per cent tribal literacy rate. For example, among the 45 districts in Madhya Pradesh the literacy rate among the tribes varies between 2.14 per cent and 28.47 per cen

Gender Disparity

In a highly stratified society like India there are numerous layers of differentiation apart from caste and class. Gender is now recognised as a more pervasive and distinct category of social stratification. In the context of literacy gender is an important aspect. The literacy rate among the tribals is not only low but also show a high level of the gender disparity. Data reveal that States which are low in general and tribal literacy are also the States with higher gender disparity.

During 1971, female literacy among tribals was 4.85 per cent at the all India level and only 0.49 per cent in Rajasthan. By 1981 it had increased to 8.05 per cent at the all India level and 1.20 per cent in Rajasthan. Despite massive efforts by the Government and non-Government agencies it was still 18.19 per cent at the all India level and 4.42 per cent in Rajasthan in 1991. The States of Andhra Pradesh with 8.68 per cent and Rajasthan with 4.42 per cent have remained in the bottom of the female literacy table among the tribals. On the other side, States like Mizoram (78.74), Nagaland (54.51), Sikkim (50.37), Kerala (51.07), have more than 50 per cent literacy among the female population. It is significant that Andhra Pradesh which has a low tribal literacy than Rajasthan, has a higher literacy rate among the tribal female population.

Primary Education: Access and Participation

As it has been mentioned earlier the tribal communities normally reside in interior, underdeveloped and inaccessible areas. Demographically tribal habitations are small in size, scattered and are sparsely populated. Nearly 63.4 per cent of tribal habitations have less than 300 people covering one fourth of total tribal population. While 22 per cent of tribal habitations have less than 100 inhabitants, the population covered by these habitations is only 3.82 per cent of the total tribal population. Because of these problems most of these villages are bereft of basic infrastructural facilities like transport, communication and other basic amenities. Formal education like other infrastructure was not available to these people and localities for a long time. A conscious effort to expand educational facilities began with the introduction of tribal sub-plan approach and got a major boost with the formulation of National Policy on Education (1986). In the backdrop, this section attempts to examine the status of acd availability of schools in tribal areas.

Data from the two surveys (1986 and 1993) clearly show that the number of habitations having schools beyond two kilometers is fast decreasing. In almost all the tribal concentration States, the number of schools within one km. of the habitations has increased and higher percentage population coverage is achieved. The Sixth All India Educational Survey (1993) shows that 78 per cent of tribal population and 56 per cent of tribal habitations have been provided primary schools with in the habitation. Another 11 per cent of tribal population and 20 per cent of their habitations had schools within the range of less than one-kilometer distance.

Comparing access conditions in tribal areas with that of the rural habitations in general one finds that the difference is only marginal. Around two thirds of rural habitations i.e. (64.80 per cent) have primary schools within the habitation or within a distance of half a kilometer covering 85.50 per cent of total rural population as against 56.33 per cent and 78.73 per cent tribal habitations and their population, respectively.

In view of difficult terrain, geographical and ecological barriers in tribal areas the distance of more than half a kilometer is a difficult proposition for young children to attend school. In fact, the distance of one kilometer and above between the school and habitation means that practically these habitations and inhabitants lack access to primary schools given the tribal context. Thus, a little more than one fifth of total tribal population are constrained by this problem. Further, 10 per cent of the tribal habitations have schools beyond two kilometers.

The States of Mizoram and Gujarat have the highest percentage of population and habitations covered by primary schools within the habitation. A huge 95 per cent of total tribal population and 85 to 90 per cent of tribal habitations of the States are provided with primary schools within the habitations. While the State of Bihar occupies the lowest position in terms of population coverage and habitations in providing primary schools within the habitation. In the States of Andhra Pradesh, Rajasthan, Orissa, and Madhya Pradesh the percentage of habitations and population served by primary schools within the habitation were not only relatively less but also a large number of the habitations and population have access to schools only at a distance of more than one km.

Several innovative efforts have been made during the 1990s to increase access to population living small habitations. For instance in Madhya Pradesh, the number of formal primary schools have increased from 16, 548 from 1990-91 to 18, 716 in 1998-99. During the same period 1,757 alter tribal schools, 10,626 EGS schools and 1,133 TWD schools have been established. These take the total number of schools from 19,295 in 1992-93 to 34,131 in 1998-99. Visakhapatnam district in Andhra Pradesh, which has a large concentration of tribal population has also witnessed a similar phenomenon where the educational facilities in last eight years had increased significantly through the establishment alter tribal schools with active community partnership.

Enrollment

Enrollment is not an independent variable in the sense that it is dependent on factors such as availability of school, its regular functioning, regularity of teachers as well as on parental willingness, their perception of the value of education and their capacity. The participation of tribal children in education is very low in comparison to others. Enrollment of tribal children was about 9 million in classes I-V during the year 1997-98.

One observes a positive trend with respect to participation of girls in education among the STs. For instance, the proportion of girls has increased from 36.5 per cent in 1989-90 to 43 per cent in 1997-98 at all India level. The northeastern States like Mizoram, Nagaland and West Bengal have more or less equal proportion of boys and girls among the total enrolled tribal children at the primary stage. The girls' enrollment shows a positive growth in all the tribal concentrated States. The State of Rajasthan shows the highest increase in girls enrollment with 64 per cent increase during the 1990s. Their proportion to the total enrollment has increased from a mere 23 per cent in 1989-90 to 35 per cent in the year 1997-98. Similar trend could be observed at the upper primary classes also.

Several innovative interventions such as appointment of local women as teachers in the Shiksha Karmi project, micro-level planning and community mobilisation under the Lok Jumbish project and several NGO efforts at grassroots level seem to be the major reasons for the significant improvement in girls' enrollment in Rajasthan. Some of the recent micro level evidences show that the interventions and initiatives like mid day meal scheme, creation of self help women groups, environment building programmes under different projects, appointment of local tribal teachers, developing partnership between school and village communities in school management had helped in raising awareness level among tribals to realise the importance of education and adopt a positive attitude towards girls' education (Sujatha, 1998).

Retention

Enrollment has no meaning unless the students are retained in the system for prescribed number of years to complete the primary level of education. However, in tribal areas high levels of absenteeism, large scale failure in year end assessment and alarming drop-out rate contribute to slow progress of education among tribals.

Learner Achievement Levels

All most all the studies on learners achievement levels in India have showed that the tribal students in primary classes had lower achievement scores compared to non-tribal population (Govinda and Varghese, 1993, Varghese 1994, Sujatha 1998, Prakash, 1998). The low achievement levels among tribals were attributed to school related variables as in the case of non-tribal students. However, the tribal students had additional disadvantages arising out social and locational factors that affect

Dropout Rates of Scheduled Tribes (Class I-V) in Tribal Concentrated States

State / Union Territory	*1991-92*		
	Boys	*Girls*	*Total*
1. Andhra Pradesh	66.65	71.95	68.64
2. Bihar	70.96	71.81	71.26
3. Gujarat	53.98	66.51	59.39
4. Madhya Pradesh	31.00	52.27	38.59
5. Maharashtra	56.24	63.88	59.48
6. Orissa	78.03	74.14	76.81
7. Rajasthan	73.01	84.20	75.92
8. West Bengal	62.47	69.68	65.07
9. Arunachal Pradesh	62.21	58.19	60.71
10. Assam	65.13	67.10	66.00
11. Meghalaya	68.00	67.95	67.99
12. Mizoram	57.91	58.37	58.13
13. Nagaland	45.83	49.23	47.42
14. Tripura	70.78	73.72	72.03

Source: Education Profile of States/Union Territories, Govt. of India MHRD (Department of Education), Planning and Monitoring.

their achievement levels. In other words, performance of tribal students varies among different schools irrespective of their location, family background and management type of the school (Sujatha, 1998). A silver lining in this regard is that the achievement levels of tribal children showed slight improvement during the period from 1993 to 1998 as revealed by the baseline studies conducted under DPEP. (Prakash, 1998)

However, this marginal improvement is not sufficient to achieve educational parity in terms of levels of achievement between tribal and non-tribal students and it must be admitted that the tribal students still have a low achievement levels and fall a long way behind the expected level of achievement. The gap between the tribal and non-tribal students in achieving competency is very big to say the least. This is a major concern and requires strategic intervention.

Achievement Le vels (Class-I) of Scheduled Tribe Students in Different States

Districts	*1994-95*		*1997-98*	
	Language	*Mathematics*	*Language*	*Mathematics*
Madhya Pradesh				
Satna	3.65	1.58	5.58	3.72
Rewa	4.18	2.74	4.58	4.51
Sidhi	4.54	2.35	5.35	5.04
Tikamgarh	3.93	2.13	5.70	7.12
Chattarpur	3.39	2.16	5.15	5.29
Panna	2.37	1.45	4.60	5.24
Maharashtra				
Aurangabad	5.21	3.24	7.24	6.35
Nanded	3.79	2.79	5.67	5.02
Parbhani	5.46	3.14	6.27	6.27
Assam				
Darrng	12.32	7.15		
Dhubri	12.12	10.11		
Karbi Anglong	NA	NA		
Morigan	15.12	10.34		

**Source:* Base Line Assessment Survey (NCERT) and Mid-Term Assessment Survey by Ved Prakash.

Problems of Tribal Education

The review clearly brings out that inspite of constitutional guarantees and persistent efforts tribal communities continue to lag behind the general population. The reasons for this can be categorized as external, internal and socio-economic and psychological. The external constraints are related to the problems and difficulties at the policy level, planning, implementation and at administration level. Internal constraints refer to problems associated with schools system, content, curriculum, medium of instruction, pedagogy, teacher related problems, academic supervision and monitoring. The third set of problems relate to social, economic and cultural background of tribals and the psychological problems of first generation learners.

External Constraints

The perspective adopted for education development among the tribal communities, fails to properly address the specific disadvantages characterising the tribal population. For instance, the population and distance norms formed by the Government have not been beneficial to the tribal locations because of their sparse population and sporadic residential patterns. Further, in formulating policies and programmes for tribal education it is essential to understand the complex realities of the tribal life and the expectation of tribals from the system and this has never been done either by the tribal welfare department or by the education department. Consequently, no worthwhile policy for tribal education has been formed.

One of the major constraints of tribal education at planning level is the adoption of dual system of administration. The tribal welfare department deals with tribal life and culture and administers the development work at the local level including education. But the tribal welfare department lacks expertise in educational planning and administration in general and academic supervision and monitoring in particular. On the other hand, the education department is the sole authority for planning of education development at the state level. They formulate implementation guidelines and instructions regarding curriculum, textbook, teacher recruitment, transfer policies and so on. In this, the education department tends to form uniform educational policies for the whole state. The school calendar is a case in point where vacations and holidays cater to the need of the formal school set up in a non-tribal context with little consideration for local context and festivals of the tribals. This lack of sensitivity to the problems and the failure in understanding the tribal social reality coupled with the faulty selection and appointment of teachers in tribal areas have resulted in poor performance and teacher absenteeism among tribal schools. Under the system of dual administration, absence of coordination and complimentarily as well as inadequate scope for reciprocal use of respective expertise and experiences between the two departments has invariably stunted educational development among the tribals.

Internal Constraints: The internal problems of tribal education refer to the quality of school provision, suitable teachers, relevance of content and curriculum, medium of instruction, pedagogy and special supervision. A majority of schools in tribal areas are without basic infrastructure facilities. Normally, the school buildings in tribal areas are with thatched roofs, dilapidated walls and non-plastered floors. Research evidences shows that a large number of tribal schools do not have teaching learning materials and even blackboards. In tribal areas the opening of a school is equated with the posting of a teacher and same is the case with the ashram schools. It is found that in most of the ashram schools which are residential in nature there is not enough space for the children to sleep. Consequently, the classroom turns into the dormitory and vice-versa. Due to lack of minimum sanitary provisions it is not uncommon to find that many children studying in ashram schools are afflicted by contagious diseases like scabies, diarrhea etc. leading to high dropout rate. The schools in tribal areas just function within a bare minimum facility.

Content and Curriculum

Though the demand for changing the content and curricula to suit the tribal context has been an old one, no serious effort has been made in this direction in any state except for some sporadic pilot projects. The uniform structure and transaction of curriculum has put the tribal children at a disadvantage. In respect of pedagogy, it has been found that the rigid systems of formal schooling, which emphasize discipline, routine norms, teacher-centred instruction, etc., have made the children wary of the school. This goes against the culture of free interaction, absence of force as embedded in tribal ethos and culture prevalent at home. This has led to sharp division between home and school leading to lack of interest among the children towards school and research findings have shown this as a major factor behind non-enrollment.

Another area is the inherent fear of tribal children towards the teacher and their inability to establish a communication link with the teacher and this is reflected in low attendance and high dropout. This could be tackled to a great extent by using the regional language as the medium of instruction. The

Constitution of India allows the use of tribal dialect (mother tongue) as the medium of instruction in case the population of the said tribe is more than one lakh. But this has not been adopted on the pretext of feasibility and viability of introducing and sustaining such a change. In recent years, some efforts have been made for preparing primers in tribal dialects but again they have been nullified in the context of inter tribal rivalry, hierarchy etc. and also being on a very small scale incapable of influencing the mainstream practices.

Socio-Economic and Cultural Constraints

In a broad sense, these socio-economic and cultural factors can be outlined as poverty and poor economic conditions, social customs, cultural ethos, lack of awareness and understanding of the value of formal education, conflict and gap between the home and school etc. Studies on educational deprivation of tribals have inevitably linked it to their poor economic condition and poverty. The main occupation of tribals is agriculture, practiced either through the method of shifting cultivation or terrace cultivation where the productivity remains very low. Consequently, children play an important role contributing directly or indirectly to the family income by participating in family occupation and household works like cattle grazing, fuel and fodder collection etc.

Even though elementary education is deemed free and additional incentives are given to the children, in practice, it is not free due to several reasons. First, the incentive schemes do not have full coverage and thus have a limited value at the community level. Secondly, many of the benefits do not reach the hands of the beneficiary. Thirdly, even though incentives like slates, uniforms and other aids are given, they are of poor quality and do not reach in time thus nullifying the entire purpose. It should also be noted that considering the impoverished economic status of the tribals even the small amount of private expenditure involved in procuring writing material, clothing etc. become a serious burden on the family. Under these circumstances it is not surprising if education is not given priority. In an economy dominated by struggle for survival options are limited. Since, education does not provide any visible and immediate benefit and tribals do not see beyond their present state, the participation of tribal children in education also become limited. Another reason for low participation is the opportunity cost involved, as majority of the non-enrolled children are required to work in the households or on family occupations. Even if the economic contribution of children is indirect, they certainly facilitate the participation of parents in economic activity.

In recent years the efforts of the Government are directed towards improving economic conditions of tribes by introducing various developmental programmes and schemes, mostly related to agriculture, horticulture, cattle rearing etc., backed by subsidies, monetary and non-monetary inputs. A critical analysis of development programmes and their effect on tribal households shows that, till the tribal

Development vs. Education

In order to introduce permanent cultivation among shifting cultivators, the Government initiated orange and coffee plantation under the horticulture scheme in Andhra Pradesh. For this, the households were given two acres of forest land, and orange plants were supplied free of cost. For taking care of the plants, they were paid Rs.100 per month in the form of rice and other things. With some persuasion the tribals accepted the scheme as it had visible monetary benefit as well as getting some more land. But accepting a new scheme in addition to their traditional cultivation, means demand for more labour, which, in turn, brings change in the structure in the family labour. Work distribution pattern among the members of the household plays a crucial role in the success of the new scheme that they have accepted. This situation comes into conflict with the children's participation in education as their help in household work or in cultivation becomes essential. In another incident, a sheep rearing project was introduced and some of the tribal households were given a unit of sheep. Usually axe fell on education of children. For the household, direct benefit from sheep rearing is more attractive to improve their economic condition than the long-term benefits of education households reach a threshold level of income and land size, the economic development programmes can come into conflict with other activities like education. In a way it can be said that these development programmes, seems to be adversely affecting the education of tribal children (Sujatha, 1994).

Poor health is another major hindrance in the promotion and participation of tribal children in education. Contagious diseases like scabies, eye infection, malaria, diarrhea, etc. are common in tribal areas, which too affect the children's attendance at school. Further, some tribal communities are seasonal migrants and their absence in a particular place for a year lead to absenteeism among their children and makes it difficult for them to effectively benefit from schooling.

Perspectives for the Future

Education of the tribals cannot be left merely to short term plan strategies. It is important that planners take a long term view which is embedded in a meaningful policy framework. Following are some important points emerging from the review.

- Emphasis should be on quality and equity rather than quantity as it has been done during the past. The prime focus should be on provision of quality education that makes the tribal communities economically effective and independent.
- Looking at the tribal context it is of absolute necessity that the school schedule be prepared as per the local requirement rather than following a directive from the State. It has been found that vacations and holidays are planned without taking into cognizance, local contexts and thereby unnecessarily antagonizing tribal communities and keeping them out of school.
- Though it has been highlighted time and again no concrete step has been taken to provide locally relevant materials to tribal students. Availability of locally relevant materials will not only facilitate faster learning but also help the children to develop a sense of affiliation to the school.
- In order to make education effective and sustainable building partnership between the community and the Government. Results from pilot projects in Andhra Pradesh shows that community partnership not only augments state expenditure on education but also

guarantees supervision and monitoring thus addressing an intractable problem for the State.

- Environment building is of immense importance in the context of educational development among tribal communities. Community awareness and community mobilization which are the core elements in should receive adequate importance and attention.
- Decentralization of education management is another aspect that needs special consideration in the context of tribal areas. In fact, considering the geographical terrain and communication problems in tribal areas, it is crucial to restructure the existing system of educational management Adaptation.

3

Isolated Communities and Ignored Claims: Tribal Children's Right to Education in India

—Archana Mehendale

Indigenous communities of India are commonly referred to as tribal or adivasi communities and are recognized as Scheduled Tribes under the Constitution of India. Although the Constitution does not define Scheduled Tribes as such, it designates these communities as those which are scheduled in accordance with Article 342 of the Constitution. According to Article 342 of the Constitution, the Scheduled Tribes are the tribes to tribal communities or part of or groups within these tribes and tribal communities which have been declared as such by the President through a public notification. The criteria followed for specification of a community, as scheduled tribe are indications of primitive traits, distinctive culture, geographical isolation, shyness of contact with the community at large, and back wardness. At present, 533 tribes in India have been notified under Article 342 of the Constitution with the largest number of 62 tribes belonging to the State of Orissa.

Socio-Economic and Demographic Profile:

As per the 1991 Census, the Scheduled Tribes (ST) account for 67.76 million representing 8.08 percent of the country's population. Of this, 1.32 million (1.95%) belong to Primitive Tribal Groups (PTG) who are more marginalised than the St population.The ST population is estimated to have reached 88.8 million in 2001 which is 8.6% of the country's total population in 2001.The Scheduled Tribes are spread across the country and reside mainly in forest and hilly regions. The proportion of Scheduled Tribes within general population varies across States/

Union Territories and indicates heavy concentration in certain parts such as Mizoram (94.7%) Lakshwadeep (93.2%), Meghalaya (85.5%), Dadra and Nagar Haveli (78.9%). States of Kerala (1.1%), Tamil Nadu (1%) and Uttar Pradesh (0.2%) have a low percentage of Scheduled Tribe population in comparison to the general population. Since Independence, the percentage of ST population has steadily increased following the growth in general population.

It is also important to note that large majority of tribals lin India are landless and do not have a sustainable source of livelihood. The 1991 Census figures reveal that 42.02 percent of the Scheduled Tribe population were main workers (those who were employed for more than 183 days in the preceding year) of whom 54.50 percent were cultivators and 32.69 percent agricultural labourers. Thus, about 87 percent of the main workers from these communities were engaged in primary sector activities. While a majority of those employed do not receive even the statutory minimum wages, tribal women are found to be doubly exploited since they are paid even less than the tribal lmen. It is thus not surprising that poverty is widely prevalent among tribal population in India. Even when the overall levels of poverty for tribal population have reduced between 1993-94 to 1999-2000 from 51.94% to 45.86% among the rural tribal population and 41.14% to 34.75% among the urban tribal population, two important trends can be observed. Firstly, the rate of decline in poverty among the STs is much lower than that among the general population and secondly, the gap between poverty rates among tribal and general population is widening. A number of Scheduled Tribes living below poverty line have been provided economic assistance to enable them to rise above the poverty-line. However, this assistance has decreased from Rs. 9.98 lakh during 1999-2000 to 8.81 lakh during 2000-2001. The sex ratio among the STs, although significantly higher than the general population, has been slowly declining. While there were 982 tribal females for every 1000 tribal males in 1971, lkthe 1991 Census shows that there are only 972 females for every 100 tribal males. This could be indicative of their poor access to health services.

Educational Status of Tribals in India

Tribal children, like several marginalised groups of children in India, are trapped in an intergenerational vicious cycle of poverty, illiteracy and deprivation. This is evident in extremely poor adult literacy rates which are reproduced as low educationlevels among the children from ST communities. This section presents some key data points on educational status of ST communities as a whole as well as schooling status of tribal children. The literacy rate of Scheduled Tribes is abysmally low at around 29.60 percent, as against the national average of 52.21 percent. A review of literacy rates among ST population in comparison with that of the general population indicates a growing gap between literacy rates of these two communities.

It is also important to note that the 1991 literacy rates for ST are almost equal to the literacy rates of the total population in 1971! Female literacy is another significant indicator of educational development within any social group. Research studies have shown the importance of female literacy and education in uplifting the socio-economic parameters of a given society. In the context of tribal women in India, illiteracy is to highly prevalent that their engagement with the mainstream society is seriously limited. While more than three-quarters of ST women are illiterate, 77 districts in India have tribal female literacy rates lower than ten percent and 14 districts have less than three percent tribal female literacy rate.

Inter-state differences in the literacy rates of tribal population is evident with tribes from North Estern States of India showing high literacy rates. The highest literacy rate among tribals in Mizoram (82.73%) is attributed to a spread of Christian missionary educational linstitutions and a strong matrilineal family system amongthe khasi and Garo tribes belonging to the State. Low literacy rates are seen among the tribals from Madhya Prades (21.54%) and Orissa (22.31%).

The above data shows that the gross enrolment ratio for Classes 1-5 and Classes 1-8 has declined from 1990-91 to 1999-2000 for the total population, but in the case of ST population; it has decreased for Classes 1-5 (except for girls) but has improved for Classes 1-8. But there still remains an almost five percentage point gap between the enrolment of ST girls and non-

ST girls wherein less than half of ST girls are not even enrolled in schools. Yet, this large scale enrolment of ST children in schools has been on account of wide scale government efforts to universalize education and a growing demand among the tribal communities to access formal education system, perhaps as a means to achieve inclusion in the mainstream. However, this has had it own ramifications. While schools as institutions and teachers as critical agents have remained fundamentally unchanged, the school atmosphere has not always become conducive to accept and retain these children in schools. As we shall see later in this lpaper, tribal children's school experience lis an important variable which determines whethere the child continues to be in school lor decides to drop out.

The problem of drop outs persists among all categories of children in India. However, in the context of children studying in Classes 1-10 the gap between the ST and total population in reduction of drop-outs has widened from 1990-91 to 1998-99. The reduction in the drop out rates could be because of various incentive schemes run by the State Governments for education of ST children such as those providing free books, uniforms and scholarships in government schools. But schemes such as those providing for hostels for ST boys and girls are not implemented fully by the States owing to lack of financial resources and therefore fewer ST children pursure high school education. The policy of reserving special seats for ST students at higher education levels is not widely availed since a large number of ST students do not even reach those levels and drop out at lower levels of school education. Even the Ashram schools (residential schools for St boys and girls) started by the Government in 1990-91 are poorly maintained and sometimes lack even the basic facilities. Given the low levels of literacy among the ST population, several children from these communities happen to be 'first generationlearners' and in the absence of State support for helping them cope with studies, very many children drop out of the schools. This disproportinonately low representation of ST children at higher levels of education compounds the existing disparties among Indian society.

Lack of proactive governance in favour of the STs is not linked only to lack of resources. Governmental indifference and lack of political willl are largely responsible for the callous state of affairs. The unutilized amount for tribal welfare for the years 1998-2001 for alll the states combined was Rs. 40546 lakhs. States with lhigh proportion of St population also had high amounts of unutilised funds with Bihar (Rs. 8113.26 lakhs), Jharkhand (Rs. 4742.62 lakhs), Madhya Pradesh (Rs. 4721.61 lakhs) and Gujarat (Rs. 3721.72 lakhs) topping the order.

The School Experience

At school, the experiences of tribal children range from discrimination to a sense of complete alienation. Students from ST communities encounter a series of obstacles including commuting long distances to school in hostile environmental conditions, abuses and discrimination from teachers and fellow students from non-tribal backgrounds, difficulty in comprehending the language of instruction and negotiating space of themselves which was denied historically.

Children's denominational identities have always affected their school experiences. Ideally, the school teacher must playa a vital role in supporting the struggles of first-generation learners. But it is found that although there is formal inclusion in the mainstream education system in the sense that children are officially enrolled, the teachers are often found to question to 'reducibility' of tribal children, revealing that nothing much has changed in the perceptions held about the 'other' by teachers who are generally drawn from mainstream social groups.

Research shows that tribal children are often subjected to overt discrimination by non-tribal upper caste school teachers who view them as 'slow learners' unable to learn despite several repetitions; as 'unclean' and are therefore given tasks of sweeping and swabbing the schools unlike non-tribal upper caste children who may be asked to fetch water or lock the school. Teachers also demean tribal children by calling their parents 'drunken', with no interest in schools and education. Untouchability is also found to prevail in schools, where upper caste teachers and students refuse to drink water from the same tap as the tribal children before washing it thoroughly. Even play activities and school transactions are sometimes segregated on the basis of these identities. The tribal children are repeatedly subjected to variable abuse at the hands of upper caste teachers and this has a critical impact on the way these first generation students view themselves as learners.

Since the tribal languages are distinctly different from the medium of instruction in schools (which is usually the respective State language) tribal children often find it extremely difficult to cope with their studies and homework. This lack of language skills acts as a serious impediment when the teacher is a non-tribal and makes no effort to link the two linguistic experiences for the child. Aspirations among tribal children are also low considering that there are not many formally educated persons in such ammonites. The inability to secure jobs amongst tribals who have completed formal education have lead some to get disillusioned with the education system and question the futility of spending several years struggling to get educated. Some consider school-educated children as unfit to carry out their hereditary occupations thereby rendering them 'useless' in their traditional lives. Yet, the motivation of a large number of tribal children to walk hours to reach school, tolerate the rebuke of teachers and fellow students, their efforts to identify with a language and curriculum that is alien to their own life worlds and their struggles to break free of their historical marginalization is definitely striking.

A Question of Tribal Rights

In several societies, children's rights are intrinsically linked to respect for human rights and it would be almost impractical to separate rights of children from those of their families and communities. Fulfillment of third generation of rights i.e. group or community rights is often imperative considering that it is not children's rights alone but those of an entire community which are under extreme risk. By bestowing children from such social group's rights that are not enjoyed by their families or communities, superficial lines get drawn between children and their families or communities while making a farce of realizing children's rights. It also presumes that children's rights can be respected while the rights of their parents and communities are persistently violated. However, as we shall see below, children's rights remain unfulfilled so long as the position of their social group is not improved. In the Indian context too, tribal children's rights are more likely to get realised if rights of tribal communities are holistically recognized and fulfilled. The following problems faced by tribal communities in India make it extremely difficult for tribal children to gain entry and sustain within the mainstream education system.

Displacement: Forced or voluntary eviction of tribals from their homes and habitats has been a serious problem since Independence. Large scale projects such as large dams, power plants. Industrial units, large mining projects undertaken on tribal lands for the 'larger public good' very often provide little to the displaced communities. For years, questions have been raised about the unsatisfactory manner in which they have been rehabilitated Research shows that between 1951 and 1990, a population of 21.3 million persons have been displaced in the states of Andhara Pradesh, Bihar, Gujarat, Maharashtra, Madhya Prades, Rajasthan and Orissa. Of this, 8.54 million are tribals (40 percent of the total) and of those only 2.12 million (24.8 percent) tribals have been resettled so far.3 In the absence of appropriate rehabilitation, displaced communities are uprooted and forced to migrate to newer areas. While they may settle down on forestlands in the new villages or in urban slums in case they migrate to cities, their settlement is considered illegal and they are therefore denied even the basic civic amenities. Children belonging to families of displaced tribal families are never able to continue schooling even if they were enrolled initially, and usually end up in wage employment in order to support the family's fresh set of challenges.

Land Alienation: Among tribal communities, land and its natural resources are sacrosanct and hold significant place in their socio-cultural and religious life. It is also the main source of livelihood and Minor Forest Produce (MEP) is known to help several communities to survive. Given the vulnerability of tribal communities in India, several of them have had to part with their treasured resource for reasons ranging from acquisition of land for public purposes, encroachments by non-tribals or 'outsiders', forcible evictions, etc. The Ministry of Rural Development data shows that as many as 4.65 lakh cases of alienation of tribal land covering an area of 9.17 lakh acres were registered in the states of Andhra Prades, Assam, Bihar, Gujarat, Himachal Pradesh, Karnataka, Madhya Prades,

Maharashtra, Orissa, Rajasthan and Tripura in January 1999. Of these, only two lakh cases were disposed in favour of 1.56 lakh tribal families covering an area of 5.31 lakh acres. Among the states, land alienation is high in Andhra Pradesh (2.79 lakh acres), Madhya Pradesh (1.58 lakh acres), Karnataka (1.30 lakh acres), and Gujarat (1.16 lakh acres). An absence of political and administrative will to identify and hand over alienated land back to the tribals is considered to be a major obstacle in ensuring that the tribal communities get what is due to them. While on the one hand, tribals continue to loose their land to so-called large developmental projects, without being compensated or restored with lands adequately, questions are being asked about the so-called benefits of these projects percolating to the tribals themselves. In fact, due to lack of education and vocational training amongst tribals, projects set up in tribal areas rarely absorb the local tribals in employment. In many cases, tribals migrate at different times of the year to find employment Children from such migrating families are either never enrolled in schools due to frequent transfers, or end up discontinuing education for the period that they are away which has an adverse impact on their educational attainments.

Tribal communities in India have been historically deprived of access to resources and opportunities, including the opportunity to get educated. The present efforts of the Indian government to bring these children into formal schools fails at two levels. Firstly, because it is not able to enroll all tribal children and provide them access to good quality functional schools. In some states, the government has started providing alternate schools run by untrained local youth which is opposed by many education activities, since it is a poor and sub-standard system given out to those who are already marginalised. Secondly, even when tribal children are enrolled into schools, the education system besides doling out some incentives does not do much to improve the school environment, which will treat these first-generation learners with respect and dignity. Instead, tribal children are made to put up with an offensive and insulting climate that continuously discriminates and alienates. For such historically deprived communities, providing access to education is simply not enough, the government has to take a proactive role in creating overall conditions and opportunities that will facilitate their transition and breaking of the intergenerational cycle of poverty and illiteracy. A sensitive cadre of teachers and bureaucracy is definitely required to make the difference. At another level, educational deprivation must be seen in the context of overall deprivation of the community and hence emphasis must be placed on improving women, providing basic civic amenities such as fuel, water and sanitation are preconditions to advancements of rights of tribal children. Unless the government undertakes urgent steps to address these issues, its proclamations on child rights would remain examples of empty rhetoric and its actions would effectively continue to exclude those already sidelined. Following the increasing gap between the rich and the poor in the country, the gap between the tribal and non-tribal children is also widening rapidly, thereby further isolating the isolated. Respecting their claims at the outset should set the ball rolling in the right direction.

4

Contextualizing Classrooms in Tribal Area Schools : An Empiricial Experience

—Mahendra-K.-Mishra

Introduction

The National Policy of Education 1986 and Programme of Action 1992 envisaged for education of scheduled tribe and scheduled caste children and has specified objectives and strategies. The cultural variations and the gap of home language and school language, understanding space and time from tribal point of view and construction of knowledge from ones own cultural context are some of the points which determine the education of scheduled tribe children. Cultural plurality is the basis of contextual differences in primary education. School as a system is to propagate knowledge and wisdom to open gateway to education and understand the meaning of ones own world around her.

In a multicultural, multiethnic and multilingual society, using a culture free textbook or adopting common curricula with a dominant language challenges the efficiency and competencies of the children of different groups. The cultural context and the common curriculum content in a language other than the mother tongue of the children is not only a contradiction in learning system but also a serious threat in cognitive development of the child. The content must have a context and this must support the language of thought and language of speech of the children, if it has to be a child centered learning. A child understand her own environment from her own mother tongue, around her own cultural context, and in the school the same experimental knowledge helps her to enter in to a new world from unknown knowledge. Association of experience with the classroom knowledge helps her in constructing a broader knowledge in her mind.

In Indian situation, the content and process need to be adaptable for the children of special needs. Due to the gap of home language and school language, also the content with out context, the pedagogy in tribal situation have a serious setback, and in many a places unable to reach the targeted children, let alone to speak of desired goal. As a result of which the competence and the performance of the children achieving the minimum levels of learning has become a far-reaching dream.

The National Curriculum Framework for School Education (NCFSE) advocates for using culture specific, and teaching pedagogies through mother tongue. The NCFSE, in favour of school education writes, "Pedagogy is perceived not merely as a source of instruction but as a culture or as a set of sub-cultures, which reflect different contexts and different teaching behaviour- inside and outside classrooms." (P.18 of NCFSE) as cultural specificity should get embedded in the pedagogical practices which should be evolved for tribal, rural, urban and other ethnic groups and communities."

In the context of education of tribal children at primary stage where the gap of home language and school language is high the non-contextual pedagogy fails to cater to the need and in these case, language as a medium of instruction determine the teaching. The question of content, process, teaching and learning comes when the issues of language is addressed at first.

Therefore National Curriculum Frame work recommends that mother tongue or regional language should be children's first language to be learnt right from the first standard (p.39). The reason being "their natural creativity and imagination must be encouraged and fostered that will make them realize the basic difference between their verbal language and the language of mathematics. Thus, learning of language should find a central place in the total educational process." *(P38)*

On the light of the above objectives, the aim of this paper is to examine the situation of the tribal area

Education of Tribal Children in Primary Stage: An Overview

Tribal population in Orissa constitutes one fourth of the total population in Orissa. There are sixty-two tribes having twenty-two distinct ethnic languages among the fourteen primitive and transitory tribal people in the State. Out of 314 Blocks 118 Blocks have more than 50% tribal population and have been declared as tribal sub plan area.

Tribal language is distinct from the Oriya language. At present, the Santal, Munda, Ho, Saora, Kishan, Khadia, Didayi, Gadaba, Bhumia, paroja, Mundari, Kuvi, Kui, Bonda, Juang, Kutia, Dongria kondh, and Bhunjia form the major ethnic groups. They have their home language and the children speak these languages in their home and society. They also construct their knowledge through their mother tongue.

Attitude of non-tribal teachers towards tribal children and, tribal language is stereotyped. The social distance is high. Teachers impose their own culture too the tribal children. Teacher's perception towards tribal culture is indifferent. Teachers from tribal communities have detribalised to the extent that they don't understand the role of mother tongue in teaching in primary stage. No teacher either from tribal or non-tribal communities have raised this issue that how the tribal children face difficulties in understanding the school language and how the language gap hampers the construction of knowledge.

Tribal children are not exposed to school language at the primary stage. Even the content of the book is alien to them since it is non-contextual. The content and the process as well do not attract the tribal children. The socio-cultural environment of a tribal child is different from others. The children of tribal areas see, feel, and understand their visible world through their language. Their language of thought and language of speech is entirely different from the textbook language. The meaning of using the space and time in a tribal area is not reflected either in the teacher's behaviour or in the content.

Fear and threat of unforeseen challenge is another aspect, which interdict the tribal children to attend the school. Even in the Ashram Schools, the children's self image or self-confidence is not built properly so that a tribal child can maintain his self-image and feel his self esteem.

Classroom content and process in teaching in non-contextual. Language is alien. Communication is a big issue between teachers and the children. The purpose and meaning of teaching by the teachers and learning by the learners become meaningless. Teaching is one sided, teacher centered. When the teacher does not understand the language of the child, the child-centered approach is far reaching goal.

Teachers performance: Teachers perform their duties with out understanding the learning difficulties of the children. Even they rarely discuss their teaching difficulties in the monthly center meetings. In the total process education of children of special needs is almost absent.

Academic support in addressing the bi-lingual classroom, preparation of tribal Oriya bi-lingual teaching learning materials is not undertaken at teachers training level. Continuous upgrading the knowledge of teachers on language teaching, understanding the diversities of socio-linguistic aspects are not taken up as a priority area. In stead the common curricula is used for all children irrespective of cultural or linguistic diversities.

Teacher training Institutes are yet to take up academic support to the Block level and District level.

State language policy (three language formula) on using of mother tongue is lacking. Therefore the diverse cultural and linguistic areas of the state has also been ignored, and it is hoped that a common curricula is to serve the purpose, which is no – contextual and from pedagogic point of view it is not child centric, but teacher centric.

Lack of long term planning and sustainable efforts to implement the education of tribal children at the academic domain.

Parental attitude towards teaches the children in mother tongue.

State Intervention on education of SC/ST in DPEP :

After introduction of DPEP in Orissa during 1996-97, education of tribal children was taken up as one of the interventions. The experience was like " we make the road by walking". With the help of Academy of tribal Dialects and culture, and also with some eminent tribal educationists, the issues, strategies and intervention were conceptualized. The steps taken up on this intervention was more of experiencing than a camera ready Programme. The learning was initiated from the dialogue with the teachers of tribal areas. Experience of the teachers led to identify the needs of the tribal education.

The first workshop with the teachers was the identification of training needs of tribal area teachers. Major issues discussed in that workshop were

(*a*) Gap of home language and school language

(*b*) Non –contextual text books,

(*c*) Teachers lack of knowledge on bi-lingual education

(*d*) Teachers attitude towards tribal language and children,

(*e*) Lack of academic support from the top

(*f*) Lack of course content in the teacher training Programme to address tribal children as a special focus group

When the initial attitudinal assessment was administered it was found that the teachers have make beliefs on tribal language and tribal children as followings:

Learning From the Past

The NCERT, New Delhi during 1985 undertook the education of tribal children for Saora children in Orissa. Textbooks for Class I and Class II were prepared for language and Arithmetic in Saora and Oriya language. But the effect of using these primers is not available in the field or in the State.

Thereafter, the SCERT, Orissa also prepared some area specific primers in tribal languages with the help of Academy of Tribal Dialects and culture. But due to lack of a concrete plan of action in the field level, the books were distributed among the children, but the teachers did not use it considering it supplementary readers for tribalchildren.

The main reason is that when a classroom with majority of tribal children and minor non-tribal children are found, teachers have given importance to teach them in regional language and the question of teaching the children's language in children's language is-ignored.

(*i*) Tribal language is inferior to the Oriya language

(*ii*) Mother tongue should not be used in the classroom

(*iii*) Children should be discouraged to use mother tongue in the class rooms

(*iv*) Tribal children are docile

(*v*) Tribal children are weak in arithmetic in comparison to others

(*vi*) If a child use mother tongue he will be dull

(*vii*) There is no science in the village

(*viii*) Arithmetic isn't used in the village

(*ix*) Illiterate people don't have knowledge

(*x*) Girls are dull in arithmetic

(*xi*) Tribal children are afraid of schools

(*xii*) Knowledge is found in the books only

(*xiii*) There is no knowledge beyond text book

(*xiv*) Oral Folktale/song/riddles are not knowledge because they are not written texts

All these statements were administered and found that about 70% teachers are with in these make beliefs and 30% teachers have differed to it. The initial attitude of the teachers towards the tribal children, tribal language and learning were captured to know the mind set of the teachers.

The findings of the workshop were that teachers should be trained up. The need for the training was that:

- Tribal children are first generation learners
- Tribal children do not have a study atmosphere at home as their parents are non-literate

- There is a visible disparity among the tribal and non-tribals
- The ethnic prejudices and biases are high in society and school as a result of which the tribal children have little hope of competing with non-tribal children
- Most of the teachers working in the tribal areas are non-tribal and have a number of beliefs and assumptions on tribal society, people and tribal children.
- The ethnic biases among teachers, the traditional process of teaching learning, lack of knowledge on tribal culture and society among the teachers and their inability to relate to the children in their language and socio-cultural context are the main reasons for educational backwardness of the tribal children.

Hence it was felt that teachers teaching in tribal areas must possess a healthy attitude towards tribal language and culture. They must be free from any type of biases and prejudices, which may come in the way of their interaction with children.

Therefore it was resolved that unless the attitude of teachers is changed and a new vision towards tribal children and culture is developed, a simple content based and processed oriented pedagogy will not serve the purpose. Attitudinal training aimed at making the teachers rethink their traditional teaching practices and styles, questioning their personal beliefs and assumptions which they initially took for granted and remove some of these prejudices- thereby making them more endearing to the tribal children and culture. This automatically reflects in enrollment, retention and greater achievement.

To address these issues a training module on attitudinal aspect was devised with the resource persons in whom the tribal area teachers were a part of it. The training module was consists of the following content.

- Initial attitudinal assessment on language,
- Understanding about the children,
- Likes and dislikes of children,
- To make know that the natural land cultural environment o f tribal children are enriched with context specific content

- Knowing that the children construct their knowledge from their own cultural context
- To know how language is learnt in context
- Use the community resources for pedagogical improvement
- To explore the rich folklore of the tribal community to use them for teaching learning materials,
- Understanding tribal society and ways of using local knowledge for classroom teaching
- Ways in which the village can be made a living classroom for a tribal child

After this the training module was prepared and 320 master trainers were trained up. These master trainers were the teachers from the field. They trained up the teachers in the field. This was a one-slot training, which gained momentum, and many teachers had their opinion that they could get a new vision to see their children potential and the special needs of tribal children.

The universal demand and need from the teachers were that unless the tribal children are provided with context specific books and materials, teaching learning is not possible.

This led to another step. Preparation of primer for the tribal children was initiated. The attitudinal training was immensely helpful for such a process. Teachers from tribal communities were come forward to prepare the primers.

The changing scenario of introducing new pedagogical vision in current years has provided the teachers on child centered, activity based and participatory pedagogy. This helped the teachers to find away for the tribal primers. The experience of Ekalavya, DPEP- I states and the expertise of language pedagogists was helpful to prepare the primers and the language-materials.

Linguistic Mapping and Survey

Meanwhile before preparing the primer linguistic mapping and survey was taken up to assess the gap of home language and school language. The extent of the study was to know the followings:

1. Reconnaisance of language variations typological and areal
2. Identification and classification of speech varieties

Grasping of different forms of speech on the basis of structural and genealogical affinities, mutual; intelligibility and geo-physical distribution

Evaluation of bi-lingualism; its nature and extent Evaluation of the process of Oriyanisation and tribalisation in operation in the tribal language speaking communities in tribal dominated areas.

The main areas covered under the questionnaire were language proficiency, language use, language maintenance, and shift, language identity, teacher's attitude towards tribal language and culture, and student's attitude towards schoolteacher.

The findings of the linguistics survey and mapping in 26 Blocks with linguistic diversities are:

Villages with 100% tribal people speak their mother tongue and the children of those villages don't have any access to Oriya language Parents are exposed to Oriya language through market Children in school do not understand Oriya language; they are also reluctant to speak Oriya language in the class The gap of language in Gajapati, Rayagada is high in comparison to Kalahandi and Keonjhar.

5

Strategies for Tribal's Education : A Pschyo-Social Approach

—Arockia Maria Michealraja

Education is a most powerful instrument for achieving an egalitarian type of the society. The framers of constituent, therefore, took a special care of the condition in which the people from under privileged communities are provided several safeguards for the promotion of their educational and economic interests. Education cannot change in any fundamental way unless we change our basic patterns of thinking and interacting so that learning can become a way of life. Teachers, parents, administrators, district resource and community people are coming together throughout hundreds of school communities to learn how to revitalize their schools with a process known as "Tribes." Evaluation of Tribes Learning Community Schools has examined the impact of the Tribes process on student behaviour, academic performance, school culture, and teacher collegiality. Studies have shown that: Tribes TLC has a positive impact on classroom environment, teachers report spending less time managing student behavior, students are significantly less likely to be referred for disciplinary problems, the Tribes process helps teachers address performance and content standards, students in well-implemented classrooms score significantly higher on standardized tests than students from comparison groups, teachers report increased staff collegiality and planning. "Responsive Education" is an essential pedagogy for academic achievement and school reform. It is the synthesis of artful teaching practices. It is based on understanding the critical developmental needs of a student age and cultural group. The

Goal of this paper is to engage all teachers, administrators, students and families in working together as a learning community that is dedicated to caring and support, active participation and positive expectations for all students.

Introduction

Education of ST children to considered important, not only because of the constitutional obligation but also as a crucial input for total development of tribal communities. Education of Scheduled Tribe children is considered important, not only because of the constitutional obligation, but also a crucial input for total development of tribal communities. The literacy levels of the Scheduled Tribes according to the 2001 census is 47.10% as compared to overall literacy rate of the total population i.e., 65.38%,which shows a dismal picture of Scheduled Tribes education. So long as there is a gap between the literacy levels, the position of Scheduled Tribes will remain backward. Most tribal children do not understand the textbooks, which are generally in the regional language. The appointment of non-tribal teachers in tribal children's schools is another problem. The teachers do not know the language the children speak and children do not understand the teacher's language. The issues pertaining to tribal education

The spread of education among the weaker sections of our society is vital as education is a prime requisite for socio-economic development. The policy to promote educational interests of the weaker sections of the people, especially the Scheduled Castes and Scheduled Tribes, has been enshrined in our Constitution as a Directive Principle of State Policy. Therefore, the main thrust continues to be on education. The general level of literacy is very low and is lower still in the case of Backward Classes. To conclude in the words of Swami Vivekananda - "The Real India lives in the Villages. Unless we are able to uplift the Tribal and the backward classes, India faces to dark future. Along with their economic improvement they have to be raised culturally and spiritually."

Education for the marginlized people, as for anyone else in India, has today become a matter of great importance. Ever since

India gained independence a considerable amount of money and resources have been spent so that the unprivileged, undeveloped and neglected marginlized people could get a fair deal. It has been generally recognized that India being a welfare state cannot afford to leave a particular section of the population behind in the field of education, as indeed in any other field. This would be against the principle of democratic development of the country there is hardly any necessity, therefore to emphasize the need and importance of education for these people. Everyone everywhere feels these needs. An earnest endeavor is being made by all concerned at all levels to bring these less privileged people, the scheduled tribes, on the same educational level as that attained by the more advanced community of India (Ambhaist, 1991).

Empowerment is about people - both women and men - taking control over their lives: becoming conscious of their own situation and position, setting their own agendas, creating space for themselves, gaining skills, building self-confidence, solving problems, and developing self-reliance. It is not only a social and political process, but an individual one as well - and it is not only a process but an outcome too. Realizing that Scheduled Tribes are one of the most deprived and marginalised groups with respect to education, a host of programmes and measures were initiated ever since the Independence. Elementary education is a priority area in the Tribal sub-plans from the 5th Five Year Plan.

Normally Ashram schools are residential schools for tribal children from a cluster of habitations. Based on the Gandhian philosophy of self-reliance, it was first experimented by Thakkar Bapa, a Gandhianin Panchamahal district of Gujarat in the pre-independence days (Ananda, 1994). Ashram schools were found effective as (i) it was not feasible to open full fledged schools in very small and scattered habitations (ii) it created congenial atmosphere for teaching learning as it is assumed that the tribal households do not have such an environment and (iii) it helped to develop the total personality of the child and impart vocational skills to improve employment opportunities. Ashram schools generally provide admission to children from habitations at least 6-8 kms away from the school. If children from nearby villages are admitted, they are not provided with boarding. The curriculum of Ashram schools includes agriculture and other life skills in addition to general subjects. Many parents in Jharkhand, Orissa and Gujarat preferred Ashram schools as they provided free food, clothing and boarding. Some parents said that education of their wards in Ashram schools was not obstructed, when parents migrated for work (Jha & Jhingran, 2002).

Education of ST children is considered important, not only because of the Constitutional obligation but also as a crucial input for total development of tribal communities. One of the super goals of Serva Shikshan Abiyan is to "bridge all gender and social category gaps at primary stage by 2007 and at elementary stage by 2010". The issues and challenges in tribal education can be categorized as external, internal, socio-economic and psychological. The external constraints are related to issues at levels of policy, planning and implementation while internal constraints are with respect to school system, content, curriculum, pedagogy, medium of instruction etc. The third set of problems relates to social economic and cultural background of tribals and psychological aspects of first generation learners. The literacy level of Scheduled Castes and Scheduled Tribes is very low compared to the general literacy rate. Recognizing that education provides opportunities for a permanent change in the socio-economic status of these people, this Government gives top priority to education. Hence out of a sum of Rs. 448.91 crores provided in the Budget Estimate for 2004-2005 to this Department, more than70% is earmarked for schemes related to education. There is a need to evolve sensitive model of tribal education rooted in the psychological strengths of tribal children.

The term 'Scheduled Tribes' first appeared in the Constitution of India. Article 366 (25) defined scheduled tribes as "such tribes or tribal communities or parts of or groups within such tribes or tribal communities as are deemed under Article 342 to be Scheduled Tribes for the purposes of this constitution". Article 342, which is reproduced below, prescribes procedure to be followed in the matter of specification of scheduled tribes. Education cannot change in any fundamental way unless we change our basic patterns of thinking and interacting so that learning can become a way of life. Teachers, parents, administrators, district resource and community people are coming together throughout hundreds of school communities to learn how to revitalize their schools with a process known as "Tribes." Evaluation of Tribes Learning Community Schools has examined the impact of the Tribes process on student behavior, academic performance, school culture, and teacher collegiality. Studies have shown that: Tribes TLC has a positive impact on classroom environment , teachers report spending less time managing student behavior, students are significantly less likely to be referred for disciplinary problems, the Tribes process helps teachers address performance and content standards, students in well-implemented classrooms score significantly higher on standardized tests than students from comparison groups, teachers report increased staff collegiality and planning.

In a multicultural, multiethnic and multilingual society, using a culture free textbook or adopting common curricula with a dominant language challenges the efficiency and competencies of the children of different groups. The cultural context and the common curriculum content in a language other than the mother tongue of the children is not only a contradiction in learning system but also a serious threat in cognitive development of the child. The content must have a context and this must support the language of thought and language of speech of the children, if it has to be . hild centered learning. A child understand her own environment from her own mother tongue, around her own cultural context, and in the school the same experiential knowledge helps her to enter in to a new world ok unknown knowledge. Association of experience with the classroom knowledge helps her in constructing a broader knowledge in her mind. In Indian situation, the content and process need to be adaptable for the children of special needs. Due to the gap of home language and school language, also the content with out context, the pedagogy in tribal situation have a serious setback, and in many a places unable to reach the targeted children, let alone to speak of desired goal. Education cannot change in any fundamental way unless we change our basic patterns of thinking and interacting so that learning can become a way of life (Mishra, 2001).

Teachers, parents, administrators, district resource and community people are coming together throughout hundreds of school communities to learn how to revitalize their schools with a process known as "Tribes". Along with a wide range of educators they realize that improving education ultimately means:

- Making the emotional, physical and intellectual growth of each and every student the primary focus of all planning and action
- Altering the deep rooted negative patterns of interaction within the school system

Whether a classroom, school, district or other organization, collaboration is difficult unless the learning community uses:

- A community building process
- A common set of collaborative skills
- Small groups for inclusion and wide participation

Without these, the supportive components for change (caring, inclusion, individual recognition and participation) cannot happen. Peter Senge, author of The Learning Organization Made Plain, asserts that "virtually all important decisions occur in groups. The learning units of organizations are teams, groups of people who need one another to act." 2 Moreover, without a process, the use of collaborative skills and peer group structures, the overall school community will have difficulty achieving common goals on behalf of students. The whole school community needs to: (1) gain knowledge on how to reach and teach the diversity of today's students; and (2) learn how to build a positive environment that gives all students inclusion, a sense of being valued, meaningful participation and experiences of success.

Evaluation of Tribes Learning Community (TLC) Schools has examined the impact of the Tribes process on student behavior, academic performance, school culture, and teacher collegiality. Studies have shown that: Tribes TLC has a positive impact on classroom environment, teachers report spending less time managing student behavior, students are significantly less likely to be referred for disciplinary problems, the Tribes process helps teachers address performance and content standards, students in well-implemented classrooms score significantly higher on standardized tests than students from comparison groups, teachers report increased staff collegiality and planning.

"Responsive Education" is an essential pedagogy for academic achievement and school reform. It is the synthesis of artful teaching practices. It is based on understanding the critical developmental needs of a student age and cultural group.

Our Questions were

1. How does teacher perception and student perception compare with the implementation of the Tribes process in the classroom?
2. How do teacher, resource teachers, administration, and the perceptions of classified staff compare with the implementation of the Tribes process school-wide?
3. What recommendations (strategies and activities) would be useful to grade level teachers (grades 3-6) and administrators/school leadership groups to strengthen the implementation of the Tribes process?

Origin and Design Stages

The process, known simply as "Tribes," and more specifically as "Tribes Learning Communities," was developed by Jeanne Gibbs at a time when concerned educators in eighteen school districts of Contra Costa County, California, were seeking ways:

- to prevent substance use and abuse, and other behavioral problems
- to demonstrate improvement in academic test scores, and
- to stem the tide of teachers leaving the profession

Un-anticipated outcomes:

- Teachers realized that they could also teach core academic content in small groups - thereby reaching and involving all of the students in a classroom.
- Individual teachers and whole schools began to request training in cooperative group learning.

Current Model: Tribes Learning Community

Ever-growing inquiries and training requests from schools throughout the United States and Canada led to the development of Center Source Systems, TLC. in 1995. The task of the new organization was: (1) to develop a research-based whole school model, and (2) to create a capacity-building training system - based on the long-standing philosophy and process of Tribes.

Philosophy and Goal

We believe that:

- The goal of education is to develop greatness in young human beings, active constructive citizens who are valuable contributors to society. To educate is to call forth all aspects of a student's human development - intellectual, social, emotional, physical and spiritual.
- Intellectual, social and emotional learning is an interdependent growth process. It is influenced daily by the quality of the systems in a student's life.
- Schools of excellence are student-centered. They have caring cultures, supportive structures and pedagogy that respond and support the stages of development and the diversity of students' learning needs.
- School reform depends upon the whole system working together as a learning community - a school community committed to continual reflective practice towards improvement and educational excellence.

The philosophy and concepts above are the foundation of the dual mission and goal statement of Tribes Learning Community schools:

The Design of the Whole School Model

The design moves the four philosophy beliefs forward into a clear action plan framework for school reform. The four-fold philosophy and four-step framework is grounded in a synthesis of a wide-range of literature and research on human development, child and adolescent development, elements of ideal cultures for learning, resilience, cognitive theory, brain compatible learning, multiple intelligences, cooperative group learning, project learning/constructivism, multicultural/gender equity, democratic group process, school climate, classroom management, reflective practice, system change, professional development and authentic assessment. approximately 16 research-based components for effective pedagogy and school reform.

> "building a culture for school-based reform means uprooting many old assumptions about learning - to make way for new beliefs about how students 'become smart'.
>
> *- A. Anne Wheelock*

The Developmental Process of Tribes

The purpose of the following graphic is to illustrate the research-based framework for the school renewal process. Brief discussions on the four strategies and the literature on which they are based follow.

1. A Caring Culture
2. The Community of Learners
3. Responsive Education - Student-Centered Active Learning

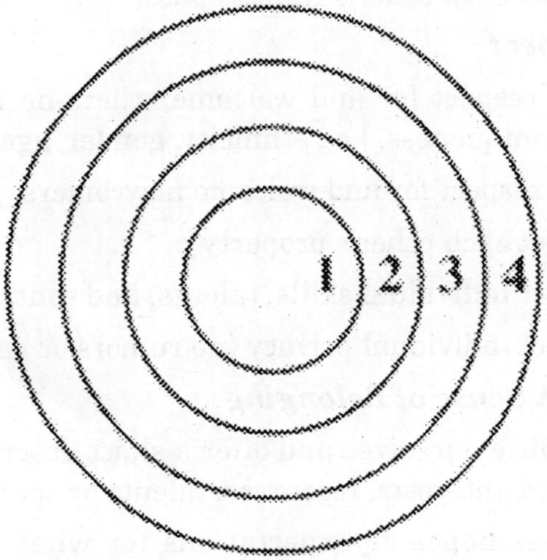

Description of Components

Beginning Tribes

- Meet in small groups and a community circle to relate as peers.
- Take time to build a sense of belonging in the group.

- Make sure that everyone participates equally.
- Use Tribes inclusion strategies.

Attentive Listening

- Pay attention and look at the person who is speaking.
- Know when and how to take turns speaking in the group.
- Paraphrase what people have said to let them know they have been heard.
- Use appropriate body language in response to the speaker, like nodding and smiling.

Appreciation/No Put-downs

- Avoid put-down remarks and actions.
- Compliment, appreciate, and recognize each other's gifts and talents.

Right to Pass

- Choose how much we will share about ourselves in a group activity.
- Respect each other's right to pass.

Mutual Respect

- Show respect for and welcome others-no matter what their uniqueness, i.e., ethnicity, gender, age, etc.
- Show respect for and welcome newcomers.
- Respect each other's property.
- Respect individual skills, talents, and contributions.
- Respect individual privacy (no rumors or gossip).

Inclusion - A Sense of Belonging

- Introduce ourselves and offer a short description of our feelings, interests, resources, talents or special qualities.
- Express hopes or expectations for what will happen during the group's time together.
- Listen to others, not only for what they say but how they feel.
- Reflect on our experiences.
- Feel a sense of belonging and being a part or the group.

Influence - To Feel of Value

- Participate in setting goals for the group
- Feel comfortable in saying what we think and feel.
- Respect people's differences.
- Build on each other's strengths.
- Think about how we can contribute to the group.
- Work together to make decisions so that everyone feels they can influence others.
- Work to resolve, rather than avoid uncomfortable problems and conflicts that begin to separate members.

Community - Working Together Creatively

- Solve problems creatively.
- Work together successfully to complete tasks.
- Share leadership in the group and share responsibility.
- Assess improvements and reflect upon individual and community experiences.
- Take time to celebrate achievements and successes.

Use of Processing Questions

- Incorporate Tribes' cooperative strategies in my content areas/curriculum.
- Use reflection/processing questions.

Student Learning and Development - Re-Focusing

Although the goal of the majority of schools today is to have higher student achievement on standardized tests, the promise of that happening depends upon the school community as a system: (1) becoming student-centered (Comer, Meier, Darling-Hammond), and (2) learning how to reach and teach the diversity of students (Dewey, Johnson, Wheelock, Goodlad, Gay). The primary focus of the Tribes school is not computer literacy, not a reading program or preparation for year-end tests - although all may be addressed and sequenced into the school's action plan. The focus is on the students. All policy, structures, decisions, curriculum and pedagogy depend upon the response to one question: "How and to what extent will 'this' support the learning and developmental needs of these students?" Even to begin to know how to respond to the on-going question, the

Tribes school staff becomes an on-going collaborative "learning community." They up-date their knowledge and perspectives on children's development, resiliency, cognitive learning and multiple intelligences. Rather than teachers taking courses on their own, the whole staff learns together to better identify and respond effectively to the diversity of students' cultures and needs, and to use multiple ways to accelerate the inseparable interdependent triad: academic, social and emotional learning.

A Caring Culture - Re-Culturing

"It is only by reculturing a school beforehand or along with any restructuring effort that meaningful improvement can be made." –Michael Fullan

Given that the focus of a Tribes school is student-centered, the next question becomes, "How do we create an ideal culture for learning?" Comprehensive studies (Werner, Bruner, Meier, Fullan, Gay) verify that the culture must be safe and caring. The culture in Tribes school communities is based on the three well-proven principles that foster human resilience: caring relationships, positive expectations and beliefs, and opportunities for participation and contribution (Benard). Its components are those of an ideal learning culture. Namely, it is participative, proactive, collaborative, communal and given over to constructive meaning (Bruner, Fosnot). The safe and caring culture is created and sustained by the students, teachers and the whole school community through daily use of the four previously mentioned Tribes Agreements:

- Attentive Listening
- Appreciation/No Put Downs
- The Right to Pass
- Mutual Respect

The responsibility to honor and to monitor the agreements is transferred from the teacher to the tribes. Signs are posted throughout the school community, student groups and school meetings begin with reminders of "how we want to be while we work together." The agreements and the step-by-step community building process of Tribes assure that every student has inclusion (belonging to a small peer group), a sense of identity and value, and a community of supportive peers and adults.

The Community of Learners - Re-Structuring

"The new model of school reform must seek to develop communities of learning grounded in communities of democratic discourse."
- Linda Darling-Hammond

The culture is activated and sustained throughout the many small learning groups in which the students, teachers, administrators, support staff and parents are involved. Many teacher teams are involved in planning active learning curriculum, decision-making, problem-solving and authentic assessment. A leadership team - composed of the principal, core teachers and the school or district's Certified Tribes TLC on-site or district trainers - coordinate overall action planning, implementation and assessment. They too are an inquiry group, raising questions and learning together. The same inquiry group process moves throughout teacher and parent groups. Training opportunities, courses and events are identified to the leadership team. As much as possible, just as with student tribes, integration and alignment of curriculum, problem-solving and decision-making is transferred to faculty and parent groups. District resource coordinators and the Certified Tribes Trainers participate and facilitate as needed. As learning areas are identified, the core leadership team is informed. Additional courses and special training is arranged by the school or district Certified Tribes TLC trainer (See Application, Part C: Training and Implementation). The democratic community-building approach based on the caring culture fosters collegiality, school spirit and achievement.

Responsive Education - Active Learning

"Rather than being powerless and dependent on the institution, learners need to be empowered to think and learn for themselves. Thus, learning needs to be conceived of as something a learner does, not something that is done to a learner."
-Catherine Fosnot

"Responsive Education" is an essential pedagogy for academic achievement and school reform. It is the synthesis of artful teaching practices. It is based on understanding the critical developmental needs of a student age and cultural group. Its sole purpose is to enable more students to acquire knowledge in a lasting and meaningful way. Crafting a caring culture and trusting small active learning communities throughout a school gives all students the opportunity to excel (Johnson).

The Center Source Systems professional development courses and training prepare teachers to be responsive to how the students of the school best can learn and grow socially, emotionally, spiritually (inner development) and intellectually. Depending upon their respective stages of development, ways of learning and culture. Teachers teach core academic content through well-proven active learning strategies (cooperative learning strategies, project learning, group inquiry, research, composition projects, debates, team performance and peer assessment.) Tribes materials provide teachers with approximately 175 group strategies (or structures). Reflection on what was learned and how it was learned is an on-going practice after every group learning experience. Cognitive research validates that this maximizes the recall of information and concepts (Caine, Johnson, Jensen). Tribes Learning Community teachers use traditional direct instruction as well as active learning. However, once they recognize and experience the positive results of cooperative learning (validated by more than 1000 studies), the majority use classroom tribes as much as possible.

A set of twelve group skills are learned so that students can work well together. Separate time is not needed to teach the skills. They are demonstrated and woven into curriculum learning tasks one or two at a time as "social learning objectives" that students assess along with assessing the "content learning objective." The responsibility to achieve both the content and social learning objectives is transferred by the teacher to the classroom tribes at the beginning of the academic task. The partnership role of students and teacher working consistently together institutionalizes the culture and "responsive education" pedagogy. The collaborative school community moves toward significant school reform and educational excellence.

Suggestive Conclusion

There is a need to evolve sensitive model of tribal education rooted in the psychological strengths of tribal children. Studies indicate that, in comparison to other groups, hunters and gatherers possess a high level of visual and tactual differentiation, they demonstrate capacity for fine judgement of shape and size of stimuli as well as spatial relations, and produce the categorization of an array of objects. These abilities are greatly required for success in science, art, music, dance, athletic activities, and vocations like carpentry, tailoring, wood and stone crafts. These skills need to be utilized not only for education of tribal children in schools, but also in the broader economic spheres of tribal life. Such attempts will be helpful in generating and promoting the sense of competence, self-efficacy, self-respect, and positive self-image among tribal children in general (Mishra, 2002). As for all other population groups and areas, community mobilization and awareness generation on issues of enrolment, education of girl children, retention of children in schools and school involvement are carried out in tribal areas. The specific features of such mobilization in tribal areas have been or are use of tribal/folk art forms, Meetings of mothers and family meetings and involvement of tribal youth volunteers Leaflets posters, Kalajathas, and videocassettes in tribal languages etc.

6

Indigenous Education in Karnataka : Issues and Constraints

—Nanjunda D.C.

Scheduled Tribes in India are more like the "indigenous" or "native people" in other parts of the world. The population of Scheduled Tribes in India according to 2001 census is 8.43 crore. Education of Scheduled Tribe children is considered important, not only because of the constitutional obligation, but also a crucial input for total development of tribal communities. The literacy levels of the Scheduled Tribes according to the 2001 census is 47.10% as compared to overall literacy rate of the total population i.e., 65.38%, which shows a dismal picture of Scheduled Tribes education. So long as there is a gap between the literacy levels, the position of Scheduled Tribes will remain backward. Lack of education may lead to child exploitation, child labor, population explosion, etc., so the need of the hour is to bring quality education through 100% school enrolment and retention with more emphasis on the girl child education. I have given some suggestions for imparting quality education among the Scheduled Tribes in order to uplift themselves and to overcome the socio-economic problems.

The spread of education among the weaker sections of our society is vital as education is a prime requisite for socio-economic development. The policy to promote educational interests of the weaker sections of the people, especially the Scheduled Castes and Scheduled Tribes, has been enshrined in our Constitution as a Directive Principle of State Policy. Therefore, the main thrust continues to be on education. The general level of literacy is very low and is lower still in the case of Backward Classes. To conclude in the words of Swami

Vivekananda - "The Real India lives in the Villages. Unless we are able to uplift the Tribal and the backward classes, India faces to dark future. Along with their economic improvement they have to be raised culturally and spiritually."

Empowerment is about people - both women and men - taking control over their lives: becoming conscious of their own situation and position, setting their own agendas, creating space for themselves, gaining skills, building self-confidence, solving problems, and developing self-reliance. It is not only a social and political process, but an individual one as well - and it is not only a process but an outcome too. Realizing that Scheduled Tribes are one of the most deprived and marginalized groups with respect to education, a host of programmes and measures were initiated ever since the Independence. Elementary education was a priority area in the Tribal sub-plans from the 5th Five Year Plan. Education of ST children is considered important, not only because of the Constitutional obligation but also as a crucial input for total development of tribal communities. One of the super goals of SSA (serva skshan abiyan) is to "bridge all gender and social category gaps at primary stage by 2007 and at elementary stage by 2010". The issues and challenges in tribal education can be categorized as external, internal, socio-economic and psychological. The external constraints are related to issues at levels of policy, planning and implementation while internal constraints are with respect to school system, content, curriculum, pedagogy, medium of instruction etc. The third set of problems relates to social economic and cultural background of tribals and psychological aspects of first generation learners. The literacy level of Scheduled Castes and Scheduled Tribes is very low compared to the general literacy rate. Recognizing that education provides opportunities for a permanent change in the socio-economic status of these people, this Government gives top priority to education. Hence out of a sum of Rs. 448.91 crores provided in the Budget Estimate for 2004-2005 to this Department, more than 70% is earmarked for schemes related to education. There is a need to evolve sensitive model of tribal education rooted in the psychological strengths of tribal children.

Traditionally referred to as adivasis vanbasis tribes, or tribals, Schduled Tribes constitute about 8% of the population of India. There are about 573 Scheduled Tribes living in different parts of our country, having their own languages, which are varied from the one spoken in the State where they live. There are more than 270 such languages in India. According to the 2001census, the tribal population in India is 74.6 million. The largest number of tribals is in Madhya Pradesh (16.40 million), followed by Orissa (7 million) and Jharkhand (6.6million). There were 16 million Scheduled Tribe children (10.87 million of 6-11 years and 5.12 million of 11-14 years) as of March 2001, out of the total child population in India of about 193 million in the age group of 6 to 14 years (Selected Educational Statistics—2000-01, Government of India). Education of Scheduled Tribe children is considered important, not only because of the Constitutional obligation but also as a crucial input for total development of tribal communities and also for the economic development of a country. One of the challenges in providing education to tribal children is to setting up school facilities in small, scattered and remote tribal habitations. The majority of the Scheduled Tribes live in sparsely populated habitations in the interior and in inaccessible hilly and forest areas of our country. So an attempt is made by the researchers to discuss and analyze the problems of tribal children's education in India since tribal children are neither culturally inferior nor cognitively less competent than the children of other groups.

Education has limited connotation. It is largely concerned with the existing formal structure of education and the institutionalized methodology of imparting knowledge to individuals. Within this very system exist many sub-groups of individuals with specific needs and tribals are one of them. In fact tribals form a large group of individuals in the Indian society. For several historical, economic and social reasons the scheduled groups have remained economically backward and socially retarded even to this day. The ST population accounts for 8.6% of the total population of the country. There are many constitutional provisions and legislative support available for safeguarding the welfare and the interests of STs. In addition planned developmental efforts have also taken place through Five-Year plans. Despite the concern reflected inthe Indian

Constitution and the developmental efforts initiated for the welfare and the development of STs., their socio-economic and political development is still far below the others and therefore much more needs to be done in this direction, including their empowerment – educational, social, economic and political – with due regard to their special identity – culturally, habitation ally, traditionally – and in terms of the tribals

Indian Constitution identifies for special consideration certain ethnic minority groups, traditionally referred to as tribes or tribals, as Scheduled Tribes who constitute around 8 per cent of the total population of the country. There are 49 Scheduled Tribes living in different parts of the state. Most of the tribal communities have their own languages different from what is spoken in the State where they are located. There are more than 70 such languages. The tribal languages in India belong to all major language families among which the Austric, the Dravidian, Tibeto-Chinese, Indo European families are the dominant ones.

One of the distinguishing features is that majority of them live in scattered habitations located in interior, remote and inaccessible, hilly and forest areas of the country. Nearly 5-6 per cent of tribal habitations have less than one hundred population and more than 10 per cent have 100 to less than 200 population, while others have less than 300 people.

Who are STs

The term tribe or tribal or adibasis is not defined anywhere in the Constitution although according to the Article 342, ST represents the tribe or tribal communities that are notified by the President. Tribes are not part of the traditional Hindu caste structure. STs in India are more like the "indigenous" or "tribal people" in other parts of the world defines Scheduled tribes as people who (*i*) claim themselves as indigenous to the soil; (*ii*) generally inhabit forest and hilly regions; (*iii*) largely pursue a subsistence level economy; (*iv*) have grate regard for traditional religious and cultural practices; (*v*) believe in common ancestry and (*vi*) have strong group ties. However, all characteristics do not apply to all tribal communities. Tribals are not homogenous groups. There are at least four groups of

STs – hunting-gathering group, agricultural group, irrigation-agricultural group and industrial wage earning group.

The Scheduled Tribes are tribes notified under Article 342 of the Constitution, which makes special provision for 'tribes, tribal communities, parts of, or groups within which the President may so notify'. There is no definition of a tribe in the Constitution but one may distinguish some characteristics that are generally accepted: self-identification, language, distinctive social and cultural organisation, economic under-development, geographic location and initially, isolation, which has been steadily, and in some cases, traumatically, eroded. Many tribes still live in hilly and/or forested areas, somewhat remote from settlements. Many stereotypes flourish about the tribal persona and tribal society. Many of the tribal people are undeniably economically under-developed, and the process of their marginalisation can be traced to the intrusion of British colonialism, which quickly detected in the forest that was home to tribals, great potential for appropriation of resources. Exploitation of forest-lands by both the British and the zamindars resulted in the clearing of huge tracts for commercial crops such as tea, coffee and rubber and allowing contractors to fell trees in the very heart of the forest.

These actions deprived the tribal people of their livelihoods because many of them were hunters and gatherers of forest produce. The interaction with the outside world brought the tribal people face to face with problems they were not equipped to cope with, such as alcoholism and sexually transmitted diseases. In the post-Independence period, while the Constitution protected the rights of the Scheduled Tribes and accorded them reservation in the legislature, educational institutions and government jobs, other 'development' activities, such as the construction of large dams or the sale of timber, led to the further marginalisation of some tribes. The scenario is therefore a mixed one. It may be necessary to use natural resources to improve the living conditions of the people of the state, but it must be done in a manner that is sensitive to ensuring the protection of the environment, which provides a livelihood to tribal people. Apart from the Scheduled Tribes, there are 75 indigenous groups in India known as 'Primitive Tribal Groups'. The Tenth Plan of the Central Government observes that these vulnerable communities have experienced a 'decline in their sustenance base and the resultant food insecurity, malnutrition and ill-health has forced them to live in the most fragile living conditions and some of them are even under the threat of getting extinct'.

The government of India have taken –up in right earnest the duty of educating the 25 million Adibasis of the country, with the object of helping them to become absorbed in the larger Indian society. This is a very difficult but a very necessary task. The difficulty is partly due to the differences in the cultural levels of the various tribes, and partly due to the intra tribal social solidarity which can be an obstacle to the integration of the Adibasis with the Indian society. The Adibasis cannot therefore be expected to rise to the full stature of citizenship immediately. Neither would any large-scale and sweeping legislation bring about the desired end. It can be done only by a gradual process of adjustment for which a suitable type of education has to be planned and carried out.

Education of Scheduled Tribe children is considered important, not only because of the constitutional obligation, but also a crucial input for total development of tribal communities. The literacy levels of the Scheduled Tribes according to the 2001 census is 47.10% as compared to overall literacy rate of the total population i.e., 65.38%,which shows a dismal picture of Scheduled Tribes education. So long as there is a gap between the literacy levels, the position of Scheduled Tribes will remain backward. Lack of education may lead to child exploitation, child labor, population explosion, etc., so the needof the hour is to bring quality education through 100% school enrolment and retention withmore emphasis on the girl child education. I have given some suggestions for impart ingquality education among the Scheduled Tribes in order to uplift themselves and to overcome the socio-economic problems.

The spread of education among the weaker sections of our society is vital as education is a prime requisite for socio-economic development. The policy to promote educational interests of the weaker sections of the people, especially the Scheduled Castes and Scheduled Tribes, has been enshrined in our Constitution as a Directive Principle of State Policy.

Therefore, the main thrust continues to be on education. The general level of literacy is very low and is lower still in the case of Backward Classes. To conclude in the words of Swami Vivekananda - "The Real India lives in the Villages. Unless we are able to uplift the Tribal and the backward classes, India faces to dark future. Along with their economic improvement they have to be raised culturally and spiritually."

India is one of the major countries having larger concentration of tribal groups in the world. Among the tribals, primitive tribal groups are highly vulnerable. These groups are still isolated from the main stream of civilized society. They are small in number and still having pre-agricultural technology. The rate of literacy among them is extremely low. Different people are exploiting these primitive tribal groups in different ways. Both Govt. and NGOs have implemented several policies and programmes for the uplift ment of these tribals. It was thoughtful of the Govt. of India to have constituted evil committees to suggest measures for the welfare and development of the Tribes implemented during different plan periods. But the result is not very significant and encouraging because of rigid traditional aspects of these tribals. Some time their dwelling places would be beyond reachable. Tribal development has been given one of the major attentions by all the Governments in India during all five years plans on account of the socioeconomic backwardness of the tribals. Also a lot of provisions have been brought into the Constitution to safeguard their basic interests. Planning Commission (1991) has remarked that 'tribal welfare should aim at the prospective within reasonable time and an advancement of the social and economic life of the tribes with a view to their gradual integration with the rest of country should be on a footing of equality'. It is noted that the total number of Scheduled Tribe (ST) population of India constitutes about 10.08 per cent of the total population as per the 2001 census. Out of this more than 63 per cent tribes are spread only in five States of the country. Recent study says the total number of such Scheduled Tribals is 643 in India (Singh, 1992). All Scheduled Tribe groups are entitled to have many benefits directly from the Governament, with reservations for them in many sectors of development. Moreover the Constitution enshrine a number of important provisions for the safeguard and promoting the interests of Scheduled Tribes in the country. Though number of efforts have been made for over all development of Scheduled Tribes it was noticed that some groups are still in the backward stage. Further the situation has deteriorated with administrative restrictions having been imposed on collection or utilization of forestland resources that the tribals traditionally depend upon. The major objective of this paper is to prepare a solid background for discussion for vanishing tribal education. Further this paper will look for such avenue where some of the suggested poicy implications can play significant role in improving tribal education in general.

Primitive Tribal Groups (PTG)

The first attempt was made in 1931 to identify the PTG in the country. The group of tribals who have the following characteristic features have been classified into primitive tribal groups 1) still practicing pre-agricultural level of technology 2) extremely low level of literacy3) near stagnant or diminishing populations. Till today 75 groups have been identified in 16 states and Union Territories. The problems of Indian tribals can be classified into two types.1 problems of major tribes and 2 problems of primitive tribes. But in India both of them are mixed up together and that's why no significant achievement could be made in solving the problems of primitive tribes. In recent years they are facing some serious problems like lack of basic facilities including; poverty, illiteracy, lack of medical facilities, unreachable to NGOs, lack of essential agricultural technology ·etc. In the resent past Planning Commission had issued some guide lines to the States that tribal development plan should emphasize on the following aspects 1 elimination of expatiation of all form 2 rapid social and economic development 3 improving their organizational capabilities and narrowing down the gap between the levels of development of the tribals and others through by providing proper education. Also the Commission suggested that the Integrated Area Development Plan fousing on the specific problems of the tribal people must be implemented vigorously emphasizing on the cultural fabrics of the respective tribes.

Profiles of Primitive Tribals of Karnataka

Jenu kuruba and Koraga tribals have been identified as PTGs in the Karnataka State. Jenu kuruba tribe is concentrated around Mysore, Chmarajanagar and Kodagu districts of the state. Total population of this tribe is around 24654 (2001 Census). Literacy rate is extremely low. Usually they are living in hamlets made out of bamboo and huts with there own judicial system. They believe in magic, sorcery and witchcraft. Neither polygamy nor polyandry is practiced. Besides working with raton and bamboo, collection of minor forest products like herb, honey, roots and fruits are their major occupations. Poverty exists more in this group.

Koraga is a very primitive tribal group in the Karnataka State. They are concentrated in Dakshina Kannada and some parts of the Udupi district of the state. They also live in some patches of Kerala and Karnataka border. The Koraga live mostly in rural areas. Sussman (2004) has rightly said 'they were compelled to lead a segregated life from the immediate multi-ethnic, multi-religious neighborhood till few decades back owing to the sever untouchability prevailed in the 'region' (To the great extent they very much believe in magic and witchcraft and local medicine men. Their total population is around 19784 (2001Census). Neither polygamy nor polyandry is being observed. The Koragas remain extremely backward socially, economically and educationally. They have there own rich culture and traditional heritage. Their traditional occupation is basket making. Few percentage of the population lives in semi urban areas.

Education- A Tool for Development

Opening of the tribal areas in the wake of modern developmental process have brought in juxtaposition two distinct value systems – one based on inherent tradition and ignores and the other on technology and innovations. Harmonious synchronization of the two systems is highly essential for the rapid development of tribals (Jha, 1995). In this crucial moment education plays a vital role. Education is a backbone of every society. It is a tool for social change. In the past education was one of the main consideration for hierarchical classification in the Hindu society. Rapid population growth impedes educational development in several ways. Most obviously it produces a rapid increase in the school age population. To spread the education among marginalised sections of society has been a formidable task in India. However, with the advent of modernization, the education of tribals has undergone a different phase. Under the influence of globalization, the tribal education and culture has been tremendously influenced. The uniuquence, of the tribal culture which enriches the country's culture mosaic, is fast disappearing and even getting distorted under powerful influences of the dominant urban culture. While dealing with the poor educational attainment of tribal children to formal schooling, researchers tend to emphasis the economic marginalization of these comminutes, their illiterate home environments, and inadequate facilities for education and culturally the alien nature of the school system. Lack of education is largely responsible for the exploitation and pitiable plight of the tribals. Due to this, the tribals have not been able to take advantage of new development. The above mentioned factors explain how level of education among the tribal children. Another important factor is the school process. This is most crucial because heavy drop outs and almost stagnation of tribal children within a year of admitting to primary school has been reported since last decade. A large proportion of the poorer tribal children, on account of the rising cost of the schooling and economic burden cannot afford to benefit from education. Most of the tribals tend to use their children for ancillary service that would bring in some added income for their starving families (Mishra,1998).

According to the 2001 Census the average literacy rate of two PTGs is 28.6 per cent. It is very painful and to note that the literacy among these two tribals increased to only 7.45 per cent during the period 1961-1971. More unfortunate is that during the same period female literacy grew by less than three per cent. As per the table Jenu kuruba tribe has very low literacy rate when compare to the Koraga. Even though Jenu kuruba tribe is in a more advantage situation, its literacy rate is comparatively low than Koragas. In both the cases female literacy rate little bit higher than males.

Table 1. Literacy Status of PTGs of Karnataka

PTG	*Total Population*	*Total Literate*	*Male-Literates*	*Female-Literates*	*Male*	*Female*	*Total*
Jenu kuruba	27597	4033	3172	2161	15.10	19.29	17.09
Koraga	11566	3543	1678	1865	27.82	29.38	28.06

(Source: Mohanty, 2002)

Table 2. Enrollment of P T G students by sex in Primary Stage in Karnataka

Year	*Boys*	*Girls*	*Total Percentage*
2000-01	1876	1098	23%
2001-02	1798	1003	15%
2002-03	1894	987	16%
2003-04	2006	998	13%
2004-05	1983	1009	11%
2005-06	1872	991	7%
% growth rate			
Annual compound growth rate			

Reasons for low literacy rate

(a) Disparity in the existence of the schools

Compared to the other major tribals of the state these primitive tribal groups are a more disadvantaged population. As for as non-existing facility within a habitation is concerned, one can find that other major tribes of the State are placed in a favorable situation relative to their total population. Looking at the disparity condition in terms of deprivation, more children of primitive tribal group school age children are deprived of a primary school within their habitations. Children belonging to the other major tribes like *Soligas, Betta kuruba* and *Male kudiya* are in a better position than the PTGs thay have atlest one Ashram or Jeneral school within their habitations (Shukla, 1998). However so for as the number of habitations without a school is a concerned PTGs child are highly in a disadvantaged position. In general primitive tribal children should have to commute more than 3-Km distance to attend a school. In some case it is even more. Distance is also one of the major drawbacks in case of providing education to the people who are still away from modern world. Many of the parents don't like to send their children especially of their girl children to school, which is quite for away from their original habitation. Finally while a large population of the country school age children still face the disadvantage of distance between their own habitation and the location of a primary school, the more disturbing situation is this disadvantage is high in case of PTGs habitations in the tribe belt of Karnataka.

(b) Language-A Medium of Instruction

The tribal situation in India presents a varied and complex picture and poses peculiar problems of social and economic developemnt. Demographically speaking, there are more than 244 scheduled tribes with many sub-groups speaking some 100 languages /dialects. Most unfortunate thing is that major portion of government's resources is diverted to concessconal provisions and little is left for the development of tribal education, language and culture of these two PTGs. The striking aspect that emerges from the scanty data on languages in primary education is the almost total absence of tribal language in schools. The attitude of our policy planners towards these tribal people appears to be one of assimilation. Little is being done to preserve their culture. Our policy scientists have almost all-major and minor tribes suffer with this kind of negligence. Not much work has been done to find out minimum and maximum resistance into their culture. Linguistic experts have made no attempt to standardize tribal languages by developing scripts, elaborating lexis and writing grammars and dictionaries in tribal languages. Till today there has not been any serious efforts to provide basic education in their respective mother tongues. No proper curriculums have also been framed based on tribal culture and tradition. Present education system does not orient the tribal children towards perusing their own mode of life. In phonology and syntax, the tribal languages are quite different from the medium of instruction like Kannada except in certain mutually borrowed lexical items due to their close contacts over a long period of time. This is one of the vital reason responsible for these PTGs poor literacy and dropout problem among tribal children (Pasayat, 1995).

(c) Urban Biased

The success of one's education largely depends on the motivation. Basically tribals are living with low socio-economic status. Obviously the level of motivation and self-esteem will be comparatively low among tribal children. The main reason for this problem is current education system is more or less urban based non-tribal and absence of culture specific. Even though these tribals are emotionally attached to their local cultural norms Govt. has no interest in providing education which is more suited to the tribal children. Modern teaching methodologies, content of the text, appointment of non-tribal teachers and parameters for evaluations have become *Grains of Iron* to the low motivated tribal children. Implementation of uniform textbooks both for urban and tribal children are one more hit to them. The theory, concepts, values alien to tribal people is generally contained in the textbooks which generates negative attitude and a big blow to the learners' self-confidence. There is no attempt to take stock of the existing situation regarding instructional materials in tribal languages. Education policy documents also have not delt on the magnitude of tasks that are involved in the preparation of primers and textbooks for tribal children and have not outlined the concrete steps that have to taken in this direction. The increasing tendency for tribal people to retain the regional language as their mother tongue is only one indicator of their growing vulnerability in the face of these larger social processes (Singh, 1995).

The problem of dropout persists among all categories of children in both urban and rural India. However, in the context of children studying in Classes 1-10 the gap between the ST and total population of dropouts has widened from 1990-91 to 1998-99.The reduction in the dropout rates could b because of various incentive shames run by the State Govt. for edition of ST children such as providing free textbooks, uniforms and scholarships in Govt. schools. But schemes such as those providing for hostels for ST boys adngirls are not implemented fully by the State owing to lack of financial resources and therefor fewer ST children pursue high school education and very few up to the college level. The policy of reserving seats for ST students at higher education levels is no widely availed since a ledge number of ST students do not even reach those levels and dropout at lower levels of school education. Even the Ashram shools run by both Govt. and NGOs are poory maintained and sometime lack even the basic facilities. Given the low level of literacy among the ST population, several children from these comminutes happen to be 'first generation learners' and in the absence of State support for heaping them to cope with studies, many children drop out of the schools. This disproportionately low representation of ST children at higher level of eduaion compounds the existing disparities in Indian society. Lack of proactive government in favor of the STs is not linked only to lack of resources. Govt. indifference and lack of political will are largely responsible for the state of affair (Mathru, 1996).

(d) Inaction of teachers

Lack of social mobility and the problem of inter-cultural communication are major retarding factors in tribal education. As the teacher and the taught in the tribal areas belong to different cultures the communication barrier becomes almost insurmountable. The late Humayun Kabir had rightly remarked that even the best system of education is bound to fail without an efficient and resourceful teacher. Most of the teachers appointed in tribal areas are a disinterested a lot due to various problems faced by them such as lack of proper residential facility, good salary, communication facility and social distance from the tribal people.

Thus the teacher feels isolated and unhappy and a disgruntled teacher is, certainly, not the best communicator of modern ideas and messages to tribal children. So even though the government has come up in recent times with various plans and programmes to improve the educational lot of the tribals, there is not much result to show as there is lack of sincerity on the part of the officials charged with the implementation of these programmes. In fact a credibility gap has emerged between such officials and the tribal people. If all these problems are to be tackled successfully, the government has to bring about a change in the basic orientation in tribal education.

Teachers are the real directors of every tribal school. There was a time in India where teachers were equal to the God. The major problem is that Govt. is recruiting teachers from the urban area to teach tribal children. A report say that only 0.56% of teachers is basically from either Anthropology or Sociology discipline. Majority of the teacher are from non-tribal community. Many of them have studied only in English medium schools and they even don't know the regional language properly. In this situation how one can expect to teach the relatively disadvantaged tribal children down to their level. More unfortunate thing is that many schools don't have teachers for all the subjects. Even though many NGOs are hiring trained teachers to teach at tribal schools many of them even don't have any basic degrees in education like BEd/ TCH. Some of the teachers are prejudious about the performance of the tribal children. As they are the only literate persons having some political connections in the tribal areas, they neither fulfil their duties properly nor the concerned higher officers dare to take any action against them for dereliction of their duties.

(e) What teacher says?

Many of the teachers are of the opinion that tribal children cannot understand the modern Kannada language. Content of the text is too standard to their level. Few of them will complain about the ignorance of the parents. More over teachers are facing many problems in the tribal areas. Proper residential and medicinal facilities are a nightmare. Higher education for their children some time will not possible. Since many primitive tribal hamlets live deep in to the forest some time it will be humanely impossible to reach the school due to the lack of appropriate transport. More over feed back from the students is completely absent. No proper laboratory facilities to teach Science effectively. Teachers raised and brought up in a more sophisticated urbanized society would find it difficult to adjust themselves to the cultural shock that generates communication gap.

(f) Parents' apathy

Tribal community feels childhood or adulthood largely depends not on the physical age but on the degree of responsibility that children could successfully fulfill. Apart from that children's responsibilities towards the family and the contributions they make are significant and much important while conceptualizing the above mentioned terms. In tribal society children from the early age will be engaged in cooking food, fetching water, siblings care, support in the field, collection minor forest food, grazing etc. Decision to give a chance to a child to spend happy childhood is not isolated from other aspects of household decision making nor are they purely household based. They reflect the norms and values of the wider community within which the tribal household is located and the social and economic possibilities which local contexts offer to different categorized of households. Hence, parents may think sending child to school means dislocation of traditional pattern of earning livelihood and of division of labour in their societies. Most vital problems of low literacy among tribal children is that children are considered by parents as economic assets to the family.

Education of tribal girl children is more neglected because of deep-rooted beliefs, traditions and mid-sets. Educationalist philosophers use the concept of false consciousness to refer to the existence of beliefs and values that individuals socialize into and operate upon. It can be argued from that the universalist perspective that the parents believe that girls need to be socialized into their adult roles as children and the formal education has no meaning for them.

The question of how elementary education can and be made universal has not received the attention it deserves. We think that issues should be highlighted. Recent study has shown that an alarmingly large number of children do not become literate even after four years of primary education especially in both rural and tribal areas (Sharma, 2002). Hence, total school effectiveness and actual learning have to be the central theme rather than secondary concern for universal education. Further, more important is that how effective schools are and successive learning basically depend not only on school level inputs but also on many vital factors outside the school. Basic infrastructures of Ashram Schools in tribal areas are worst than any thing in many southern districts of Karnataka. Many schools even don't have hard roofs. Hostels are ruining. Unavailability of play ground, lab and library and separate toilets are most common in many tribal schools where children of these two PTGs are learning. Absence of extra curricular activities makes children learning as a kind of unavoidable burden. Since tribal children are completely different from urban children or atleast from rural children learning should be a joyful experience for them other wise simply they may be dropouts. For genuine universal elementary education the impact of the wider context on schooling has to be understood in a better way.

Absence of Central Monitoring Unit

Absence of effective monitoring unit on the tribal schools is one of the major drawbacks in case of development of tribal education. Concerned inspecting staffs hardly visit to the tribal schools. Some time even only one time in a year. This makes teacher to lack commitment to their profession. Some people reported that teacher' visit one or two times in a weak to the schools only. This is also due to low level of motivation, inspiration and commitment among the inspecting staff, which are again matched, by the low level of motivation and interest among the teachers. This is the high time that Govt. should think to strengthen or establish Centralized Monitoring Unit especially for Tribal School and better unit chief from either Anthropology or Sociology background.

In the light of above discussion we may conclude that on one hand, economic backwardness is responsible for the low percentage of literacy in the younger generation and on the other social backwardness and lack of social consciousness are responsible for low percentage of children attending schools. When the school going children are few it can be well understood that higher education will be a rare phenomena in these PTGs. Hence, along with other development it is also necessary that we should create some awareness about significance of education among tribles the facilities available to them for education and the role of education in their upliftment of socially economically and politically condition of the tribal community.

Policy Implications

Some suggestions to handle the educational problems of Primitive Tribal groups are made based on the fieldwork and review of previous literature. These are brought out in this section.

1. There are many basic difference can be seen between major tribals and primitive tribals in case of India. Hence, the Govt. should bring a new educational policy especially for primitive tribals. It must be culturally and geographically specific. Moreover educational experts should be very sensitive while framing the policies which should not destroy the social solidarity of the tribes and kill their zest for life.

2. It is well revealed fact that modern education cannot cater to the basic needs of the tribes. Modern education

system cannot deem to have held much relevance for them since they are from the outer world. During our fieldwork it has been revealed that tribals consider 'culture as their first educator'. Hence there is a need to identify the areas of minimum and maximum resistance to innovations in their culture and vital linkage to their cultural fabric. Once we identify enough space we can imbibe education in to their culture.

3. It is the high time to have special education programme made for tribal children in consonance with the privileged cultural pattern and also in keeping with the needs and resources of the area concerned in order to secure the maximum amount of tribal children participation. Moreover new education programme should be in a the position to assert the existing perception, behaviour and action in education seeking process and culturally determined attitude towards use of different system of education.

4. The state Govt. should construct a Textbook Commission especially for tribal education developemnt. While framing the textbooks experts should focus on three-impordent prospectvies 1 Linguistic 2 Instrumental 3 and the Culture. From the primary level itself all text materials should be in their respective mothertongue. There is need to evolve scripts, grammar, and as well as appropriate vocabulary to communicate 'school knowledge'. Proper training should be given in tribal language, culture and society to the non-tribal teachers working in the tribal areas.

5. Lack of good quality teachers in sufficient numbers resulting in high pupil teacher ratio may be an important factor in explaining the variations of educational status in these two PTGs in education. Given the inaccuracies in enrolments and the attendance/absence of teachers, probably pupil teacher ratio may not be efficient and meaningful variable representing the quality of tribal education.

6. Ashram Schools should have a multi-purpose complex. If, possible there should be a provision for selling and

buying of consumer goods and minor forest products. Further Ashram Schools initially must emphasis on the service rendered to the primitive tribals than on costly building. 'In the initial stage provision should be made for a Kacha thatched Ashram type building rather than a pucca building' (Mohnthy, 2003).

7. The socio economic context, along with the development dimension is an integral part of school effectiveness. On the other hand it is difficult to ensure good school quality in less developed tribal areas. On the other hand, it is found that area type affects learning directly by influencing poverty levels and also opportunities and motivation for learning. The impact of the area type on schools and learning is such that no description or analysis of schools can be meaningfull with out a parallel understanding of the area type (rural (1) hamlet of major tribals or primitive tribals)

Conclusion

If we go through from the other angle, the problems of intensity of dropouts have been increasing day by day among tribal students. The next question is once they become dropouts what will be the next plan? What will be their day-to-day context? How do their parents react for this? In our fieldwork it is revealed that many dropout children have become child workers. Many of them are working with their parents in the field and in some big estates. Of cource, there are many reasons for children dropouts even from the primary stage. Suppose if Govt. ready to overcome all these problems modernize the tribal education system will parents send their children to school? The Anthropological study on dynamic model of tribal child labour suggests that, their decision to send to work today depends not only on current consideration such as the marginal productivity of child'work but also on expected returns to work compared with alternatives such as school attendance. The finding that farm size increase dropout suggest that at given levels of household income, the return to work relative to the return to school is a significant determinant in sending their children to school. A naturally policy implication is therefore to invest in raising the return to education. In addition to general investment in improving school supply such measures may include reducing labour market discrimination against tribal women and raising awareness to reduce inhibiting social norms. policise that improve the function of labour market in rural and tribal areas may reduce the dropouts, especially that of girls. Given the recent expansion of micro credit programmes, it is pertinent to note that developing tribal financial market many have positive spillover effects, encouraging development of land and labour market. The growths of tribal action market will not only counter the substation effect highlighted here, it may also generate overall income growth and reduce tribal inequalities. If so parents may not mind in sending their children to school.

While implementing the tribal development plans especially in case of education care should be taken to see that the cultural traits of primitive tribes are not disturbed with in the process of their interaction with the mainstream of nation life. More over a careful watch on the trends set in motion, which should not destroy the social solidarity of the tribes and kill their zest for life should be the part and parcel of every tribal developmental policies. Further there should be a lot of scope for prioritizing their needs, solving their own problems and raising their own resources to meet their urgent needs in all schemes by using their knowledge got from the schools. Finally it can be said that educational activities will have to be simultaneous with economic advancement in such areas as are in contact with urban and civilized, or partially civilized, centers. In such areas however, where the tribes are not in such contact and are economically stable, education should have top priority. But in all such cases where economic disintegration has processed far and deep and the number of such cases is quite large economic rehabilitation must get very high priority

7

School Absence Among Tribal Children : Whare Rubber Hits the Road?

—Nanjunda D.C. and Steven Wind

The policy to promote educational interests of the weaker sections of the people, especially the Scheduled Castes and Scheduled Tribes, has been enshrined in our Constitution as a Directive Principle of State Policy. Therefore, the main thrust continues to be on education. The general level of literacy is very low and is lower still in the case of Backward Classes. All over the world, Education is powerful avenue for advancement of socio-economic status and social change. India has large sizable proportion of tribe those in may respect lag behind their non-tribal counterparts. Recognizing the importance of education, Government of India is giving much attention to their education but education has made little progress among the tribal. The poor socio-economic situation, illiteracy of the tribles plays major role in high rate of non attendance of students in school as well as drop out in from school. The tribal students do not get any motivation, aspirations, and guidance from their parents. They are made to work in the fields, look after the siblings and help in the household activities. Village does not have high school and transportation is not available. Since there is insufficiency of teachers, classrooms and poor attendance of the students, the teacher faces lots of problems. This paper discusses about school absence among the tribal children with special references to Karnataka

Introduction

The term 'Scheduled Tribes' first appeared in the Constitution of India. Article 366 (25) defined Scheduled Tribes as "such tribes or tribal communities or parts of or groups within such tribes or tribal communities as are deemed under Article 342 to be Scheduled Tribes for the purposes of this constitution". Article 342, which is reproduced below, prescribes procedure to be followed in the matter of specification of scheduled tribes. Education cannot change in any fundamental way unless we change our basic patterns of thinking and interacting so that learning can become a way of life. Teachers, parents, administrators, district resource and community people are coming together throughout hundreds of school communities to learn how to revitalize their schools with a process known as "Tribes." Evaluation of Tribes Learning Community Schools has examined the impact of the Tribes process on student behavior, academic performance, school culture, and teacher collegiality. Studies have shown that: Tribes TLC has a positive impact on classroom environment, teachers report spending less time managing student behavior, students are significantly less likely to be referred for disciplinary problems, the Tribes process helps teachers address performance and content standards, students in well-implemented classrooms score significantly higher on standardized tests than students from comparison groups, teachers report increased staff collegiality and planning. "Responsive Education" is an essential pedagogy for academic achievement and school reform. It is the synthesis of artful teaching practices. It is based on understanding the critical developmental needs of a student age and cultural group. The Goal is to engage all teachers, administrators, students and families in working together as a learning community that is dedicated to caring and support, active participation and positive expectations for all students.

In spite of sixty years of independence and more than fifty five years of planned development and social provision for accelerated socio economic development of weaker sections, the gap in literacy levels among the general population and the socially disadvantaged sections is persisting and in some cases this gap is further widening. There were 16 million ST children [10.87 million of 6-11 years and 5.12 million of11-14 years) as of March 2001, out of the total child population in India of about 193 million in the age group of 6 to 14 years. [Selected

Educational Statistics – 2001 Government of India] – Education of ST children to considered important, not only because of the constitutional obligation but also as a crucial input for total development of tribal communities. Most tribal children do not understand the textbooks, which are generally in the regional language. The appointment of non-tribal teachers in tribal children's schools is another problem. The teachers do not know the language the children speak and children do not understand and the teacher's language. The issues pertaining to tribal education.

The population of Scheduled Tribes in India according to 2001census is 8.43 crore. Education of Scheduled Tribe children is considered important, not only because of the constitutional obligation, but also a crucial input for total development of tribal communities. The literacy levels of the Scheduled Tribes according to the 2001 census is 47.10% as compared to overall literacy rate of the total population i.e., 65.38%, which shows a dismal picture of Scheduled Tribes education. So long as there is a gap between the literacy levels, the position of Scheduled Tribes will remain backward. Lack of education may lead to child exploitation, child labor, population explosion, etc., so the need of the hour is to bring quality education through 100% school enrolment and retention with more emphasis on the girl child education. In this paper have given some policy suggestions for impart inequality education among the Scheduled Tribes in order to uplift themselves and to overcome the socio-economic problems.

India is one of the few countries in the world having the largest tribal concentration. The tribals of this country are having fascinating rich cultural heritage and played a significant role in enrichment of composite culture. The objective and comparative studies of pre-literate societies and their contribution to great indigenous culture of India is essential before they are totally eclipsed in the fast changing cultural canvass of India. Such in-depth, comparative and analytical studies may throw light and provide missing cultural links in understanding complex Indian heritage.

The spread of education among the weaker sections of our society is vital, as education is a prime requisite for socio-economic development. The policy to promote educational interests of the weaker sections of the people, especially the Scheduled Castes and Scheduled Tribes, has been enshrined in our Constitution as a Directive Principle of State Policy. Therefore, the main thrust continues to be on education. The general level of literacy is very low and is lower still in the case of Backward Classes. To conclude in the words of Swami Vivekananda - "The Real India lives in the Villages. Unless we are able to uplift the Tribal and the backward classes, India faces to dark future. Along with their economic improvement they have to be raised culturally and spiritually."

The Scheduled Tribes represents one of the most economically impoverished and marginalized groups in India. Karnataka has a high proportion of the tribal population. Education of tribal women is recognized as indispensable for their growth and development. The education of tribal women according to 2001 census, the Scheduled Tribe female literacy is 8.07%as compared to the male literacy of 12.68% in Karnataka. So long as there is disparity between male and female in education levels the difference between the position of men and women would continue to exist. The tribal women's access to education in the country is inadequate and discriminating because of ignorance, lack of motivation, etc.. Thus education is the key catalyst to the development of human resources. Lack of education is largely responsible for the exploitation and pitiable plight of the tribal women. For the tribal, education disseminates knowledge, knowledge give inner strength, which is very essential for the tribal for attaining freedom from exploitation and poverty. So due to ignorance arising out of illiteracy, the tribal have not been able to take advantage of new economic opportunities. Empowerment of women covers aspects such as education, economic status etc. Abolition of gender based discrimination in all institutions and structures of society and participation of women in policy and decision process at domestic and public level are sew dimension of women empowerment.

Despite the significant progress that has been made the past 15 years in achieving universal primary education, approximately 1.5 million children do still not go to school.

Especially in South India figures are alarming. Children who do not go to school in South India constitute more than one third of all children who are not enrolled in school the agree India. If we look at the net primary school enrolment ratio (1998-2002) we see that in India only 91% of the boys in the 6-10 age group were enrolled, for girls this figure was 76% (Bellamy, 2004). It is important to keep in mind that these figures relate to children who are officially enrolled in school, but who are not necessarily attending. Looking at the net primary school attendance these numbers go down to 80% for boys, and 73% for girls. However, the attendance lists kept by teachers are not always accurate, and the actual attendance figure might be even lower. When we then look at UNICEF's gross secondary school enrolment ratio (including all children, regardless of age) the figure is 56% for boys, and only 40% for girls. Only a segment of the total number of children, which are not enrolled in school, can be found in the statistics of working children. There are thus a number of children that are excluded from these figures. These children can be classified as nowhere children, a term coined by D.P. Chaudhri (1997). According to the Planning Commission of the Government of India, deriving their figures from the Census of India, incidence of tribals was 5.4 percent while incidence of nowhere children was 45.2 per cent in 1991. There has been a shift from the research-focus on tribals alone to the out-of school segment as a whole, which thus includes nowhere children. In order to design policy to also get these children in school, it is important to learn how they are spending their time. For this purpose IREWOC initiated a project on nowhere children in four Indian states: Andhra Pradesh, Bihar, Chhattisgarh, and Karnataka. The results presented in this paper are derived from qualitative research that was conducted in three tribal areas in Karnataka between September and December 2007.

An attempt has been made in this present research paper to analyze educational status of the tribal children in Karnataka. Data on completion rate, repetition rate, dropouts rate, attendance rate, transition rate and enrolment rate for primary schoolchildren have been collected from the report of the Sarva Shiksha Abhiyan (SSA) during the year 2005 to 2007.

Methodology

This proposed research consisted of three major components; in-depth schools studies, community norm study and an institutional ethnography. Data collected from five sources: household members, teachers, adults (18-25-age group) ashram schools students other community members and tribal welfare officials and NGOs. Following types of data collection method have been used to conduct this present study

1.Case Study 2. Interview 3. Participant observation 4. Ethnography 5. Unobsturive method 6. Content analysis

Analysis of data

Data analysis had incorporated both qualitative and quantitative data sets to insure triangulation of result. The *qualitative data* has been analyzed using *NUD* IST* database software and The *quantitative data* has been analyzed using SPSS software.

Result and Discussion

Karnataka, 8th largest state of India, with a total population that constitutes only 8.65% of India's population as a whole, is one of the most sparsely populated states. Being one of the driest regions, Karnataka is also among the poorest states of India. It is a predominantly rural state, with agriculture and animal husbandry as the most important sources of income.

Karnataka is one of the least performing states in terms of tribal literacy. The state also has a tremendous gender gap in terms of both school enrolment and literacy demand: Several factors are essential in identifying the reasons for absence of children in school. We will first give an overview of demand-factors such as livelihood strategies, poverty, gender, caste, family crises, which we found were crucial. Looking at livelihood strategies it appears that during seasons with a great demand for agricultural labour, such as the crop-cutting season, the attendance of children, especially girls, decreases. These children are not found in the field, but are required to stay home to take over household duties such as caring for siblings, so that the mother is able to go to the field to do wage work. Like the 10-year-old Rangi, (name changed) oldest daughter of parents who are out in the field all day during the crop-cutting season, told me: "I have to be here to take care of my brothers, because who else is here to do this?" However, we cannot simply argue that children do not go to school only because parents have to do agricultural work. Similarly, where as many children can be found in the field looking after cattle, it is not the case that these children do not go to school, because they have to look after cattle. Often other factors are operational. In some cases parents might be aware of the importance to educate their children and try to send their children to school, but if the children are reluctant, the parents might lack the determination to make sure their children are indeed going to school. Here it is important to recognize the social capital of a child: if a child is surrounded by one or more educated relative who encourages him to go to school, it leads to increased motivation for the child to learn and to go to school regularly. The 12-year-old Seam explains: "But my uncle is literate, and he always encourages me to go to school. We want to continue the tradition of being literate in the family. We want to continue studying in the future and go outside the village to be a doctor". Likewise, if a child is not blessed with a learning environment at home, he or she is prone to fail and eventually to drop out of school. Migration occurs in various forms in the tribal areas. It can have both negative and positive consequences for the education of children.

In some cases, especially with temporary migration of the whole household, the effects on the education of a child are negative, especially when the household leaves the village for a couple of months every year, and the child needs to leave school, and falls behind. However, temporary migration of only the father to the city in search of work could be positive, as it can also lead to increasing awareness about education for both boys and girls. Economical problems within the household do lead to absence of children in school. These may be a result of a crisis in the family, for example the illness or even death of a parent. This often results in the burden of working, in order to feed the household, falling on the shoulders of the child. Sons, suddenly the "man of the household", are required to tend animals, either their own or those of others in order to make money, and girls, especially the oldest daughter, have to stay home doing household chores, or are sent to the field to do agricultural work, especially during crop-cutting season. The 13-year-old

Manchavva had to dropout of school when his father fell ill. His father complains: "I do not want this for my child, but if I die, Manchhva needs to know how to be the man of the household. He is the oldest, and thus the only one who can do this work". Caste also influences whether children are sent to school in societies in Karnataka. The sub caste system is still of significant importance among Karnatakan tribes, especially in the northern areas. The traditional perception that tribles do not recognize the importance of education does not hold true anymore. Yet, there are still certain castes that, because of traditional work arrangements, do not send their children to school, and these include upper castes as well. For example, we found Soliga boys and girls expected to help out in the household of a socially higher ranking family member. Gender also plays a role. In general, there are more boys than girls attending school regularly. Of the total number of children enrolled in any school up to class V in the three tribal areas, 55% are boys. The difference is especially apparent on upper-primary level, where only 32% are girls 22%. For this there are various explanations.

For example, it is often considered not safe for a girl, once she is a teenager and thus sexually vulnerable, to go out side the village for her education. Another reason given for keeping girls at home is related to household chores. In some cases it is a necessity for girls to stay home and, for example, take care of their younger siblings. This is often a result of economical crisis. In other cases household chores are looked upon as a good preparation for a girl's married life. Marriage then is another important reason behind gender discrimination. Quoting the seventeen-year-old Macha : "Education is useless for girls, because they are just living in our houses doing female chores. For us boys it is useful, so we can get a job". Some parents do not recognize how education can help their daughter in her future life, while others are reluctant to invest in her, since she is going to her husband's house after her marriage, like a father expresses: "But I cannot afford a good education for all my children, and in the future, the girls will be married off to another house, while the boys stay in my house". Thus, when a family has money for only one child's education, they will prefer to spend it on the boy. However, within some castes more and more people are interested in the amount of education the potential spouse of their child has received. Therefore, there is often overlap between the factors gender and caste mentality. The supply-side of education. The next section will deal with supply-factors, since the quality of offered education is crucial when parents decide between sending their children to school, or keeping them at home. In all sample tribal areas, all children, disregarding caste, have access to the same educational facilities. These facilities are within reach of the children. Government school buildings are often built just outside the village, whereas private school owners have been able to open their schools in buildings in the middle of the village. The location of the school influences the parents when deciding to which school they should send their children. Especially small children are more likely to be sent to a school that is nearby the house. In a village, situated. This number only reflects on children who are attending school within their village, thus excluding the children who are attending a school outside the village. Also, keep in mind that these are enrolment figures and do not say anything about attendance along a busy road which has to be crossed by many people in order to reach the government school, a father wants to postpone sending his two youngest sons to school, "since they are too young and scared to cross the main road".

In the three tribal areas that were included in the research, the general perception of villager son the quality of education offered by the government is negative. Most villagers prefer the private school to government schools, but complain that they cannot bear the costs of private education. They believe that teachers are more committed and that children learn much more than children who are enrolled in a government school. In some schools, there are too few teachers appointed for too many children. Appointed teachers are usually present, and thus teacher absenteeism, a problem regularly mentioned in the literature, did not occur during our research, apart from the absence of teachers due to other government programmes, which they are required to attend. The fact that teachers reside outside the village and leave as soon as the school hours are over (or even earlier) makes communication between parents and teachers difficult. It thus would be better if teachers were appointed in their own village. Another issue is the lack of female teachers. There were only a few female teachers in the schools. This is unfortunate, since female teachers often serve as a role model for girls, as one of the teachers explained. The presence of female teachers could positively influence the enrolment and attendance of girls. The ten-year-old Radha told me she aspired to be a "madam in school". Among the children in all tribal areas, there is a fear of punishment by the teachers for skipping school, for not knowing the right answers or for not being clean or properly dressed. But children, as well as their parents and other villagers, also complained about the limited knowledge they actually gain after finishing a number of classes. When a parent asked a boy who studies in class ten to speak English to me, he replied (in Marwari, their local language): "If the headmaster does not even know how to speak English to her, then why should I?" Quoting a twenty-year-old from another village: "If you ask someone here who is enrolled in class V to read or write, he will not be able to do so, because he does not learn this in school". However, some parents did not blame the school: "My youngest daughter Sannavva is in class III, but cannot count until twenty. Radha is in class IV, and cannot even read a book properly. But my oldest daughter Pinki could do all these things when she was at their age. As opposed to the other two girls, Pinki was very studious and always did her homework. She studied in the same school as Radha and Kabita, and she is doing fine. So I do not blame the teachers". Both children and their parents mentioned the financial aspect of education as an obstacle. While primary education is supposed to be free, in all schools children were expected to pay fees. The fee structure however, is not transparent. Fees differ according to gender, caste, and class-level, and also per village. Furthermore, teachers and parents give different accounts on the exact amount that has to be paid for "admission" or "building maintenance". Boys of a general caste in class IV and V for example were expected to pay a yearly fee of Rs. 60. Some households complained about having to pay the government schoola yearly fee of Rs. 151. In addition to these school fees, there are also the expenses for school uniforms (to have a uniform made is Rs. 150-200) and stationary, which constitute a hugeburden on the household's finances. Government schools were, however, still cheaper than private schools. These charged the children a monthly fee of Rs. 30-70. In the three tribal areas an average wage is Rs. 50 for one day of agricultural work or labour in a stone factory.

Suggestive Conclusion

The problem of absence of children can unfortunately not be solved just by raising the quality of the offered education. Quality of education is not a sole reason for not sending children to school. But when the performance of school is inadequate, children may only be sent when their duties are not required elsewhere; for example, in the household or herding the cattle. For some, school attendance then becomes a residual activity. In other cases, when parents decide the money required for a child's education can better be spent on other basic requirements, children might drop out altogether. Droping out might also be a result of failure in standards. And once dropped out, it is unlikely the child will find its way back into the education system. Explanations for this might be the reluctance to go over the same curriculum again, and often they find that they just get used to working. Closing remarks: When children who are out of school, for whatever reason, are not required to help out in the household, they can be found roaming around their house or in the village, and we might then consider them as nowhere children. It goes without saying, that these nowhere children also do some work to help their parents out in the household. But this work is not the reason that keeps them out of school. It is clear that the issue discussed here is a complex one. Overall, the awareness of the importance of education is present among all villagers, regardless of caste. We have seen that many factors can lead to the non-attendance of children in school, and more than often there is overlap. Both parents and children also seem to be convinced that the child will do the same work as their parents. Thus, the absence of a (government) job-perspective for children also leads to a preference to keep them at home and to prepare them for their future occupation as animal-herder, agricultural labourer, or in some cases shopkeeper.

Programmes like community mobilization, strengthening VECs/PTAs/MTAs and involving NGOs to reach out of school tribal children would need to be re-visualized in a more tribal specific context. Keeping in mind the poor socio-economic background of tribal children, a re-assessment is required on how free the primary education is for the tribal child and what further measures are required to be taken to make their education totally free. Capacity Building at All Levels As was expressed by the experts there is a need for training and orientation to administrators, resource persons, teacher-trainers on different aspects of tribal education. However it would be wrong to say that there is a dearth of experts at State/district level. Rather, what is required at present is that the State resource persons should be identified and trained by the national core group in developing separate training modules for administrators, teacher-trainers and teachers. It was recognized that the teachers working in tribal are as required special pedagogical training to tackle the special needs and problems of tribal children, especially as the present pre-service and the in-service training modules are found to be devoid of any special component of tribal education. Even though it was realised that a more powerful and demanding Vets/PTAs/MTs would exercise indirect control over school functioning (e.g. regulating effectively the incentive schemes etc.), the State nodal persons were lacking any directives regarding how to make these bodies more powerful. All the State strategies have included community awareness campaign. But the community awareness modules developed by the State or district components were not found effective. A fundamental error was pointed out in conceptualizing the awareness campaign. It was assumed that the tribal parents are not aware of the free primary education being provided by the Government. But as revealed by the State nodal persons, the tribal parents are aware of it but they are not convinced of the relevance of this education for their children. Thus, emphasis should be placed on convincing these parents about the relevance of primary education for their children. However, pedagogical revolution backed by adequate compensation of the tribal parents for their labour loss, and a suitable academic calendar would convince the parents of the utility of primary education for their children. Although it was long back decided to have adequate representation of tribal parents in Vets as well as PTAs, not much has been achieved in this regard. Besides, many of the tribal villages do not have either VECs or PTAs.

Relevance of Pedagogy

Continue of the debate around quantity verses quality of education still is on. Before this, policymakers should note that quality and quantity are intertwined and cannot be separated. It is real sense of urgency. Differences expressed pertained to the placement of priorities for the achievement of universal education, and are in turn related to the broader views held on the nature of the challenges. If state is really interested in the eradication of tribal illiteracy or at least mind to minimize the problem it must and should seriously think about the quality of primary education at present. Probably a new population policy may help in this regard. Resources need to be targeted at expanding provision if Govt. think providing alternative income generation programmes to the poor parents who would like to send children to work, then resource will have to diverted to making the curriculum relevant and of high quality. Given the manifest failure of the standard schooling system to include hard-to –reach children, special efforts need to be made in this area and particular attention should be given to first generation learners. Some noted that high rates could put off many aspiring to secondary and higher levels of education, thus eroding the incentive to send children regularly and consistently to school. Without providing of universal coverage and equivalent standards in terms of quality, it is not feasible or just to penalize parents who do not send children to school. Clearly, meaningful and genuine universal elementary education is associated not only with universal access to well-functioning schools but also with certain out-of –school initiatives. Children have varying capacities, apart from individual intelligence, depend on factors such as adequate nutrition good health and freedom to attend school regularly. It follows that thee prerequisite have to be ensured for effective and genuine universal education.

To conclude, how elementary education should be made universal is central to the concern for making it universal? It is necessary to make sure that such education is effective. Apart from the need to scrutinize the education system, non-educational measures that prepare children for education and facilities the process of learning are also needed. India is one of the countries having largest number of tribals in the world, also country having highest percentage of dropouts at higher primary level. Poverty and overpopulation are intertwined with this problem (Sharma, 1998). At the same time, it has pioneered a number of different educational models for addressing the problems of hard to reach children, models which reflect a shared value given to the welfare of children and the need to ensure their right to education, but very different philosophies and modalities. If we seriously try with this model with some addition or subtraction suiting our culture and traditions which are more effective and under what circumstances, we believe that the experiences, of India will have made a major contribution to a long standing problem beyond boundaries.

India is one of the few countries in the world having the largest tribal concentration. The tribals of this country are having fascinating rich cultural heritage and played a significant role in enrichment of composite culture. The objective and comparative studies of pre-literate societies and their contribution to great indigenous culture of India is essential before they are totally eclipsed in the fast changing cultural canvass of India. Such indepth, comparative and analytical studies may throw light and provide missing cultural links in understanding complex Indian heritage.

8

Education Among Tribal Communities in Maharashtra

—Hemant Apte and Rinzi Lama

The Indian Constitution assigns special status to the tribal communities as Scheduled Tribes (STs). They constitute about 8 per cent of the Indian population. The literacy rate among the Scheduled Tribes is only 29.60 per cent compared to general population which is 52.21 per cent (1991 census). The female literacy rate among ST is 18.19 per cent as against the overall female literacy which was 39.29 per cent (1991 census). ST population in Maharashtra currently constitutes about 10 per cent of the total population. Population survey data of Adivasi Utthan Karyakram shows highest literacy rate for total population for Pardhan (73 per cent), Korku (62 per cent) and Mahadev koli (60 per cent) tribal groups. Lowest literacy was among PTG Katkaris (24 per cent) followed by the Bhil (27 per cent) and Madia Gonds from Ethapalli (31 per cent). Kolam, another PTG has higher literacy rate (55.9 per cent) as compared to the other two PTGs.

Gender wise analysis shows (50 per cent) males and only (35 per cent) females were literate. Among males, Korku and Mahadev koli had highest literacy rate (70 per cent each) while Madia (37 per cent), Bhils (33 per cent) and Katkari (31 per cent) had lowest literacy. Among females, Korku (53 per cent) and Mahadev Koli (50 per cent) had high literacy rate while Madia (23 per cent), Bhil (21 per cent) and Katkari (16 per cent) had lowest literacy. The highest number of school children in the age group 6-14 years was among Mahadev Kolis (83 per cent) followed by Gond and Korku (80 per centeach) and Kokna (77 per cent). Mahadev Koli boys reported highest school attendance rate (85 per cent) and among girls Mahadev koli tribe had (81 per cent) girls attending school followed by Gond and Korku (79 per cent each). The data presented in this paper brings out the need for a more focused regional or state level intervention

Introduction

Education is a process beginning at birth, of developing intellectual capacity, manual skill and social awareness especially by instruction. It is a term which refers to the process of imparting literacy, numeracy and a generally accepted body of knowledge (Hodder, Arnold, 2004). Formal education is of prime importance as it serves as the means to the end i.e. the development of the country. Efforts are made by the Government to educate the citizens of our country by introducing various schemes to that effect. However, the process of formal education is affected by various socio cultural factors. There exist a numbers of problems due to which the imparting of education to all hasn't been possible till date. Alienation from the society, lack of adequate infrastructure like schools, hostels and teachers, abject poverty and apathy towards irrelevant curriculum are some of the problems related to education. This problem is more severe among the tribal population residing in the country today.

The Indian Constitution assigns special status to the tribal communities as Scheduled Tribes (STs). Traditionally, referred to as *Adivasis, Vanbasis* (original inhabitants, forest dwellers). STs constitute about 8 per cent of the Indian population. There are 573 Scheduled Tribes living in different parts of the country, having their own dialect, which are different from State language. There are more than 270 such dialects in India. According to the 2001 census, the tribal population in India is 74.6 million. The largest number of tribal population is in undivided Madhya Pradesh 16.40 million (now divided into Madhya Pradesh and Chattisgarh), followed by Orissa 7 million and Jharkhand 6.6 million.

The tribal people are identified for their unique way of life, their customs, traditions, beliefs and practices. Though the condition of tribal communities has inched towards national mainstream over years, yet majority of scheduled tribes continue to live below poverty line, have poor literacy rate, suffering from malnutrition and disease and are vulnerable to displacement. The Draft National Policy on Tribal people has tried to look into the problems of tribal population with the aim of addressing each of their problems in a concrete way. "The main objective is to facilitate an overall development and welfare of the tribal people through empowering them- educationally, socially, economically and politically while recognizing their special identity- culturally, habitationally, traditionally and in terms of their age old rights and privileges." Facilitating the educational development of tribal people is one of the aims of this policy.

The literacy rate among the Scheduled Tribes is only 29.60 per cent as compared to general population which is 52.21 per cent (1991 census). The female literacy rate among ST is 18.19 per cent as against the overall female literacy which was 39.29 per cent (1991 census). There is high incidence of illiteracy especially among female ST population and also among primitive tribal groups, need for medium of instruction in tribal dialects, heavy dropout rate etc. are some of the problems faced by the tribal people. However, the draft National policy also provides some measures to be taken to promote education among them.

There are many schemes for promoting education among tribal communities like Ashram (residential) school in Tribal Sub Plan (TSP) areas, vocational training in tribal areas, education of ST girls in low literacy pockets, postmatric (Post School Graduation) scholarship etc. These schemes have started to bring the tribal population at par with the general population facilitating the overall holistic development of the country. Ministry of tribal affairs is also implementing schemes of national overseas scholarship for higher studies abroad, book bank, coaching and allied and upgradation of merit for the benefit of ST students.

Methodology

In consonance with Mahatma Gandhi's concern about Adivasi reflected in his constructive programmes and

Jawaharlal Nehru's Panchshil about integrated tribal development, ITDP-special authority for tribal development (Integrated Tribal Development Program), and Tribal Sub Plan have been devised in India. There are a plethora of schemes of development at the National, State and District levels, which are primarily implemented by respective departments for their sectors. The integration, networking and linkages continue to be a major hurdle in effective implementation. Although 73rd Constitution amendment has bestowed more authority to tribal Gram Sabha (statutory village council), the Panchayati Raj Institutions (PRIs) which means democratic institution at the district, sub district and village level, in tribal areas are not functioning to the desired effect. Almost the entire tribal populations in ITDP areas continue to be Below Poverty Line (BPL). This raises issues of equity and human development.

The Scheduled Tribe population in Maharashtra currently constitutes about 10 per cent of the total population. Tribal people have been living in geographical isolation as a result of which some of them who are designated as primitive tribes or who live in the hilly tracts are in a state of time freeze. Tribal people are usually referred to as backward, meaning their lack of capacity to utilize the opportunities of development offered to them. The crucial issues in their development are therefore not related only to providing infrastructure and schemes of development but to develop their capacity to utilize them at par with other citizens of the State.

Among the tribal communities in Maharashtra, there are gradations of backwardness amongst the ethnic groups. The primitive groups such as Madia Gonds, Kolams and Katkaris in Maharashtra are at the bottom of the deprivation scale. Similarly, the Bhils in hilly tracts of Akkalkuwa and Dhadgaon in Nandurbar district, Warli, Dhor Koli and Thakar in Jawhar and Mokhada (District Thane) and Korku in Amravati district are relatively more backward.

Poverty issues among the tribal people have always been compared with poverty in the general main land population. Tribal poverty has come into sharp focus since their food sources from the forest have kept on dwindling, mainly due to forest development policies. Since tribal people have basically been the collectors of food and not primarily the producers of food, land as a productive asset and property is a recent concept. As a result of the primitive methods of cultivation, food security has become a major problem with these tribal communities.

Malnutrition, infant and child mortality is the major problem in the tribal areas. Since 1990, every year child deaths in the tribal area are attributed to the problem of malnutrition. These deaths have occurred in different tribal pockets and have remained in focus. Illiteracy levels, high percentage of BPL families, livelihood are other key issues in tribal development.

Adivasi Utthan Karyakram (AUK) (Comprehensive and Sustainable Human Development of the Tribal people of Maharashtra).

Comprehensive and Sustainable Human Development of the Tribal people of Maharashtra in local language is Adivasi Utthan Karyakram (AUK).

It is on this background; Adivasi Utthan Karyakram was initiated as a partnership program between Government and Non Governmental Organizations (NGO), namely Comprehensive Rural Health Project, Jamkhed and Maharashtra Association of Anthropological Sciences, Pune. Tribal Development Department, Government of Maharashtra sponsored the programme, which is implemented by the two organizations.

AUK is aimed at developing the model for comprehensive and sustainable tribal development. The main emphasis of the project is on Maternal and child health with a focus on prevention of child malnutrition and mortality. The program covers about 150.000 tribal population spread over 250 villages predominantly tribal sub districts from seven districts of Maharashtra state. It also includes three Primitive Tribal Groups in the State viz. — Katkari, Kolam and Madia. Programme components include health and nutrition education with special focus on Ashram Schools and Anganwadis (hamlet based activity centers of ICDS (Integrated Child Development Scheme), livelihood and income generation activities, Organisation of Community based organisations (CBOs) like self help groups, youth clubs, farmers clubs, training of traditional birth attendants, herbalists and other traditional healers, village level elected representatives; Programmes for increasing awareness about self identity, cultural identity etc. The Adivasi Utthan Karyakram was commenced in September 2004. The programme gained momentum from January 2005, when village volunteers started their work in respective villages. To achieve the goal, village level male and female volunteers were selected by the villagers themselves. These volunteers are regularly trained on the issues of health and other development. These village volunteers are expected to act as catalysts for social development, who will bring the change in the tribal society which will become sustainable.

The survey was not initiated immediately after the commencement of the project for the reason that the AUK should not be perceived by people as merely a survey project. Hence after the confidence building measures by village volunteers in the community and after the rainy season baseline survey was conducted. The Baseline Survey was organized during the period November 2005 - January 2006. In the Baseline survey about 1.5 lakh populations has been covered which is 1.75 per cent of the total tribal population of Maharashtra and nearly 3.5 per cent of the tribal population living in the Tribal Sub Plan areas. The survey has covered all the major tribal groups in the State of Maharashtra. Hence the survey could be said to be representative of the total tribal population of Maharashtra. Findings of the baseline survey will help policy planners to develop the comprehensive policy for tribal development.

Survey Tools

Household schedule, schedules for pregnant and lactating mothers, anthropometric measurements were prepared.

Training of Trainers

In the month of October 2005, three day training workshop was organized at Karjat field unit for training the trainers for the survey. Household schedule was discussed in details.

Investigators

Local tribal youths in the age group of 20 - 35 years were hired as investigators at respective field units. Most of them belonged to villages under AUK. These youths had knowledge of local conditions and were fluent in local dialect. At each field unit about 20 investigators were selected. Many of the investigators were educated upto college level. In some sub districts, educated AUK volunteers also worked as investigators. All the AUK volunteers attended the survey training which helped them to know the survey process and investigators.

Survey Training

In each sub district three day training workshop was organized to train the investigators. Investigators wrote down the questions to be asked in local dialect. Pilot testing was done to test the investigators. Pilot survey forms were scrutinized and mistakes were discussed with the investigators. Investigators who showed poor performance were omitted from the survey team.

Survey

Actual survey was conducted at respective field units as per the plan. Survey commenced from November 2005. Survey team covered all the households and moved from village to village. Village volunteers from AUK assisted the investigators and helped them in data collection. Supervisors checked completed forms everyday. Incomplete forms were returned to the investigators for corrections. At the beginning of the survey there were more incomplete forms. The quality of the filled forms was improved as investigators gained experience. In each sub district survey process was completed within 10 - 15 days. Village volunteers of AUK and investigators conducted anthropometric survey in December 2005-January 2006.

Data Entry and Analysis

Completed forms were sent to the Central Coordination Unit for the data entry. An outside agency was hired for the data entry. Data entry process for nearly 29000 families was completed in the month of October 2006. After the data entry was completed, data were converted into MS Excel files. Data files were cleaned and gaps in the data were filled by referring to the survey forms and basic family data. Data analysis was carried out using MS Excel and SPSS 10 packages. Anthropometric data was analysed using WHO Anthro 2005 package. Sub district wise and tribe wise frequency tables were prepared.

Data

The tribal populations of Thakar, Mahadeo-Koli, Katkari, Warli, Kokna, Dhor koli resides in Thane district. The other tribes such as Bhil and Parwa are present in the district of Nandurbar, Korku and Gond in Amravati; Mahadeo koli, Thakar in Ahmednagar; Madia Gond, Gond and Pardhan in Gadchiroli; Kolam and Gond in Yavatmal and Katkari and Thakar in Raigad.

Literacy rate

Highest literacy rate for total population was observed for Pardhan (73 per cent), Korku (62 per cent) and Mahadev koli (60 per cent) tribal groups. Lowest literacy was observed for PTG Katkaris (24 per cent) followed by the Bhils from Satpuda region (27 per cent) and another PTG Madia Gonds from Ethapalli, who live in the jungle (31 per cent). Kolam, another PTG has a much higher literacy rate (55.9 per cent) as compared to the other two PTGs.

In absolute numbers, highest graduates belonged to Mahadev koli (130), Bhil (129) and Kokna (101) community. Bhils also have the highest number of postgraduates (57) followed by Mahadev kolis (45).

The three PTG groups had 18 graduates in total- Katkaris (3), Kolam (7) and Madia (8). Among PTG, only two individuals who had learnt upto post graduation belonged to Madia.

Gender and Education

Gender wise analysis shows that (50 per cent) males and only (35 per cent) females were literate. Among males, Korku and Mahadev koli had highest literacy rate (70 per cent each) while Madia (37 per cent), Bhils (33 per cent) and Katkari(31 per cent) had lowest literacy. The third PTG viz. Kolam had (58 per cent) literate males and were comparatively better placed than other two PTGs. Numberwise, Bhil and Mahadev koli tribes had 108 male graduates each followed by Kokna (90 per cent). Bhil (53) and Mahadev koli (43) males had completed their post graduation.

Among females, Korku (53 per cent) and Mahadev koli (50 per cent) had high literacy rate while Madia (23 per cent), Bhil

(21 per cent) and Katkari (16 per cent) had lowest literacy. There were only 76 female graduates out of which 22 and 21 belonged to Mahadev koli and Bhil tribe respectively. There were only 9 females who had completed their post graduation, out of which 4 belonged to Bhil and 2 belonged to Mahadev koli community.

It is clear from the educational status that the three PTG communities were lagging behind the other tribal groups. The three PTGs had lowest education. Only one female had graduated from Katkari and Madia community while Kolam had only two females who had completed the graduation. None of the female has completed post graduation from these communities.

Educational status of children in 6-14 year age group

Out of the total 37303 children in the age group of 6-14 years, 22450(60 per cent) children were going to school while remaining (40 per cent) were out of school children. The highest number of school children in the age group 6-14 years was observed for Mahadev kolis (83 per cent) followd by Gond and Korku (80 per centeach) and Kokna (77 per cent). On the other hand only (47 per cent) Dhor koli, (41 per cent) Katkari and (39 per cent) Bhil children were attending the school at the time of survey.

Gender and Schooling (6-14years)

There were (64 per cent) boys in the age group of 6-14 years who were learning in school at the time of survey. Remaining (36 per cent) boys were out of the school at the time of the survey. Fifty seven percent girls in the age group of 6-14 years were learning in school while (43 per cent) were out of school.

Mahadev koli boys reported highest school attendance rate (85 per cent) followed by Gond and Korku (81 per cent) each. Lowest percentage for school going boys in this age group was observed for Dhor koli (48 per cent), PTG Katkaris (44 per cent) and Bhils (44 per cent). Comparatively other two PTG were positioned better in education with (75 per cent) Kolam and (60 per cent) Madia boys attending the school in this age group.

Among girls Mahadev koli tribe had (81 per cent) girls attending the school followed by Gond and Korku (79 per cent each). There were only (45 per cent) Madia, (39 per cent) Kakari and (33 per cent) Bhil girls in the age group of 6-14 years were attending the school at the time of survey. Girls from other PTG Kolam were positioned well as (72 per cent) were attending school.

Central and State governments have assured "education for all": for children in the age group of 6-14 years. Scheme of "Sarva Siksha Abhiyaan" has been launched for the same. There is need to have concentrated efforts to bring all children to school especially girl.

Efforts have been made by the Government to improve the education among the tribal people. However, inspite of all these efforts the illiteracy rate still remains high among the tribal population.

The category of ST in the national sample surveys and census represents all tribes living in different parts of the country pooled in a single category. This poses a problem in identifying the disparity that exists among different tribes in a state or in the region. These data, presented here would help in a more focused planning and implementation of programs for the STs. It further helps in understanding the differentials in education with respect to their geographical location that is tribes of the plains and forest dwelling tribes.

Other than location, there are many reasons for the non attendance of students in the schools. The teachers being from the mainstream tend to impart education pertaining to the mainstream. Other than this the students are faced with various social and cultural factors which act as barriers in the uptake of education. Study was conducted aiming at mapping the existing provisions for primary education in the tribal areas as well as their utilization by the recipient population. It was carried out in seven states viz. Assam, Karnataka, Kerala, Maharashtra, Madhya Pradesh, Orissa and Tamil Nadu. The aspects studied include educational infrastructure and facilities available, status of teachers in tribal areas, status of curriculum and teaching learning materials, use of tribal language, status of school enrolment and school dropout, monitoring, evaluation and community participation. This study revealed a number of reasons for children not going to school regularly. The reasons given were financial work, household work and health problems. In addition to these other problems included agricultural work, school atmosphere, teachers' behaviour, children's failure in examination and unwillingness of the parents.

In a study of tribal education in Adilabad District, E. V. Rathnaiah investigated the attitude of Gonds to school education. In the course of this investigation he found that in the opinion of the teachers interviewed 13.7 percent of parents were positively cooperative, 56.3 percent were favorable to education but not active, 23.7 per cent were indifferent, 1.3 percent were unfavorable, and 5 per cent were antagonistic. The reasons given by parents for not sending their children to school include, need for help in household work (35.7 per cent), occupation with herding cattle (30 per cent), children's lack of interest in education (25.3 per cent) and ill health (6.6 per cent).

In the opinion of the teachers questioned, the reasons for the poor enrollment of tribal children in schools were Lack of interest in education among parents (64.5 per cent), Poverty (31.5 per cent) and Lack of interest in education among children (4.0 per cent).

Even more important factors impeding the spread of education among tribal children are the distance of many villages from the nearest school and the limited admission in ashram schools. There are many villages whose children would have to walk five or six kilometers to attend a school, and there are not enough boarding schools to accommodate more than a fraction of the children from villages without primary schools in the vicinity.

Discussion

The whole issue of education is mainly focused on the overall development of the country, particularly "mainstreaming" of the tribal population. There have been different approaches in this matter namely- the Immersion approach, Ashram school, Transfer approach and the Integrational approach. In the immersion approach there is no difference in the curricular content and medium of instruction between the main stream schools and tribal schools. The tribal children are taught in the dominant language of the state and the values, skills and knowledge are those desirable to the main stream society. (Annamalai, Tribal Development and Education)

The Ashram schools provide residential facilities to tribal children who are drawn from nearby villages. This facilitates the children to focus on studies along with their peers. It also helps them to maintain their interest in continuing education.

All the above three approaches are visible in the society today. Annamalai further states, "What is required in fact is an Integration approach where the curricular content needed for success in the 'main stream' society is integrated with the distinctive tribal curriculum without supplanting it throughout the entire schooling period. This approach will produce bicultural and bilingual enriched students."

As cited earlier, the atmosphere of the school and the teacher's behavior stand as a problem. Therefore what is required is the change in the attitude of the teachers towards the students. The distinction between tribal and mainstream needs to be resolved by the teachers so that they can teach them with no biases in their minds.

Another challenge in providing education to tribal children relates to setting up school facilities in small, scattered and remote tribal habitations. The majority of the Scheduled Tribes live in sparsely populated habitations in the interior and in inaccessible hilly and forest areas of the country.

Education is an institution which has its great importance. However, various socio-cultural factors influence the uptake of education. Factors such as occupation, the lifestyle of the population, their attitudes etc. determine the acceptance or the non acceptance of education among them. The gender differences among them and the attitude towards the female child plays an important role in the literacy rate. So a change in the attitude of the people on the above issues becomes important. Along with this, the attitude of the mainstream population (teachers imparting education to tribal children) towards the tribal population also needs a change. So an Integrational approach as a whole is the requirement of the day to improve the literacy among the tribal population. The data presented in this paper brings out the need for a more focused regional or state level interventions within the framework of the National policy.

9

Status of Scheduled Tribes : A Case Study of Karnataka* (India)

—*Nanjunda D.C., Annapurna, M., Venu Gopal P.N. and Jyothi Lakshmi S.*

Introduction

The Scheduled Tribes are tribes notified under Article 342 of the Constitution, which makes special provision for 'tribes, tribal communities, parts of, or groups within which the President may so notify'. There is no definition of a tribe in the Constitution but one may distinguish some characteristics that are generally accepted: self-identification, language, distinctive social and cultural organisation, economic under-development, geographic location and initially, isolation, which has been steadily, and in some cases, traumatically, eroded. Many tribes still live in hilly and/or forested areas, somewhat remote from settlements. Many stereotypes flourish about the tribal persona and tribal society. Many of the tribal people are undeniably economically under-developed, and the process of their marginalisation can be traced to the intrusion of British colonialism, which quickly detected in the forest that was home to tribals, great potential for appropriation of resources. Exploitation of forest-lands by both the British and the zamindars resulted in the clearing of huge tracts for commercial crops such as tea, coffee and rubber and allowing contractors to fell trees in the very heart of the forest. These actions deprived the tribal people of their livelihoods because many of them were hunters and gatherers of forest produce. The interaction with the outside world brought the tribal people face to face with problems they were not equipped to cope with, such

* This is not an original work of the authors. It has been downloaded from various websites.

as alcoholism and sexually transmitted diseases. In the post-Independence period, while the Constitution protected the rights of the Scheduled Tribes and accorded them reservation in the legislature, educational institutions and government jobs, other 'development' activities, such as the construction of large dams or the sale of timber, led to the further marginalisation of some tribes. The scenario is therefore a mixed one. It may be necessary to use natural resources to improve the living conditions of the people of the state, but it must be done in a manner that is sensitive to ensuring the protection of the environment, which provides a livelihood to tribal people. Apart from the Scheduled Tribes, there are 75 indigenous groups in India known as 'Primitive Tribal Groups'. The Tenth Plan of the Central Government observes that these vulnerable communities have experienced a 'decline in their sustenance base and the resultant food insecurity, malnutrition and ill-health has forced them to live in the most fragile living conditions and some of them are even under the threat of getting extinct'. In Karnataka, the Koragas of Dakshina Kannada district and the Jenu Kurubas who are concentrated in the districts of Mysore, Chamarajnagar and Kodagu are classified as 'primitive tribes'. Population The tribal population of Karnataka increased to 34.64 lakh in 2001 from 19.16 lakh in 1991.The decadal growth rate during this period is a high 80.8 per cent, caused not by a spurt in fertility rates but by the addition of several new tribes to the Scheduled Tribes (ST) category. The decadal growth rate is higher for females (81.9 per cent) than for males (79.8 per cent). The highest decadal growth rate occurred in Mysore district (around 328.0 per cent), Bagalkot (261.6 per cent), Dharwad (201.1 per cent) and Belgaum (193.0 per cent).The decadal growth rate is negative in Dakshina Kannada (-2.9 per cent). Raichur (18.1 per cent) has the highest percentage of ST population followed by Bellary (18.0 per cent), while Chitradurga (17.5 per cent), which had the highest percentage of ST population in 1991 came down to third place in 2001 on account of its bifurcation.The reverse is true of Raichur. Bellary has the highest population of Scheduled Tribes as a percentage of the ST population in the state (10.6). The tribal population of Karnataka increased to 34.64 lakh in 2001 from 19.16 lakh in 1991. The decadal growth rate during this period is a high 80.8 per cent, caused not by a spurt in fertility rates but by the addition of several new tribes to the Scheduled Tribes category.

The Scheduled Tribes who constitute the weakest sections of our society have been subjected to economic exploitation and social discrimination for ages. This unfortunate situation has been largely responsible for their abject poverty, illiteracy and overall backwardness. Due to social disabilities arising from the practice of untouchability against the Scheduled Castes and geographical isolation in the case of the Scheduled Tribes, they have been alienated from the rest of the comm- unity as a result of which they have been forced to lead a life of economic and social subjugation. An idea of the enormity of the problems facing SC and ST can be gathered from the demographic profile which indicates that these two unprivileged groups constitute about one-fourth of the total population of the country. The 1991 Census of India revealed that the population of SC & ST was 13.82 crores and 6.78 crores respectively accounting for 16.48% and 8.08% of the total population of the country. Further, the census data also revealed that SC & ST children between the ages of 0-6 years constituted 19.63% and 20.18% respectively of the total SC & ST population. This means that about one-fifth of their population belongs to this vulnerable and formative age group. It may, therefore, be advisable for the planners to focus their attention particularly on this age-group and provide for larger investments in the areas of education, nutrition, health, etc., in order to prepare them better to face challenges in the subsequent years as a part of the mainstream Indians.

Despite the increased pace of urbanisation, India continues to be predominantly rural in character especially in the context of SC & ST. Out of the total SC & ST population of the country, as much as 81.28% and 92.61% respectively live in rural areas. Considering the fact that a majority of the SC & ST population live in rural areas where incidence of poverty is more acute, the thrust of planning should be directed towards this significant rural section of their population.

According to the 1991 Census 77.11% and 90.03% SC&ST workers were engaged in the primary sector of the economy, 9.83% and 3.85% respectively in the secondary sector and 13.06% and 6.12% respectively in the tertiary sector. In terms of work participation rate, the SC & ST compare favourably with the total population. However, considering the extent of poverty amongst SC & ST, it becomes imperative that the occupations in which they are engaged generate insufficient income. The other conspicuous feature with relation to the occupational classification is that 49.06% of the main workers among SC and 32.69% among ST were engaged as agricultural labourers. Another interesting fact comes to light on analysing the data relating to distribution of working population by sex. While the work participation rates of male SC & ST workers are higher (51.48% for SC and 54.74% for ST) compared to female participation rates (25.98% for SC and 43.71% for ST), the SC & ST female participation rates are significantly higher than that of their counterpart in the total population. This difference is even more conspicuous in respect of ST female workers. This only confirms that the SC and ST women have to work in greater numbers because of economic compulsions.

Eradication of poverty and raising the standard of living of SC & ST persons have been the most important objectives of the country's economic planning. In the initial years of our planning it won presumed that the economic growth to be realised through planned efforts would by itself ensure that benefits would reach the poorer sections of the population which is commonly known as the 'trickling down' or percolation theory. However, this was not to be and from experience the planners realised that unless specific plans/programmes/schemes were formulated in respect of the poorer sections of the society, especially SC & ST, the main objective of eradication of poverty through economic planning would not be achieved. It was also real- ised that mere economic growth need not lead to better standard of living for all sections of the population, especially SC and ST, which constitute the bulk of the poorer sections of our population.

Tribal Sub-Plan

Against the background of the above realisation by the planners the Tribal Sub-Plan was formulated in the context of welfare and development of ST and the strategy was adopted during the Fifth Five Year Plan. The Plan basically aimed at not only the economic development of ST but also their protection from various kinds of exploitation. At present the Tribal Sub-Plan is being implemented in 18 States and two Union Territories, viz., Andhra Pradesh, Assam, Bihar, Gujarat, Himachal Pradesh, Jammu & Kashmir, Karnataka, Kerala, Madhya Pradesh, Maharashtra, Manipur, Orissa, Rajasthan, Sikkim, Tamil Nadu, Tripura, Uttar Pradesh, West Bengal, Andaman & Nicobar Islands and Daman & Diu. Keeping in view the fact that the ST are by and large concentrated in pockets, the strategy of the TSP was implementing the plan by identifying such pockets of tribal concentrations. Presently 194 Integrated Tribal Development Projects (ITDPs) have been launched and each of these has a contiguous geographical area of a Block or Tahsil where more than half of the population belong to the ST. In addition to this, 250 Modified Area Development Approach (MADA) pockets have been selected in the country in which population in a contiguous area is at least 10,000 and 50% of them are tribals. Seventy five Primitive Tribal Groups (PTGs) have also been identified for the purpose of their alround development.

One of the positive gains since the adoption of the TSP strategy has been that it has ensured separate financial outlays for utilisation' on schemes and programmes which exclusively benefit the ST. The earmarking of funds has also contributed significantly to increasing the size of the plan in terms of financial resources. The achievements can be appreciated from the fact that while during the Fifth Plan period the size of the TSP of the States implementing them was Rs.759.33 crores accounting for only 4.29% of the total State Plan, it increased to Rs. 3019.74 crores in 1992-93 (about four fold) and represents 12.27% of the total State Plan size. The following table shows the flow of funds from State Plans to Tribal Sub-Plans during the Fifth Five Year Plan onwards:

Sex ratio

The sex ratio for Scheduled Tribes (972) is higher than the all-India average (964) for STs as well as the state average (965) according to the 2001 census. There has been a perceptible improvement in the sex ratio of STs since 1991 when it was 961. Among the southern states, Kerala performs well with 1,021 followed by Tamil Nadu (980). Andhra Pradesh is below

Karnataka with 971. The child sex ratio for the 0–6 age group is also higher (960) than the state average of 946. Culturally, there is greater gender equity among the Scheduled Tribes compared with the general population, which is largely shaped and driven by a male-dominated discourse that prioritises son preference. Across districts, one impressive finding is that Udupi (1023) has a sex ratio higher than Kerala's followed by Kodagu and Bagalkot (996) while Bangalore Urban, typically, has the lowest sex ratio (913) followed by Haveri (941), Dharwad and Bijapur (944) and Bidar (950). In Bellary, which has the highest proportion of ST population to the state's ST population, the sex ratio is 985 while Raichur, which has the highest percentage of ST population to the total population, is in fourth place with 993 (Appendix Tables: Series 10). Literacy It is a well-accepted fact that access to knowledge is crucial to improving the human development status of people. Improvements in literacy levels have positive spin-off effects, such as better health indicators and an increase in productivity, which can increase the income levels of poor people significantly. The literacy rate of STs in Karnataka is a cause for concern, as it has consistently been lower than that of the total population.The literacy rate among Scheduled Tribes, which was 36.0 per cent in 1991, increased to 48.3 per cent in 2001, while the state average moved up from 56.04 to 66.64 per cent. The gap between the literacy rate of the total population and the ST population is very wide, although there has been a marginal decline of about 1.6 percentage points in the last decade. The decennial literacy rate of the ST population has increased at a faster pace (12.3 per cent) than the rate for the total population (10.6 per cent). The literacy rate of urban STs (64.6 per cent) is higher than the overall literacy rate of STs and compares quite favourably with the state average. The female literacy rate among STs in 1991 was 23.6 per cent and it increased to 36.6 per cent in 2001. While it has increased at a faster pace than the male literacy rate (the increase during the decade was 13.0 percentage points for females and 11.8 percentage points for males) the gap between the ST male and female literacy rate declined only marginally, from 24.3 in 1991 to 23.1 in 2001, which is slightly higher than the gap between the male and female literacy rates for the total population (22.92 in 1991 and 19.22 in 2001). The literacy rate for ST women is the lowest in the state in comparison with all women as well as Scheduled Caste women. The literacy rate for rural ST women is a low 33.3 per cent compared with 56.9 per cent for men. Overall, the Scheduled Tribes in the state have markedly lower literacy rates than other groups. The fact that they are above the all-India average in respect of men and women is, of course, an indicator that Karnataka has performed better than many other states in this respect. However, the literacy status of the STs in Karnataka, which is in marked contrast to the improvements in literacy of other social groups, is a matter of concern and needs strong policy initiatives to push up literacy levels significantly. Dakshina Kannada district (72.95 per cent) has the highest literacy rate followed by Bangalore Urban (72.83 per cent), Udupi (69.62 per cent),Uttara Kannada (62.74 per cent), Shimoga (62.11 per cent), Tumkur (59.69 per cent) and Chikmaglur (58.84 per cent).The literacy rate is the lowest in Raichur (29.01 per cent), followed by Gulbarga (32.40 per cent) and Kodagu (40.37 per cent). While the literacy rate of Scheduled Tribes has improved in the decade 1991-2001, they still have a long way to go before they catch up with the rest of the population. The ST literacy rate in The literacy rate of STs in Karnataka is a cause for concern, as it has consistently been lower than that of the total population.

Though the literacy rate for women has increased at a faster pace than for males, it is still problematic because it is so much lower than the literacy rate for all women in 2001. Districts that have high literacy rates have also done well with regard to STs with the exception of Kodagu. This is clear when we look at the statistics of districts with low literacy rates, such as Raichur (48.81) and Gulbarga (50.01), where the literacy for STs is also poor (29.01 and 32.40 respectively). The low literacy level suggests that the programmes of the Education Department have not had the desired effect on this very vulnerable sub-population. More concerted efforts are required to bring STs' literacy on par with the state average, at the very least. Culture-specific curricula would be a step in the right direction.Since illiteracy and poverty are factors that play off one another to create a cycle of deprivation, ensuring greater cohesion at the gram panchayat level between anti-poverty programmes and school enrolment/retention drives would provide the poor with viable ways to access education. Education Low literacy rates are matched by less than satisfactory educational attainments across all levels of primary, secondary and tertiary education. Many schools in tribal areas suffer from high dropout rates. Children either never enrol or attend for the first three to four years of primary school, only to lapse into illiteracy later. The attrition rate is quite strong at various levels of the educational system thereafter. The first step in the education ladder is enrolment, where performance is high for most social groups, except STs. For instance, the gross enrolment ratio (GER) in 2001, for STs for Classes I–VIII (90.12) was significantly lower than the GER for all students (98.81) and SCs (104.57).This inequality is heightened even more by the gap between the GER for south Karnataka (110.62) and north Karnataka (74.21). The GER for girls (103.64) is also much better in the southern districts than in north Karnataka (70.22). In that respect, the GER of the Scheduled Tribes in south Karnataka more closely approximates the overall GER of other social groups. The northern districts are caught up in a cycle of deprivation: they have the highest levels of ST population and also have poor human development indicators. Among districts, Bangalore Urban (319.10) and Bijapur (270.65) had high GERs, but then, the proportion of ST population in these districts is not significantly high. Districts with high ST populations did not perform well: Bellary (76.47), Raichur (58.21) and Bidar (48.76) are well below the state average. Kodagu has the lowest (73.41) GER in south Karnataka, followed by Davangere (76.23), Chamarajnagar (86.02) and Chitradurga (87.03). It is noteworthy that the ST population of Chitradurga and Davangere forms a significant percentage of the state's total ST population.

Since illiteracy and poverty are factors that play off one another to create a cycle of deprivation, ensuring greater cohesion at the gram panchayat level between anti-poverty programmes and school enrolment/retention drives would provide the poor with viable ways to access education. Unequal access to schooling is further exacerbated by the fact that ST children stay in school for the least amount of time, as indicated by the mean years of schooling. Scheduled Tribe children have the lowest levels of achievement (4.166 years) compared with SC (4.235 years) and non-SC/ST (4.458 years) children. Not surprisingly, in this context, then, ST children also constitute the highest percentage of out-of-school children (2.42), compared with the state average of 1.54 per cent. The percentage of out-of-school ST girls (2.67) is the highest across all categories (Table 10.2).The Sample Survey of ST households conducted by the Department of Economics and Statistics in 2004,which elicited responses from persons in the age group 9–35 years, found that the principal reasons for females dropping out of school were (i) to work at home and (ii) their parents could not afford to pay for their education. The reasons are identical to the ones adduced to SC girls and indicate that the poor cannot afford the high opportunity costs of education. Girls are the first to be pulled out of school to work at home and take care of siblings to enable their mothers to work. In such cases, families do not find the many incentives offered by the government such as free uniforms, text books and even scholarships, an adequate compensation for lost wages. For boys, family work is the main reason for dropping out.

Akshara Dasoha, the recently introduced midday meals programme for school children, will have a more sustained impact on ensuring enrolment and retention hereafter. Enrolment in secondary education is lower than in primary education. This is part of a pattern of attrition, which increases with levels of education and occurs across all social groups. The GER, in Classes I–X, in 2000-01, was 81.17, which was considerably lower than the GER for SCs (94.31) and all students (89.95).The differential between boys (85.59) and girls (76.51) was also higher than for SCs and all students. As with primary education, there is a marked disparity between the GER for south Karnataka (100.10) and north Karnataka (66.03).While a similar regional trend exists for all students and SCs, the disparity is not as high as it is with STs; Gulbarga (32.86), Bidar (43.06) and Chitradurga (77.93) were all below the state average. GER for Bellary and Raichur (61.89 and 43.89), which have the highest proportion of ST population, is very poor. What are the outcomes for students who overcome the barriers of poverty and gender and stay the course? Surprisingly good, if performance in school examinations is taken as an indicator of educational attainment. Scheduled Tribe students performed well in the Class VII examinations in 2002, with a pass percentage of 88.25, which was higher than the pass percentage of all students (87.31) and SC students (87.87). Girls (89.41) had an edge over boys (87.39) as in all social groups. The inference is that girls will perform well academically, if they are enabled to overcome the socio-economic constraints that keep them out of school. This is apparent when we look at the percentage of students who passed the S.S.L.C (Class 10th) examinations from 2001–2005 where ST girls have outperformed ST boys, SC boys and SC girls (Table 10.3). In 2005, ST girls had a pass percentage of 55.18, which is higher than the percentage of ST and SC boys and SC girls. This outcome only serves to support the earlier finding that the performance of girl students in general, and ST girl students in particular, is exemplary, once they make it past the roadblocks. As the Sample Survey (DES: 2004A) found, the dropout rate increased with levels of education. In the sample surveyed, there were only 0.18 per cent women graduates and 1.40 per cent male graduates, and only 0.02 per cent ST women were post-graduates. Scheduled Tribe students, in general tertiary education, cluster primarily in government.

Unequal access to schooling is further exacerbated by the fact that ST children stay in school for the least amount of time, as indicated by the mean years of schooling. In 2003-04, STs constituted 4.46 per cent of students in government colleges and 2.80 per cent in private aided colleges. There is a marked disparity in the enrolment of boys (3,209) and girls (1,652). This gap in male and female enrolment in general degree courses is uniform across government and private aided colleges. The percentage of ST students in engineering colleges averaged 0.1 per cent from 1996 to 2000 and went up to 1.7 per cent in 2002-03. Scheduled Tribes enrolment in engineering diploma courses is a minimal 0.2 per cent (Annual Reports, DTE; Annual Report VTU 2002-03).This places young ST graduates in a disadvantageous position when they seek jobs in a market that wants trained technical professionals. They are ill-equipped to take advantage of the IT-fuelled boom in jobs in Karnataka. Economic status Historically, the tribal economy was based on subsistence agriculture and/or hunting and gathering. However, since the tribal people treated land as a common resource, they rarely had land titles, and thus, lost their lands to outsiders when exploitation of forest resources began to take place on a significant scale. This ensured that a majority ended up as small and marginal landholders. The 2001 Census data reveals that around half the ST population is in the workforce. Women constitute about 41.7 per cent of the workforce. More than 85 per cent of the working population is in rural areas. The distribution of main workers (76.4 per cent) is concentrated in the rural parts of the state where a high 51.5 per cent work. Bellary has the highest percentage of main workers (11.5 per cent) followed by Raichur (7.8 per cent). The highest percentage of ST marginal workers lives in Raichur (11.7), which also has the highest proportion of the ST population to the total population, clearly indicating their highly precarious livelihood status. Land holdings The data analysed in this section shows that STs largely own low-productivity assets: the principal asset being their own labour. This scenario is exacerbated by their low literacy and lack of vocational skills, which pushes them into jobs with poor remuneration, where men, women and children, between them, earn insufficient wages, as represented by their monthly per capita expenditure.

Urban STs are slightly better placed than their rural counterparts. According to the 2001 Census, 7.65 per cent of STs are cultivators,11.86 per cent are agricultural labourers and 4.70 are in household industry. The largest percentages of ST women are in household industries (58.80) and agricultural labour (57.90). Only 29.89 per cent of ST cultivators are women here, but ST ownership of medium and large holdings is a low 7.9 and 1.0 per cent respectively. The majority of STs have small units with low productivity, which are so economically unviable that landholders are compelled to work as wage labour to survive. Sources of income. The NSS (1999-2000) data shows that the largest percentage of rural ST households (12.8) reported rent as a source of income, followed by wages/salaried employment (9.7), cultivation (7.7), fishing and other agricultural enterprises (6.7). In Andhra Pradesh, which has a significant tribal population, 11.4 per cent derived income from fishing and other agricultural activities and 8.9 per cent from cultivation. An analysis of the income levels of STs in the Sample Survey (DES: 2004A) reveals a wide gap of more than 100 per cent between STs in urban areas and their rural counterparts. The annual per capita income of rural STs is Rs. 4,768, as compared with Rs. 10,987 for urban STs. The percentage of families below the poverty line in the rural ST population is 40 while it is 25 for the urban ST population. Rural Scheduled Tribes had the lowest monthly per capita expenditure (MPCE) of Rs. 404, compared with Rs. 419 for all social groups and much lower than the average MPCE of Rs. 500 for all rural groups. In urban Karnataka, the MPCE for STs was Rs. 634, which was again below the state average MPCE of Rs. 911. Not surprisingly, the MPCE of STs is the lowest in rural areas given their concentration in rural areas and their dependence

The Sample Survey shows that while 57.39 per cent of rural ST households owned agricultural land, a high 74.35 per cent of it was not irrigated. The percentage of total area irrigated in the state to gross area sown was 21 per cent (2002-03).

The decline in rural expenditure is disturbing and could be the effect of the increasing casualisation of labour. Healthcare Data on health, except for NFHS surveys, does not contain information disaggregated by social groups on a regular basis. Lack of data is a constraint when it comes to tracking the health indicators of the ST population. This section uses data from the NFHS surveys and the Sample Survey to develop a profile of the health and nutritional status of STs in the state. The Sample Survey estimated the crude birth rate (CBR) at 22.79, which is marginally higher than the state average of 21.8. The crude death rate (CDR) is estimated at 8.50 which is again higher than 7.50 for the general population. The CDR is lower for STs than SCs (9.12) in the state. Most of the health indicators show deterioration in the health of women and children. The health status of the tribal population is not on par with the rest of the state's population. The infant mortality rate (IMR) of STs (64.37) is much higher than the state average (52.0); the IMR for STs is marginally lower than the IMR for SCs (64.74) and there is a marked difference between male (75.84) and female IMR (54.48). The Sample Survey found that the principal causes of death among infants are diseases of the circulatory system (49.06 per cent) and respiratory system (23.45). Disturbingly enough, NFHS data for 1992-93 and 1998-99 shows regressive trends with the total fertility rate increasing to 2.38 from 2.15, the post-neonatal mortality rates to 21.9 from 18.0, the child mortality rate to 38.9 from 38.0 and the under-five mortality rate to 120.6 from 120.3. Only the neonatal mortality rate fell to 63.2 from 67.6.

National Family Health Survey-2 Karnataka 1998-99, November 2001 present a grim picture of the health status of ST women and children. There are many reasons for infant and maternal deaths: the mother's age at the time of delivery, her nutritional status, access to antenatal care (ANC) and postpartum healthcare are all significant factors that determine whether women and their infants will survive the challenges posed by pregnancy and childbirth. The Sample Survey reveals that the most reproductive age group among STs in Karnataka is 20–29 years, which accounts for about 71.0 per cent of births. Given this data, the age of the mother is probably a lesser contributory factor than undernutrition and lack of access to healthcare services. Antenatal Care: Here too, women's access to antenatal care has either worsened or remained static. The percentage of tribal women receiving no antenatal care has increased to 28.2 per cent from 21.4 per cent during the period 1993-98. Pregnant women receiving antenatal care from registered medical practitioners also showed a decline from 53.6 per cent to 48.5 per cent during the same period. While the percentage of women not getting tetanus toxoid vaccinations at any time showed only a negligible increase from 33.0 per cent to 33.4 per cent, those receiving iron and folic acid showed a slight increase from 61.6 per cent to 63.3 per cent. This leaves a very large number outside the purview of antenatal care and the protection it affords to the mother and her infant. Institutional deliveries Ensuring that women receive professional care during childbirth and in the postpartum period will greatly reduce infant and maternal deaths caused by prolonged or complicated labour, eclampsia, haemorrhage, infections, etc. The NFHS data indicates that there was a marginal increase in institutional deliveries from 26.8 per cent in 1992-93 to 31 per cent in 1998-99.The Sample Survey (DES: 2004) suggests that the situation has improved significantly with the percentage of births receiving some kind of professional care being a high 63.36 per cent, with another 24.08 per cent attended by trained dais. While this is a good development, the outcomes in terms of lowered IMR and MMR are yet to become visible. The inaccessibility of ST habitations, combined with high absenteeism of medical staff in primary healthcare centres, further contribute to the difficulties that tribal people have in availing basic health facilities. Genetic and other diseases There are also certain genetic disorders and deficiency diseases specific to tribal areas such as GEPD and sickle cell anaemia. Malaria, tuberculosis and sexually transmitted diseases are other areas of concern. Cases of HIV/AIDS too have made their appearance among the tribal

Human Development in Karnataka

Given the isolation of some tribes, their traditional healing systems should be allowed to complement modern medical care practices. Many ST habitations are located in remote areas in the forest where immediate attention by trained medical staff is rarely available when it is most needed, so traditional healthcare can fill this breach. Nutrition The nutritional status of an individual depends partly on income but also on awareness of the importance of the nutritional content of food. The diet of ST women is likely to be low in terms of consumption of fruit (39.8 per cent), eggs (49.4 per cent) and chicken, meat, fish (26.6 per cent). Their consumption of milk/curd is higher than that of SCs, but less than OBCs and others, and contains some amount of pulses, beans, green leafy vegetables and other vegetables. If this is juxtaposed with data relating to the consumption patterns of (i) poor women whose consumption of milk, curd, fruit and vegetables is less than that of high income women and (ii) rural women whose consumption of milk, curd, fruit and meat is below that of urban women, then it is not surprising that ST women have very poor nutritional levels (NFHS-2,1998-99).Malnutrition is of many kinds: there is protein-energy malnutrition and micronutrient malnutrition caused by inadequate dietary intake, as well as intake of food insufficient in protein and micronutrients. Mal- and under-nutrition are reflected in the statistics relating to height and body mass. Among rural women, 9.4 per cent were below the mean height (which is on par with OBCs and others and less than SCs) and 49.0 per cent were below the body mass index

(BMI), which is much worse than for all social groups. At the all-India level, 13.5 per cent were below the mean height and a high 46.3 per cent were below the BMI, which is poorer than SCs (42.1), OBCs (35.8) and others (30.5). Given their poverty levels, ST women have very high levels of under-nutrition. Tribal children also suffer from sharp levels of under-nutrition. Policies directed at reducing under-nutrition among children and women must also target the dietary intake of adolescent girls in addition to focusing on pregnant and nursing mothers. Government programmes include ICDS, for children in the age group 0–6, pregnant women and nursing mothers, the public distribution system (PDS), which provides 10 kg of rice and wheat at Rs.3.0 per kg to the poor and midday meals for school children. The midday meals scheme is a big step in the right direction but, unfortunately, it does not address the nutrition needs of out-of-school children, many of whom are girls. Another cause of poor nutrition could be the declining access of the tribal people to forest areas, which had earlier provided them with food rich in protein and micronutrients. Nutrition security through kitchen gardens is an intervention that would pay rich dividends. Family planningAwareness of birth control methods is relatively high among ST married males (48.0 per cent) and married females (45.0 per cent). Permanent forms of birth control appear to be the preferred mode, with 26.30 per cent women and a low Another cause of poor nutrition could be the declining access of the tribal people to forest areas, which had earlier provided them with food rich in protein and micronutrients.

The brunt of family planning is borne by women, possibly because they have a higher stake in not becoming pregnant frequently and because men are not prepared to take equal responsibility for birth control, or possibly, because healthcare providers find it easier to target women.

Sanitation: An unsanitary environment contributes to the proliferation of disease, leading to high morbidity rates, which reduces productivity and affects the earning capacity of individuals. The poor sanitary condition of ST households is highlighted by the 2001 Census data, which shows that 79.71 per cent of households do not have latrines and 61 per cent do not have any kind of drainage facilities. A high 90.3 per cent of rural ST households and 41.7 per cent of urban households do not have latrines, although it must be noted that the rest of the population is not well situated either, since the state averages are 82.5 per cent for rural and 24.8 per cent for urban areas. About 42 per cent ST households have a bathroom in the house, as against 58.9 per cent of the total population at the state level and 36.1 per cent at the all-India level. In Karnataka, STs have better sanitary facilities than their counterparts at the all-India level, but this is only a matter of degree. A low 11.18 per cent of ST settlements/villages have community latrines, about 30.5 per cent of households have open drains and only 8.6 of households have closed drainage. A high 58.0 per cent habitations lack storm water drains. Drinking water Tap water constitutes the main source of drinking water for 53.7 per cent ST households (58.39 for all households). Access to drinking water by tap within the premises is higher for all households (24.1) than for STs (12.7) and SCs (12.6). A slightly higher number of ST households have access to tap water near the premises (Census: 2001).Almost 89.0 per cent of ST villages surveyed have a drinking water facility within the village and the sources comprise bore-wells with hand pumps, mini water supply and piped water supply schemes. Three out of four villages have adequate drinking water supply during all seasons (Table 10.14). Housing The percentage of STs living in permanent houses (43.7 per cent) is lower than the corresponding figures for SCs (51.1) and all households (54.9) according to the 2001 Census, About 39 per cent dwell in semi-permanent houses compared with 35.6 per cent for all households and 36.6 per cent for SCs. A higher percentage of rural STs live in semi-permanent houses (43.4) than urban STs (23.1) who live predominantly in permanent houses (66.9). There is little difference between STs and all households, with reference to building material used. A high percentage of STs (84.4 per cent) owned their houses, compared with 78.5 per cent for all households. House ownership is highest in rural areas (91.9 per cent). This can be attributed to the very progressive state and Centrally-sponsored housing programmes (Ashraya, Ambedkar, Indira Awaas), which clearly have had visible outcomes. Almost 89.0 per cent of ST villages surveyed havea drinking water facility within the village and the sources comprise bore-wells with hand pumps, mini water supply and piped water supply schemes. Three out of four villages have adequate drinking water supply during all seasons.

State Policies

The Department of Tribal Welfare was formed specifically to address the needs of STs in Karnataka. Its budget is part of the budget of the Department of Social Welfare. Tribal Sub-Plan The concept of the Tribal Sub-Plan (TSP) and its counterpart the Special Component Plan (SCP) emerged in the National Fifth Five-Year Plan. The Tribal Sub-Plan was first introduced in 1976-77 when it was implemented in five Integrated Tribal Development Projects (ITDP) in the districts of Mysore, Chikmaglur, Kodagu and Dakshina Kannada (including Udupi). In 1992, it was extended to all districts in the state. The objectives of the TSP are poverty alleviation, protection of tribal culture, education, healthcare and providing basic minimum infrastructure. Poverty alleviation includes programmes in agriculture, animal husbandry, sericulture, horticulture, village and small industries as well as all employment-generating schemes such as Swarna Jayanthi Swarozgar Yojana (SJSY). Pooling TSP funds Under the TSP, departments earmark three per cent of their plan budget for expenditure on tribal development. However,as in the case of the Special Component Plan for Scheduled Castes, some departmental schemes were not particularly relevant or effective and ended up being symbolic gestures to the development of STs. The TSP funds were first pooled in 1991. In 'pooling', funds earmarked under TSP are partially or completely withdrawn from the department. The resultant corpus is then utilised to finance three strategic areas: housing, education (construction of hostels) and financing irrigation wells and The Department of Tribal Welfare was formed specifically to address the needs of STs in Karnataka.

Micro industries: The objective here is to utilise local skills for the promotion of micro industries like bee-keeping, minor forest produce, tribal crafts, sericulture, and carpentry. An investment varying from Rs. 500 to Rs. 25,000 generates an income of about Rs. 30–40 per day. Self-help groups: Self-help groups (SHGs) have radically changed the micro-credit systems in rural areas.Tribals, who form a large percentage of rural agricultural labour, and subsistence farmers find it difficult to source credit from financial institutions and are likely to benefit from the SHG philosophy. Self-help groups promote savings and microfinance among members, but they also have other objectives such as social empowerment and gender equity. The Stree Shaktiprogramme of the department of Women and Child Development has 1,19,621 ST women members in 1,00,000 SHGs. *The role of NGOs in tribal development:* There is growing realisation of the need to develop a healthy partnership between the government and the non-governmental organisations (NGOs). The role of NGOs in tribal welfare activities, though small, has been responsible for introducing qualitative changes in the lives of the people. Vivekananda Girijana Kalyana Kendra, Swami Vivekananda Youth Movement, DEED, FEDINA, CORD,Samagra Grameena Ashrama, Janashikshana Trust, Chintana Foundation, DUDI, Samvriddi/Krupa,Vanavasi Kalyana Ashramaare some of the NGOs involved in tribal development in Karnataka. *Community based organisations:* It is possible to make development works more effective and sustainable through an engagement with the local community, which has a better understanding than non-tribals, of its own socio-economic needs, traditions and culture. Their participation in programmes, funded by government and voluntary organisations builds confidence in the people to utilise the services thus offered and provides feedback for modification and re-orientation of programmes. In Chamarajnagar district, the tribal people's organisations are known as sanghas.They actively Under the IPP-9 project, the Health Department and NGOs trained tribal girls as Auxiliary Nurse and Midwives (ANM) and they were posted to sub centres in remote tribal areas.These ANMs are now providing good healthcare services to tribal women and children. The government-owned primary health centres at Gumballi and Thithimathi, were handed over to Karuna Trust and Vivekananda Foundation respectively and are run as model PHCs.In B.R. Hills, VGKK, an NGO, is promoting the traditional knowledge systems of tribals and has integrated traditional healthcare system with modern medicine. Tribal knowledge of herbal medicines is being promoted. NGO experiences in tribal health. Source: Author. participate in issues concerning tribals, such as preventing forest fires, illegal quarrying, smuggling and poaching. Their participation in programmes such as sustainable harvesting of NTFP through participatory resource monitoring, value additions to the NTFP and conservation of bio-diversity has helped to reduce the exploitation of minor forest produce by outsiders. Concerns Some state programmes have been very successful in providing services to the Scheduled Tribes, e.g. free housing, drinking water supply and electrical connectivity to ST households. There is a gamut of programmes designed to address the problems of school dropouts (ashram schools, scholarships, free text books and uniforms, midday meals) and income poverty through the many poverty reduction programmes. Unfortunately, the degree of effectiveness in terms of programme implementation that one sees in these sectors is not evident in the three critical areas of health, education and poverty reduction.

The magnitude of the problem is so great that a large percentage of Scheduled Tribe families is still poor and lacks access to resources that would improve their education and health status. It can be said, based on some of the indicators discussed above and in chapter 2, that the human development status of the Scheduled Tribes is more than a decade behind the rest of the population of the state and they are the poorest and most deprived of all sub-populations in the state. The role of NGOs in tribal welfare activities, though small, has been responsible for introducing qualitative changes in the lives of the people. Tribal participation in programmes such as sustainable harvesting of NTFP through participatory resource monitoring, value additions to the NTFP and conservation of bio-diversity have helped to reduce the exploitation of minor forest produce by outsiders.

Their literacy rate is the lowest for all social groups and female literacy, which is a low 36.6 per cent when compared with the state average of 56.9, places ST women far behind a population that is, itself, disadvantaged to start with. There are disparities between ST students and others at every level and along all indicators of educational attainment: enrolment and retention in primary education and subsequent participation in secondary and tertiary education. One bright feature is the fact that girls perform well scholastically once they clear the hurdles to the deceptively simple acts of first enrolling and secondly, being allowed to stay on in school. The health of the tribal people has not improved significantly over the previous decade. Their IMR (64.37) is worryingly higher than that of the total population (52.0) of the state. This scenario can be partly attributed to the inadequacy of institutional support. Both antenatal and post-partum care by skilled attendants is not adequately available to the tribal people, especially those who live in remote or inaccessible habitations. State functionaries have not focused sufficiently on these vulnerable people to ensure a reduction in maternal and infant deaths. Under-nutrition levels among children are severe enough to lead to stunting. The occupational distribution shows that the majority of the tribal people are small and marginal farmers and agricultural labour. Their holdings are unirrigated and therefore economically unviable. The Scheduled Tribes also have very low monthly per capita expenditure compared with the rest of the population. Access to MFP and NTFP is critical to the survival of certain tribes, who live in or around forests, most of which are now classified as wildlife sanctuaries.

Recommendations

Develop a comprehensive policy on tribal development, which derives inputs from people at the grassroot level to ensure sustainable development that is ecologically sound, people oriented, decentralised and culturally acceptable. Ensure the collection and collation of disaggregated data to enable benchmarking and monitoring. Conduct a rapid survey of the health status of the tribals and prepare region-specific and tribe-specific health plans. Relax norms for primary health centres and sub-centres in tribal areas and make allowances for geography and population. Select tribal girls for training as ANMs and post them to sub-centres located in predominantly tribal areas. They could also be trained in traditional medicine and health practices, thus encouraging and integrating traditional healing systems into modern medicine. Encourage nutrition security by promoting kitchen gardens. Focus on genetic diseases. Ensure 100 per cent antenatal care coverage and immunisation of women and children. Provide secondary and tertiary care, transport facilities for emergency services and obstetric care. Ensure greater access to education through convergence of the services of several departments: Education, Rural Development and Labour to monitor child labour, track dropouts and provide local employment to their parents. Include tribal culture, traditional knowledge systems, tribal history and vocational skills training in the school curriculum. Involve tribals in biodiversity conservation; encourage them to grow fruit trees on degraded forest-lands; allow sustainable harvesting of the non-forest produce for their livelihood, without endangering the biodiversity of the forest. Encourage need-based economic activities that use locally available raw materials and assist in marketing of finished goods. Provide more budgetary support to the land purchase scheme. Promote organic forming, conservation of traditional seed. Empower tribals at village level to participate effectively in Gram Sabhas, by promoting community based organisations. Develop a comprehensiv policy on tribal development, which derives inputs from people at the grassroot level to ensure sustainable development that is ecologically sound, people oriented, decentralised and culturally acceptable. Include tribal culture, traditional knowledge systems, tribal history and vocational skills training in the school curriculum.

Acknowledgements

1. Various reports Govt. of India.
2. Various websites.
3. Annual Report of Various Research Organisations in India.
4. Karnataka Census Report.
5. Karnataka Human Development Report, 2005.

10

Education of the Indigenous Children in India : Few Stylized Facts

—*Manoher Shetty*

Background

The Indian Constitution assigns special status to the Scheduled Tribes (STs). Traditionally referred to as adivasis, vanbasis, tribes, or tribals, STs constitute about 8% of the Indian population. There are 573 Scheduled Tribes living in different parts of the country, having their own languages different from the one mostly spoken in the State where they live. There are more than 270 such languages in India.

The term tribe or tribal is not defined anywhere in the Constitution although according to the Article 342, ST represents the tribe or tribal communities that are notified by the President. Tribes are not part of the traditional Hindu caste structure. STs in India are more like the "indigenous" or "tribal people" in other parts of the world. Mishra (2002) defines Scheduled tribes as people who (i) claim themselves as indigenous to the soil; (ii) generally inhabit forest and hilly regions; (iii) largely pursue a subsistence develop economy; (iv) have grate regard for traditional religious and cultural practices; (v) believe in common ancestry and (vi) have strong group ties. However, all characteristics do not apply to all tribal communities. Tribals are not homogenous groups. There are at least four groups of STs – hunting-gathering group, agricultural group, irrigation-agricultural group and industrial wage earning group (Mishra, 2002).

Accordingly to the 1991 census, the tribal population in India is 67.8 million. The large stnumber of tribals is in undivided

Madhya Pradesh (16.40 million), followed by Orissa (7 million) and Bihar (6.6 million). However, the largest proportion of tribals in total population is in Mizoram (95%), followed by Lakshadweep (93%), Nagaland (88%), Meghalaya (86%) and Arunachal Pradesh (64%). Nine States – Madhya Pradesh, Chattisgarh, Orissa, Jharkhand, Maharashtra, Gujarat, Rajasthan, Andhra Pradesh and West Bengal – together account for more than four-fifth of the tribal population in India.

Tribals are Heterogeneous Groups

Tribals are not homogenous groups. Different tribes, even if living in the same village, maintain exclusive identities. Socialization is generally endogamous and they identify more with people belonging to their tribe rather than to those living in the same village or area. There is also a sense of being 'superior' to others in many tribes. For instance, the Gonds in Sidhi villages prefer to socialize only in their own community and do not consider the Kols and the Baigas equal to them. Similarly, the Bhumiyas at Mulasar village in Orissa look down upon the Parojas and the Kandhas, and the Kharwars in Ukamad village in Jharkhand do not consider the Korwas as equals. However, this seldom leads to any form of exploitation and cannot be compared with the practice of untouchability. This is more to do with an isolated existence and separate territoriality in the past. The Soligas in Maddur Colony consider themselves 'superior' to Kurubhas whereas the Jenukurubhas feel they are superior to 'others'. The Kunbis and Warlis in Mahal Village in Dangs district in Gujarat also consider each other 'different'(Jha & Jhingran, 2002).

There are 16 million ST children (10.87 million in 6-11 years and 5.12 million in 11-14 years) as on March 2001, out of the total child population of about 193 million in the age group of 6 to 14 years in the country (Selected Educational Statistics – 2000-01). Realizing that Scheduled Tribes are one of the most deprived and marginalized groups with respect to education, a host of programmes and measures were initiated ever since the Independence. Elementary education is a priority area in the Tribal sub-plans from the 5th Five Year Plan. Education of ST children is considered important, not only because of the Constitutional obligation but also as a crucial input for total development of tribal communities. Another important development in the policy towards education of tribals is the National Policy on Education (NPE), 1986 which specified among other things the following:

- Priority will be accorded to opening primary schools in tribal areas.
- There is need to develop curricula and devise instructional material in tribal language at the initial stages with arrangements for switchover to regional languages.
- ST youths will be encouraged to take up teaching in tribal areas.
- Ashram schools/residential schools will be established on a large scale in tribal areas.
- Incentive schemes will be formulated for the STs, keeping in view their special needs and lifestyle.

NPE, 1986 and Programme of Action (POA), 1992 recognized the heterogeneity and diversity of the tribal areas, besides underlining the importance of instruction through the mother tongue and the need for preparing teaching/learning material in the tribal languages. Working group on Elementary and Adult Education for Xth Five Year Plan (2002-07) emphasized the need to improve the quality of education of tribal children and ensuring equity, besides further improving the access.

STs and Literacy

The literacy rate for STs has gone up from 8.5% (male – 13.8%, female – 3.2%) in 1961 to 29.6% (male – 40.6%, female – 18.2%) in 1991 and to 40% (male – 59%, female – 37%) in 1999-2000 as per the 55th Round of NSS.

Elementary education is a priority area in the Tribal sub-plans from the 5th Five Year Plan. Education of ST children is considered important, not only because of the Constitutional obligation but also as a crucial input for total development of tribal communities. One of the super goals of SSA is to "bridge all gender and social category gaps at primary stage by 2007 and at elementary stage by 2010". Hence out of a sum of Rs. 448.91 crores provided in the Budget Estimate for 2004-2005 to this Department, more than 70% is earmarked for schemes related to education. There is a need to evolve sensitive model of tribal education rooted in the psychological strengths of tribal children.

States with large proportion of STs like Mizoram, Nagaland and Meghalaya have high literacy rate while States with large number of tribals like Madhya Pradesh, Orissa, Rajasthan and Andhra Pradesh have low tribal literacy rate (Sujatha, 2000). For instance, tribal literacy in Madhya Pradesh was 7.6% in 1971, 10.7% in 1981, 21.5% in 1991 and 36% in 1999-2000 (NSS 55th Round) – all below the national average for tribal literacy. The disparity among various States in terms of tribal literacy rates is high ranging from 82% in Mizoram to 17% in Andhra Pradesh (India Education Report; 2002). As many as 174 districts(out of 418 districts in the country in 1991) in 1991 have ST literacy rate below the national average of 29.6%. Tribal literacy in 17 districts (7 in Uttar Pradesh, 4 in Madhya Pradesh, 3 in Rajasthan, 2 in Assam and 1 in Orissa) is below 10% while in 3 districts, it is more than 90% (2 in Himachal Pradesh and 1 in Bihar). Lalitpur district of Uttar Pradesh has the lowest ST literacy – 4.8%. Data reveal that States, which are low in general and tribal literacy are also States with higher gender disparity (Sujatha, 2000). The female literacy among STs has increased from just 3.2%in 1961 to 37% in 1999-00. As per 1991 Census, female literacy of tribals is high in Mizoram (79%), Nagaland (55%), Sikkim (50%) and Kerala (51%), compared to Andhra Pradesh (8.7%), and Rajasthan (4.4%). There were 119 districts in the country in 1991 where ST female literacy rate was below 10%. Most of them were in Madhya Pradesh (27), Uttar Pradesh (27), Bihar (20), Rajasthan (20) and Andhra Pradesh (11). Although disaggregated data on tribal literacy from the 2001 census is not available yet, there isan indication that tribal literacy especially that of women may go up as most of the states with large number of STs have reported substantial increase in the literacy rate in the 2001 Census. NSS 55th Round (1999-2000) also gave indication of the rising trend of tribal literacy in India.

Strategies and Approaches in SSA

The National Programme of Sarva Shiksha Abhiyan (SSA), which aims to achieve Universal Elementary Education (UEE), has a special focus on education of the tribal children. Tribal children are an important constituent of the Special Focus Group (SFG) under SSA; other focus groups include girls, SCs, working children, urban deprived children, children with specialneeds, children below poverty line and migrating children. These groups are not mutually exclusive and they overlap. One of the super goals of SSA is to "bridge all gender and social category gaps at primary stage by 2007 and at elementary stage by 2010". The broad strategies under SSA reiterate that there will be a focus on participation of children from SC/ST and minorities, urban deprived children, children with special needs, working children and children in the hardest to reach groups. The Sarva Shiksha Abhiyan (SSA) recognizes the varied issues and challenges in tribal education in view of the heterogeneous structure of tribal population in the country. The issues and challenges in tribal education can be categorized as external, internal, socio-economic and psychological. The external constraints are related to issues at levels of policy, planning and implementation while internal constraints are with respect to school system, content, curriculum, pedagogy, medium of instruction etc. The third set of problems relates to social economic and cultural background of tribals and psychological aspects of first generation learners. STs are at different levels of socio-economic and educational development. STs in North Eastern States and those settled in urban and semi-urban areas are comparatively better placed. The problems of education of the ST children vary from area to area and tribe to tribe. Therefore, SSA emphases on area specific and tribe specific planning and implementation of interventions, which could meet the learning needs of ST children. The planning teams at the State and district levels under SSA have been sensitized about the approach adopted and provisions made in the SSA framework for the education of ST children. The assessment of the problems issues and challenges relating to/of tribal education is made through the household surveys and micro planning exercise. The plans are developed by the districts based on the findings as well as the secondary data.

The 'Manual of Appraisal of Plans' brought out by the Ministry of Human Resource Development has outlined appraisal issues with respect to planning of interventions for theeducation of tribal children. Monitoring tools have also been developed to ensure that programmes for education of tribal children are implemented as planned. A checklist to address the equity issues specially focusing the education of ST children has also been developed. Some of the interventions being promoted in States under SSA include:

- Setting up schools, education guarantee centres and alter tribal schools in tribal habitations for non-enrolled and drop out children.
- Textbooks in mother tongue for children at the beginning of the primary education cycle, where they do not understand the regional language. Suitably adapt the curriculum and make available locally relevant teaching learning materials for tribal students.
- Special training for non-tribal teachers to work in tribal areas, including knowledge of tribal dialect
- Special support to teachers as per need
- Deploying community teachers
- Bridge Language Inventory for use of teachers
- The school calendar in tribal areas may be prepared as per local requirements and festivals.
- Anganwadis and Balwadis or creches in each school in tribal areas so that the girls are relieved from sibling care responsibilities.
- Special plan for nomadic and migrant workers.
- Engagement of community organizers from ST communities with a focus on schooling needs of children from specific households.
- Ensuring sense of ownership of school communities by ST communities by increasing representatives of STs in VECs / PTAs etc. Involving community leaders in school management.
- Monitoring attendance and retention of children.
- Providing context specific interventions eg. Ashram school, hostel, incentives etc.

Provisions under SSA

SSA provides for Rs. 1.5 million per district per year for specific interventions for education of SC/ST children. It also provides free textbooks upto Rs. 150/- for girls and SC/ST children (SSA framework for implementation, 2002). The other components under the broad framework of SSA which have an impact on the education of tribal education are (i) school/EGS like alter tribal facility to be set up within one kilometer of all habitations; (ii) upgradation of EGS to regular schools after two years; (iii)mainstreaming camps, bridge courses/residential camps for out of school girls SC/ST children under the alter tribal and innovative education component; (iv) provision of process based community participation with a focus on the participation of women and SC/ST; (v) free mid-day-meal to all children at primary stage; and (vi) interventions for early childhood care and education.

Universalizing access

One of the challenges in providing education to tribal children is with respect to setting up schooling facilities in small, scattered and remote tribal habitations. The majority of the Scheduled Tribes live in sparsely populated habitations in interior, and inaccessible hilly and forest areas of the country. Nearly 22 per cent of the tribal habitations have population less than 100 while more than 40% have population of 100 to 300. The rest have population of 300 to 500 (Sujatha, 2000).

Relaxed Norm on Setting up Schools

One of the reasons for poor access to schooling in tribal areas before 1980s was the high norm on population, number of children and distance for opening new schools. Most of the States have relaxed these norms to enable setting up schools even in small tribal hamlets. This, along with other measures has improved access in tribal areas. For instance, Andhra Pradesh has relaxed norms to set up schools in habitations even with 20 school-age children. Some States Karnataka etc. have lowered the population size norm, especially for tribal areas. EGS centers can now be established even with 15 children. In remote tribal habitations in hilly areas of North Eastern States and Jammu & Kashmir, EGS schools can be opened even with 10 children.

The Sixth All India Educational Survey (1993) shows that 78 per cent of tribal population and 56 per cent of tribal habitations have been provided primary schools within the habitation. In addition, 11 per cent of tribal population and 20 per cent of tribal habitations have schools within less than 1 km radius. About 65 per cent of rural habitations covering 86 per cent of the total rural population have primary schools within the habitations or within a distance of half kilometer, as against 56 per cent of tribal habitations with 79 per cent of tribal population.

Mizoram and Gujarat have the highest percentage of population and habitations covered by primary schools within the habitations. As high as 95 per cent of tribal population and 85 to 90 per cent of the tribal habitations in the States are provided with schooling facility within the habitation.

According to the Sixth All India Educational Survey (1993) there are about 176,500 habitations without schooling facilities, mostly in tribal habitations and habitations of hardest to reach groups. The situation regarding access has now improved substantially, thanks to the schemes like NFE/Education Guarantee Scheme and Alter tribal and Innovative Education (EGS& AIE), DPEP and Sarva Shiksha Abhiyan. More than 70,000 education guarantee centers and alter tribal schools were opened under the District Primary Education Programme (DPEP), EGS schemes and other programmes in the State over the last 10 years. In addition about 116,000 new primary and upper primary schools were opened since 1996-97 – as number of schools increased from 767,000 in 1995-96 to 883,000 in 2001-02 (Abstract of Educational Statistics 2001-02).

Subsequent to this statistical report, SSA sanctioned in the last two years over 85,000 new schools. In addition 300,000 EGS centers and equal number of alter tribal and innovative education centers were sanctioned to benefit more than 14 million never enrolled and out of school children. Many of these new schools, EGS centers and alter tribal schools have been sanctioned in the tribal habitations, improving the schooling access. As per the latest estimate (2003-04), there are about 81,000 unserved habitations in the country. The largest number of unserved habitations without primary schools is in Bihar

(14200) followed by Orissa (13100), Assam (12300), Rajasthan (8000), West Bengal (6600) and Andhra Pradesh (4100). These unserved habitations are being covered under Sarva Shiksha Abhiyan.

Considered the position of access to schooling in tribal areas in States. Madhya Pradesh has setup EGS schools in every habitation having at least 40 children. The majority of these EGS schools are located in tribal areas. Andhra Pradesh has gone one step further by deciding to setup community schools called 'Mabadi' in every habitation with at least 15 children. In Javadu hills of Tiru district of Tamil Nadu, access to formal schools was a major problem for the tribal population. The State has opened a number of forest schools in these areas. In Kerala, over 100 multigrade centres have been set up in small tribal habitations, which have at least 20 children. In Gadchirauli and Dhule of Maharashtra, there were many tribal habitations where children do not have access to schooling. Contract schools have been set up in these habitations. In Gujarat, there are many districts with significant tribal population, which migrate with children in search of work. The State has adopted strategies like summer camps, seasonal hostels and salt farm schools for covering children in such areas. Bridge Courses are run for such children to ensure that children could be readmitted to formal schools. In Himachal Pradesh, Sirmour district experimented with mobile teachers for migrating Gujjar children in Nohrudhar education Block. There are residential Ashram Schools for tribal children in many States including Madhya Pradesh, Gujarat, Andhra Pradesh, Rajasthan, Jharkhand, Orissa, Chhattisgarh, Maharashtra and Karnataka etc.

Ashram Schools

Ashram schools are residential schools for tribal children from a cluster of habitations. Based on the Gandhian philosophy of self-reliance, it was first experimented by Thakkar Bapa, a Gandhian in Panchamahal district of Gujarat in the pre-independence days (Ananda, 1994). Ashram schools were found effective as (i) it was not feasible to open full fledged schools in very small and scattered habitations (ii) it created congenial atmosphere for teaching learning as it is assumed that the tribal households do not have such an environment and (iii) it helped to develop the total personality of the child and impart vocational skills to improve employment opportunities.

Ashram schools generally provide admission to children from habitations at least 6-8 kms away from the school. If children from nearby villages are admitted, they are not provided with boarding. The curriculum of Ashram schools includes agriculture and other life skills in addition to general subjects. Many parents in Jharkhand, Orissa and Gujarat preferred Ashram schools as they provided free food, clothing and boarding. Some parents said that education of their wards in Ashram schools was not obstructed, when parents migrated for work. In Bihar emphasis is on opening Apana Vidyalayas in tribal dominated villages for non-enrolled/dropout children. The Angana Vidyalayas for 9+ girls have also been set up on a priority basis in SC/ST dominated areas. In Assam about 1200 AS centres are run in tribal and tea garden estates. Apart from setting up of alter tribal schools for remote habitations, the alter tribal schooling strategies under SSA have also targeted out of school children in tribal areas and pockets.

Universalizing Participation

Out of the ST child population of 16 million in the age group of 6-14 years, more than 14 million (11 million at primary stage and 3 million upper primary stage) ST children are attending schools during 2000-01 (Selected Educational Statistics 2001-02). This means about 2 million ST children were not attending school during 2001-02. The enrolment of scheduled tribes at the primary and upper primary in the last 20 years from1980-81 to 2000-01 increased by 2.4 and 4.2 times respectively. There has been a clear positive trend with respect to participation of ST girls in education. Their enrolment increased by 3 times at primary and 6 times at upper primary stage during the same period. The share of tribal girls in the total school going tribal children at the elementary stage increased from 32.1% in 1981 to41.2% in 2000-01. The Gross Enrollment Ration (GER) of ST children is now about 96 to 100% at primary stage and 88 to 89% at elementary stage.

Oases of Universal Education

The school participation of children, especially tribal children, is influenced by interplay of arrange of factors at school, society and family. For school participation, ideally, all the three factors should be positive or at least one or two factors should be strongly favourable. There are a few oases of universal education in the country. One such area is the tribal blocks of Dondi and Dondi Lohara Blocks in the Durg district of the newly formed Chhattisgarh State. In Dondi, out of the child population (6-14 years) of 24,518, the enrolment is 24,404. There are only 104 out-of-school children in the block. The net enrolment ration (NER) at primary stage isan almost impossible figure – 99-79%. The drop out rate is just 0.76% and completion rate is as high as 96.4% (DISE 2003, Durg). Dondi Lohara, the adjacent tribal block is another island of excellence in UEE. It also has similaral most impossible educational indicators. Of the child population of 33,471, there are only 103 out-of-school children. The NER at primary stage is 99.24% and at upper primary 99.58%. The drop out rate is only 0.58% and completion rate 94.42% (DISE 2003, Durg). I could not see a single out-of-school child in the fields, roads and ponds of Dondi and Dondi Lohar blocks during my three-day field visit in August, 2003. But one afternoon I saw an 11 year old boy grazing cattle in the Karre forest area in the Dondi Lohara block. When I approached him, the boy started running but I chased him. He was not an out-of-school child. A grade 4student from the neighbouring district, he had come to spend 2-3 days with his uncle in Dondi Lohara.What sets apart Dondi and Dondi Lohara – the islands of UEE – from the rest of the country? There are several reasons. Firstly, the hugely successful total literacy campaign in the Durg district in 1989-91 created a positive perception on value of education. Secondly, most of thechildren are second-generation learners, which reflects the parental interest in education. Thirdly, there are no social inequalities among social groups and there is no social exclusion or socialdisharmony. Fourthly, most of the tribals and dalits have land holding and therefore, they are not affected by poverty or economic deprivation. (Zachariah, 2003)

Education – Social Norm in Kerala

Kerala is another example where the main driver of high school participation of tribal children is societal factors. In Kerala, the societal norm in favour of education even among STs

– had emerged long back. There were several factors – socio-potential awakening, absence of social inequalities and social exclusion and snowballing effect of the benefits of education – which helped to evolve social norms. When asked why she sends her children to school, a mother in the tribal hamlet of Kozhikodamoor (hamlet) in Attapady block of Palaghat district in Kerala was baffled. She had not thought about it and did not know what to say. Where else the children should go other than to the school, she wondered. Sending children to school is a social norm in Kerala, the State that has achieved cent percent literacy and where the health and HDI indicators are comparable to that of United States. (Zachariah, 2003)

Convergence between the tribal welfare department and the education department is also critical for enhancing and ensuring school participation of STs. In many States schools in tribal areas are run by the tribal welfare department or tribal development authorities while the curriculum, textbooks, school calender, examination are set by the education department. Moreover, synergy of replication, opening of new schools, residential camps etc. leads to larger coverage and outreach of tribal communities.

Quality Improvement

Most of the States address the issues related to teachers' attitudes, medium of instruction, textbooks and materials, curriculum and pedagogy, and teaching-learning process in tribal areas. An increasing number of researches strongly advocate the use of the mother tongue or home language as media of instruction in early stages of education. This assumes greater significance in the context of education of tribal children because their mother tongue is often quite distinct from the prominent languages in the State or regional languages. ST children face problems wherever teachers do not speak their dialect at all. From the perspective of language, it is desirable to have a local teacher from the same tribal community (Jha & Jhingran, 2002).

Though Research evidence also favour bilingual or multi lingual schooling in view of its positive consequences for cognitive development and social interaction processes, itwould need special treatment for tribal children to be able to cope. The Constitution of India allows the use of tribal dialect (mother tongue) as the medium of instruction if the population of the tribe is more than 100,000. Assam was the first State to prepare teacher training modules and separate teaching learning materials for the Bodo tribal language in 1995. Bodo is also a medium of instructions in somedistricts of Assam. The work on tribal language materials was undertaken through DIET staff and BRC/CRC coordinators who belonged to the tribal community. Resource material in Bodo language has been prepared and all workbooks at primary stage have been translated/adopted in Bodo language. In Golpara district, Garo medium workbook has been translated/adopted and distributed in the schools.

Most of the States have taken up activities for quality improvement of tribal area schools. One ofthe issues identified by the States was the problem faced by tribal children whose home languagewas very different from the regional language, which was the medium of instruction at theprimary level.

In Karnataka a text book for class I & II has been developed and introduced for Soliga language. A handbook has been developed for sensitization of teachers towards social and cultural specificities of tribal societies. In Maharashtra tribal language dictionaries have been developed. Language resource groups have been set up for Bhili, Pawara, Madia, Gondi etc. Bridge material has been developed in Dhule district. Kerala has developed bilingual language materials at district level in Kasarkode, Waynad, Malapuram and Palakkad. Orissa took initiative to develop a comprehensive strategy for education of tribal children as early as 1997. The State has initiated a number of activities for addressing the quality improvement of tribal education.

Quality Improvement: Orissa

A large number of teachers have undergone attitudinal training which has had a significant impact on the attitudes of non-tribal teachers towards tribal children. Continuing efforts are being made to sustain the impact of the attitudinal training through block and cluster level meetings of teachers by including items for discussion on these issues in the monthly meetings. A linguistic survey and mapping has been completed by the Academy of Tribal Dialects and Culture in 4 districts viz. Kalahandia, Gajapati, Raygoda and Keonjher. The State has also explored the use of folklore in primary education, which would help to tap the rich tradition in arts, crafts, music, songs, etc. in tribal societies. Stories and riddles have been collected for use by the teachers and classrooms.

- Seven Tribal Primers in seven tribal languages i.e. Saora, Santali, Kui, Kuvi, Koya, Bondaand Juanag.
- Teachers' handbook of the 7 tribal language primers
- Saora self reading materials
- Picture dictionary in tirbal languages
- Training module on how to use the tribal primer in classroom.
- 16 folk stories developed in Saora (tribal language) and Oriya for both teachers and children.
- Conversation chart with about 100 commonly used sentences in Oriya Saora was prepared and distributed.

Andhra Pradesh has developed bilingual dictionaries and teacher training has been organised in Warangal and Vizianegarem districts. For use of the bilingual material, Research studies have also been undertaken on the issue of language and Maths learning by tribal children. It has been decided to use the multi-level kits developed for tribal areas in Vishakapatnam district in other tribal areas also. Gujarat has developed dictionaries in Dangi and Bhili dialects. A local work glossary in Dangihas been prepared and distributed in schools for class I-IV in Dang district. Similarly a local word glossary in Adivasi dialect has been prepared for class I-IV in Banaskantha district and distributed in schools. The Vidyasahayaks were given training on the use of these dictionaries.

Gujarat has also initiated extensive work for preparation of TLM in tribal languages. The TLM developed include flash cards for different languages and also cards for mathematics. These have been supplied to all school in tribal areas. Bridge Language

Inventory has also been introduced in Ho and Mandavi languages in Ranchi district of Bihar.

The acceptance of Teachers by the community as one among them is critical for increasing the schooling participation in tribal areas. An understanding of and respect for tribal cultures and practices are important for teachers to gain this acceptance. The presence of tribal teachers, especially from the same community, has shown and improved school participation of ST children. Coming from the same community, it is believed that the teachers would understand and respect the culture and the ethos with much greater sensitivity. Studies suggest that teacher motivation contributes more to teaching – learning process than teacher competence (Vaidyanathan and Nair, 2001).

Realising the importance of having teachers from the local community many States have appointed community teachers or para teachers as they are popularly referred to. The deployment of community teachers was first experimented in the late Seventies in NFE and later in the formal school with the Volunteer Teacher Scheme of Himachal Pradesh (1984). Nineties saw spurt in the appointment of community teachers, who are from the local community and appointed by the gram panchayat for Village Education Committees. Different States have different schemes for appointing community teachers.

The issues relating to classroom transaction are difficult as they deal with well entrenched attitudes and prejudices of teachers as well as seemingly intractable problems of the huge difference between home and school language. Attempts have been made to address the first issue through training programme for teachers. However, more emphasis on attitudinal training of teachers on the lines of Orissa is required in most of the States. The second issue has been addressed mainly through the BLIs and primers in tribal languages. There may be a problem of acceptance of the tribal language as a medium of instruction in the tribal communities, therefore, adequate dialogue with tribal communities and their leaders is required to prepare them on this issue.

Poverty, deprivation, poor economic condition, low earing, struggle for survival, dependence on forest products, seasonal migration are some of the other road blocks in providing universal education to scheduled tribes. Jha and Jhingran (2002) says that

"One incidence of illness in the family, one year of drought or the transfer of a teacher –anything can bring a change in circumstances and may mean discontinuation in the schooling of these tribal children". All most all States have scholarships, incentives and allowance for ST children to offset their private cost of education and encourage school participation. These measures have been found fruitful, but timely provision of these incentives is important.

Children helping parents in their work is a social norm in many tribal communities. The involvement of children in livelihood activities – cattle grazing, collection of forest productions etc. – makes it difficult for them to attend school. Girls, apart from taking part in agricultural activities and collection of forest products are commonly engaged in sibling care. (Jha and Jhingran, 2002).

Learning Achievement

Earlier studies on learning achievement of tribal children at primary classes had shown lower levels of achievement compared to non tribals (Govinda and Varghese 1993, Varghese 1994,Sujatha 1998, Prakash et al. 1998), although empirical evidence suggest that tribal children do possess the basic cognitive abilities and psychological dispositions for successful participation in schools. The low achievement levels among tribals are attributed to school-related variables as in the case of non-tribal students.

Tribal students had additional disadvantages arising out of social and location factor (Sujatha,1998). Singh (1996) and Singh and Jayaswal (1981) have argued that low levels of parental education, occupation, income and deprivation, are mainly responsible for poor performance of tribal children in the school. Other roadblocks include negative parental attitude to education, less parental support in schoolwork, low level of motivation and poor self-esteem of children. Sinha and Mishra (1997) argue that tribal children can perform well in school if the intervention programmes directed at them can overcome their deprivation. However, learning achievement surveys conducted in DPEP show that in a majority of the districts the gap between achievement levels of ST children and other children has been reduced to less than 5%. The situation is better in language than in Maths.

There is a need to evolve sensitive model of tribal education rooted in the psychological strengths of tribal children. Studies indicate that, in comparison to other groups, hunters and gatherers possess a high level of visual and tactual differentiation, they demonstrate capacity for fine judgement of shape and size of stimuli as well as spatial relations, and produce the categorization of an array of objects (Mishra et al., 1996). These abilities are greatly required for success in science, art, music, dance, athletic activities, and vocations like carpentry, tailoring, wood and stone crafts. These skills need to be utilized not only for education of tribal children in schools, but also in the broader economic spheres of tribal life. Such attempts will be helpful in generating and promoting the sense of competence, self-efficacy, self-respect, and positive self-image among tribal children in general (Mishra, 2002).

Community Mobilization/involvement

As for all other population groups and areas, community mobilization and awareness generation on issues of enrolment, education of girl children, retention of children in schools and school involvement are carried out in tribal areas. The specific features of such mobilization in tribalareas have been / are:

- Use of tribal/folk art forms (Kerala, Assam, Bihar, Orissa)
- Meetings of mothers and family meetings and involvement of tribal youth volunteers
- Organization of meetings in tribal 'haats' / bazaars and use of tribal fairs and festive occasions to discuss primary education issues (Assam, Gujarat).
- Involvement of traditional tribal organizations in the mobilization effort (Assam, Orissa).
- Involvement of the community including VECs members in documentation of local folklore, history, traditional medicine, agricultural practices (Assam).

11

Tribal Education : A Case Study of Katkaris in Maharashtra

—Anjali Kurane

All over the world, Education is powerful avenue for advancement of socio-economic status and social change. India has large sizable proportion of tribe those in may respect lag behind their nontribal counterparts. Recognizing the importance of education, Government of India is giving much attention to their education but education has made little progress among the tribal. The present study has tried to present an overall educational profile and problems of the education of the katkaris. The poor socio-economic situation, illiteracy of the katkari parents' plays major role in high rate of non attendance of students in school as well as drop out in from school. The literacy rate is low 21.01% among the Katkaris and they are backward in many ways. Most of the katkaris migrate seasonally to work in coal and brick manufacturing factories and work as woodcutter in forest. This seasonal migration rate is very high 70.65%; and significant. The Katkaris do domestic work in the landowner's house. They collect and sell the forest products for their livelihood. They borrow money from the landowners and repay that by doing farm work without pay. They are known for their alcoholism and cold- heartedness for strangers. The Katkari students do not get any motivation, aspirations, and guidance from their parents. They are made to work in the fields, look after the siblings and help in the household activities. Village does not have high school and transportation is not available. Since there is insufficiency of teachers, classrooms and poor attendance of the students, the teacher faces lots of problems for teaching the students. More planned efforts are required to provide basic infrastructure, general scheme of poverty alleviation and employment generation should be implemented for them to reduce their seasonal migration in the haunt of job. Efforts should be taken to create the awareness among them. A great deal of Anthropological study of the Katkaris is necessary for designing an effective pedagogy for them.

Introduction

All over the world, Education as an instrument of socialization and is also play important role in the removal of social economic disabilities, reduces discriminations and attain better advancement of socio-economic status in society and is powerful avenue for social change. Education has a fundamental role in all round and harmonious development of individual, society and nation by reducing poverty, ignorance, exclusion, oppression, superstitions, prejudices and old unreasonable and nonrealistic social taboos. It directly influences one's attitude, opinion, and behavior pattern and adds dignity, grace, and prestige. It is a major basis for socio-economic progress of individual and Society and one of the important avenues for achieving social mobility. According to Hans (1964) "Education probably the most important medium of all because of its influential aspect. Education changes behavior. People and nations are as they are because of their educative process..."

India is multicultural and multi classed society includes the large sizable proportion of the caste and indigenous and ethnic population of tribe. Since independence our nation has achieved multifaceted socio- economic progress but is yet to be completed. Social reformers of our nation had put considerable faith in education as they had recognized the role of education as an effective instrument for bringing about not only the economic progress but also for reducing casteism and caste conflict that would lead to social changes and to development of a society

India has to play multiple role in achieving equity and social justice for the certain castes and tribes those are at different level of socio-economic development that need special provision to be gradually at par with the others. The Government of India has strengthen the educational program, is giving high – priority and providing all opportunities in the field of education and made it accessible to the deprived and backward sections of the Indian society.

Tribal constitute a substantial portion of the India's population and in many respect they lag behind their nontribal counterparts. Recognizing the importance of education in bringing about the changes in the tribal's socio-economic condition, the Government of India is giving much attention to their education.

Education will help to retain the enriched cultural heritage of the tribal of the country by influencing their attitude, behavior and aspiration and providing them necessary skill, knowledge, values, attitude, for realization of enriched culture.

But Irrespective of the best efforts of the Government tribes are even today remained backward. Education has made little progress among the tribal, the result have not been satisfactory. And incase of some tribal even the rate of literacy is on the decrease. Tribal education in India is beset with a multiplicity of problems some of which are really very complex and need a deliberate, systematic approach for their solution.

At present juncture the development of the backward section should be priority and that could be by giving special attention to their education. As Development of our nation depends on the proper and homogeneous development of all the section of our society and not a particular section of the society, in turn depends on the effective attention on the education and educational progress of the weaker section that is tribal of our society.

The present study has tried to present an overall educational profile the katkaris and focuses on the problems of the education the Katkaris.

Location of the Study

The present study, ethnographic fieldwork was conducted in Chikhalgoan group gram panchayat consisting six villages or padas, namely namely Unehere, Karanjai, Ghodgaon, Keshavnagar, Dharanachi Wadi, and Chikhalgoan. These six villages are located in the Sudhagad Taluka, of Raigad District of Maharashtra state. The Chikhalgaon group gram panchayat is west to the Pune and is very near to Pali that is one of the 'Ashtavinayak' places; holy place for Ganesh devotees, Pali is about 114 km away from Pune. It takes approximately three to four hours to reach Pali from Pune and from Pali it takes another twenty minutes to reach the Chikhal Goan. The distance of various padas is 2 km to 7 km from the main Chikhalgaon village. Unhere pada is situated very near to Chikhalgaon approximately 4.5 km. This place is known for hot spring. Unhere is completely dominated by Katkaris. Karanjai pada is 4 km and Ghodgaon pada is 7 km from Chikhalgaon and are located on the hilltop so there is no proper tar road to go these places. In Ghodgaon pada there are katkaris as well as Thakars. In the Keshavnagar pada Maratha community is dominant and is 2 km. from Chikhalgaon, where as dharanachi wadi pada is about 3.5 km. and has only eleven families of Katkaris and five families of Thakars. Chikhalgaon gram panchayat is dominated by the Katkaris. The data is collected from all six padas. There are total 80 families of the Katkaris in Chikhalgaon group gram Panchayat.

People under Study

In Chikhalgaon group gram Panchayat different tribal communities such as Katkaris, Thakars, as well as upper caste Hindus such as Marathas, and Agris are inhabited. The present study conducted on the Katkari community. They are known as one of the primitive tribes residing in Raigad District and Thane district of Maharashtra State.

The Katkaris are originated in Maharashtra but in search of work and livelihood they migrated to Rajasthan and Gujarat, therefore today they are also found in Rajasthan and Gujarat. The term katkari is derived from the Marathi word "Kat". Their traditional occupation was "Kat Karane" or "Kat padane" that means making of catechu, so they were "makers of catechu" from the bark of a "khair" tree or Acacia tree and hence the name "Katkari". "Kat" is used in 'Pan' or 'betel leaf". The Katkaris are reported to be Bhil tribe origin. Their dialect contains some words common among Bhils and their customs to some extent indicates Bhil origin. According to them, they were descended from the Vanaras to whom Shri Ram took with him in his expedition against Ravana. Though they speak Marathi, their language is mixed traces of Marathi, Hindi and Gujarathi.

The Katkaris are classified into two groups "Son Katkaris" and "Dhor Katkaris". According to them that initially there was no division among the Katkaris but many generation ago under the stress of famine some of the Katkaris started eating carcasses and since that time the two section have been distinct namely "Son Katkari" and "Dhor Katkari", The Katkari including "Son Katkari" and "Dhor Katkari", were first notified as scheduled tribes against the name "Kathodi" or "Katkari" under constitution order, 1950.

Today the katkaris are teetering on a brink of extinction. They are landless; most economically backward peoples and live in abject poverty. They were used to live in forest; the basically peoples of jungle but as forest land became less and less living in forest became very hard for them and they started working as farm laborers. At present they are engaged in charcoal making, and brick making, and mainly working as bonded laborers on their masters field. Almost all The Katkaris still wear their traditional dresses. They are known for their alcoholism and cold- heartedness for strangers.

Educational Status of the Katkaris

Study has tried to present the over all picture educational profile of the Katkaris staying in Chikhalgoan Group Gram Panchayat.

There are two types of Institutions (a) Anganwadi school and (b) Zilla Parishad school providing formal education in Chikhalgoan Group Gram Panchayat villages.

Anganwadi School

There are all together two Anganwadi School established in 1995 under the chikhalgoan group gram panchayat one at chikhalgaon village itself and other at the Unhere pada. The Anganwadi School is a nursery school, running a special program for children ranging from age 0 to 6 yrs. It is the basic institution which provides free education along with the nutritious one time meal per day and medicine.

Infrastructure

Anganwadi held in the one room of someone's house made up of bricks. In the classroom a very big mirror has hanged on the wall, intention is that children should see their own full image in the mirror, and they should know that how do they look like, and thus to learn to maintain cleanliness of themselves. The teachers also encourage the parents to keep their children clean and sent them regularly to the Anganwadi. The social reformers Photos such as Dr. Ambedkar and Mahatma Phule also put on the walls of the classroom.

Teacher

The school is run by one lady teacher studied till 9th standards and one lady worker or helper qualified 4th standard. These lady teachers get training at Pali for three months and get the salary of Rs.1400/- per month while the lady helper get Rs. 700/- per month.

Total Number of Katkari students

At present there are 22 Katkari students at chikhalgoan Anganwadi and eight students at Unnhere anganwadi so all together there are 30 Katkari students out of which 18 boys' and 12 girls are there.

School Timing

Everyday the Anganwadi school timing is from 11 am to 2 pm except on Saturdays that is a half day from 9 am to 12 pm. The classes usually begin with a Saraswati vandana that is Hindu Goddess prayer.

Functions

(a) Provision of the writing material:

The students are given pencil, chalk and slates for writing and are taught how to read and write with the help of the picture chart pasted on the walls of the classrooms that consist of picture of various fruits, animals, alphabets, and numbers. The teacher tries to teach them with the help of the action songs, poems and dance. The teacher does not conduct regular monthly or yearly examination but sometimes ask them oral questions. The students do not have school uniform.

(b) Provision of the meal:

Along with the formal education the students are provided one time nutritious meal a day at 1pm. This meal contains khichadi that is prepared from rice, dal and oil. The lady helper does all the work of organizing classroom and meal such as sweeping and cleaning the classroom and the premises, filling of water in the buckets, cleaning the utensils and preparing meal for students and she also takes care of them. Monthly a truck brings all the required food materials and medicines from Pali. During the rainy season the foodstuffs are brought together for 3-4 months.

(c) Provision of the health care facilities:

Another important function of the Anganwadi is to provide health care facilities to the students. Anganwadi carry out various immunization programs such as giving polio drops, B.C.G. vaccination. Weight of the students is taken every month, but in case of malnourished students it is monitored every week. The Anganwadi also maintain the records of the births, deaths and diseases in the village. The medical team comes from PHC Pali every two months to visit the Anganwadi and try to create awareness of various diseases and health, hygiene and sanitation among the students and parents. A supervisor comes once in two months from Pali to check the smooth running of the school. Thus the Anganwadi plays multiple functions in the field of formal education and health care of the students. However the Katkari students are not regular to the Anganwadi. Most of them, parents as well as students come and show interest only in the food but not at all interested in education and school.

Zilla Parishad School

There are two Zilla Parishad Primary School from classes' first to fourth standard under the Chikhalgaon Group Gram Panchayat; has been established in 1994 -95, one is at Chikhalgaon village itself and the other at Unhere pada.

Infrastructure

At both the places, Chikhalgoan as well as at Unhere the school has its own a small separate building made up of bricks and cement. There is only one class room at Chikhalgoan and two class rooms at Unhere. Both the schools have toilet and a small playground. At Chikhalgoan School , all the students from standard first to standard fourth seat together on the mats in one classroom. On the walls many picture charts for Ist to IV std. have pasted. In this classroom there is only one common black board for Ist to IV standards, only one cupboard where they have kept 30 books, the Gram Panchayat has donated these 30 books to school, comprising text books, illustrations and story books. These books are used by both teachers and students and they call it as there library. There are two chairs and one table for teaching staff and Head master. All students of std. Ist to Std. IV, teacher, and headmaster seat together in one room. The Headmaster doesn't have separate room for himself. The school doesn't have hostel facilities and it is Marathi medium day school but the students are also taught English from the Ist std. At Unhere, though school has two small classrooms the seating arrangement of the students is similar of Chikhalgoan School that all the students from std. Ist to std. IV seat together on mat in one classroom and Headmaster is having separate room.

Cleaning of the School

In both the school, peon or helper or worker is not there to look after the cleanliness of classrooms and school premises, for filling up the drinking water and other day to day work. The task of cleaning and filling up water is allocated to all students turn by turn. Everyday some students come early to sweep and clean the classroom and playground and they also fill up water in the container kept in the corridor for the drinking purpose for all the teachers and the students. They bring water from nearby well.

Facilities

(a) Provision of the School Uniforms:

Students are having compulsory school uniforms, for girls blue skirt and white shirt and red ribbon to tie their hair, and brown shorts and white shirt for boys that is provided free. Students both boys and girls do not wear any kind of footwear.

(b) Provision of the Textbooks and Writing material:

The students are provided free books, pencils, slates and chalks.

(c) Provision of the Meal:

The students were given a meal everyday at 1pm. The food consists of rice and dal or Khichdi of dal and rice.

Number of Teachers

Both the schools are run by two eligible qualified teachers, where one is the headmaster and the other is a teacher. Both the Headmasters, of Chikhalgoan and of Unhere Zilla Parishad Schools, have qualified D.Ed. and get salary of Rs. 8000/ per month. The teachers are Graduates and after selection they had taken the training of 3 months at Pali and get a salary of Rs. 3000/ per month. All the selected teachers undergo the training program of three months at Pali.

Total Number of Katkari Students

There are total of 42 katkari students in Chikhalgoan Zilla Parishad Primary school, out of which 22 are males and 20 are females. While at Unhere Zilla Parishad primary school only six Katkari students are studying out of which 4 are males and 2 are females and the remaining almost all students are from upper caste Maratha caste and few from Thakars and Agri.

The classwise distribution of the Katkari students at Chikhalgaon Zilla Parishad Primary School:

Class	*Total Number of Students*	*Male*	*Female*
I	20	11	9
II	9	5	4
III	8	4	4
IV	5	2	3

The classwise distribution of the Katkari students at Unhere Zilla Parishad Primary School:

Class	Total Number of Students	Male	Female
I	3	2	1
II	1	1	0
III	2	1	1
IV	0	0	0

School Timing

Everyday the school starts at 11 am and it goes up to 5 pm. except Saturday that is half day school from 10 am to 1 pm. Morning assembly for 20 minutes is conducted everyday. The students are asked to assemble in the corridor where they sing the National anthem first and then Saaraswati prayer. The teacher writes the thoughts of the day on the blackboard that is kept in the corridor.

The Methods of Teachings

Only one teacher conducts the classes for Ist to IV standard at a time. Four different subjects are taught simultaneously to four different standards for 35 minutes that is one subject is taught for 35 minutes. In this way they have classes of 8 period everyday with two breaks one is short breaks of 10 minutes and other is lunch break for half an hour. The medium of education is Marathi, since most of the katkaris speak Marathi; most of the students say that they well understand teaching. At the end of the day they again pray that closes the class hours. Home work is also given to the students but they stress more on the class work and don't do home work at all. In such situation proper discipline is not maintained, the students are not given proper attention. Since one teacher teaches simultaneously to different standards quality of education is very low. In addition to this teacher take leave whenever he wants according to their own wish. And there is no proper inspection and supervision of the school from the higher authorities.

Competitions

Apart from the studies the students also take part in various competitions such as story telling, poem recitation conducted within a school among different classes or with nearby school.

The students play games like kabbadi, khokho, hopping, high jump, long jump throw ball, athletics. They have sports week once a year where they take part in inter school competitions or competition within a school among the different classes are held every year.

Examination

Written exams are conducted four times a year that consist of two unit tests, terminal examination and final examination. And the marks of all the exams are added together in the final and the percentages are taken. But no student is failed till the 4th standard.

Problems Faced by the Teachers

The teachers complain that the sufficient numbers of rooms and sufficient numbers of teachers are required for run the school. Since there is insufficiency of teachers and classrooms they also face lots of problems for teaching the students. In addition to this constantly trainings for teachers are held at Taluka place and that is compulsory for them to attend. And since there is only one teacher, school remains open without teacher. The students' attendance also happens to be a big problem.

Problem Faced by the Students

The parents being illiterate do not think education is necessary for their children. They do not give any importance to education, and do not have any aspirations for it but they sent their children to school only for food. The students do not get any motivation from their parents. And they also get less time for studies as they are made to work in the fields, look after the siblings and help in the household activities.

Five Katkari students those are studying in fourth standard said that the Chikhalgoan village does not have high school so even few of these katkari students want to take a secondary education they have to go to near by Ashram school that is Government organization and provides free education or high school at Pali that is about six to seven km away from the village, and transportation is not available, so they have to walk everyday for six-seven km.

Though the Ashram school provides free boarding and lodging facilities to the tribal students, the Katkari students usually do not stay there because they got lots of work, for their parents keeping children in the boarding school is not affordable. In the Chikhalgaon there are total nine katkari students studying in secondary out of which six are males and three are females, and four male katkari students studying in higher secondary Ashram school. All they walk for two hours daily to reach the Ashram school and come back.

Problems faced by the Parents

Since all the Katkaris are laborers, who earn their daily wages for their lively hood they expect their children to help them and consider them as economic assets. So they make their children to work along with them that making the children to miss their classes. They hardly have any time or no time for their children.

Reasons for Drop-outs and less attendance

There are some major socio-economic factors those are affecting the formal education of the Katkari students and that could be the reason for their dropouts and less attendance in the school. The major drop out rates is among the age group of 10 to 13 years.

Economic Factors:

(a) Poverty and bonded labor:

All 80 katkari families of Chikhalgoan Group Panchayat are Below Poverty Level (BPL), stay in abject poverty and are landless people; mainly working as daily wages agricultural bonded labor. First and most important sources of income for the Katkaris are daily wages paid for agriculture labor.

Land of Chikhalgon group gram panchayat is fertile and good for cultivation of rice and millet. Total fertile land in Chikhalgaon is 1968.85, acres and Unhere it is 664.67 acres. But out of this only about 0.37% of land is owned by negligible katkaris staying at Unhere pada. Almost all the katkaris are landless people and they work as a farm laborer and bonded labor on land owned by Maratha upper caste people during rainy season. Men and women get only Rs. 40/ daily along with the meal twice a day as daily wages. There is no difference in pay scale for men and women. But some time women are engaged in household work, collecting and selling wood and grazing livestock, if any, except during rainy season when land cultivation is done, women are indulge in farm work. This less wages are not enough for their sustenance and are unable to meet their needs, except for daily bread anyhow and therefore they except the contribution from their children also and they consider their children as economy assets and at an early age they are forced to work and do not give importance to education and get them out of the school. The children help their parents by looking after the goats and their young siblings, fetch the water and fuel when their parents go out for work and engage in some kind of domestic work to provide economic help to their family. The katkaris spend whole day long hours on farm work and hardly get any returns. Their poor economic conditions force them to seek job outside their village, when there is no farm work.

Only five Katkari families from Unhere Pada own some land where they practice very primitive agriculture and cultivate rice, millet, sweet potato, that they use for there own consumption but they get very less and hardly enough to satisfy their own family's need from such primitive agriculture. And these families also work as farm labor when needed.

The education of the Katkari children takes places in the most uncongenial home environment. The katkaris say that their immediate need is food and not education and that education does not produce immediate economic results.

They strongly feel that if there is money then only education is possible.

The Katkari children are at the great disadvantage as they do not get any motivations, aspirations, guidance from the parents, they are entirely depending on the school for guidance. These children are helpless and ignorant.

(b) Seasonal migration:

Most of the katkaris migrate seasonally to nearby places such as Chiplun, Nagothana to work in coal manufacturing and brick manufacturing factories. And are paid on monthly or sometimes weekly basis. The Katkaris working in brick making industries are paid approximately Rs. 1600 - 1800/ per month, depends upon the amount of work done and number of absenteeism; At Chiplun they also work as woodcutter in forest for 8 months during winter and summer.

Migration rate

This migration rate is very high; so significant.

Seasonal	*Migration %*	*Permanent Migration %*
Katkaris	70.65%	29.35%

The whole katkari family migrates to new work place; they take their children along with them to that forces the children to leave their school.

Since the katkakari want only immediate economic returns, they only look for the labor job and they take up the opportunity whenever it comes. They do not even inform to the school while migrating and do not bother much about information they get from the teachers about the importance of education. Their poor economic condition is responsible for developing such attitude in them.

(C) Other Sources of Income:

1. Domestic work:

There is no secondary occupation like goat domestication, poultry. When there is no agriculture work; the Katkaris do domestic work such as fetch water from well, household repair works in the Marathas house. And they are paid according to the nature of work, but most of the time it is maximum Rs. 40/ per day. Most of the time children are engaged in domestic work such as cleaning the utensils, and sweeping.

2. Collection and selling of the forest products for livelihood:

Chikhalgoan is surrounded by forest that provides much valuable products that Katkaris use it as their livelihood. They collect wood of Garuli and Bharjamun and that they sell at the rate is Rs. 5 – Rs. 6 per kg. to private contractor, whose truck comes every alternate day, in the early morning to collect it. The wood of Garuli and Bharjamun is used for preparation of medicine. The Katkaris eat Kadu karande that is available in the forest and use Nivdi wood as a fuel. Mostly the Katkari women and children are engaged in the collection of the forest products and while selling it to contractor katkari men are present

3. Livestock:

Livestock is very important source of income for katkaris. And some Katkaris have livestock. Live stock mainly consists of goat and poultry.

Animal Census:

Animal	*Number*	*%*
Goat	149	36.07%
Poultry	74	17.91%

For the celebration of festivals such holi, Sarvapitri Amavasya and some life cycle events such as marriage, childbirth, death they need money and whenever such extra money is needed livestock if any, is sold.

Livestock	*Selling price in Rs.*
Goat, depending on physical condition	Rs. 1000-1200/
Hen	Rs. 50/
Cock	Rs. 100/

Most of the time children are engaged in looking after the goat. During the school time they will go to grazing livestock.

Social factors

1. Alcoholic:

The katkaris are known as an alcoholic tribe. Katkaris men as well as women consume alcohol regularly almost daily after the day's work. Certain recreational activities and special occasion like wedding, births, deaths, and reunion involve massive and extravagant consumption of alcohol. Though most of the children do not drink alcohol, they show indifference towards users and believe that they will be indulging in the activity once they are grown up. Drinking liquor everyday is spontaneous reaction to their continuous social and economic exploitation and not related to any kind of religious belief. They also consumed tobacco by chewing and rarely smoked. Most of the time, the katkaris borrow money from their landowners to buy liquor. This money has to be repaying by doing farm work without pay. This one of the main reasons that the katkaris becoming more and more poor and economically backward. The Katkaris life is just to work the whole day as a daily wages, earn little and flirt that earnings in the evening in liquor, nothing remains for the next day. They are known for their alcoholism and cold- heartedness for strangers.

Educational Profile of the Katkaris staying in Chikhalgaon Group Gram Panchayat:

Category	*Males*	*Females*
Illiterate	178	164
Anganwadi	18	12
Primary	26	22
Secondary	6	3
Higher secondary	4	Nil
Graduate	Nil	Nil

Total population of the village – 433

The total male population – 232

The total female population -201

Percentage of the female literacy – 22.56 %

Percentage of the male literacy – 30.33%

The literacy rate is low 21.01% among the Katkaris.

Conclusion

There are many reasons such as long isolation, primitive ways of life, and socio-economic problems of the Katkaris behind the slow growth of education, very low literacy, and they are backward in many ways. The poor financial condition and socio-economic situation of the katkari parents plays major role in high rate of non attendance of students in school as well as drop out in from school. The katkaris parents are illiterate, therefore ignorant about importance, value and utility about the education so they do not give much importance to the education, and are adverse to education to their children. They stay in abject poverty, are below poverty level and are landless people; mainly working as daily wages agricultural bonded labor. First and most important sources of income for the Katkaris are daily wages paid for agriculture labor. They give more emphasis on the labor work where they get a meager sum of money to survive their daily lively hood and expect that their children should help them in their work as they consider their children as the economic assets and hamper their education.

Most of the katkaris migrate seasonally to nearby places such as Chiplun, Nagothana to work in coal manufacturing and brick manufacturing factories and work as woodcutter in forest. This seasonal migration rate is very high 70.65%; and significant. They do not even inform to the school while migrating and do not bother much about education. Their poor economic condition is responsible for developing such attitude in them. There is no secondary occupation like goat domestication, poultry. When there is no agriculture work; the Katkaris do domestic work such as fetch water from well, household repair works in the Marathas house. They collect and sell the forest products for their livelihood. Some Katkaris have livestock that is very important source of income for them. During festivals and life cycle events when extra money is needed livestock is sold. Most of the time children are engaged in looking after the goat during the school time. The katkaris are known as an alcoholic tribe. The Katkaris life is just to work the whole day as a daily wages, earn little and flirt that earnings in the evening in liquor, Most of the katkaris spent their earnings on alcohol, festivals, marriages, and death rituals. They borrow money from the landowners and repay that by doing farm work without pay. And becoming poorer and economically backward. They are known for their alcoholism and cold-heartedness for strangers. The education of the Katkari children takes places in the most uncongenial home environment as katkaris' immediate need is food and not education and that education does not produce immediate economic results.

The Katkari strongly feel that if there is money then only education is possible. The Katkari students do not get any motivation, aspirations, and guidance from their parents as their parents being illiterate do not think education is necessary for their children. They sent their children to school only for food. The katkari students are more attracted to home environment as get less time for studies as they are made to work in the fields, look after the siblings and help in the household activities, celebration of festivals and some life cycle events. The Katkari children are helpless and ignorant. They have become home homesick that divert their attention from the school. Few of these katkari students want to take a secondary education but Chikhalgoan village does not have high school so they have to go to near by Ashram school that is Government organization at Pali that provides free boarding and lodging facilities to the tribal students, but it is about six to seven km away from the village. And the Katkari students usually do not stay there because they got lots of work, for their parents keeping children in the boarding school is not affordable. And since transportation is not available, they have to walk everyday for six-seven km. for two hours daily to reach the Ashram school and come back.

Since there is insufficiency of teachers and classrooms and poor attendance of the students, the teacher also faces lots of problems for teaching the students. In addition to this constantly trainings for teachers are held at Taluka place and that is compulsory for them to attend. And since there is only one teacher, school remains open without teacher. During rainy season the teacher face lots of problem to come to school as the teachers live outside the village and transportation facilities are very poor. Sometimes situation arises when students come to attend the school and teacher is absent and vice versa.

The education of the Katkaris does not depend only on the facilities provided by the Government of Maharashtra but also depend on the sincerity and combine efforts on the part of the teachers, katkari students and parents' equally. Unless the katkari parents and students themselves should understand that education is of use to them and will provide better employment opportunities will help them to improve their economic condition, they will not become serious about education. Therefore efforts should be taken to create the awareness among them through various associations and groups.

Though Maharashtra Government taking efforts in the education sector, there is needed to improve literacy and education level, as it is a priority area for action to improve overall status of the Katkaris. Much more planned efforts are required to provide basic infrastructure and facilities such as roads, communication and transports for the Katkaris staying in this area as education is suffering because of lack of basic infrastructure. As the katkaris are living below poverty line, they need a secure year round occupation. Therefore general scheme of poverty alleviation and employment generation should be implemented for katkaris, and such scheme will support to improve their income and reduce their seasonal migration in the haunt of job. Land allowing act for them will help them to become independent and to improve their economic conditions. There is need to create an awareness about their basic and important rights, urge to pursuit knowledge in them and also for entire and psycho temporal development of them for their own benefits and empower them through various camps, lectures, seminars, group and co-operative activities. A great deal of Anthropological study of the Katkaris is necessary for designing an effective pedagogy for them and for better achievement of the educational goals.

12

Awareness of the Prevention of Atrocities (Scheduled Tribes) Act, 1989—A Perspective

—Enanalap Periyar

Tribal communities are considered as early settlers or autouchonese groups of people; it is at the same time true that they are also non-static or itinerant groups owing to many compelling circumstances. Due to various factors, the isolation gaps among the groups disappeared and they are found to obliterate the transformational phases. It is true as well that they have no permanent crystalline structures belonging to one stage of historical or social development (Bhowmick: 1982). The Scheduled Castes and Scheduled Tribes (Prevention of Atrocities) Act of 1989 is a milestone in the history of Tribal communities. Without this Act, People cannot fully develop as human beings. Historically, education is an instrument of development and a factor for social change. Nowadays, the scheduled tribes are degraded by the literate people in the Government Institutions. The literate people also don't aware about The Prevention of Atrocities Act, 1989. Generally students are becoming a future Government. So the awareness of The Prevention of Atrocities Act, 1989 should be educated to the college students.

Aim of this study was to have more general awareness of The Scheduled Castes and Scheduled Tribes (Prevention of Atrocities) Act of 1989 and its future prevalence in the college students. This act is a old in India, But research into the awareness of The prevention of Atrocities Act, 1989 is still in its initial phases, this study aimed to increase the awareness of The Prevention of Atrocities Act, 1989. A sample of 60 college students were selected for this present study in Tirunelveli

District by employing a non-probability sampling technique - namely Purposive sampling. The objective of the study is to examine the nature of awareness of college students about The Scheduled Castes and Scheduled Tribes (Prevention of Atrocities) Act of 1989 in Tirunelveli district, to investigation of perpetration and victimization of college students under The Prevention of Atrocities Act, 1989. The study primarily focused to analyze the college students' willingness to participate in the awareness programme of this Act. The suitable recommendations were made accordingly.

Need and the Significance of the Present Study

Violation and lack of awareness about The Scheduled Castes and Scheduled Tribes (Prevention of Atrocities) Act of 1989 is predominantly considered as a serious issue. In Colleges, the teasing is a part of certain culture. Even though school teasing are college teasing is prevalent in the name of ragging we do not give the connotation of teasing in the Indian context though there new laws regarding ragging in schools and colleges, teasing per se has not been condoned. Off late there is a rise of teasing of scheduled tribes students has increased. The study of the awareness of The Scheduled Castes and Scheduled Tribes (Prevention of Atrocities) Act of 1989 was conducted among the college students of Tirunelveli district. The present study tries to fill the gap in the literature of Indian sociology in general and Indian criminology in particular.

Limitations

In common with the investigations cited in the introduction, all samples are non- random and as such generalization to other survey results cannot be made. Nor can generalization be made to the entire population of victims of The Scheduled Castes and Scheduled Tribes (Prevention of Atrocities) Act of 1989. An unknown number of individuals may not define themselves as victims of Atrocities Act or perpetrators, or if they do so, they may be unwilling to come forward and speak openly about their experiences. This survey is the only of its kind so far conducted in Tirunelveli district. The scope of the studies limited only to specific colleges of Tirunelveli district. In future the researchers should conduct a holistic research within entire Tamil Nadu or India whichever permissible and compare the intra-regional and inter-regional disparities and disputes to widen the scope for a holistic perspective on Tribal Community Development. This study also had constraints like to time and finance. Also the researcher could not able to draw exact data from many students because many of them were unwilling to participate in the research due to fear of their corresponding teachers and parents. Only students who were willing to participate in this research were contacted and taken as respondents for this study.

Related Review

An Act to prevent the commission of offences of atrocities against the members of the Scheduled Castes and the Scheduled Tribes, to provide for Special Courts for the trial of such offences and for the relief and rehabilitation of the victims of such offences and for matters connected therewith or incidental thereto.

Statement of Objects and Reasons:

The Statement of Objects and Reasons appended to the Bill while moving the same in the Parliament, read as under:

> "Despite various measures to improve the socio-economic conditions of the Scheduled Castes and Scheduled Tribes, they remain vulnerable. They are denied number of civil rights. They are subjected to various offences, indignities, humiliations and harassment. They have, in several brutal incidents, been deprived of their life and property. Serious crimes are committed against them for various historical, social and economic reasons."

Be it enacted by Parliament in the Fortieth Year of the Republic of India as follows:

The Scheduled Castes and the Scheduled Tribes (Prevention of Atrocities) Act, 1989 is an Act to prevent the Commission of offences of atrocities against the members of the Scheduled Castes and the Scheduled Tribes and to provide for special Courts for the trial of such offences. By exercising inherent powers Courts are empowered to compound offences under SC & ST (Prevention of Atrocities) Act, 1989 and Protection of Civil Rights Act, 1955. Public Prosecutor is the officer of the Court who has to essentially assist the Court in dispensing justice. Sec.

18 of the Act specifies that Sec. 438 CrPC has no application to persons committing an offence under the Act.

Preliminary

1. Short title, extent and commencement:

(1) This Act may be called the Scheduled Castes and the Scheduled Tribes (Prevention of Atrocities) Act, 1989 or Act.

(2) It extends to the whole of India except the State of Jammu and Kashmir.

(3) It shall come into force on such date as the Central Government may by notification, in the Official Gazette.

2. Definitions (1) in this Act, unless the context otherwise requires

(*a*) "Atrocity" means an offence punishable under Section J

(*b*) "Code" means the Code of Criminal Procedure, 1973 (of 1974);

(*c*) "Scheduled Castes and Scheduled Tribes" shall have I meanings assigned to them respectively under Clause (24) and Clause (25) of Article 366 of the Constitution ;

(*d*) "Special Court" means a Court of Session specified as a Special Court in Section 14 ;

(*e*) *"Special Public Prosecutor"* means a Public Prosecutor specified as a Special Public Prosecutor or an advocate referred to in Section 15;

(*f*) Words and expressions used but not defined in this Act. and defined in the Code or the Indian Penal Code (45 of 1860) shall have the meanings assigned to them respectively in the Code, or as the case may be, in the Indian Penal Code.

(2) Any reference in this Act to any enactment or any provision thereof shall, in relation to an area in which such enactment or such provision is not in force, be construed as a reference to the corresponding law, if any. in force in that area.

Offences of Atrocities

3. Punishments for offences of atrocities:

(1) Whoever, not being a member of a Scheduled Caste or a Scheduled Tribe:

(*i*) Forces a member of a Scheduled Caste or a Scheduled Tribe to drink or eat any inedible or obnoxious substance;

(*ii*) Acts with intent to cause injury, insult or annoyance to any member of a Scheduled Caste, or a Scheduled Tribe by dumping excreta, waste matter, carcasses or any other obnoxious substance in his premises or neighbourhood ;

(*iii*) Forcibly removes clothes from the person of a member of a Scheduled Caste or a Scheduled Tribe or parades him naked or with painted face or body or commits any similar act which is derogatory to human dignity;

(*iv*) Wrongfully occupies or cultivates any land owned by, or allotted to, or notified by any competent authority to be allotted to, a member of a Scheduled Caste or a Scheduled Tribe or gets the land allotted to him transferred;

(*v*) Wrongfully dispossesses a member of a Scheduled Caste or a Scheduled Tribe from his land or premises or interferes with the enjoyment of his rights over any land, premises or water;

(*vi*) Compels or entices a member of a Scheduled Caste or a Scheduled Tribe to do "beggar" or other similar forms of forced or bonded labour other than any, compulsory service for public purposes imposed by Government;

(*vii*) Forces or intimidates a member of a Scheduled Caste or a Scheduled Tribe not to vote or to vote to a particular candidate or to vote in a manner other than that provided by law;

(*viii*) Institutes false, malicious or vexatious suit or criminal or other legal proceedings against a member of a Scheduled Caste or a Scheduled Tribe;

(*ix*) Gives any false or frivolous information to any public servant and thereby causes such public servant to use his lawful power to the injury or annoyance of a member of a Scheduled Caste or a Scheduled Tribe;

(*x*) Intentionally insults or intimidates with intent to humiliate a member of a Scheduled Caste or a Scheduled Tribe in any place within public view;

(*xi*) Assaults or uses force to any woman belonging to a Scheduled Caste or a Scheduled Tribe with intent to dishonour or outrage her modesty;

(*xii*) Being in a position to dominate the will of a woman belonging to a Scheduled Caste or a Scheduled Tribe and uses that position to exploit her sexually to which she would not have otherwise agreed;

(*xiii*) Corrupts or fouls the water of any spring, reservoir or any other source ordinarily used by members of the Scheduled Castes or the Scheduled Tribes so as to render it less fit for the purpose for which it is ordinarily used;

(*xiv*) Denies a member of a Scheduled Caste or a Scheduled Tribe any customary right of passage to a place of public resort or obstructs such member so as to prevent him from using or having access to a place of public resort to which other members of public or any section thereof have a right to use or access to;

(*xv*) Forces or causes a member of a Scheduled Caste or a Scheduled Tribe to leave his house, village, or other place of residence; shall be punishable with imprisonment for a term which shall not be less than six months but which may extend to five years and with fine.

(2) Whoever, not being a member of a Scheduled Caste or a Scheduled Tribe:

(*i*) Gives or fabricates false evidence intending thereby to cause, or knowing it to be likely that he will thereby cause, any member of a Scheduled Caste or a Scheduled Tribe to be convicted of an offence which is capital by the law for the time being in force shall be punished with imprisonment for life and with fine ; and if an innocent member of a Scheduled Caste or a Scheduled Tribe be convicted and executed in consequence of such false or fabricated evidence, the person who gives or fabricates such false evidence, shall be punished with death;

(*ii*) Gives fabricates false evidence intending thereby to cause, or knowing it to be likely that he will thereby cause, any member of a Scheduled Caste or a Scheduled Tribe to be convicted of an offence which is not capital but punishable with imprisonment for a term of seven years or upwards, shall be punishable with imprisonment for a term which shall not be less than six months but which may extend to seven years or upwards and with fine;

(*iii*) Commits mischief by fire or any explosive substance intending to cause or knowing it to be likely that he will thereby cause damage to any property belonging to a member of a Scheduled Caste or a Scheduled Tribe, shall be punishable with imprisonment for a term which shall not be less than six months but which may extend to seven years and with fine;

(*iv*) Commits mischief by fire or any explosive substance intending to cause or knowing it to be likely that he will thereby cause destruction of any building which is ordinarily used as a place of worship or as a place for human dwelling or as a place for custody of the property by a member of a Scheduled Caste or a Scheduled Tribe, shall be punishable with imprisonment for life and with fine;

(*v*) Commits any offence under the Indian Penal Code (45 of 1860) punishable with imprisonment for a term of ten years or more against a person or property on the ground that such person is a member of a Scheduled Caste or a Scheduled Tribe or such property belongs to such member, shall be punishable with imprisonment for life and with fine;

(*vi*) Knowingly or having reason to believe that an offence has been committed under this chapter, causes any evidence of the commission of that offence to disappear with the intention of screening the offender from legal punishment, or with that intention gives any information respecting the offence which he knows or believes to be false, shall be punishable with the punishment provided for that offence; or (*vii*) Being a public servant, commits any offence under this section, shall be punishable with an imprisonment for a term, which shall not be less than one year which may extend to the punishment provided for that offence and it explains,

4. Punishment for neglect of duties
5. Enhanced punishment for subsequent conviction
6. Application of certain provisions of the Indian Penal
7. Forfeiture of property of certain persons
8. Presumption as to offences
9. Conferment of powers
10. Removal of person likely to commit offence
11. Procedure and failure of person to remove himself from area and enter there on after removal
12. Taking measurements and photographs, etc., of persons against whom the order under section 10 is made.
13. Penalty for non- compliance with order under section
14. Special courts
15. Special public prosecutor
16. Power of State Government to impose collective fine
17. Preventive action to be taken by the law and order machinery
18. Section 438 of the Code not to apply to persons committing and offence under the Act.
19. Section 360 of the code or the provision of the Probation of Offenders Act not to apply to persons guilty of an offence under the Act:
20. Act to override other laws
21. Duty of Government to ensure effective implementation of the Act.
22. Protection of action taken in good faith:
23. Power to make rules.

Methodology

The fundamental aim of the study is to impart adequate general awareness of The Scheduled Castes and Scheduled

Tribes (Prevention of Atrocities) Act of 1989 and its future prevalence amongst college students. This Act by itself is an old amongst very many Acts coined in India, but research into the awareness of the prevention of Atrocities Act, 1989 is still in its initial phases, this study aimed to increase the awareness of The Prevention of Atrocities Act, 1989. The study is an exploration of the scheduled Tribal student's issues. The primary focus is one the examination of nature of awareness of The Scheduled Castes and Scheduled Tribes (Prevention of Atrocities) Act of 1989 prevalent in the college students in Tirunelveli districts. The secondary focus is on the investigation of perpetration and victimization of college students under The Scheduled Castes and Scheduled Tribes (Prevention of Atrocities) Act of 1989. The third purpose of the study is to analyze the college student's willingness to participate in the awareness programme of The Scheduled Castes and Scheduled Tribes (Prevention of Atrocities) Act of 1989.

Objectives of the Study

1. To examine the nature of awareness of The Scheduled Castes and Scheduled Tribes (Prevention of Atrocities) Act of 1989 prevalent in the college students in Tirunelveli districts.
2. To investigate the perpetration and victimization of college students under The Scheduled Castes and Scheduled Tribes (Prevention of Atrocities) Act of 1989.
3. To analyze the college students willingness to participate in the awareness programme of The Scheduled Castes and Scheduled Tribes (Prevention of Atrocities) Act of 1989.

Universe and Sampling Design

The Universe of the present study consists of students from various colleges of Tirunelvei district belonging to the Arts and Science students. Convenient sampling techniques are the method used in the study. It is a kind of non-probability sampling. A total 60 respondents were taken as sample for the study. Samples were identified from the various college of Arts and Science.

Tools and Techniques for Data Collection

A semi-structured Interview schedule was prepared by the researcher for this study. The researcher used Interview schedule instead of questionnaire to record informal observations as well. The Scheduled Castes and Scheduled Tribes (Prevention of Atrocities) Act of 1989 is new one to the college student and it is hypothesized that most of the college students would not know the meaning of the prevention of Atrocities Act. So there was a need to explain the prevention of Atrocities Act and get answers from the respondents. Hence, the interview schedule was framed and administered on college students. It was used to find out the profile of the students and their awareness on Prevention of Atrocities Act, and also to investigate the perpetration and victimization under the Act and their willingness to participate in the awareness programme of this Act. Each question described the awareness level on prevention of Atrocities Act and responses were recorded and ranked to reflect the range of 'Yes' and 'No'.

To obtain participants, a list of co-education colleges in Tirunelveli district was made. In total 60 college students were selected by the researcher for the present study. The researcher went to each colleges and selected students by purposive sampling and then the questions were asked to them and they were added in the interview schedule.

Analysis of Data

In this research work, the percentage analyses were adopted to examine the awareness of The Scheduled Castes and Scheduled Tribes (Prevention of Atrocities) Act of 1989. Questions 1- 4 employed to understand the profile of students. Questions 5 – 8 highlighted on awareness of the Act. Questions 9a and 9b concentrated that perpetration and victimization of students under The Scheduled Castes and Scheduled Tribes (Prevention of Atrocities) Act of 1989. Questions 10 – 11 focused on willingness of students participation towards the awareness programme related to the Act.

Major findings

- Majority of the respondents were male students (53.33%)

- Majority of the respondents were from the age group of 16- 19 (60%)
- Majority of the students were interviewed from the professional course (Dept. of Police Science and Criminology). (36.67%)
- Majority of the students did not know about The Scheduled Castes and Scheduled Tribes (Prevention of Atrocities) Act of 1989 (71.67%)
- 13.33% of the students only know about this act as used to development of ST's. (N = 17)
- 13.33% of the students were ST students (N= 60)
- 100% of the ST students were teased in college. (N = 8)
- 50% of the respondent (ST) were verbally abused by other community students (N = 8)
- Majority of the respondents involved in the abusing of Students (86.54 %).
- 57.14% of the respondents verbally teased the ST students (N = 7)
- Majority of the respondents interested to study The Scheduled Castes and Scheduled Tribes (Prevention of Atrocities) Act of 1989 as a subject (55%)
- 57.14% of the respondents felt about this act need not to their life.
- Majority of the respondents willfully participated in the awareness programme of The Scheduled Castes and Scheduled Tribes (Prevention of Atrocities) Act of 1989.

Conclusion

This study explores a new important issue in India related to awareness of The Scheduled Castes and Scheduled Tribes (Prevention of Atrocities) Act of 1989. The preliminary analysis of a survey data collected from college students sheds light on this evolving issue. The first important issue was on the awareness levels and it was found that to a large extent college students were unaware about Scheduled Tribes and Scheduled Castes and the Act pertaining to it i.e., Scheduled Tribes (Prevention of Atrocities) Act of 1989.

In this study 100% of the ST students report that they have been victimized during college study. Initially the researcher thought that the ST students' socio economic background might be a major factor that the richer of other student's background they might involved in victimization. One possible explanation is there college climates – That is , perhaps no effective policy toward perpetrating or controlling programmes. Another explanation may be that abusing is becoming increasingly severe in terms of the scope and the extent in large area. Future researchers should conduct a holistic and in-depth study on Tribal Community Development to examine this issue.

Recommendations

(A) State

- Make it a priority to learn about The Scheduled Castes and Scheduled Tribes (Prevention of Atrocities) Act of 1989 and what the colleges can do to help keep ST students safe from victimization.
- The state should announce severe punishment to the perpetrators under The Scheduled Castes and Scheduled Tribes (Prevention of Atrocities) Act of 1989.
- The state may provide projects related to The Scheduled Castes and Scheduled Tribes (Prevention of Atrocities) Act of 1989 to all Universities.

  (The research scholars can engage the P.G students through action research projects and study about Scheduled Castes and Scheduled Tribes (Prevention of Atrocities Act of 1989.))

(B) Colleges

- The college management may devise clear-cut rules for violation of Atrocities Act, use on college grounds - include all forms of teasing under these rules, so as to ensure students to operate within their boundaries.
- The college may educate students about the impact of teasing of ST students can have on themselves and their peers and work with them to identify strategies for preventing violation of ST students.

- The college teachers should learn to detect signs of teasing ST students, including changes in a ST students' behaviour or personality, loss of interest in class activities, changes in their behaviour, communication and reluctance to attend classes.
- The college may create a disciplinary cum redressal cell for protecting the ST students from the other student violations.

(C) Students

- Let ST students know that they can talk to the college management about issues like teasing - whether the problem is occurring in college grounds.
- The students should provide their willingness to study The Scheduled Castes and Scheduled Tribes (Prevention of Atrocities) Act of 1989.
- The students must not downsize the SC / ST students on humanitarian grounds.

  (Student's should ensure humanity and also imbibe all possess basic human rights like as "Be with brotherhood" within a secular democracy)

ANNEXURE

Table 1. Distribution of Respondents According to Sex

Response	*Frequency*	*Percentage (%)*
Male	32	53.33
Female	28	46.67
Total	60	100%

Table 2. Distribution of Respondents According to Age

Response (in years)	*Frequency*	*Percentage (%)*
16 – 19	36	60.00
20 – 23	16	26.67
24 – 27	08	13.33
Total	60	100.00

Table 3. Distribution of Respondents According to Course

Response	*Frequency*	*Percentage (%)*
Arts	21	35.00
Science	17	28.33
Others	22	36.67
Total	60	100.00

Table 4. I have known about the prevention of Atrocities Act

Response	*Frequency*	*Percentage (%)*
Yes	17	28.33
No	43	71.67
Total	60	100%

Table 5. I have known this Act, via

Response	*Frequency*	*Percentage (%)*
Name only	08	47.06
Used to ST's	04	23.53
No idea	05	29.41
Total	17	100.00

Table 6. I am a Schedule Tribes student

Response	*Frequency*	*Percentage (%)*
Yes	08	13.33
No	52	86.67
Total	60	100%

Table 7. I have been victimized by other students under the prevention of Atrocities Act

Response	*Frequency*	*Percentage (%)*
Yes	08	100.00
No	00	00.00
Total	08	100%

Table 8. I have been victimized, via

Response	*Frequency*	*Percentage (%)*
Physically	00	00.00
Verbally	03	37.50
Psychologically	04	50.00
Others	01	12.50
Total	08	100.00

Table 9. I have teased ST students

Response	*Frequency*	*Percentage (%)*
Yes	07	13.46
No	45	86.54
Total	52	100%

Table 10. I have abused ST students, via

Response	*Frequency*	*Percentage (%)*
Avoid them	01	14.29
Verbally	04	57.14
No Idea	02	28.57
Total	07	100.00

Table 11. I like to study the Act as subject

Response	*Frequency*	*Percentage (%)*
Yes	33	55.00
No	07	11.67
No answer	20	33.33
Total	60	100.00

Table 12. Why don't I like to study?

Response	*Frequency*	*Percentage (%)*
It Need not to my life	04	57.14
Useless	01	14.29
No Idea	02	28.57
Total	07	100.00

Table 13. I like to participate in awareness programme of the prevention of Atrocities Act

Response	*Frequency*	*Percentage (%)*
Yes	33	55.00
No	07	11.67
No answer	20	33.33
Total	60	100.00

Table 14. Why don't I like to participate?

Response	*Frequency*	*Percentage (%)*
It Need not to my life	04	57.14
Useless	01	14.29
No Idea	02	28.57
Total	07	100.00

13

Educational Issues of Primitive Tribes in Maharashtra

—*Dr. Rohin D. Tribhuwan and Jayshree A. Patil*

India has 698 Scheduled Tribes, out of which, 75 groups, have been classified by the Ministry of Tribal Affairs, Govt.of India, as Primitive Tribal Groups. The social, economic, educational and political status of these PTGs is different from the other progressing tribes. This paper highlights the educational issues of the PTGs in Maharashtra viz. Katkari, Madia & Kolam. Katkaris are the poorest tribe in the state and their literacy rate as compared to the Madias' and the Kolams' is very low. Statistics provided in the paper reveal both micro and macro literacy rates and educational issues of the PTGs' of Maharashtra. This paper also recommends strategies such as visits of Ashram and Zilla Parishad school teachers to the hamlets of these groups and use of folk media to communicate the significance of education so as to motivate these groups to send their children to primary, high school and higher educational institutions.

Introduction

The Ministry of Tribal Affairs, Government of India, has declared 75 Tribes as Primitive Tribal Groups, out of the 698 scheduled Tribes in the country. The GOI's criteria for classifying the 75 groups as PTGs (Primitive Tribal Groups) are as follows:

(*i*) Primitive tribes have low levels of literacy.

(*ii*) Their populations are declining or stagnant.

(*iii*) Lastly, they have pre-agriculture level technology.

The 75 P.T.Gs are geographically distributed into 15 states / union territories, given below is a list of GOI's approved list of Primitive Tribal Groups in India.

Table 1.1. GOI's approved list of Primitive Tribal Groups

Sl. No.	*State*	*Primitive Tribes*
1	Andhra Pradesh	1. Bodo Gadaba
		2. Bondo Poraja
		3. Chenchu
		4. Dongaria Khonds
		5. Gutob Gadaba
		6. Khond Poroja
		7. Kolam
		8. Konda reddis
		9. Konda Savaras
		10. Kuttiya Kondhs
		11. Parangiperija
		12. Thoti
2.	Bihar & Jharkhand	13. Asur
		14. Birhor
		15. Birjia
		16. Hill Kharia
		17. Korwa
		18. Mal Pahariya
		19. Pahariyas
		20. Sauria Pahariya
		21. Savar
3.	Gujarat	22. Kathodi
		23. Kotwalia
		24. Padhar
		25. Siddi
		26. Kolgha

Sl. No.	*State*	*Primitive Tribes*
4.	Karnataka	27. Jerur Kuruba
		28. Koraga
5.	Kerala	29. Cholanaikan (A Section of Kattunayakan)
		30. Kadar
		31. Kattunayankan
		32. Kurumbas
6	Madhya Pradesh	33. Koraga
	& Chattisgarh	34. Abujh Maria
		35. Baiga
		36. Bhaira
		37. Hill Korwa
		38. Kamar
		39. Sahariya
		40. Birhor
7	Maharashtra	41. Katkari (Kathodi)
		42. Kolam
		43. Madia
8	Manipur	44. Maram Naga
9	Orissa	45. Bihor
		46. Bondo
		47. Didayi
		48. Dongria-Khond
		49. Juang
		50. Kharia
		51. Kutia Khond
		52. Lanjia Saura
		53. Lodha
		54. Mankirdia

Sl. No.	*State*	*Primitive Tribes*
		55. Paudi Bhuyan
		56. Saura
		57. Chuktiya Bhunjia
10	Rajasthan	58. Sahariyas
11	Tamil Nadu	59. Kattu Naickans
		60. Kotas
		61. Kurumbas
		62. Irulas
		63. Paniyans
		64. Todas
12	Tripura	65. Reangs
13	Uttar Pradesh & Uttaranchal	66. Busax
14	West Bengal	68. Birhor
		69. Lodhas
		70. Totas
15	Andaman and	71. Great Andamanese
	Nicobar Islands	72. Jarawas
		73. Onges
		74. Senteneless
		75. Shompens

It would be right to note at this juncture that internationally the use of the term 'primitive' is not widely used. Terms like "indigenous" or "tribal" people are used. We personally feel that, there is a need to give academic thought to the above mentioned criteria for classifying a tribe into Primitive Tribal Group category.

Primitive Tribes In Maharashtra

Maharashtra ranks second in the country as regards the size of tribal population is concerned. The total population of tribals in Maharashtra, as per 2001 census is 85.77 lakhs. There are 45 Scheduled Tribes in the State, out of which three tribes namely; Katkaris, Kolams and Madias have been classified as PTGs. The Katkaris are found in the Sahyadri region, in western Maharashtra. They predominantly found in Raigad, Thane, Pune, Nasik, Ahmednagar, Sindhudurg, Ratnagiri and few other districts.

The Kolams are mostly found in Yavatmal and Nanded districts, while the Madias are found in Gadchiroli district. Table No. 1.3 presents the population of the three communities.

Educational Issues of PTGs.

In their book captioned, Development of Primitive Tribes in Maharashtra, Tomar Y.P.S. and Tribhuwan Robin (2004), have revealed that the Socio-economic and educational status and needs of the Katkaris, Kolams and Madias vary from each other. Furthermore, their study pointed out the need, for further research into educational issues of these three groups in the State. Keeping this background in view, the present paper highlights the educational issues of PTGs in Maharashtra.

Aims of the Study

The aims of the paper are :

(*i*) To compare micro and macro level literacy status of the Katkaris, Kolams and Madias.

(*ii*) To highlight the educational problems of the said tribes.

(*iii*) Finally, to suggest strategies to motivate and attract these groups to take up primary, secondary and even higher education.

(II) RESEARCH METHODOLOGY

Locale of the Study

The present study was conducted in six hamlets of the Primitive Tribal Groups of Maharashtra, namely Katkaris, Madias and Kolams. These six hamlets are geographically located in three districts namely Raigad, Yavatmal and Gadchiroli. Table number 1.2 gives details of the same.

Table 1.2. Districts, blocks and hamlets selected for the study.

Sr.No.	District	Block	Village	Hamlet
1.	Raigad	(1) Pen	(1) Khaparpada	(1) Khairaswadi
			(2) Ambivali	(2) Shitulwadi
2.	Yavatmal	(2) Kelpur	(3) Dhaipod	(3) Dhaipod
			(4) Karnjpod	(4) Karanjpod
3.	Gadchiroli	(3) Bhamragad	(5) Dhaipod	(5) Zuvi
			(6) Medampalli	(6) Hindabhatti
	3 Districts	3 blocks	Six villages	Six hamlets

Target population

As mentioned earlier the present study was carried out among the Katkaris, Kalams and Madias of Maharashtra. Table 1.3 presents tribe and hamlet wise number of respondents selected.

Table 1.3. Tribe & hamlet wise number of respondents selected

Sr.No.	Tribe	Hamlet	Males	Females	Total
1	Katkari	1] Khairaswadi	15	5	20
		2] Shitulwadi	21	5	26
2	Kolam	3] Dhaipod	25	4	29
		4] Karanjpod	22	3	25
3	Madia	5] Zuvi	24	3	27
		6] Hindabhatti	22	3	25
	Total	—	129	23	152

Method of Data Collection

(A) Primary Data—An interview schedule was designed to gather relevant data from the heads of the household. Besides this, Focus Group Discussions with students, Teachers of Zilla Parishad and Ashram Schools were held so as to get an understanding of the educational issues of Primitive Tribes in Maharashtra.

(B) Secondary Data—Books, journals and articles on the educational issues of PTG is Maharashtra were referred. The

Bench Marks Survey conducted by the Tribal Research & Training Institute was useful in understanding the state level educational scenario of the three tribes.

Sampling procedures

Since the hamlets studied were small, the researchers selected 100% sample.

Analysis

Both quantitative and qualitative data collected was analyzed manually.

(III) FINDINGS

(A) Literacy Rates of PTGs : A macro level scenario.

Before getting into the macro level literacy scenario of the PTGs in Maharashtra, let us take a glance at the decadal growth of PTGs in Maharashtra. Table No. 1.4 presents details.

Table 1.4. Decadal growth of PTGs in Maharashtra

Sr.No.	*Particulars*	*Census Year*			
		1961	*1971*	*1981*	*1991*
1.	Katkaris	135893	146785	144602	202203
2.	Kolams	43555	56061	118073	147843
3.	Madia (estimated)	42720	53400	66750	83437
	Total P.T.G.	222114	256246	359425	433483
	Total Tribal Population	2397159	2954249	5772038	7318281
	Percentage of P.T.Gs	9.26	8.67	6.22	5.92

Note : Madia is a sub-tribe of 'Gond" tribe, hence separate census figures for Madia are not available.

From the above table, it is evident that, the population of in increasing every decade. This trend does not support the criteria of stagnant or declining populations as one of the key characteristics of Primitive Tribal Groups.

Literacy Status of PTGs

The Tribal Research & Training Institute, Pune, conducted a Bench Mark Survey of P.T.G.s in Tribal – Sub-Plan areas of Maharashtra State during he years 1996-1997, reveals macro-level literacy scenario of the Katkaris, Kolams and Madias. Table number 1.5 presents the same.

Table 1.5. Literacy Rates of P.T.G.
In T.S.P. Areas of Maharashtra

Sr.No.	Details	Total Tribal Population	Population Above 6 years	Literate Population	Percentage
1.	All Tribes	3415091	2799636	1025731	36.64
2.	All P.T.G s	207723	170024	42533	25.03
	(a) Katkari	68421	57119	9356	16.38
	(b) Kolam	62397	51240	18899	36.88
	(c) Madia	76905	61665	14298	23.19

From table number 1.5, it is clear that the literacy rate of the Katkaris is lowest i.e. 16.38%, meaning their illiteracy rate is 83.62%. The literacy rate of Madias is 23.19%, of course illiteracy rate is 76.81%. Finally, the Kolam literacy rate is higher than Katkaris and Madias and even higher than all tribes and all P.T.G s. Table 1.6 presents sex wise literacy level of P.T.Gs in Maharashtra.

Table 1.6. Sex wise literacy level of PTGs in Maharashtra.

Sr.No.	Sex	Literacy rate of PTGs as per BMS			
		Katkari	Kolam	Madia	P.T.G.
1.	Male	21.70	45.66	30.19	31.97
2.	Female	10.70	27.83	16.09	17.86
	Total	16.38	36.88	23.19	25.02

Source: BMS 2001, Table No. 3, P.T.G. series.

Interestingly, the literacy rate of females among Katkaris is 10.70%, Kolams is 27.83 and Madias is 16.09% and general literacy rate among PTG females is 17.86%. The illiteracy rate of Katkari females is highest i.e. 89.30%; followed by Madia females i.e. 83.91%; and Kolam females i.e. 72%. Comparatively Kolam females are better placed literacy status wise.

The literacy rates of Katkari males are 21.70%, Madia males 30.19% and Kolam males 45.66%. Here again Kolam males are better placed. Illiteracy rates of Katkari males is 78.30%; Madia males 69.81% and Kolam males is 54.34%. The striking feature of the above statistics is the lowest level of literacy and highest level of illiteracy of the Katkari tribe. This is because of semi-nomadic trend of the tribe, Utter Poverty and bonded labour.

(B) Literacy Rates of P.T.Gs : A Micro level scenario.

Primary data collected in six hamlets of all the three P.T.Gs in Maharashtra following scenario.

(i) Literacy Status of Katkaris

Table number 1.7 reveals the educational status of Katkaris in Khairaswadi and Shitulwadi in Pen Tahsil in Raigad district.

Table 1.7. Educational Status of Katkari Respondents

Sr.No.	*Educational level*	*Number*	*Percentage*
1	Illiterates	42	91.30
2.	Primary	2	4.36
3.	High school	1	2.26
4.	Higher secondary	1	2.26
	Total	46	100

Statistics in table 1.7 are self explanatory. 91.30% of Katkaris from both the hamlets are illiterate; while 4.36% have studied upto primary; 2.26% high school & 2.26% higher secondary. Not a single soul has gone above gradation or Master level.

Table 1.8. Sex wise literacy level of Katkaris in Khairaswadi & Shitul wadi.

Sr. No.	*Education level*	*Number*			*Percentage*		
		Males	*Females*	*Total*	*Males*	*Females*	*Total*
1	Illiterate	33	9	42	91	90	91
2	Primary	1	1	2	3	10	4.34
3	High school	1	-	1	3	-	2.26
4.	Higher secondary	1	-	1	3		2.26
5.	College	-	-	-	-	-	-
	Total	36	10	46	100	100	100

Sex wise illiteracy percentage of Katkari males is 91% & females are 90%. These micro level statistics of sex wise illiteracy among Katkaris are almost same as the State Level statistics as per B.M.S. The state level illiteracy of Katkari females is 89.30%, while among the males it is 78.30%.

(ii) Literacy Status of Madia

Table number 1.9 presents educational status of Madia respondents from Zuvi and Hindbhatti villages of Bhamragad block, Gadchiroli district.

Table 1.9. Educational Status of Madia Respondents

Sr.No.	*Educational Level*	*Number*	*Percentage*
1.	Illiterate	49	94.24
2.	Primary	1	1.92
3.	High school	1	1.92
4.	Higher secondary	1	1.92
	Total	52	100

Table 1.9 reveals that 94.24% of the respondents are illiterate while the remaining 5% have take up education up to higher secondary. Furthermore, table 1.10 highlights sex wise literacy rates among the Madia respondents studied. Table 1.10 shows that 93.47% of Madia male respondents are illiterate while 100% of female respondents are illiterate.

Table 1.10. Sex wise Literacy Status of Madia Respondents

Sr. No.	*Educational Level*	*Number*			*Percentage*		
		Males	*Females*	*Total*	*Males*	*Females*	*Total*
1.	Illiterate	43	6	49	93.47	100	94
2.	Primary	1	-	1	2.17	-	2
3.	High school	1	-	1	2.17	-	2
4.	Higher Secondary	-	-	-	-	—	-
5.	College	1	-	1	2.17	-	2
	Total	46	6	52	100	100	100

(iii) Literacy Status of Kolams

As compared to the Katkaris and Madia, Kolams are better placed educationally. Tables 1.11 and 1.12 reveal it all.

Table 1.11. Educational Status of Kolam Respondents

Sr.No.	*Educational Level*	*Number*	*Percentage*
1.	Illiterate	27	50
2.	Primary	18	33
3.	High school	8	15
4.	Higher Secondary	-	-
5.	College	1	2
	Total	54	100

Table 1.11 reveals that only 50% of the Kolam respondents studied were illiterate, while 33% studied up to primary and 15% upto high school. This only indicates the progressive nature of Kolams as compared to the Katkaris and Madia. Table 1.12 reveals that both males and females share 50% of illiteracy rate.

Table 1.12. Sex wise literacy rates of Kolam respondents

Sr.	*Educational*	*Number*			*Percentage*		
No.	*Level*	*Males*	*Females*	*Total*	*Males*	*Females*	*Total*
1.	Illiterate	23	4	27	50	50	50
2.	Primary	16	2	18	35	25	33
3.	High school	7	1	8	15	12.5	15
4 .	Higher secondary	-	-	-	-	-	-
5.	College		1	1	-	12.5	2
	Total	46	8	54	100	100	100

(B) Educational Problems of P.T.G.

Focus group discussions with key informants of all the three tribes such as parents, teachers of Zilla Parishad and Ashram Schools, Project Officers of Integrated Tribal Development Projects etc. revealed following educational problems of the three tribes. Table number 1.13 reveals the same.

Table 1.13. Tribe wise educational problems of P.T.Gs in Maharashtra.

Sr.No.	*Tribe*	*Problems*
1.	Katkaris	• Semi-nomadic nature:- Members of Katkari tribe are semi-nomads. They move out of their villages for six months to work as brick kiln labourers, hence cannot send their children to schools. • Landless- 85 % of the respondents were landless, whereas, at the state level 83% have been found to be landless. This aspect of landlessness, forces them to migrate. • Poverty- Bench Mark Survey of TR & TI shows that 97.14% of the Katkaris were below the poverty line. Poverty is one of the major constrains of illiteracy among the Katkaris. • Illiteracy of Parents- If parents are illiterate, they do not realize the significance of education. • Domestic help and Case of little Ones- Teenaged Katkari children, especially the Girls have to contribute in domestic help as well as taking case of little brothers and sister at home as well as at the brick kilns. • Early Age at Marriage- Katkari girls get married between the age 14-17, while boys get married between the age 15-20. This is why they drop out from schools.

Sr.No.	*Tribe*	*Problems*
		• Teenagers as earning members- Since there are no economic assets such as land, live stock, good house etc, they have adapted to semi-nomadism. The parents ultimately depend on teenagers to work at the brick kilns. • Money More Precious than Education:- Some respondents told us that our basic needs are food, shelter & clothes, for which we need money. We have to work for money.
2.		• Forest & Inaccessible Villages:- Madias live in forest & inaccessible villages. Schools are away from hamlets. Fear of wild animals is one factor that prevents the Madias from sending the children to schools. • Language Barrier:- Most Madia children do not speak Marathi & Hindi. They find it difficult to cope up with Marathi language, in the school. • Lack of Interest:- Some Parents said their children are not interested in studies. • Distance to Schools:- High schools & colleges are far away from Madia habitats, hence long distance becomes a barrier. • Lack of Awareness:- Lack of awareness & motivation is yet another factor that keeps the Madia away from formal education.

Sr.No.	Tribe	Problems
3	Kolams	• Economic inability: Kolams are better placed as compared to the Madia and Katkaris. They are aware of educational significance, however, some of the respondents said, for ten years Ashram schools of Tribal Development Department provide us with free books, notebooks, uniforms, food etc. and suddenly after xth grade, we are left to take case of their higher educational expenses. Hence, very few children go for higher education. • Poverty, illiteracy of parents, lack of awareness regarding significance of education etc. are the main reasons of low level literacy among the Kolams.

(IV) Conclusions:

As compared to the general population the literacy rates of Primitive Tribal Groups are very low. The gap between literacy rates of general population and primitive tribes is increasing over the decades. Efforts should be made to reduce this gap. Simultaneously, development of PTGs in domains of economic, social, health, nutrition, political and cultural life can help them to develop interest in education.

(V) Recommendations:

(1) Efforts must be made by Government as well as Non-Government agencies to implement integrated development programs, for every Katkari, Madia and Kolam family at the same time. Basic facilities and amenities such as food, shelter, clothes, employment, land on lease etc. are very necessary.

(2) Parents should be motivated and convinced.

(3) Mobile Schools for semi-nomadic groups like Katkaris will be a boon to their children.

(4) Creating awareness among them about Ashram School and Government Hostel Programs.

(5) Establishing Ashram Colleges for P.T.Gs and other tribes.

(6) Creating awareness of Eklavya Residential Schools, for P.T.Gs among them.

VI] References:

(1) Jain N.S. and Tribhuwan Robin, 1995

An overview of Tribal Research Studies, T.R. and T.I.

(2) Jain N.S. and Tribhuwan Robin, 1996

Mirage of Health and Development, Vidyanidhi Publication, Pune.

(3) Tomar Y.P.S. and Tribhuwan Robin, 2004

Development of Primitive Tribes in Maharashta, T.R. and T.I. Pune.

(4) Primitive Tribes of Maharashta at a Glance, 2001

Bench Mark Survey, TR and TI, Pune.

14

Formal Education and Pardhi Tribe's Culture in Mulshingi of Kolhapur

—*Dr. Arvind Kumar Jha, IFS*

Phase Pardhis were settled in villages like Mulshingi near Kolhapur town of Maharashtra by *Chhatrapati Shahuji Maharaj* in 1917 for helping him in hunting. These villages gradually got engulfed in the expanding township. Pardhis have undergone a process of enculturation and development that was expected to be positively accelerated by the impact of education. Formal education's structure as well as content, however, has been very different from Pardhis' indigenous knowledge and traditional patterns of its assimilation. The cultures of the school as well as the surrounding urbanized environment have also been different from the cultural ethos of the tribe. The inherent qualities, skills and knowledge inherited from their forefathers, over time, were considered apparently of not much relevance in the urban milieu and the prevalent value system deciding the percepts of stratification based on formal learning kept them at the lowest rung and priority in the society which has definitely imposed inherent limits on their social mobility. The heavy quantum of drop outs, dislike for manual work, unfair and unjust competition with the urban populace for livelihoods, non availability of jobs related to their traditional competencies, clamor for Government jobs, and overall massive unemployment and related frustrations are just some of the symptoms of the cultural divide. The need is to reevaluate the complex question of trade-off between loss of indigenous knowledge of Pardhis and their exposure to formal education and ensure that the Pardhis become functional in their 'niche' that is invaluable for the society at large.

Introduction

The word Pardhi in Maharashtra is said to be derived from the Marathi word 'paradh', which means hunting. Pardhis have at least eleven variates classified according to their occupational characteristics and tools and methods employed for hunting. The Pardhi tribe has been classified as "hunters and fowlers" in the caste index of 1891. They were notified as criminal Tribe by the British Government but were denotified in 1952 after India's independence.

Although the main endogamous divisions of Pardhis are Phanse Pardhi, Haran Pardhi, Mir, Korchar, Wagri, Shikari or Bhil Pardhi, Langoti Pardhi, and Takankars but occupational distinctions classifying them into eleven types are seemingly more prominent. In fact the distinction arising out of settled life adopted by some Pardhis, for instance in Kolhapur district in Maharashtra State due to initiatives of Chhatrapati Shahuji Maharaj, is also coming up prominently against the 'nomads' in this regard. The 'nomads' are also called as 'Pal Pardhis' by the Phase Pardhis of Kolhapur and are seen as a distinctly different group having an inferior position as compared to those who have settled down.

Location of the Study

As one moves towards the settlement of Pardhis located in Mulshingi area just adjoining Kolhapur Municipal limits, the Pardhi women and children come forward curiously asking for the purpose of visit. There are very few male members present in the village. They have all gone on work, it is revealed by the children in a chorus. The approach road to the settlement is about 100 meters from the main road and is flanked by pucca houses of non-Pardhis. After being convinced that there is no danger in allowing us into the settlement, three Pardhi young men escort us into the same.

The settlement retains the typical formation of Pardhi dwellings, and consists of mainly two rows of houses running parallel and facing each other. The houses are made of brick and are small. Almost every house has colorful drawings and designs made in a variety of pattern on the front wall and the premises are kept quite clean. There exists a temple on one end of the ground between the rows of houses.

The temple built in the space between the rows of dwelling serves as a common place for social gathering and meetings also. A rectangular space filled with ash and charcoal in front of the temple was conspicuous. The people said that they walk on the lighted charcoal during Navaratri. This custom is clearly an adaptation by the Pardhis of local religious tradition. The surnames of some the Pardhis interestingly have some Muslim names also but they follow Hindu religious practices.

The land for the settlement was granted by Chattrapati Shahuji Maharaj to the Pardhis who were called primarily to assist him in hunting. The Pardhi families were granted land in Alagwadi, Kankanwadi and Khandal villages also in the year 1917. Records show that Pardhis in the name of Shri Anji Jafal, Agna Mahaku, Jalgar Mavalya, Ajnya Bebya and two others received ten acre land each in Khandal. Hujura Murti, Ujal Zalya and three others, and Babal Daulta received eight acre land each in Alagwadi, and Lalya Jalal, Malya Bodal, Ijarat Uttam, Ango Darya, Jalal Saklu, Matya Matkal, Mainsha Ajan and eight others received about four acres of land each in Kankanwadi. It is interesting to note that the names and surnames of some of the Pardhis appear as those belonging to Muslims. Presently, however, the main surnames in the settlement are found to be Kale, Chauhan, and Powar.

These Pardhis identify themselves with 'Phase Pardhis' and have contempt for 'Pal Pardhis' who are described by them as wanderers who dwell in cone shaped tents. Marriages cannot take place between them and Pal Pardhis. They expressed that they actually are descendents of a higher 'Kul' of Pardhis and proudly narrate that they have moved into the area on the request of Chhatrapati Shahujee Maharaj. They express great reverence for him.

Indigenous Knowledge of the Paradhis

Pardhi tribe possesses a very rich content of indigenous knowledge. Indigenous knowledge has been defined as the aggregate of experience and percept of any ethnic group. This forms the basis for decision making whenever the group faces familiar or unfamiliar challenges and problems. This knowledge develops and gets consolidated through a process of absorption of the relevant aspects of experiential as well as shared knowledge into the cultural stream of the group. The indigenous knowledge gets firmed up though the above process over a long time and it is an important, critical, and substantial aspect of the culture of any society. Hunting as the livelihood system has traditionally been practiced by male Pardhis only and they not only prepared various kinds of nets and traps but use and maintain them very efficiently. Earlier most of nets were made of horses and other animals' hair but now nylon threads have replaced almost all animal produce and vegetative fibers in this context. The variety of nets and traps are also nothing but the translation of indigenous knowledge of Pardhi community into objectified forms. It is the indigenous knowledge of Pardhis about their intricate relation with the natural resource base that precisely makes them the masters of remarkable traditional intellectual property.

The tools used for hunting by the Pardhis have evolved over time as have the hunting related skills and techniques. They depended primarily on the type/category and behavior of prey, vegetation, terrain, and also whether the prey had to be caught alive or dead. For household daily consumption, for example, killing of prey could be a favored option but if hunting is primarily for commerce, it is desirable that the prey must be caught alive and also maintained as such. This had led to the development of techniques related to rearing and maintenance of wildlife in captivity as well as under transit and this was a part of indigenous knowledge available with the Pardhis. The variety of nets and traps with Pardhis are nothing but the translation of indigenous knowledge of the Pardhi community into an objectified form.

Pardhis' occupational division got developed, sustained, and recognized through association in the hunting expeditions employing specialized hunting methods. In addition, skills of trapping and preparation of various types of traps matching the behavioral aspects of specific target animals and their habitats gave rise to specialization amongst the Pardhis. The patronage to hunters and hunting as a sport and profession seems to have contributed significantly in establishing the identity of various types of Pardhis.

Skills of Pardhis developed over time have behind them the components of knowledge of wild animal behavior, seasons of breeding, rearing of captured animals, and wild life habitats. The Pardhis also possess the personal and group qualities of bravery, stealth, planning for hunting, grit, perseverance, tact and knowledge of hunting tools and equipment maintenance. The Pardhis also have the skill of attracting game by making false calls of various birds and animals like Partridge, peacock, quail, hares, young and old jackals, foxes etc. All the above form the core competencies characteristic of Pardhi tribe.

Interestingly enough the indigenous knowledge existing as informal but well implemented self-imposed rules governing relationship between Pardhis and the faunal resource base has been attempted to be formalized and expressed through various wildlife conservation related legislations by the Government from time to time, albeit without recognizing their well deserved intellectual property rights.

The earlier Wildlife related Acts of 1912, 1951 and 1972 tended to gradually but decisively hijack the resource base from the Pardhis but the 1991 amendment to the Wildlife (Protection) Act banning all hunting led, in effect, to the ultimate usurpation of the natural resource in question. It also throttled the legal possibility that was available, though to a limited extent, to the Pardhis as a means of sustenance and survival.

Any such usurpation without provision of an appropriate altertribal means of livelihood obviously leaves hardly any natural livelihood options for the people dependent on such natural resource. Some continue stealthily with their profession with or without the connivance of the authorities, while some have migrated to areas that may provide relatively less harsh options.

Impact of education and urbanization:

With time, however, things have changed. The Pardhis of this settlement under the influence of urbanization do not look like typical pardhis and their life style and day-to-day work overtly appear like those of any other lower middle class people. These Pardhis hardly have any chance of making their traditional skills survive for want of game and those going occasionally into forest areas are often afraid of openly attempting hunting. The treasure, accordingly, of the related skills objectified in terms of preparation of snares, nets and trapping instruments including hunting techniques and personal traits of the Pardhis is on the path of extinction.

As regards traditional occupational characteristics of the people, it is revealed that the men-folk do not go for hunting anymore because there are hardly any forests left nearby, there are very few animals in the forests and also because the forest department staff catches and harasses those who go to hunt.

The population of Pardhis settled in Kolhapur, having been constantly exposed to the option of education as well as to the influences of the urban society, seem to have lost the indigenous knowledge and has many characteristics that are no more purely typical of Pardhis as a tribe. The basic skills of hunting are not passed on to the next generation although some of them have retained various types of traps etc. just for tradition sake. They did not show the hunting implements perhaps because of fear of being publicized and later seized by the Forest Department people.

An analysis of life and world-view of Pardhis of Kolhapur indicates that education as well as urbanization and modernization processes have significantly influenced them. Majority of Pardhi women in this settlement wear their typical traditional colorful dress and ornaments where as Children and men folk have adopted modern attire. Traditional turban has disappeared and some people wear Gandhi cap now. The dresses are generally cleaner and much better in comparison to those worn by Pardhis in relatively remote settlements. Their traditional lifestyle gradually becoming unsustainable, a combination of alien occupations is per force being increasingly adopted by the Pardhis today just for survival and sustenance. Further, the fact of socio-cultural dynamics of Pardhi community trapped so strongly in the 'macro versus micro' approach of wildlife management and in the 'man versus animal' dilemma of wild life protection, unfortunately, seems to indicate that they, as a unique social entity, may perish along with all skills and indigenous knowledge.

Currently there are about 400 children in this settlement in about 155 families, Total population -726 out of which only about 120 children are going to school. The nearest school is in Mulshinghi itself. There is one student in class 11th and three are in the first year B.A. The residents express that they do not have enough resources for sending their children for higher education. In the class Ist to IIIrd, there are 70 students with 45 boys and 25 girls. Class IVth to VIIth has 25 students with 15 boys and 10 girls. Class VIIIth to Xth has 15 students all of which are boys. The attrition is 50 in the class Ist to IIIrd and 25 in the class VIIIth to Xth. The overall enthusiasm of the children regarding attending school is low.

The children seemed to keep good health and there is a consciousness regarding general hygiene. As regards relatively grown up children, they have higher expectations and a craze for Government service. Some of them however, expressed that they would like to go for small trade or business.

As regards employment, presently there are 20 persons employed in various jobs. Six are employed in Maharashtra State Electricity Board; eleven works as peons in various organizations, two works as clerks in Banks and one is employed in Survey work. There are forty women employed in cotton yarn industry as labor. Most of the womenfolk basically remain at home only but some do go for work on wages in the nearby households. While majority of youths are drop outs and are educated up to various secondary classes, they are unemployed as they do not like to go for manual works. The adults, both male and female, go to work as manual labor. Some are engaged in petty business, dairy and trade but they constantly clamor for Government job. They are not able to get the benefits of reservations as they lack awareness as well as the basic qualification in most cases.

It is important to note the effect of formal education on the Pardhis of Mulshingi. The formal educational content as well as school culture is very different from their own cultural patterns. There is a heavy quantum of drop outs despite the fact that there is a school within the locality. The students who have touched books do not wish to do manual work. There is a clamor for Government jobs and they have to compete with the urban populace for livelihoods. The inherent qualities, skills and knowledge descended onto them from their forefathers and possessed by them are not of relevance in the urban milieu. The prevalent value system based on formal learning keep them at the lowest rung of the society. This is typified by their employment level in the present social and economic structure and obviously has imposed limits on their social mobility. Kolhapur and nearby Districts like Sangli have zoos which can utilize the skills of Pardhis. Similarly the forest department can employ their competencies in management. These areas appear to be completely away from their reach and there is no conscious efforts made to document and utilize the indigenous knowledge of Pardhis.

The Pardhis of Kolhapur in majority have retained their certain cultural indicators especially those related to religion, ladies' attire, and community feeling. The area truly looks like an 'island', culturally as well as socially, in the otherwise developed city of Kolhapur today but it is apparent that the next generations of the Pardhis here might lose their original tribal identity expressed through their traditional customs, occupation, indigenous knowledge, and cultural traits and get assimilated into the so called modernity and mainstream.

The questions that emerge are "Has the trade-off between loss of indigenous knowledge and exposure to formal education been worth while in the instant case?" and "Has the replacement of traditional cultural values by modern systems been beneficial for the Pardhis as well as for the society at large?" Only time may perhaps be able to tell that!

15

Tribal Education : A Frame Work for Research, Monitor and Interventions

—Nanjunda D.C.

Unity in diversity is our main strength. Our land is cradle for various traditions, religious, ethnic, cultural, customs and linguistic groups. We can say it is more or less a plural society. Hence the researchers can get plenty of data to study cross-cultural aspects of the country. Even though India has diverse groups only few percentage has eating fruit of main stream development and a lager section of the under privileged of the society has remained near the periphery or long away from the so-called development.

One of the weakest link in the chain is strong existence of caste system in the Indian society. Caste is a foundation stone of the Indian society. Without understanding the caste no one can properly understood the Hindu society and social institutions. Experts of the opinion that Varnas are the basic reasons for the existence of complex caste system in India. Brahmins have got first place in the social stratification of the Hindu law and Sudras have got a last place. These people have now recognized as SC under the Indian constitution. They represent 17.5 per cent of the total population of India

Anthropologically speaking a tribe is a social group (Jha, 2001). The tribal people constitute an out caste group (Mishra, 1999). The members of these groups live in common territory, using common dilated posses cultural homogeneity. Experts of the opinion that as per these characteristics it is not very easy o locate many tribal groups in India who posses all these outstanding characteristics Further many tribal group have been recognized as scheduled tribal in our fifth schedule of the constitution.

The term 'Scheduled Tribes' first appeared in the Constitution of India. Article 366 (25) defined scheduled tribes as "such tribes or tribal communities or parts of or groups within such tribes or tribal communities as are deemed under Article 342 to be Scheduled Tribes for the purposes of this constitution". Article 342, which is reproduced below, prescribes procedure to be followed in the matter of specification of scheduled tribes.

Literary speaking these people is commonly called Adivasi. It means original inhabitants, or tribal peoples comprise a substantial indigenous minority of the population of India. Tribal people are particular numerous in the Indian states of Orissa, Bihar, Jarkalnd and in other northeastern part of the country.

Traditionally referred to as adivasis, vanbasis, tribes, or tribals, Scheduled Tribes constitute about 8% of the population of India. The scheduled tribes lie mostly in isolated, and mostly inaccessible hilly areas. These regions are relatively underdeveloped and poorly integrated with the rest of the regions. They have not much cultural contact with the rest of population and have thus remained closed static societies. They have also thus maintained their characteristic way of living.

There are about 573 Scheduled Tribes living in different parts of our country, having their own languages, which are varied from the one spoken in the State where they live. There are more than 270 such languages in India. According to the 2001census, the tribal population in India is 74.6 million. The largest number of tribals is in Madhya Pradesh (16.40 million), followed by Orissa (7 million) and Jharkhand (6.6 million). There were 16 million Scheduled Tribe children (10.87 million of 6-11 years and 5.12 million of 11-14 years) as of March 2001, out of the total child population in India of about 193 million in the age group of 6 to 14 years (Selected Educational Statistics – 2000-01, Government of India). Education of Scheduled Tribe children is considered important, not only because of the Constitutional obligation but also as a crucial input for total development of tribal communities and also for the economic development of a country. One of the challenges in providing education to tribal children is to setting up school facilities in small, scattered and remote tribal habitations. The majority of the Scheduled Tribes live in sparsely populated habitations in the interior and in inaccessible hilly and forest areas of our country. So an attempt is made by the researchers to discuss and analyze the problems of tribal children's education in India since tribal children are neither culturally inferior nor cognitively less competent than the children of other groups.

Indian Constitution and STs

The constitution provides various safeguards in favour of the scheduled tribes. These may be broadly divided into two parts viz., (a) protection and (b) development. Protection of interest of scheduled tribes is very essential for their development. The protective provisions are contained in articles 15(4), 16(4), 19(5), 23,29, 46, 164, 330, 332, 334, 335, 336, 339(1), 371(a), 371(b), 371(c), fifth schedule and sixth schedule. Articles 16(4) and 19(5) are exceptions to the fundamental rights, rights of equality and freedom guaranteed under part lll of the constitution. Provisions relating to development of scheduled tribes are contained mainly in article 271(1) first provision and 339(2).

In spite of sixty years of independence and more than fifty five years of planned development and social provision for accelerated socio-economiç development. The term 'Scheduled Tribes' first appeared in the Constitution of India. Article366 (25) defined scheduled tribes as "such tribes or tribal communities or parts of or groups within such tribes or tribal communities as are deemed under Article 342 to be Scheduled Tribes for the purposes of this constitution". Article 342, prescribes procedure to be followed in the matter of specification of scheduled tribes as development of weaker sections, the gap in literacy levels among the general population and the socially disadvantaged sections is persisting and in some cases this gap is further widening. There were 16 million ST children [10.87 million of 6-11 years and 5.12 million of11-14 years) as of March 2001, out of the total child population in India of about 193 million in the age group of 6 to 14 years. [Selected Educational Statistics – 2001Government of India] – Education of ST children to considered important, not only because of the constitutional obligation but also as a crucial input for total development of tribal communities. Most tribal children do not understand the textbooks, which are generally in the regional language. The appointment of non-tribal teachers in tribal children's schools is another problem. The teachers do not know the language the children speak and children do not understand the teacher's language. The issues pertaining to tribal education

Scheduled Tribe in India are more like the "indigeneous" or "tribal people" in other parts of the world. The population of Scheduled Tribes in India according to 2001census is 8.43 crore. Education of Scheduled Tribe children is considered important, not only because of the constitutional obligation, but also a crucial input for total development of tribal communities. The literacy levels of the Scheduled Tribes according to the 2001census is 47.10% as compared to overall literacy rate of the total population i.e., 65.38%,which shows a dismal picture of Scheduled Tribes education. So long as there is a gap between the literacy levels, the position of Scheduled Tribes will remain backward. Lack of education may lead to child exploitation, child labor, population explosion, etc., so the need of the hour is to bring quality education through 100% school enrolment and retention with more emphasis on the girl child education. I have given some suggestions for imparting quality education among the Scheduled Tribes in order to uplift themselves and to overcome the socio-economic problems.

The spread of education among the weaker sections of our society is vital as education is a prime requisite for socio-economic development. The policy to promote educational interests of the weaker sections of the people, especially the Scheduled Castes and Scheduled Tribes, has been enshrined in our Constitution as a Directive Principle of State Policy. Therefore, the main thrust continues to be on education. The general level of literacy is very low and is lower still in the case of Backward Classes. To conclude in the words of Swami Vivekananda - "The Real India lives in the Villages. Unless we are able to uplift the Tribal and the backward classes, India faces to dark future. Along with their economic improvement they have to be raised culturally and spiritually."

The Government of India have taken up in right earnest the duty of educating the 25 million Adibasis of the country, with the object of helping them to become absorbed in the larger Indian society. This is a very difficult but a very necessary task. The difficulty is partly due to the differences in the cultural levels of the various tribes, and partly due to the intra-tribal social solidarity which can be an obstacle to the integration of the Adibasis with the Indian society. The Adibasis cannot therefore be expected to rise to the full stature of citizenship immediately. Neither would any large-scale and sweeping legislation bring about the desired end. It can be done only by a gradual process of adjustment for which a suitable type of education has to be planned and carried out.

As per the 1991census, the scheduled tribes (ST) account for 67.76 million representing 8.08percent of the country's population. Of this, 1.32 million (1.95%) belong to primitive tribal groups (PTG) who are marginalised than the ST population. The ST population is estimated to have reached 88.8 million in 2001which is 8.6% of the country's total population in 2001. The scheduled tribes are spread across the country and reside mainly in forest and hilly regions. The proportion of scheduled tribes within general population varies across states/ union territories and indicates heavy concentration n certain parts such as Mizoram (94.7%), Lakshawadeep (93.2%), Meghalaya (85.5%), Dadra and Nagar Haveli (78.9%). States of Kerala (1.1%), Tamilnadu (1%), and Uttar Pradesh (0.2%) have low percentage of scheduled tribe population in comparison to the general population. Since Independence, the percentage of ST population has steadily increased following the growth in general population.

Education has limited connotation. It is largely concerned with the existing formal structure of education and the institutionalized methodology of imparting knowledge to individuals. Within this very system exist many sub-groups of individuals with specific needs and tribals are one of them. In fact tribals form a large group of individuals in the Indian society. For several historical, economic and social reasons the scheduled groups have remained economically backward and socially retarded even to this day. The ST population accounts for 8.6% of the total population of the country. There are many constitutional provisions and legislative support available for safeguarding the welfare and the interests of STs. In addition planned developmental efforts have also taken place through Five-Year plans. Despite the concern reflected in the Indian Constitution and the developmental efforts initiated for the welfare and the development of STs., their socio-economic and political development is still far below the others and therefore much more needs to be done in this direction, including their empowerment – educational, social, economic and political – with due regard to their special identity – culturally, habitation ally, traditionally – and in terms of the tribals' age-old rights and customs. The number of educational institutions in 1978, together with the number of pupils within the area covered by the plans for tribal development, is shown. The boarders accommodated in hostels were also given special coaching. The number of teachers in ashram schools was 1,171, and the number of teachers employed in primary, upper primary and high schools was 1,821. The number of students in receipt of post-matric scholarships was 1,950, 468 tribal students were admitted to reputable private schools and public schools, and 90 students were enrolled in the special residential school for tribals.

Truly speaking the problems of the Indian tribals can be classified in to 2 main groups; 1 problems of the major tribes and 2 problems of the minor tribes. One of the main hurdles of our tribal administrations is mixing up together. Out of many major problems like land alienation, poverty, shifting cultivation and migration the problem of solid education system has blacken their entire way towards empowerment and entry to the main stream of the sustainable development. It not only deprives them of the opportunity in the new ventures but also alienates them from their resource base.

Education cannot change in any fundamental way unless we change our basic patterns of thinking and interacting so that learning can become a way of life. Teachers, parents, administrators, district resource and community people are coming together throughout hundreds of school communities to learn how to revitalize their schools with a process known as "Tribes." Evaluation of Tribes Learning Community Schools has examined the impact of the Tribes process on student behavior, academic performance, school culture, and teacher collegiality. Studies have shown that: Tribes TLC has a positive impact on classroom environment, teachers report spending less time managing student behavior, students are significantly less likely to be referred for disciplinary problems, the Tribes process helps teachers address performance and content standards, students in well-implemented classrooms score significantly higher on standardized tests than students from comparison groups, teachers report increased staff collegiality and planning "Responsive Education" is an essential pedagogy for academic achievement and school reform. It is the synthesis of artful teaching practices. It is based on understanding the critical developmental needs of a student age and cultural group. The Goal is to engage all teachers, administrators, students and families in working together as a learning community that is dedicated to caring and support, active participation and positive expectations for all students.

After the independence of India in 1947, sincere efforts were made by the government to improve the economic and social life of the tribals through the spreading of education. In fact, education has occupied an important place in the Tribal sub-plan. Some of the steps taken for this purpose were- (1) opening of schools, Balwadis, and Angan Kedras in tribal areas; (2) establishing community centers; and (3) granting financial assistance to tribal children. Soon it was realised that these measures are not sufficient for the progress of tribal education for the following reasons;

(1) problem of providing free and compulsory education to all 6 to 13 year old tribal children by establishing sufficient number of schools in the remote tribal areas; (2) problems regarding the unfavorable negative attitude of the tribal parents towards the education of their children. The formal education, given to the tribal children in the schools, does not bring any immediate return. It is therefore natural that the parents develop a negative attitude towards it which indirectly lead to high drop out rates. Besides these, some of the major problems regarding tribal education are

(1) the problem of getting educated men and women teacher from the same tribal group;

(2) the problem of the medium of instruction;
(3) the problem of supervision and inspection;
(4) the problem of evaluation and examination;
(5) the problem of linking education with life;
(6) the problem of providing technical schools;
(7) the problem of providing physical facilities and amenities;
(8) the problem of providing residential schools;
(9) the problem of preparing text books;
(10) the problem of girl's education etc.

Recent survey report revealed many pertinent problems and issues related to the primary education of tribal children in triabl dominated State. The problem areas identified are inaccessibility of schools in geographically difficult areas, absence of Non Formal Education centers and Ashram Schools, lack of awareness among parents, absence of tribal language linker, lack of adequate teaching-learning materials, negligence of tribal girl child, inadequate incentives, absence of vocational courses etc. However, according to the expert's team, the State/ district strategies have begun intervening in these problem areas. Besides opening new primary as well as pre-primary schools, providing more buildings, rooms and other facilities like textbooks, dresses, and shoes have been the major interventions. A few other sensitive areas were identified to support and sustain the educational activities going on in tribal areas. One of the areas of intervention programme under State/ district strategies is mobilization/ awareness. House to house campaign and special campaign to promote girls education are viewed as helpful to tribal education. The State strategies to improve management and capacity development include setting up of BECs. However nomination was made with regard to educating and re-orienting VEC members to make this body effective. Re-orienting parents and strengthening PTAs re considered as major strategies for reducing drop-outs. The State strategies for learning improvements include preparation of handbook for tribal language, targeted interventions for girls and tribal students, free distribution of textbooks, opening of new pre-primary schools providing in-service training to Anganwadi/ Balwadi teachers, etc. The programme to improve access includes opening ofnew schools and NFE centers in tribal remote areas. Strategies Suggested for National Intervention by Kerala Team• National help is needed in preparation of textbooks for tribal children - specially with regard to which and in what form the tribal folklore and tribal history could be included intext books.•Details regarding how to standardize the curriculum developed in tribal dialect may be remarked at national level. •National directives to be given on smooth convergence of government functionaries (TWD, Education Department, Panchayat etc.) to avoid administrative bottlenecks and spread UPE among tribes.• Preparation of modules at national level to provide adequate information and special orientation to State/ district level officers in handling tribal education programme. •Direct access to the information as well as guidance from the national component by the research organisations at the State level with regard to tribal education. Poverty, lack of awareness, child labour, ill health, migration problem, unsuitable school calendar, irrelevant curriculum, unattractive and inadequate educational facilities, lack of interest among parents and teachers, language problem and gender discrimination were found to be major hurdles in enhancing learning capacity of tribal children in Karnataka. The State/district strategies aim at intervening in these problem areas. However, the salient features of tribal strategy at State/district level include preservation of culture, language and development of the community of different tribes. Thus, separate educational plan is envisaged and designed for different tribes like Beads, Jenu Kurubs and Lambanis. Formulation of separate school calendar and time table suiting the life cycle and, daily activities of the tribal students and communities are being attempted. Moreover, the State nodal persons were found to have actually moved tribal group wise in recommending the medium of instruction and the instructional materials. The textbooks re proposed to be taught in regional language in the classes/ schools having heterogeneous tribal groups; whereas tribal dialect could be used in the schools where homogenous groups of tribals study. However, phasing of instruction should be done in such a way that the tribal dialect is used as the mother tongue in the first two years of schooling and in higher classes a mix of tribal dialect and regional language is used for instruction until the latter replaces the former completely by standard V. As a result the child is gradually mainstreamed into instruction in the regional language. The teacher factors such as including provision of residential facilities to the teachers in tribal areas, project allowance and incentives for primary school teachers in tribal areas, are well comprehended by the State component. Monitoring and evaluation could take place on a mid-term and annual basis.

Policy Improvements

In most of the Indian states there is no office or department is created exclusively to handle tribal education. The National authority should take notice of this and suggest a review of the State policy in the light of this. Providing expertise and developing capacity at State/ district levels to develop modules for training and orienting teachers in tribal culture and tribal dialect. National intervention is needed for development of Tribal learning material. The National component can provide expert help from NCERT or other language institutes for developing books and curriculum at State level within objective of providing "joyful learning" to the tribal children. Slow growth of education among tribals in many Indian states is due to small and scattered habitations over vast hilly terrain, inadequate cooperation among different departments like TWD, Forest Department, Panchayat, etc., involvement of tribal children in agriculture and household work, lack of parental motivation in enrolling children in schools, etc. The State/district strategies aimed at increasing intervention in the area of improving access, environment building, capacity building and empowering Vocation Learning Centers and Continuing Education Centers. etc. Altertribal model of schooling should be adopted in all the tribal blocks under DPEP in order to improve access to schools. Motivating tribal parents through social awareness camping with the help of tribal NCC students of schools and colleges are also planned to reach out to the more difficult school age tribal children. Conducting a survey on migratory pattern of parents and starting of residential schools to retain the children whose parents seasonally migrate/or issuing certificates which are valid for continuing classes in new schools are suggested to help in bringing these other wise difficult to reach school age tribal children back in to the mainstream of education. It has increasingly been realised by the State/district strategies that empowering the teacher to buy teaching-learning materials worth Rs.500/-. orienting teachers to motivate tribal children towards formal education, monitoring effectively the existing welfare schemes and strengthening community participation will help in improving retention and learning achievements among tribal children. Intervention programmes have begun in this direction. With regard to the problem of medium of instruction in few states like Tamil Nadu have maintained that preparing tribal language linker is not necessary for the reason that almost all the tribals can speak and understand the regional language i.e. Tamil. However, the resource persons are not in agreement. Besides, the State was also silent about changes in the curriculum in the direction mentioned by other State teams however, added a few more points such as providing escort services with the help of MTCs as an innovation of DPEP, appointment and provision of special coaching for the tribal teachers recruited from the local areas, etc. Developing textbooks with crucial emphasis on socio-cultural milieu of the tribals and providing tribal culture specific in-service training to teachers and orientation programme to administrators etc. are the other interventions planned in the State

Further study has pointed out various lacunas in the education policy of most of the Indian states and expressed concern that the inter-tribal and intra-tribal disparities are not sufficiently reflected in the States component of tribal education. Hence National policies should assist the State component in re-orienting the community participation modules to make it more effective. •The Gender component of tribal education is not adequately addressed. National strategy should address this issue immediately. • States requires help from the national strategies for formulating training cells to motivate and improve the caliber of tribal teachers. National component also needs to provide expert services in developing training/ orientation module for the members of VLC/MTC and ECC. •The national component needs to remind the State component regarding the objective of utmost decentralizing of the planning processes and addressing the inter and intra-tribal and gender disparities at all stages of plan processes.

Tribal scenario in case of India seemed to have some unique features which need to be adequately addressed by the respective State as well as the national component of tribal education while planning for primary education. Negative parental attitude to education, lack of interest and motivation among teachers to problems of tribal children, lack of community participation, and language incomprehensibility are the major hurdles in spreading education among tribal children. The strategies for tribal education under DPEP include interventions in areas like increasing access to education, retaining tribal children in the school up to class V and in capacity building.

Conducting various camps to increase the awareness by using songs, skits, slogans, films and printed material developed mainly in local languages using existing structures like tribal bazaars and fairs for conducting intensive outreach campaigns to motivate tribals towards education, involving education in tribal pockets, adopting soft strategies to enter the tribal dominated tea estates and giving priorities to tribal areas must be undertaken for increasing accessibility of education to tribal children. The textbooks developed in little tribal language are in the final stages. The State strategy team should also plan to prepare teacher-training material in required language on priority basis. State strategy places equal emphasis on capacity building.

Acknowledgement

This Author is grateful to UGC and Dr. Midatala Rani for providing an opportunity to work in a Major Project on Tribal Education in Karnataka.

16

Education of Tribal Children in India and the Issue of Medium of Instruction: A Janshala Experience

— *Vinoba Gautam*

Janshala is a joint programme of the Government of India and five UN agencies (UNDP, UNICEF, UNFPA, UNESCO and ILO) for the universalisation of primary education among educationally undeserved communities. The programme is being implemented in nine Indian states. Records collected in schools in the Janshala Programme areas indicate continuing high "dropout" rates among tribal children. A major reason for this is that in most states the medium of instruction is the regional language. Most tribal children do not understand the textbooks, which are generally in the regional language. The appointment of non-tribal teachers in tribal children's schools is another problem: the teachers do not know the language the children speak and children do not understand the teacher's language. The issue of language is being debated in the context of tribal education. While some researchers argue for a uniform policy with respect to language use in schools, others perceive it as a constraint in the process of schooling. This paper examines the current policy framework of the participating states withregard to the medium of instruction in government schools in tribal areas and meeting the needs of soundeducation of tribal children in terms of the posting of teachers, development of textbooks and curricula, training of teachers, etc. The paper also presents a statistical analysis of the responses of parents, children and teachers on the issue of using the mother tongue as medium of instruction in schools and other language issues. The responses of the stakeholders have been gathered through a survey carried outrecently in fifteen Janshala blocks of five states. Introduction The Janshala Programme is a collaborative effort of the Government of India (GOI) and five UN agencies – UNDP, UNICEF, UNESCO, ILO and UNFPA – to provide programme support to the ongoing efforts towards achieving Universal Elementary Education (UEE). Janshala, a communitybased primary education programme, aims to make primary education more accessible and effective, especially for girls and children in deprived communities, marginalised groups, Scheduled Caste/ Scheduled Tribes/minorities, working children and children with specific needs. A unique feature of Janshala is that it is a block-based programme with emphasis on community participation and decentralisation. The blocks have been selected on the basis of different indicators such as low female literacy, incidence of child labour, and concentration of Scheduled Tribe (ST) and Scheduled Caste (SC) populations. Target group and primary beneficiaries: The GOI and the UN system recognize that certain sections of the population remain marginalised. Therefore it is the goal of the Joint GOI-UN System Education Programme to target girls and the marginalised population of children in selected areas and to improve their attendance and performance in primary education. Children who are marginalised by the formal education systemare usually scheduled tribes, scheduled castes, working children, those belonging to minorities, disabled children, and children in remote areas. Girls from these groups are severely marginalised. Coverage: The Programme is being implemented in nine States of India - Andhra Pradesh, Jharkhand, Chhattisgarh, Karnataka, Madhya Pradesh, Maharashtra, Orissa, Rajasthan and Uttar Pradesh - with a total of 139 blocks including ten cities under the Programme. The Programme covers nearly three million children, and 58,000 teachers in 18,000 schools. Out of 139 blocks more than 75 blocks have substantial tribal population. The proportion of tribal children is 33% of the total target group children in the project area. Education of tribal children: The Indian Constitution assigns special status to the Scheduled Tribes (STs). Traditionally referred to as adivasis, vanbasis, tribes, or tribals, STs constitute about 8% of the Indian population. There are 573

Scheduled Tribes living in different parts of the country, having their own languages, which are different from the one mostly spoken in the State where they live. There are more than 270 such languages in India. According to the 2001 census, the tribal population in India is 74.6 million. The largest number of tribals is in undivided Madhya Pradesh (16.40 million), followed by Orissa (7 million) and Jharkhand (6.6 million). There were 16 million ST children (10.87 million of 6-11 years and 5.12 million of 11-14 years) as of March 2001, out of the total child population in India of about 193 million in the age group of 6 to 14 years (Selected Educational Statistics – 2000-01, Government of India). Education of ST children is considered important, not only because of the Constitutional obligation but also as a crucial input for total development of tribal communities. An important development in the policy towards education of tribals is the National Policy on Education (NPE), 1986, which specified, among other things, the following:

- Priority will be accorded to opening primary schools in tribal areas;
- There is need to develop curricula and devise instructional material in tribal languages at the initial stages with arrangements for switchover to regional languages;
- ST youths will be encouraged to take up teaching in tribal areas;
- Ashram schools / residential schools will be established on a large scale in tribal areas;
- Incentive schemes will be formulated for the STs, keeping in view their special needs and lifestyle.

The NPE, 1986 and the Programme of Action (POA), 1992, recognized the heterogeneity anddiversity of the tribal areas while underlining the importance of instruction through the mother tongue and the need for preparing teaching/learning materials in the tribal languages. A working group on Elementary and Adult Education for the Xth Five Year Plan (2002-07) emphasized the need toimprove the quality of education of tribal children and to ensure equity as well as further improving access. The interventions being promoted in

States under Janshala include:

- Schools, education guarantee centres and altertribal schools in tribal habitations for non-enrolled and drop-out children;
- Textbooks in the mother tongue for children at the beginning of the primary education cycle, when they do not understand the regional language. Suitably adapted curriculum and the availability of locally relevant teaching and learning materials for tribal students;
- Special training for non-tribal teachers to work in tribal areas, including knowledge of tribal dialect;
- Special support to teachers as per need;
- Deploying community teachers;
- Bridge Language Inventory for use of teachers;
- School calendars in tribal areas appropriate to local requirements and festivals.
- Anganwadis and Balwadis or crèches in each school in tribal areas so that the girls are relieved from sibling care responsibilities;
- Special plan for nomadic and migrant workers;
- Engagement of community organizers from ST communities with a focus on schooling needs of children from specific households;
- Ensuring sense of ownership of school committees by ST communities through increasing representatives of STs in VECs / PTAs etc. Involving community leaders in school management;
- Monitoring attendance and retention of children;
- Providing context specific intervention e.g. Ashram school, hostel, incentives etc.

Universalizing access One of the challenges in providing education to tribal children relates to setting up school facilities in small, scattered and remote tribal habitations. The majority of the Scheduled Tribes live in sparsely populated habitations in the interior and in inaccessible hilly and forest areas of the country. Nearly22 per cent of the tribal habitations have populations of less than 100 while more than 40% have population of 100 to 300. The rest have population of 300 to 500 (Sujatha, 2000).Relaxed Norm for Setting up Schools One of the reasons for poor access to schooling in tribal areas before the 1980s was the high norm on population, number of children and distance for opening new schools. Most of the states have relaxed these norms to enable setting up schoolseven in small tribal hamlets. This, along with other measures has improved access in tribal areas. For instance, Andhra Pradesh has relaxed norms to set up schools in habitations even with 20 school-age children. Some states have lowered the population size norm, especially for tribal areas. EGS centers can now be established even with 15 children. In remote tribal habitations in hilly areas of North Eastern states and Jammu & Kashmir, EGS schools can be opened with only 10 children. The Sixth All India Educational Survey (1993) showed that 78 per cent of the tribal population and 56per cent of tribal habitations have been provided primary schools within the habitation. In addition, 11 per cent of the tribal population and 20 per cent of tribal habitations have schools within less than 1 km radius. About 65 per cent of rural habitations covering 86 per cent of the total rural population have primary schools within the habitation or within a distance of half a kilometer, as against 56 per cent of tribal habitations with 79 per cent of tribal population. Mizoram and Gujarat have the highest percentage of population and habitations covered by primary schools within the habitations. Up to 95 per cent of the tribal population and 85 to 90 per cent of the tribal habitations in the states are provided with schooling facilities within the habitation.

Quality improvement Development of culturally relevant materials in local languages Most of the states recognize the need to address issues related to teachers' attitudes, medium of instruction, textbooks and materials, curriculum and pedagogy and teaching- learning process in tribal areas. An increasing number of researchers strongly advocate the use of the mother tongue or home language as medium of instruction in early stages of education. This assumes greater significance in the context of education of tribal children because their mother tongue is often quite distinct from the prominent languages in the state or regional languages. ST children face problems wherever teachers do not speak their dialect at all. From the perspective of language, it is desirable to have a local teacher from the same tribal community (Jha & Jhingran, 2002). Although research evidence has demonstrated the positive consequences of bilingual or multilingual schooling on cognitive development and social interaction processes, tribal children would require special programs to be able to cope. The Constitution of India allows the use of tribal dialect (mother tongue) as the medium of instruction if the population of the tribe is more than 100,000. Assam was the first state to prepare teacher training modules and separate teaching learning materials for the Bodo tribal language in 1995. Bodo is also a medium of instructions in some districts of Assam. The work on tribal language materials was undertaken through DIET staff and BRC/CRC coordinators who belonged to the tribal community. Resource material in Bodo language has been prepared and all workbooks at primary stage have been translated/adopted in Bodo language. In Golpara district, Garo medium workbook has been translated/adopted and distributed in the schools. Most of the states have taken up activities for quality improvement of tribal area schools. One of the issues identified by the states was the problem faced by tribal children whose home language was very different from the regional language, which was the medium of instruction at the primary level. In Madhya Pradesh teachers' handbooks called Bridge Language Inventory (BLIs) have been prepared in 3 tribal languages viz. Gondi (Shahdol and Betul district), Kuduk, (Raigarh) and Bhili (Dhar). Identified teachers were given training in using BLISs in their classrooms. The teaching-learning package called Dham Dhama Dham was translated into Gondi and supplementary reading material, Kopal, was developed for tribal children. The class I textbook Bharati has been translated into tribal languages. Supplementary TLM for tribal children has been developed in Jhabua district using local cultural form i.e. folk tales, songs, proverbs, riddles, to make the learning process interesting. In all, 450 teachers of 311 schools have been trained to use the supplementary materials. Researches have underlined the need to develop culturally sensitive programmes of school education that can ensure the dignity of tribal groups by providing them with economically viable options for life (Sinha & Mishra, 1997). Some attempts have been made for linking curriculum with the local needs of the communities. Such curriculum would make tribal children more sensitive to local contexts and sustain them in their respective environments instead of forcing them to move out in search of another life. In Karnataka a textbook for class I & II has been developed and introduced for Soliga language. A handbook has been developed for sensitisation of teachers towards social and cultural specificities of tribal societies. In Maharashtra tribal language dictionaries have been developed. Language resource groups have been set up for Bhili, Pawara, Madia, Gondi, etc. Bridge material has been developed in Vinoba Gautam Dhule district. Kerala has developed bilingual language materials at district level in Kasarkode, Waynad, Malappuram and Palakkad. Orissa took the initiative to develop a comprehensive strategy for education of tribal children as earlyas 1997. The state has initiated a number of activities for addressing the quality improvement of tribal education. Andhra Pradesh has developed bilingual dictionaries and teacher training has been organised in Warangal and Vizianegarem districts. Research studies have also been undertaken on the issue of language and maths learning by tribal children. It has been decided to use the multi-level kits developed for tribal areas in Vishakapatnam district and also in other tribal areas. Gujarat has developed dictionaries in Dangi and Bhili dialects. A local word glossary in Dangi has been prepared and distributed in schools for class I-IV in Dang district. Similarly a local word glossary in Adivasi dialect has been prepared for class I-IV in Banaskantha district and distributed in schools. The Vidyasahayaks were given training on the use of these dictionaries. Gujarat has also initiated extensive work for preparation of TLM in tribal languages. The TLM developed include flash cards for different languages and also cards for mathematics. These have been supplied to all schools in tribal areas. A Bridge Language Inventory has also been introduced in Ho and Mundari languages in Ranchi district of Bihar. Use of Local teachers The acceptance of teachers by the community as one of them is critical for increasing schooling participation in tribal areas. An understanding of and respect for tribal cultures and practices and some amount of familiarity with the local language are important for teachers to gain this acceptance: The presence of tribal teachers, especially from the same community, has shown and improved school participation of ST children. Coming from the same community, it is believed that the teachers would understand and respect the culture and the ethos with much greater sensitivity. Studies suggest that teacher motivation contributes more to teaching – learning process than teacher competence (Vaidyanathan and Nair, 2001). Realising the importance of having teachers from the local community, many states have appointed community teachers or para teachers as they are popularly referred to. The deployment of community teachers was first experimented in the late Seventies in NFE and later in the formal school with the Volunteer Teacher Scheme of Himachal Pradesh (1984). Nineties saw spurt in the appointment of communityteachers, who are from the local community and appointed by the gram panchayator Village Education Committees. Different states have different schemes for appointing community teachers – Shiksha Karmi Scheme (Madhya Pradesh and Rajasthan), Shiksha Mitra Yojna (Uttar Pradesh), Lok Shikshak (Bihar), Andariki–Vidya Volunteer Scheme (Andhra Pradesh). Vidya Upasak Yojana (Himachal Pradesh), Shikshan Sevak (Maharashtra), Guruji (under EGS in Madhya Pradesh) Shikshak (under Basti Shala Scheme in Maharashtra) etc. It is estimated that there are about 220,000 para teachers engaged in full time schools in the country (Ed.CIL, 2001). The issues relating to classroom transactions are difficult as they deal with well entrenched attitudes and prejudices of teachers as well as seemingly intractable problems of the huge difference between home and school languages. Attempts have been made to address the first issue through training programmes for teachers. However, more emphasis on attitudinal training of teachers on the lines of Orissa is required in most of the states. The second issue has been addressed mainly through the BLIs and primers in tribal languages. There may be a problem of acceptance of the tribal language as a medium of instruction in the tribal communities, therefore, adequate dialogue with tribal communities and their leaders is required to prepare them on this issue. Conclusion The discussion presented above gives us two important lessons. One is that the cognitive qualities of tribal children have to be viewed and evaluated taking into consideration their ecological and cultural contexts that place very different demands on day-to-day life. Because of differences in the demands of tribal ecology, the patterning of their cognitive abilities shows considerable variation from those of other groups. A related and more important lesson is that tribal children are neither culturally inferior nor cognitively less competent than the children of other groups. Instead many of their skills and abilities are highly developed and extremely sophisticated.

The implications of these findings for schooling of tribal children are clear. A programme of schooling, which does not pay attention to the ecological, cultural and psychological characteristics of tribal children is highly unlikely to make any significant impact. The educational system of the dominant non-tribal population is of very limited value in the tribal cultural milieu because it does not match with the lifestyle of individuals and the needs of the tribal community. Linking school education with life in general and the needs of the tribal communities in particular is a most important step that requires serious attention. The evidences suggests that tribal children do possess the basic cognitive abilities and psychological dispositions necessary for successful participation in school. Yet tribal children have very low levels of participation and success in school education programmes. This points to our failure to develop a sensitive model of education that is rooted in the psychological strengths of tribal children. Studies indicate that, in comparison to other groups, hunters and gatherers possess a high level of visual and tactual differentiation; they demonstrate capacity for fine judgment of shape and size of stimuli as well as spatial relations and they produce fine categorization of an array of objects (Mishra et al 1996). These abilities are required for success in science, art, music, dance, athletic activities, and vocations like carpentry, tailoring, wood and stone crafts. These skills need to be utilized not only for education of tribal children in schools, but also in the broader economic spheres of tribal life. Such attempts will be helpful in generating and promoting the sense of competence, self-efficacy, self-respect and positive self-image among tribal children in general. Such attempts are also highly likely to provide tribal children with a culturally meaningful, ecologically valid and economically viable altertribal to life by reinforcing the dignity of their culture and identity. Ever increasing contact of tribals with the outside world over the years hasintroduced several changes in their culture and life. These changes are reflected in their psychological characteristics also. Studies (e.g. Mishra et al 1996) indicate that their ways of perceiving the world, categorizing objects, interpreting pictures, and strategies of learning and memory become more similar to those with whom they interact and negotiate their life in these changed circumstances. This suggests that tribal children can acquire all those skills that the members of other groups of the society possess. What is important on our part is to develop apositive frame of mind about tribal children. This is possible only through sensitivity to tribal culture and life, recognition of the cognitive strengths of tribal children, and appreciation of their personality qualities. Efforts in these directions will be very helpful in organizing the programme of tribal education as well as promoting economic and other aspects of tribal development.

Similarly a clear policy for language use in schools has to be developed. Research evidence suggests that significantly fewer students drop out of schools in which the language of tribal groups is used for instruction at the primary level. Development of primers in the tribal dialect involving content fromthe local context will go a long way in ensuring children's active participation in the learning process in school. While there is a general need for improvement in physical facilities in all schools in remote tribal regions, change in perceptions and outlooks of teachers about tribal children are equally important. Teachers must be sensitized to the cultural and behavioural strengths of tribal children and motivated to do their best for them in schools. Incentives should be initiated to attract effective teachers to work in tribal schools and to retain them there. Only such motivated teachers are likely to generate interest among tribal children towards schools education by attempting to link the contents of the curriculumwith the existing realities of tribal communities through the use of innovative technologies.

17

Institutional Care and Tribal Education: A Sociological Study on Ashram Schools in Karnataka

—*Amarnath R. Das and N. Srider*

Introduction

The Education backwardness of Scheduled tribes has its roots in the socio-economic and cultural setting in which the tribal people live. In India they remained isolated for a long time and were confined to the their traditional economic activites such as food gathering, hunting, fishing, shifting cultivation and landless agricultural labour. The primitive conditions of the tribal life, their univerability to exploitation and the existing socio psychological barriers developed through prolonged isolation, had clear manifestation in the life they led.

The tribal areas have failed to attract resource personnel and infrastructure facilities. As the areas were thinly populated, the burden on the infrastructure will be heavier. This has retarded the process of educational development of the tribal children. The education imparted to the tribal children is one of non-tribal in nature and hardly attract the tribal children. The lack of interaction with societies outside the tribal enclaves, made the tribal people develop their own sub-cultures, ethos, language, social, political and economic organisations which were predominantly 'backward'. Thus emerged was the inequality based on differential access to education.

The planning in the post-independent era stressed the all round development of the backward sections of the society, through provision of additional inputs for their educational, economic and ultimately social Upliftment. This became the national focal and also the social obligation of the national and state governments. Ashram Schools were introduced during Second Five –year plan assumed special importance during Fifth Five-year plan period. In Karnataka, within two decades, Ashram Schools went up from 62 schools with 340 students to 79 schools with 4400 pupils by 1994-95.

Ashram Schools provides conducive atmosphere for the deprived tribal students who are handicapped by their home environment and condition which are not conducive for their successful continuance of studies. Ashram School is a place of formal instructions as well as wholesome living. The teachers are expected to live with the students and to have closed, prolonged interactions so as to imbibe in them proper aspirations, attitudes, towards education and lire. The institutional care was visualised to provide proper socialization, which is not available in their disadvantaged homes. The Ashram Schools were expected to provide motivation and inspiration for the children to continue their studies without dropping midway. The education in the Ashram was to bring about all round development of the Tribal children. Life in the Ashram School, was to provide effective socialization, so as to enable them to form proper attitudes, aspirations, awareness, values towards education, employment and life.

The review of various surveys and studies by most of scholars has pointed the continued backwardnes of tribal children in education. These studies have examined the educational advancement of STs in terms of equality of opportunity. The Ashram Schools which came as a special input for the Tribal children during the Second Five Year Plan and got expanded in the Fifth Five Year Plan in Karnataka. There was no study on Ashram Schools except that of G. Ananda (1988). The studies did not examine the qualitative changes that accrue to the Tribal children through the provisin of Ashram School and raise such questions as:

1. What qualitative changes have accrued by the provision of Ashram Schools.
2. To what extent Ashram. School is functional altertribal agency of socialization to the disadvantaged tribal children to attain edccational equality.

The socio-economic variance among S.Ts has handicapped their home environment to be effective socialization agency to pave way for their educational progress. This has resulted in the provision of Ashram Schools which were perceived not merely as shelter homes to provide food, clothing, but also to be an alter tribal socialization agency to socialize the Tribal children to form proper attitudes, awareness, value-orientation for their educational, economic and above all social Upliftment.

This paper seeks to examine the aspirations attitudes, awareness, value-orientation among the tribal children to see the socialisation provided by Ashram Schools. It also examine whether Ashram has become effective functional alter tribal to the handicapped home environment of the tribal children.

Methodology

The study was conduct of on a sample of 270 inmates of nine Ashram Schools located in the four districts of the three divisions of Bangalore, Bangalore (rural), Mysore and Tumkur divisions of Karnataka State.

Results and Discussion:

1. Aspiration

The level of aspiration is psychological conduct that reflects a cognitive type of motivation of the individual. According to O.D. Pandey (1988) "the task of education is to develop right aspirations necessary for favorable character formation and to prepare him for the correct and courageous solution of the problems of life."

The table-1 reveals that 53.79% of the respondents had considered getting through the examination as their immediate aspiration. The immediate aim of 20.74% Ashramites was to continue education at any cost. Most of the respondents, in spite of being first generation learners have expressed that getting through the examination and continuing their education as their immediate aspiration. This reflects the keen interest of the tribal children in education. The aim of the remaining 25.56% of the respondents was to get better social status. From this, it is obvious that the tribal students have even recognized the importance of education as a tool that helps in enchancing their social status and mobility.

The analysis of the means chosen by the respondents to achieve their aspirations in life, has revealed that, about 58.52% of the respondents had chosen hard work as the means to attain their immediate aim; of them 28.15% aspired to take their teacher's help, as against 9.26% who were eager to take their parents help and only 4.07% wanted to take private tutions to perform better in their studies. It can be inferred that the Ashram Schools have not only succeeded in inculcating sound aspirations in the respondents but also made them evince their interest in education.

Along with the aspirations, the level of self-confidence of the Ashramites to get through the examination is also analysed. From the analysis it was learnt that nearly half of the respondents, have their studies seriously and have reported that they are certainly confident of getting through the examination.

A majority of the respondents despite facing one problem of the other in studies were confident of getting through the examinations. This is an indicator of the self-confidence of the respondents. The Ashram Schools by imbibing self-confidence in the inmates certainly enhance their chances of continuing studies. Finally, the role of the Ashram School in influencing the aspirational level of the respondents in analyzed. From the analysis of Ashram Schools in influencing the aspiration level of respondents it is clear that about two-thirds of the respondents have perceived the Ashram School as an agency influencing the inculation of positive aspirations, right aspirations in them.

2. Attitude

One of the notable problems of education of the Tribals, especially in the rural areas is that majority of the parents are illiterates and think that there is no demand for education in their environmental needs.

Their socio-economic condition is such that the parents are indifferent to education. Hence the tribal students find their families handicapped socially and economically. To overcome this handicap the Government has provided a few educational inputs. One such input is the Ashram School. These Ashram

Schools are required to function as an alter tribal socializing agency to the ill equipped home environment enabling the inmates to form proper attitudes, aspirations and value orientation.

An attitude scale consisting of positive and negative statements was prepared to examine the attitude level of the students. The attitude scale included statements pertaining to equality, special privileges, Ashram Schools facility, the benefits of schooling, traditional occupation and last but not the least education and their future. These were computed and a range of attitude score was presented.

As depicted in Table-2, the attitude of the Ashramites revealed that 72.59% of them obtained scores ranging between 49 to 60 an indicator of very favorable attitude. Next came 15.93% of respondents, who obtained scores ranging between 36-48 having favorable attitude. 7.04% of the respondents scored between 24-36 mark which is deemed as unfavorable attitude and a very small percentage of 4.44% respondents exhibited strong unfavorable attitude by scoring marks ranging between 12024. It can be emphatically inferred that the Ashram School have succeeded in inculacting lproper behaviour traits in the respondents. This is reflected by the very favourable level of attitude, the respondents had developed.

Awareness

The analysis of the awareness is aimed at knowing the level of awareness among the Ashramites about the problems of their society in general and their community problems in particular.

From the analysis, it is learnt that a majority (54.07%) of the respondents has considered poverty as the main problem of our society. To 17.47% of respondents it is illiteracy followed by unemployment (11.48%), population (10.75%) and casteism (6.29%). On the whole, the tribal people it seems have perceived poverty as the main problem of our society. Regarding the problems of Tribals as large as 74.81% hold poverty as the major problem followed by ignorance (15.19%) and illiteracy (10.00%).

Secondly, a glance at their awareness of the provisions of redressal revealed the fact that they are aware of the provisions of redressal.

Finally, the analysis of the awareness of the respondents about the reasons for their poor performance in the school, it was learnt that the STs. Are aware of the problems that haunt them? Prominent among these is their economic problem. The next in the order is poor parental motivation and lack of interest.

Despite facing a series of problems the respondents were reported confident enough in competing with other castes in education. This change in self-confidence of the tribal people has definitely been brought about by the education. Given the equality of opportunity and the needed inputs and encouragement they can come up on par with other castes in academic achievement.

3.Value Orientation

Value orientation is the process of educating and conditioning the mind to understand the values, foster them and translate them into action. An attempt has been made here to examine the value-orientation of the Ashramites. Form the analysis, it is evident that the respondents in spite of their poor socio-economic condition and handicapped home environment have developed right values in life. Of the respondents 58.52% have considered money as the most valuable thing in life. It reflects the poor socio-economic condition of the respondents. Other things considered most valuable by the respondents include happiness (19.62%), peaceful life (12.22%), power (5.56%), equality (2.96%) and liberty (1.11%).

The value attached by the respondents to education is to get knowledge and to know reading and writing. It also signifies qualifying for a job, besides getting scholarship. The value attached to employment is to earn livelihood. Besides these a tiny fraction of them had the value of contributing something productive to the society and to help their parents. On the whole two thirds of the respondents have developed right values in life.

4.Index of Socialisation

Socialisation is a process to meet twin situation of a group, to perpetuate the existing mores, norms and practices on the one hand and transference of knowledge on the other. One results into value orientation and the other in training the younger generation for all functions to be performed for the survival of the group-a family, a community and a nation. The agencies through which socialisation is carried out are also equally important-parents, peer groups, teachers, elders and religious leaders are normally accepted by the child.

As the Tribal children are handicapped by their home environment, the Ashram Schools are required to function as an alter tribal socialising agency to home. To know whether the Ashram Schools function as an alter tribal socialising agency to home, an index of socialisation containing 14 items is prepared and the respondents were required to rank their choices as to what socialises them among the three agencies of socialisation viz, home, Ashram School, and peer group.

As depicted in table-3, the first item in the index of socialisation is sanitation. The ranks given by the Ashramites for sanitation include 82.59% of the respondents have given first rank to their Ashram School followed by home (15.19%) and peer group (2.22%).

It can be inferred that as far as sanitation is concerned, the Ashram School makes good the handicap at home environment of the Tribals. The young generation not only knows the importance of sanitation through Ashram Schools but also their fellow Tribals to maintain hygienic conditions.

About 57.04% of the Ashramites have given first rank to their home as an agent socialising them with regard to eating habits followed by Ashram School (38.02%) and peer group (4.44%) When it comes to dressing habits 67.41% of the Ashramites have given first ranks to their Ashram Schools followed by home (21.85%) and peer group (13.33%).

On the whole, Ashram School with a total of 65.85% of the first ranks stands first as an agent of socialization influencing the individual practices of the respondents. Home with 22.22% of first ranks is considered as the second agency and peer group as an agent of socialisation occupies the lowest position with 11.93% first ranks.

Other items grouped under the heading social practice include conformity to norms, obedience, way of interaction, and religion. About 57.04% of the first ranks, regarding conformity to norms, have gone to the home followed by Ashram School

(31.85%) and group (11.11%). Regarding obedience 69.26% of the first ranks have been captured by home while Ashram School has captured 30.74%.

About 53.33% of the respondents have given first rank to Ashram School an agent influencing the way of interaction followe by home (30.74%) and peer group (15.93%). As large as 82.23% of the first ranks have gone to home as an agent influencing religion followed by lpeer group (13.70%) and Ashram School (4.07%).

On the whole it is clear that, as far as the social practices are concerned, the home with a shar of 66.0% first ranks occupies the first place as an agent influencing the social practices. Ashram Schools whose share of the first rank is 42.59% follow lit and the peer group with a share of 8.51% first ranks occupied the third spot as an agent least influencing the socialisation process.

Other items in the index of socialisation grouped under the heading personality development include motivation and morals.

About 67.78% of the Ashramites have given first ranks to Ashram schools as an agent of socialisation influencing motivation followed by lpeer group (17.78%) and home (14.44%).

Ashram School lis also recognised as an agent of socialisation influencing the morals of the inmates. This is evident by the 72.96% of the first ranks it got in its favour. It is followed by peer group (19.26%) and home (7.78%).

As far as the personality development items are concerned the Ashram School with a share of 70.37% first ranks is considered as the prime agent of socialisation followed by peer group (18.52%) and home (11.11%). Socialisation of values related to the attitutdes, aspirations and values that include items like value of education, dignity of labour, equality and rights are also analysed.

About 80.37% of the Ashramites perceived Ashram School as the prime agency of socialisation influencing the value of education followed by peer group (12.59%) and home (7.04%). About 61.11% of the respondents have given first ranks to the Ashram School in socialising them about the dignity of self. Peer group with (25.07%) stands second and home with (14.82%) is lpushed to the third place.

About equality, 70.00% of the first ranks have gone to the Ashram School, 17.41% have gone to the home and the rest 12.59% to the peer group. Taking into account the right, 77.04% of the first ranks have gone to the Ashram School followed by peer group (12.59%) and home (10.37%).

The share of first of the Ashram School accounts to 71.73%. It is followed by home with 16.60% and peer group with a share of only 11.67% assumes a lower importace in the socialisation of the above said items.

On the whole, form the analysis it is evident that with regard to the individual practices, personality development, formation of proper attitudes, aspirations and values a greater part of socialisation is done by the Ashram School. The influence of home has thus become secondary.

Considering the attitude of the tribal parents towards the education of their wards one can say that the tribal children are severely handicapped by their home environment.Ashram Schools have come lup as an effective socialising agent to socialise the respondents as far as their personality development, apirations, attitudes and value orientations are concerned. Moreover, greater part of the socialisation of the Ashramites is being done by the Ashram Schools.

Taking into account the overall influence of the agencies of socialisation as evident from the ranking of the Ashramites it can be emphatically said that Ashram School has been functioning as an effective socialising agent to the ill-equipped home or disadvantaged home.

To sum up, the functional analysis of the Ashram School in terms of the aspirations, attitudes, awareness and as a socialising agent of the respondents brings forth the following observations:

1. An analysis of the aspirations of the respondents has showed that the aspirations of the Ashramites are very higher than that aspired by their parents. This can be attributed to the influence of the Ashram School;

2. The parents are not interested in providing education to their children. The respondents are thus severely handicapped by the lack of parental motivation;
3. An analysis of the attitudes of the respondents has revealed that 72.59% of them had very fair attitude while 19.93% had fair attitude;
4. From the analysis of their awareness it is clear that they have perceived poverty (54.07%) as the main problem of the Indian society. Other in the order of their preference are: illiteracy (17.47%), unemployment (11.48%), population (10.75%) and casteism (6.29%);
5. About the problems of STs, 74.81% of the respondents had preceived poverty as the main problem followed by ignorance (15.19%) and illiteracy (10.0%);
6. The STs are aware of the provisions of redressal;
7. The respondents have owed their poor performance in the school to their poverty (55.33%) followed by lpoor parental motivation (34.82%) and lack of interest (11.85%);
8. An analysis of the index of socialisation reveals that a greater part of socialisation on individual practices, personality development, formation of right attitudes, aspirations is done by the Ashram Schools followed by their homes and peer group. But as far as the socialisation of social practices are concerned the home has pushed the Ashram School to the second position.

Conclusion

The above findings suggest that the Ashram School is functional enough and has attained the status to be a truly social institution of enduring nature, to replace family followed by lpeer group as an agency of socialisation. The Ashram Schools are designed to suit the tribal milieu. But adequate attention is not given to the craft based education. Given the inadequacies in meeting the tribal needs and such other limitations, the Ashram Schools can, at most be, viewed as supplementary socialising agency than as a functional altertribal to the home. This necessitates a few qualitative changes in the functioning of the Ashram Schools to make them trualy functional.

Table 1. Immediate aspirations of the respondents

aspiration	*Boys(%)*	*Girls(%)*	*Total(%)*
To get through the examination	83 (56.08)	62 (50.82)	145 (53.79)
To continue education	291 9.60	27 22,13	56 20.74
To get better social status	36 24.32	33 27.05	69 25.56
Any other	—	—	—
totsl	148 100.0	122 100.0	270 100.0

Table 2. Range of Attitude Scores of Respondents

Score and Range of Score of the Respondents	*Boys (%)*	*Girls (%)*	*Total (%)*
Very-poor (12-140)	3(2.03)	9(7.38)	12(4.44)
Poor (25-36)	8(5.41)	11(9.01)	19(7.04)
Fair (37-48)	29(19.59)	14(11.48)	43(15.93)
Very Fair (49.60)	108(72.97)	88(72.13)	196(72.59)
Total (%)	148(100.0)	122(100.0)	270(100.0)

Table 3. Percentage of 1st Ranks Obtained by the Socialising Agencies

(Percentage in Brackets)

Practices	*Item/Agency of socialisation*	*Home*	*A survey in school*	*Total (%) Group*
Individual practices	Sanitation	41 (15.19)	223 (82.59)	6 (2.22)
	Eating Habits	154 (57.04)	164 *38.52)	12 (4.44)
	Dressing Habits	50 (21.85)	182 (67.41)	29 (10.74)

Practices	*Item/Agency of socialisation*	*Home*	*A survey in school*	*Total (%) Group*
	Reading Habits	31 (11.48)	194 (71.85)	45 (16.67)
Social Practices	Confirmity of norms	156 (57.04)	86 (31.85)	30 (11.11)
	Obedience	187 (69.26)	86 (31.85)	—
	Way of interaction	144 (53.33)	83 (30.74)	43 (15.93)
	Religion	222 (82.23)	83 (30.74)	37 (13.70)
Personality Development	Motivation	39 (14.44)	11 (4.07)	48 (17.78)
	Morals	21 (7.78)	183 (67.78)	52 (19.26)
Values	Value of Education	19 (7.04)	197 (72.96)	34 (12.59)
	Dignity of Self	40 (14.82)	217 (80.37)	65 (25.07)
	Equality	47 (17.41)	165 (61.11)	34 (12.59)
	Rights	28 (10.37)	129 (70.0)	34 (12.59)

18

Problems in Educating Tribal Children: The Dongria Kondh Experience

—Akshaya K. Kanungo

After India attained her Independence and Constitution framed in 1950, the universalisation of Primary education has become one of the priorities of development. Huge amount of money earmarkedand spent on undertaking many schemes and programs that went begging with little success in areas of educational development. Analysis of the educational scenario of the country reveals that there is a huge gap between rural and urban literacy. Further going down the ladder, the educational attainment and literacy of Scheduled Castes and Scheduled tribes is far low and abnormal. Development practitioners and academia relates poverty and underdevelopment to lack of spread of education as the foremost reason. The Government at Center is always in pressure to revise policies and devise new strategies to curb the regional disparity that exists in educational development in the country. Orissa is the homeland of as many as 32 tribal communities who reside in nooks and corners of the State. Almost 13 such communities are declared as primitive, basing on their low educational achievement and economic practices. The "Dongria Kondh" which is a sub-tribe of 'KONDH' is declared as primitive tribe. They reside mostly in the Southern part of the State and known for their infamous human sacrifice during British colonization in India and even before that. They are mainly concentrated in the Niyamgiri hill ranges, which covers parts of K. Singpur, Bissam Cuttack blocks of Rayagada district. And live in hill slopes surrounded by dense forests. Their name is derived from word "Dongar" which means hill slopes where they cultivate. They have a subsistence economy based mainly on shifting cultivation and hunting gathering. Besides by now they have become skilled horticulturists. The Kondhs once infamous for their pernicious practice of human sacrifice and female infanticide identified as early as August 1836 by Mr. Russell, a British official under Madras Presidency in British Colonization in India. It was of deep concern for the British Government to stamp out the barbarous practices to restore peace and order in the territory.

The somatoscopic and anthropometric data of the Kondhs relate them to the proto- Australoid racial stock with considerable Mongoloid admixture. The Dongria Kondh mainly concentrates in the southern administrative district Rayagada, one of the 30 districts of the state of Orissa of India. Orissa is situated at the eastern part of India on the coastline of the Bay of Bengal, 500 kilometers south of Calcutta Metro. The state is known worldwide for the seat of Lord Jagannath and for the temple of Konark, music engraved on stone. The Dongria Kondh is a marginal indigenous tribal community in the state having concentrated in the plateau of Niyamgiri hill range, which covers two blocks of Rayagada District. They live in hill ranges situated at a highest of 1000-4970 feet above sea level. Two Micro projects on Dongria have been established. They cover 112 villages and hamlets and 1813 families with a total population of 8042 as per the latest survey. (*Source D.K.D.A., Chatikona and Parasali*). The male and female ratio stands as 1000:1030. There has been no enumeration of population by the State Government on Individual tribal communities since 1981. In the Rayagada Division where the Dongrias exist, Sal (*Shorea Robusta*) is the dominant species and common associates of Sal like Bija or Piasol (*Ptero carpus Arcupium*), Teak (*Tectona Gradis*), Mohua (*Modhuka Latijolia*), Kendu (*Diospyros Melanoxylon*), Mango (*Mangifera Indica*) are found in plenty. The Dongria villages and habitations are located in a tangle of thickly wooded hill ranges, which is determined by availability of perennial streams and sufficient land for shifting cultivation. A village has minimum two separate wards, one inhabited by the Dongria Kondh and the other by Domb, a scheduled caste community. The houses are generally mud-built and straw-thatched, although now a days, some brick-built straw-thatched houses are made by the Dongrias. The road communication network has not been developed much even after 50 years of independence of India. The dress and ornaments, which adore the Dongrias, are distinguishable from other sections of the tribe. Dongria males put a narrow scarf wrapped around the waist and often a leaf rolled cigarette (*pika*) will be seen tucked in the hair-knot at the back. Invariably all of them carry on axe on the shoulder and a knife is kept hanging from the waist belt. The women wear a lower garment not long enough to hide their knee. They use their chest with a small band of cotton cloth tied at the back. All these garments are woven by neighboring schedule caste community. All the male and female members wear hair-clips on their head and often pierce their ears and love to wear as many earrings as they can. The women folk wear big neck rings made up of aluminum and iron.

They beatify themselves with traditional hand-woven multi coloured embroidered scarf, which is a rare specialty of the Dongria Kondh tribe. The installation of "Dharnipenu" and her consort "Kotiasal" in the centre of the village street is a typical feature of Dongria settlement. Invariably the maiden's dormitory, which is present in each Dongria settlement also, adds to the specialties of Dongria social structure and culture. In the dormitory, the maiden girls are trained about their norms, values and taboos by a senior, often married, women who is the leader of the dormitory. The dormitory is the source of mostly cultural education orally transmitted for learning folklore, riddles, proverbs, legends, myths and songs amidst singing and dancing with boy and girl friends that take place every night. They are grown there until they attain marriageable age and by the time they acquire all the skills and knowledge that are expected from a good ideal wife/woman in their society. Dongrias have a distinct skill of horticulture, which separates them from all other tribals in the state. They know their soil condition and grow many fruits of high commercial value. They grow pineapple, banana, jackfruit, *and papaya* in plenty. They also grow high quality turmeric and ginger that has the highest demand in the state. Despite that, due to no marketing facility they often get very low price for their produce and all the profit is usurped by the middlemen. Dongrias practise shifting or *podu* cultivation as it is called. They produce varieties of crops like maize, *ganja*, *ragi*, grams, etc. They also practice hunting and gathering. Gathering of forest produce like Siali creepers, Kendu leaf, Sal leaf, seeds of Karanja (*Pongnamia glatera*) and Mohua (*Bassia latifolia*) is made for daily domestic requirements. Dongrias drink liquor very often prepared from Mohua, Sago palm juice and datepalm juice. Dongrias rear pig, cattle, buffalo, goat and fowl. These animals and birds meet their nutritional protein requirement. But most importantly these animals and birds are sacrificed before the spirits and ghosts on the occasion of propitiation on account of family members falling sick. Sickness of any sort is attributed as the effect or wrath of spirits, ghosts due to breach of norms, known or unknown. The Dongria family is normally simple nuclear family consisting of father, mother and their unmarried children. Extended families are rare due to the fact that it needs big houses to accommodate all members which is a rare probability and often dangerous on a hill top with rugged level. The Dongria family is patrilocal and patrilineal.

The Dongria Kondh have their own dialect "KUVI" which has no script. Their culture is as strengthened as any one's with songs, riddles, proverbs, myths, legends, dances and full of literacy works which are generally transmitted orally from one generation to another. Each of these piece of literature are often based on and linked to tress, animals, birds, streams, etc., in the forest which form the part of their ecology and environment. Therefore forest and tribal are in separable and forest plays the pivotal role in shaping their society and culture. The tribal people are highly religious by the fact that their society and culture is totally governed by religious beliefs and practices. They see their world full of mysteries governed by deities, spirits, and ghosts; both benevolent and malevolent. Each and every natural object; animate or inanimate is attributed to be the abode of some sort of deities, spirits, ghosts; is worshipped and propitiated with prescribed norms. Deviation of any such norm by any member of society is dealt with impurity. The Dongria Kondh family is nuclear and polygynous. The woman is more diligent and hard working in comparison to their male counterparts. She does all sorts of household work ranging from fetching water from distant streams to prepare foods for family members, from taking care of brothers and sisters to working along with other male members in the field. Therefore, she is treated as an economic asset to the family. Due to this reason girl child is preferred over boy child in Dongria Kondh community. Further the prevailing marriage practice among the Dongrias go in favor of women. The parents yield a lot of money through bride price that is given by the groom's parent as part of the marriage deal. The Dongria Kondhs being conservative and educationally backward live in relative isolation from other people of the area. However due to various state development interventions like development in communication, i.e., construction of Roadsand Bridges, opening of offices for launching of various welfare schemesand programs by Government, they are relatively exposed to the outside world. These interventions effected in thinning down of forest base and deforestation due to indiscriminate cutting of trees by unscrupulous contractors. Wide spread deforestation has led to shrinking of their subsistence base, poverty and unemployment leaving their society exposed to widespread discrimination, exploitation by other people of the area. Education (Modern) does not seem to be the priority of D. Kondh community. They disvalue formal primary education because of lack of awareness and cultural orientation. Studies on their view of a happy life reveal they certainly prefer to have more of, forestlands where shifting cultivation can be practiced, fruit bearing trees for collection and consumption, wild animals and birds to hunt and more nos. of children to work for the household and run their progeny. It is worth describing their system of education here.

In Dongria Kondh, the dormitory system is there to orient boys and girls to acquire skills and knowledge that is required to be a full phased member of their society. There are separate dormitories for boys and girls in each village. After returning from fields, they stay together in the dormitory and in an informal ways, i.e., through songs, dance, riddles, proverbs, gossip etc. which are transmitted orally from generation to generation. The whole night in spent amidst dancing and singing, travelling to other dormitories and interacting with boys and girls over there. By the by when they turn to adulthood they master their arts, traditions and customs and command respect as a bonafide member of their community. Therefore sending children to school is a worthless investment for parents. Because, not only he/she is deprived of helping their parents in sibling care and household works and learning basic skills of their society but also the family looses an able hand from the household and by thus a lot of income. If we consider the teacher and taught relationship, the teacher or instructor (most often non-tribal) is like a foreigner and looked suspiciously by the students and the community. His language, etiquetteand manners are regarded as unusual and quite different from the tribal ways of life.

The ethnocentric attitude of the teachers towards tribal society and culture also aggravates and worsen the situation. He does not have meetings and interactions with people around him to gain their confidence. He often creates fear psychosis among pupils by castigating and punishing them in classrooms using derogatory and sensitive comments about their life styles. That fear and inferiority complex created among students cause massive scale dropouts among Dongria Kondh students, specially the girls who are enrolled at an over-aged stage and close to the age of puberty. Therefore, at one end the school environment and attitude of teachers pushes them out of schools and all the other their love for freedom and forest based life pulls them out of the formal schooling environment. The situation is not better of or different where even a tribal teacher having a positive out look and dedicated approach is working. The tribal children have a year round season of forest based collection and festivals. Accompanying parents at tender ages to forest yield more forest collection of fruits, roots tubersand leaves, which in turn gives better economic property to family parental care is ample for children except sending children to school which has no tangible immediate gains for parents. There are few parents who have been mobilized and have got the conviction to educate their children. But in school the children find language as the greatest problem hence other curricular transactions meaningless.

The standard language text book, its unfamiliar contents, contexts and picturisations depicts a whole range of foreignness and unfamiliarity for which the students lack interest and achieve nothing. The teacher centered monologue class room transactions throws the pupils into absolute poor achievement in tests fear or it is sea ore of and failure in examination is another most important reasons of dropouts from school among Dongria Kondh children. Above all, the students find the subjects, contentsand contexts not linked to their real life experiences and extremely monotonous and boring. Those reasons are so strong that, even in residential schools run by Department of Welfare, Govt. of Orissa, with all sorts facilities like free food, free reading- writing materials and other basic requirements like sitting mat, uniform, blankets, beds, etc., the enrollment, attendance and achievement of students are far from satisfactory. The irony is that there is no supervision or monitoring of the works of Teachers and school management by the personnel who are supposed to be the decision-makers in the system. The lack of performance of the schooling system is always attributed to the lack of interest of the poverty and community for their children's education rather than the whole range of faulty planning and implementation by the Government.

Suggestions

The schooling facility must be provided on demand of community and community must be mobilized enough to spontaneously come forward to run and manage the school. The children should be provided text books in their own language in initial stages of their schooling and gradually they should be exposed to standard text books in state language at a later stage. The textbooks should be local specific contents, contexts and narration by which the children can relate their learning to their real life situation. The timing of the school should be as per the availability of children and holiday calendar as per the holiday pattern of the locality. The teacher belonging to the community should be posted if not a teacher having a positive attitude and some understanding about tribal community should be employed in the area. Moreover the education administrators should be more responsive and responsible to the education of the children with special needs close and continuous monitoring of schools (academicand administrative) would definitely render insights to the problem and it's solutions at the earliest.

19

Formal Education among the Mahadev Koli Community

—Jugnu Hydari and Hemant Apte

An ethnographic study was conducted among Mahadev Kolis in December, 2005, in Aghane, Done and Pimpergane villages in Ambegaon Taluka, Pune District. Observation, in-depth interviews, key informant interviews were used to collect data from school teachers, students and parents of school going children.

The main objectives were to study the various aspects of formal education, methods of imparting knowledge and bringing about awareness including structure and function of the educational institutions at the primary and pre-primary level.

There are two primary schools, run by Zilla Parishad in Done and Pimpargane, and one school set up by Shaswat (NGO) in Aghane. All primary schools have classes from 1st to 4th standard and have two teachers; one of them acts as the headmaster. School timings are between 10.30 a.m. to 5 p.m., syllabus is as per the prescription of the Education Department. Subjects that are taught include Marathi (local language), English, Mathematics, Science, Geography and History. Extra-curricular activities consist of sports. Students are provided with daily meal and nutritious food once a week. In the Government schools, scholarships provide incentive for learning. Gram Shikshak Samiti and Palak Sabha monitor the activities of the schools and performance of students.

Anganwadis and Balwadis at the pre-primary level cater to children below 6 years of age. They are taught songs, stories with morals and prayers. There is one teacher and a helper.

Ashramshalas have also been set up by the Government where students are given residential facility and are provided education up to the 8th class. Parents are becoming more aware of the importance of education and are beginning to play an active role. It is seen that more boys go for higher education than girls, as they get married at a younger age.

Introduction

From the anthropological point of view, the educational process is to be understood as a comprehensive system involving the entire community, including all agents and institutions which are explicitly educational. Education helps not only in the socialization of children and the development of human personality, but also plays a crucial role in social mobility, occupational change and most importantly, social awareness. As education is the very factor that shapes our lives to such a large extent, it is important that it be studied in every context. The present study was conducted in the Villages of Aghane, Pimpargane and Don, which are villages located in Ambegaon Tehsil of Pune district in Maharashtra and focuses on the Formal Education system among the Mahadev Koli community. The study was conducted during a stay of ten days from 13th to 24th Dec 2005.

1.1 Education - Defined:

Education as defined by Herskovitz is said to be *"That part of the enculturative experience that throughout the learning process equips an individual to take his place as a member of society."*

The word education is derived from the Latin word educare meaning "to raise", "to bring up". In recent times, the myth has arisen of its derivation from a different verb: "to lead out or "to lead forth". This false etymology is used to bolster one of the theories behind the function of education – to develop innate abilities and expand horizons.

Education can also then be said to be a process either formal or informal, which finally shapes the potential of a maturing organism.

1.2 Formal and Informal Education:

Formal education refers to an organized system of training and developing knowledge skills, mind, and character of an individual. It is thus a conscious effort by human society to impart the skills and modes of thought considered essential for social functioning. It refers to a structured educational system provided by the state for children, and occurs when society or a group or an individual sets up a curriculum to educate people.

In contrast, Informal education refers to education which takes place outside of the formally organized school, and refers to the system wherein one learns from the family, habitat and kin group. This type of cultural learning from one generation to another has three components:

1. Post-Figurative Culture: In which children are essentially educated by their parents.
2. Con-Figurative Culture: In which parents and children learn from their peers.
3. Figurative Culture: In which adults also learn from their children.

Informal education also refers to the process of enculturation. Enculturation continues throughout the life of the individual, it includes not only the training he receives but also the assimilation of such elements in his culture as he acquires by observation and assimilation.

1.3 Objectives of the Study:

- To study the structure and functioning of the schools in Aghane, Pimpargane and Don Villages.
- To try and understand the methods of teaching and imparting education to the youth as well as the syllabus and other aspects of the enculturation process.
- To understand the levels of awareness among the people and what is the extent to which education is given importance, and higher education encouraged.
- To understand the reasons for educational deprivations among the tribals as well as government efforts in the betterment of the education system.

1.4 Informal Approach to Tribal Education:

The Indian constitution gives privileged status to the disadvantaged groups, and this has been primarily done due to historical reasons. The content and orientation of tribal education has to be geared up according to the social conditioning in which the tribal people live in accordance with. Hence the main objective of traditional tribal institutions has always been to educate and train their children in economic pursuits or make them skilled in traditional occupations. Since many tribal communities have only a dialect and not a written language, most of the education is conducted through non literacy or non reading methods. The vocation and craft needed information regarding designs and techniques had to be disseminated orally and memorized by the students.

Education thus plays a crucial role in socializing and thereby controlling the new generation in certain more important and core areas of social life, and prepares them to be able to adjust to change. Education thus moulds and develops the personality of the members of the new generation, but does not necessarily mould them according to the desires of the individual. Essentially, it tries to find out what sort of personality is expected by society as a whole, and tries to mould it according to societal expectations.

As the main goal of tribal societies is the maintenance of stability and continuity, the main function of education is to transmit its cultural heritage to the new generation and mould and control it according to the norms values and traditions of society.

1.5 Education in the Indian context:

The Indian education system is largely concerned with the existing formal structure of education which according to B.A. Deshmukh refers to "an organized system of training and developing knowledge, skills, mind and character etc. of individuals" and on the other hand the institutionalized methodology of imparting knowledge to individuals". Within this very system exist many sub groups of individuals with specific needs and tribal are one of them. For several historical, social and economic reasons, the scheduled groups have remained economically backward even to this day. This is with respect to their educational levels also.

Thus, although "Formal education is the key to all round human development, despite several campaigns to promote formal education, ever since independence the national literacy rates amongst tribal is 29.60% according to the 1991 census. The female literacy rate is only 18.19% and the male literacy rate is 40.65%.

"While literacy is only a means to education and not only an end in itself, education tends to lead to economic benefits which are the results of increased ability of the individual to utilize the information acquired through the process of learning"

National Council of Educational Research and Training

Therefore any educational planning for such a vast group of individuals should aim at educating all its members at the school going age group. Education is infact, an input not only for the economic development of tribes but also for inner strength of tribal communities, which eventually would help them meet the new challenges of life.

Tribal and Indian Constitution with regard to education

Education has been recognized as one of the key mechanisms for development for tribal and society at large. The constitutional provisions for tribal education are as follows:The framers of our constitution have given certain safeties and securities to the tribal.

The constitution in Article 46 observes, "The state shall promote with special care the educational and economic interest of the weaker sections of the people and in particular of the Schedule castes and Schedule tribes and shall protect them from social injustice and all forms of exploitation".

Article 29 guarantees "Educational and Cultural rights to all citizens". Article 45 is more specific regarding obligation of the state. It directs the state to provide with a period of 10 years from the commencement of the constitution, free and compulsory education up to the age of 14 years.

Additionally, the constitutional amendment bill 86, notified on December13th, 2002 provides for free and compulsory education, as a fundamental right for all children in the age group of 6-14 years.

The National Policy on Education (1986) ensures the following:

- Tribal are included in the national program of Sarva Shiksha Abhiyan run by the ministry of human resource development;
- Schools and hostels are opened in areas where no such facilities exist;
- At least one model residential school is located in each tribal concentrated area;
- Education is linked with provision of supplementary education;
- Special incentives like financial assistance, pocket allowance, free distribution of textbooks and school uniforms are provided;
- Teaching is imparted in the tribe's mother tongue at least up to the primary level. Educated tribal youth are given employment as teachers, wherever possible, (this will obviate the need to employ teachers belonging to far off places who find commuting as difficult as staying in a village with no basic amenities);
- Curriculum and co–curriculum include aspects of meta skill up gradation of tribal children;
- Curriculum for meta skill up gradation are to include aspects of tribals games and sports, archery, identification of plants of medical value, crafts art and culture, folk dance and folk songs, folk paintings etc.;
- Emphasis is laid on vocational/education. Polytechnics are set up for studies in subjects like forestry, horticulture, dairying, veterinary sciences.

1.7 Education and the need for its Planning:

Planning for education of children coming form tribal communities is not a simple task. Though the entire educational program for tribal children is looked after by the educational department yet a comprehensive picture is hardly available.

There are many activities related with education of tribal children which are managed by other departments.

For example, in almost all states primary institutions catering to the needs of children from tribal communities are looked after by the education department while Āshram schools are the responsibility of the tribal welfare departments, and pre-primary education of voluntary agencies or social welfare departments. Besides planning for ancillary services like scholarships, stipend, hostels, free book aid, mid-day mean etc. are done at the sate level, hence in order to plan for education of tribal children, it is necessary to study the linkages between different schemes.It is sad to note that this scheme, once approved is left to operate independently and no study is conducted to assess the effectiveness of such a scheme, this sometimes results in duplication and wastage in terns of efforts and inputs.

II) Methodology and tools and techniques used for Data Collection:

Thus the main tools used for data collection were:

2.1 Observation: This was primarily non participant, and thus observation was used to record location of the schools, the infrastructure and overall condition of schools as well as facilities that were provided to the students and educational material in terms of books, pencils, slates, uniforms and other writing material. Visual aids like posters, teaching aids and charts were observed which reflected directly on the content taught to students. Extra curricular activities and games like dodge ball and *kho kho* were also observed being played outside the school.

2.2 Photography: was an extremely useful tool as it helped obtain an immense amount of visual data. Thus while analyzing data photographs helped a great deal in getting a clearer picture of what the students were taught.

2.3 Interviews: were the tool through which most of the data was collected. Informal interviews with parents, headmasters of schools and a few children were undertaken. They reflected primarily people's views on the importance of education as well as their attitude towards it. With respect to interviews taken of the headmasters, they provided an insight into the functioning of the schools, their structure, government schemes their interpretations of these and most importantly the reasons for drop outs and educational deprivation.

2.4 Interviews with Key Informants:

As every individual varies with respect to knowledge of their own social and cultural systems, key informants were limited to headmasters of the schools and students. A total of 7 Key Informant Interviews were conducted.

(I) Formal Education in the villages of Don, Pimpargane and Aghane:

Formal education in the villages of Done, Pimpargane and Aghane consists of primary and pre primary education. Primary education consists of the first years of formal, structured education that occurs during childhood.

With reference to pre primary education in the villages, there are Balwadis and Anganwadis, and in the case of primary education there is one primary school from STD.I - IV in each village.

(A) PRIMARY EDUCATION

In Aghane the Primary school was set up by Shaswat an NGO working towards all round development in the village, whereas in the villages of Don and Pimpargane the schools have been set up by the government and hence are run by the Zilla Parishad.

Description and Location of Schools

All the schools were more or less centrally located; hence they were easily accessible to most of the students. All the schools had a small area outside so that children could play and be entertained. They played games here as well as had their P.E. lessons held here. Each school had 2 classrooms, and since the schools were from STD.I - IV, one classroom would be shared among two classes, usually STD.I - II shared a classroom, and STD.III - IV shared the other. Outside the classrooms there was a verandah wherein children used to sit and write there exams, being supervised by their teacher. Each school had a flag post outside it, in front of the school. The walls of the schools, outside as well as inside the classrooms had various kinds of teaching aids like posters with geographical maps, alphabets, number names, prayers etc. for the purpose of learning; children are constantly internalizing colourful posters and other visual aids, thus enabling them to grasp concepts easily, and making learning more fun.

1.1 N.G.O. School in Aghane Village:

The primary school in Aghane was started in the year 2002 by Shaswat, and the class wise strength in 2005-06 is presented below:

Table 1. Class wise strength of the school in Aghane

Class	*Girls*	*Boys*	*Total*
Std. I	8	3	11
Std. II	3	4	7
Std. III	3	4	7
Std. IV	2	1	3
Total	16	12	28

There are usually two teachers in each school, the headmaster and an additional teacher. The teachers need to have passed the Std. XII exam or SSC exam, as well as have a Diploma in Education (DEd) The subjects taught are Math, Science, History, Geography, English, and Marathi, which is also the medium of instruction. Extra curricular activities consist of games like kho-kho, kabaddi, cricket, longjumps, and skipping. Besides these physical activities the children are taught songs, prayers, bhajans, stories with morals and poems. Arts and crafts are also encouraged. Ethno-medicine is also taught in the school.Students are provided with 2 uniforms a year, they are also provided with hair oil, soap and books. Shashwat has also set up a hostel for girls living in Pimpargane, Navade and Ahupe. In terms of meals they are provided with two meals a day, i.e. consisting of *bhaji, bhakri*, *vatana* and *bhat.* A non-vegetarian meal is provided once a month consisting of chicken and egg. Breakfast consists mainly of *rava,* and *poha*. Children are also provided with milk daily. Medical check ups are also stressed upon in the school.

1.2 The Zilla Parishad Schools in the villages of Don and Pimpargane:

The schools run by the Zilla Parishad also have two teachers each, one of whom is the head master of the school. However their appointment differs from that of the teachers in the school at Aghane. The school teachers here are appointed on the basis of merit in the D.Ed (diploma in education) exam, and by an interview taken by the *Shikshan Adhikari.*

The School in Don village was established in 1985, and the class wise strength of the school for the yr 2005-06 is as follows:

Table 2: Class wise strength of the school in Don

Class	*Boys*	*Girls*	*Total*
Std. I	2	3	5
Std. II	1	4	5
Std. III	3	3	6
Std. IV	0	3	3
Total	6	13	19

The School at Pimpargane was established in 1956, and the class wise strength of the school for the yr 2005-06 is presented below:

Table 3: Class wise strength of the school in Pimpargane

Class	*Boys*	*Girls*	*Total*
Std. I	5	7	12
Std. II	3	5	8
Std. III	2	7	9
Std. IV	0	1	1
Total	10	20	30

A comparative look at the number of students presently enrolled in the 3 schools at Don, Pimpargane and Aghane.

Table 4: Enrollment in the three schools for the years 2005-2006:

CLASS	*DON school (Z.P.)*		*PIMPARGANE school (Z.P.)*		*AGHANE school (N.G.O.)*	
	Boys	*Girls*	*Boys*	*Girls*	*Boys*	*Girls*
STD. I	2	3	5	7	3	8
STD. II	1	4	3	5	4	3
STD. III	3	3	2	7	4	3
STD. IV	-	3	-	1	1	2
Total	6	13	10	20	12	16
	19		30		28	

Thakesan Gaware, Headmaster of the Don school stated that boys usually leave and go to the Ashramshalas to study further. And hence the trend is that till STD. IV there are more girls after which, the number of boys enrolled and passing STD. X is definitely more. This may be due to the incentives provided by scholarships for the girl child to study further, and hence complete primary education.

1.3. Government initiatives in the betterment of Primary Education:

(1) Universalisation of Elementary Education - Sarva Shiksha Abhiyan: Is a historic stride towards achieving the long cherished goal of Universalisation of Elementary Education (UEE) through a time bound integrated approach in partnership with States. SSA which promises to change the face of the elementary education sector of the country aims to provide useful and quality elementary education to all children between the age groups of 6 – 10 years by the year 2010.

The main features of the programme include:

- Focus on girls especially those belonging to the Schedule Caste and Schedule Tribe communities and minority groups.
- Free textbooks for girls.
- Special coaching and remedial classes for girls and a congenial learning environment.

- Teacher's sensitization program to promote equitable learning opportunities.
- Special focus on innovative projects related to girls education. Recruitment of 50% female teachers.

(2) Midday-meal scheme: The midday meal scheme is a successful incentive program. It covers all students of primary classes in all government, local body and government aided schools in the country with the aim to improve enrollment, attendance and retention while simultaneously impacting on the nutritional status of the children.

Children are provided with meals consisting of *rice* and *dal* (100 gms) per child.

Rs.1.75 per child is spent on food. Additionally once a week banana, egg, biscuits and peanuts are also given to the children, providing them with nutrition.

The syllabus is in accordance with the SSC board. The syllabus is common to all the primary schools. The subjects include math, science, English, history, geography and Marathi which happens to be the medium of instruction.

School timings are from 10.30 a.m. to 5.00 p.m. and extra curricular activities in the Zilla Parishad school consist of physical education, where boys and girls are taught exercises, they play *kabaddi, kho-kho*, they are told stories with morals, songs, poems and *bhajans*. Work experience is stressed on terms of gardening, and children are made to stress on cleanliness.

In the school at Aghane, ethno-medicine is also taught, besides songs and stories which are related to the children. The physical education taught here consists of long jumps, high jumps, skipping among other games like cricket, *kho kho* and *kabadi*.

The students are provided with uniforms, slates, and writing material, as well as text books.

(3) Government Scholarships at the Primary level

1. **Savitribai Phule scholarship:** This scholarship provides Rs.300 per year for girls who stand 1st in class.

2. **Attendance allowance:** This scholarship provides that for every day that the girl child attends school she gets Rs.1 per day.
3. **Vidhya Vetan:** This scholarship provides that every girl studying between Std. V and Std. VII get Rs. 500 per year and boys get Rs.400.

Hence these scholarships form incentives for students to work hard and come to school, and in turn encourage parents to send their children to school.

Provisions in the form of merit scholarships, stipends and other attendance scholarships also suffer from planning. In the case of most states in India, attendance scholarships are eligible for all boys and girls belonging to tribal communities. This provision has been there for quite some time. Some communities have taken full advantage of these facilities and scholarships while others remain unchanged.

How far children avail of these scholarships is questionable. Parents continue to remain unaware of most of these schemes therefore even if their children are to avail of them, they remain ignorant of this.

1.4 Government Committees set up in schools to ensure smooth functioning:

Each Zilla Parishad school consists of a Gram Shikshan Samiti and a Palak Sabha. The NGO schools do not have these committees.

The Gram Shikshan Samiti consists of 7 members; however the number may vary from school to school. The *Sarpanch* of the village is the President of the committee, whereas the headmaster of the respective school is the secretary of the committee. The committee also consists of 2 ladies, and 3 parents as well as educated elders from the village.

The Gram Shikshan Samiti meets once every two months, and discussions take place regarding the school, facilities provided to the students, constructions for renovations in the schools, toilets etc.

In the Pimpargane School, due to heavy rains the roof of the class room had broken, thus a lot of books, slates and other stationery were damaged. Hence the Gram Shikshan Samiti had taken this up as a topic for discussion at their last meeting. The construction of new classrooms was being undertaken.

- A sum of Rs. 5000 per year is given by the government to the school, and in the meetings of the Gram Shikshan Samiti, discussions so as to how the money will be spent are undertaken.
- An additional sum of Rs. 2000 is provided by the government which is to be spent on teaching aid for the benefit of the children.
- Rs. 500 per month is given to the teachers primarily for the benefits of the students for posters charts and drawing, and coloring material and other visual aids to help them learn.

The Palak Sabha is an association consisting of parents who play an active role in the educational system, and hence help to better it. The meeting is held by the Palak Pratinidhi who is a parent appointed by the other members and basically serves to monitor the sessions of the Sabha. In all the Palak Sabha consists of about 20-30 parents who meet once every 3 months to discuss things like the progress of children, changes in the syllabus or introduction of a new subject.

(B) PRE PRIMARY EDUCATION

At the pre primary level there are Balwadis and Anganwadis set up. Although these institutions are formally established they follow informal means of teaching.

(1) Anganwadi: Anganwadis have also been set up by the govt., the Anganwadi at Don village was started in 1993. Minavittal Gare is the main teacher at the Anganwadi. It is basically like a nursery of pre-school wherein the children are sent to interact with one another. The syllabus taught is not fixed, children are taught songs, poetry, prayers. Children get a meal consisting of *khichdi, dal* and *rice* everyday.

Teachers undergo training for 3 months in a special institute in Pune; the person must have passed his/her 10th to be eligible for training in this institution.

(2) Balwadi: The Balwadi in Ahupe village was also started by Shashwat in 1997-98. In all there were 25 children, 11 girls and 14 boys, who vary between 2-6 years of age. There is one teacher who looks after the school.

Here the children learn through listening, repeating and internalizing. Songs, stories with morals are taught, children are taught to internalize what they see in their surroundings.

Children are provided with *shira* once a week, usually on a Monday. Milk is provided to them on a daily basis. Food consisting of *pulses, moong dal, matthi* and *vatane* is provided 4 times a month. (50 gms of food per student). Children are also provided with uniforms and books. Although no exams are held *Shaswat* also ensures that medical check ups take place once a month by the ANM- Madhne who lives in Tirpad.

(3) Residential School or Ashramshalas: Another special educational input for tribal education is residential schools in India. Since such institutions are very special effort in the direction of tribal education, it is generally believed that there are significant attempts in the direction of higher enrollment of tribal children belonging to the school going age group. Hence Ashramshalas are where majority of the tribal youth get basic education from Std. I – VIII. They are similar to boarding schools which provide for residential facilities within the schools.

The Ashramshala in Ahupe village was established in 1994, although Ashramshalas in general do not have the best reputation, without them majority of the tribal youth would be unable to get basic education facilities. The staff consists of a headmaster, 7 teachers, 7 female workers, 4 cooks, 4 male servants and 1 watchman. There are 28 posts in all, but some are vacant – hence only 17 people are working there presently.

Students are also provided with 3 meals in a day, at 10:00 a.m. and 7:00 p.m. they get *dal, rice, bhaji* and *chapatti* and in the afternoons they get *poha*. They are provided with uniforms, books, slates, pencils and also get a blanket and a *shatranji* besides a bar of soap and a bottle of oil. Every month girls get an additional bottle of oil. Text books as well as 2 uniforms per child are provided for a year.

Although we saw toilets being constructed, most of the children have to go to the lake to bathe, as there is no water in the toilets. Even electricity is not there in the area so students have to make do with lanterns at night.

Table 5. Enrollment in the Ashram school for the year 2005-06

Class	*Boys*	*Girls*	*Total*
STD. I	9	12	21
STD. II	8	12	20
STD. III	6	6	12
STD. IV	12	7	19
STD. V	11	14	25
STD. VI	6	18	24
STD. VII	7	8	15
STD. VIII	5	8	13
TOTAL	64	85	149

Although it is said that after STD IV more boys usually go in for secondary education, even in the Ashramshala, there are majority of girls.

Students are purposely not failed from Std. I to VII as parents stop sending them to school. The headmaster also stated 100% students go on to Std. VI & VII.

Two studies that were conducted on Ashram schools by Desai B. and Patel A. (1981) and Pratap D.R., Raju C.C and Rao M.V.M (1971) do not project a good profile of Ashram schools. Pratap D.R and Raju C.C (1973) found the working and the physical conditions of Ashram schools unsatisfactory. Some of the teachers working in these schools did not stay there and visited schools occasionally. The study pointed out that the schools were treated as a source of income rather than avenues of service.

Desai B and Patel A., (1981) found that in most of the Ashram schools; the number of children enrolled was much higher than the prescribed number. On the other hand, only 18 of the 22 ashram schools had 100% teachers and in some cases the educational qualifications of teachers was STD.VII. The study by Joshi S.T (1980) found that majority of teachers did not have specialized training for working in backward areas.

Shrivastava R.C (1981) found that unproductive and traditional type of educational system for tribal was the cause of indifferent attitude of tribal parents towards their children's education, lack of necessary facilities and equipment for teaching was the cause for the lack of motivation for education among tribal.

Table 6: Literacy rates in the villages of Don

DON Village	*Males*	*Females*
Literate	73.91%	59.02%
Illiterate	26.08%	40.97%

Table 7: Literacy rates in the villages of Aghane

AGHANE Village	*Males*	*Females*
Literate	65.15%	39.53%
Illiterate	35.57%	60.46%

Conclusion

Specific causes and factors leading to the educational deprivation of tribal.

Like all other sectors of socio-economic life, educationally the tribal people at different levels of development but on the whole, formal education has made very little impact on tribal groups. In the light past efforts, it is not shocking because prior to 1980, the Government of India had not direct programs for the education of the tribal with the adoption of the constitution, the population of education of Schedule Tribes has become a special responsibility of the central as well as the state government.

Since education is the most effective instrument for insuring quality of opportunity, the tribal people have been left far behind due to lack of education.

The problems with respect to education in the villages of Don, Aghane and Pimpargane are as follows.

(a) Inadequate Teachers: For one thing lack of suitable teachers to begin with is one of the major reasons for the slow growth of education in tribal areas. Considering there are just 2 teachers teaching 4 classes, posses a problem in it. STD. I and

STD. II both share a classroom, thus failing to give children individual attention. This is mainly due to the fact that teachers appointed do not fish to live in such remote tribal villages, even if they don't live in the village commuting to and fro becomes a huge burden on them.

(b) Inadequate Infrastructure and Lack of Facilities: In the case of Ashramshalas working and physical conditions were unsatisfactory, basic amenities like water in toilets and for bathing purposes was not available to children. Even washing of utensils and clothes had to be done at the lake nearby – in spite of toilets being constructed. Even electricity in the school was not there and hence the students had to use lanterns at night.

(c) Economic Conditions: Since most of tribal people are living in abject poverty, under subsistence economy, it is not easy for most of them to send their children to schools, thus losing healthy hands in their struggle for survival.

(d) Curriculum not in tune with their needs: Tribal children follow the state board; hence their syllabus is in accordance with the SSC board. The contents of what they study rarely appeal to them, as they come from totally different cultural backgrounds. The education system should stress on making children learn about their own surroundings, their way of life, their culture so that they can relate to what they are being taught. Keeping education in tune with their culture and surroundings is what is urgently needed in tribal areas.

According to Mr. Anand Kapoor, 8% of funds from the state are to be allotted for tribal education and at the moment only 5.11% and 6% or so are being allotted. Tribal students also face a lot of problems once they have to go in for higher education to larger cities, for one thing, language becomes a barrier, due to which they face an inferiority complex.

Hence the planning of education according to educational needs is critical. In spite of all the problems faced with respect to education, there have been cases where people have excelled like in the case of *Dr. Nandkumar Gaware, who was encouraged by his father to work hard and get an education. He stated that with the help of his uncle in Manchar he was able to study hard and in turn fulfill his father's dream of becoming a doctor.* Similarly in the case of *Yogita Pardhi, who is the wife of Chimaji Pardhi, headmaster of the Aghane School, she is still studying in Std XI and living in a hostel in Narodi. In spite of being married, she wanted to study further as she was good at her work, so she decided to continue with her education.* When asked about the opinion of people, he stated that they had mixed views about the fact that she was still studying in spite of being married.

To conclude, we all know that mass education and literacy are the hallmark of every society. Thus, education is necessary and above all is the basic ingredient in bringing about social and economic development.

In the Mahadev Koli community, it is thus observed that people are becoming aware of the importance of education, and in turn the fruitful benefits it would bring about to their society.

20

Indigenous Education in the Philippines Case Study of the Sagu-ilaw School of Indigenous Knowledge and Traditions*

—*Ricarte b. Abejuela*

Indigenous education in the Philippines has been a recent phenomenon, starting only in the past decade. Legislation supporting indigenous peoples rights as well as giving legitimacy to establishing indigenous schools were only authored in the past 8 years. The Asian Council for People's Culture assisted the different indigenous tribes in the country in setting up Schools for Indigenous Knowledge and Traditions (SIKAT). The SIKAT programme envisions a system at par with mainstream education, founded on the ways of life, traditions and culture of indigenous peoples. This paper takes a closer look at one of the SIKAT Schools – the Sagu-Ilaw SIKAT of the Bukidnon Tribe in Northern Mindanao. Sagu-Ilaw was set up in 2002 with the assistance of ACPC. Since then, despite the perennial problem of funding, it has been surviving on its own. It was designed as a tertiary type teacher-training school whose students teach the tribe's children in their respective communities. Recent linkages with the Department of Education has led to conflict over control of the school, leading the tribe to fear for the continued loss of their identity. Other linkages are currently being established for the survival and further development of the school. Key Words Indigenous Education; Indigenous Knowledge; Indigenous Traditions; Philippines; Tribal School Indigenous Knowledge Systems According to the United Nations Educational, Scientific and Cultural Organization (UNESCO) (2003), 'Local and indigenous knowledge' refers to the cumulative and complex

*Reproduced.

bodies of knowledge, know-how, practices and representations that are maintained and developed by peoples with extended histories of interactions with the natural environment. These cognitive systems are part of a complex that also includes language, attachment to place, spirituality and worldview. Many different terms are used to refer to this knowledge, these include: • traditional ecological knowledge (TEK) • indigenous knowledge (IK) • local knowledge • rural peoples'/ farmers' knowledge • ethnobiology / ethnobotany / ethnozoology • ethnoscience • folk science • indigenous science UNESCO says that these many terms coexist because the wide range of social,political and scientific contexts have made it all but impossible to for a single term to be suitable in all circumstances. UNESCO has recognized the importance of Indigenous Knowledge Systems, that it launched the Local Indigenous Knowledge Systems (LINKS) Project in 2002. As a cross-cutting intersectoral project, LINKS brings together all five programme sectors of UNESCO in a collaborative effort on local and indigenous knowledge. The LINKS Project focuses on this interface between local & indigenous knowledge and the Millennium Development Goals of poverty eradication and environmental sustainability. It addresses the different ways that indigenous knowledge, practices and worldviews are drawn into development and resource management processes. It also considers the implications this may have for building equity in governance, enhancing cultural pluralism and sustaining biodiversity (UNESCO 2003). Local and indigenous knowledge includes the sophisticated understandings, interpretations and meanings that are accumulated and developed by peoples having extended histories of interaction with the natural environment (UNESCO 2003: 1). For the vast majority of rural and indigenous peoples these knowledge systems provide the basis for local-level decision-making about fundamental aspects of day-to-day life (economic, social, cultural, ecological). Indigenous knowledge is also one of the key action themes identified by UNESCO in the UN Decade for Education for Sustainable Development (2005-2014). Indigenous and local knowledge spans several important areas. However, for this paper, it shall be limited to indigenous education in the Philippines.

Situation of Indigenous Education in the Philippines The Philippine archipelago is made up of 7,107 islands with a total area of 300,000 sq km. It has a current population of nearly 88 million people, 75% of which belong to 8 major ethnic groups and the remaining 25% are divided among different minor ethnic groups and indigenous tribes. The country has more than 110 ethnic tribes and cultural communities whose culturesand traditions are in varying states of extinction. These vanishing ancestral traditions and customary laws used to define social relationships and values and promoted efficiency of economic activities. Unfortunately, environmentally devastating socio-economic ventures, large-scale indiscriminate mining and industrial logging have brought incalculable damage to their primary source of livelihood and cultural sanctuary. The consequent destructionof their environment resulted in the further degradation of ancestral cultures which are largely shaped by the indigenous people's interaction with the natural elements. This resulting loss of their cultural identities, coupled with the devastation of their environment, have resulted in the serious economic displacement and cultural disempowerment of these communities. Tribal communities in various geographical areas are thus among the most impoverished and marginalized sectors of Philippine society (ACPC 2005). Though the Philippine republic has been in existence for more than 100 years, it hasonly been since the late 1980s and the 1990s that the government sought to address the plight of the indigenous peoples. The present constitution, which was written in 1987, in Article XIV Sec 1 states: "The State shall protect and promote the right of all citizens to quality education at all levels, and shall take appropriate steps to make such education accessible to all." Furthermore, Sec 17 also reads: "The State shall recognize, respect, and protect the rights of indigenous cultural communities to preserve and develop their cultures, traditions, and institutions. It shall consider these rights inthe formulation of national plans and policies." These mandates were unfortunately not supported by specific legislation or policies. It was not until the 1990s that further legislation was authored to protect the rights of the indigenous peoples. In October 1997, then President Fidel V. Ramos signed into law Republic Act 8371 - the Indigenous Peoples' Rights Act (IPRA). This legislation lays down the legal framework for addressing indigenous peoples' poverty. It seeks to alleviate the plightof the country's "poorest of the poor" by correcting, through legislation, the historical errors that led to the systematic dispossession of and discrimination against the indigenous peoples. The IPRA law enforces the 1987 Constitution's mandate that the State should craft a policy "to recognize and promote the rights of indigenous peoples within the framework of national unity and development" and "to protect the rights of indigenous cultural communities to their ancestral lands to ensure their economic, social and cultural well-being" (Asian Development Bank 2002: (13). The IPRA law also serves as the basis for the establishment of indigenous schools. Section 28 of the IPRA law states: "The State shall, through the National Commission on Indigenous People (NCIP), provide a complete, adequate and integrated system of education, relevant to the needs of the children and young people of ICCs/IPs." Section 30 further states: "The State shall provide equal access to various cultural opportunities to the ICCs/IPs through the educational system, public or cultural entities, scholarships, grants and other incentives without prejudice to their right to establish and control their educational systems and institutions by providing education in their own language, in a manner appropriate to their cultural methods of teaching and learning. Indigenous children/youth shall have the right to all levels and forms of education of the State." However, even with these recent legislation on indigenous peoples and indigenous rights, there remains very few indigenous schools in the country. In the Philippines, education is divided into formal and non-formal education. The formal sector is further divided into three levels: primary, secondary and tertiary. Each can be private or public. Ever since the Americans established the public school system in the country, no efforts were done on establishing schools that utilized indigenous knowledge. In fact, it was required in all schools that the American system be used – language and all. All Filipinos were required to learn only in English. It was only in the past 20 years that Filipino has been reintroduced as a language of instruction inschools, though English still has preference. Tribal regional languages have never been encouraged, much less those of the indigenous peoples. Only a handful of indigenous schools are in existence, all of them due solely on the efforts of the tribal elders, often with very minimal support from the government – if any. Schools for Indigenous Knowledge and Traditions Among the organizations in the country that promoted indigenous learning is the Asian Council for People's Culture (ACPC). It was ACPC that came up with the SIKAT Programme. SIKAT is the Filipino word for 'rising' and at the same time theacronym for 'Schools for Indigenous Knowledge and Traditions'. The combination of both meanings expresses well what the SIKAT programme is all about. It envisions asystem at par with mainstream education, founded on the ways of life, traditions and culture of indigenous peoples, as a stepping stone to promote sincere development of the communities (Meneses 2004:1). The idea for the development of a culturally-responsive education was first expressedin 1999 by several of the indigenous leaders present in one of ACPC's trainings.

ACPC decided to facilitate the building of a national network of indigenous community educators who would develop and promote a dynamic and culturally responsive curriculum for indigenous communities. This inter-tribal council of elderslaunched the movement for the promotion of indigenous education. They then put forth a document – the Kalinga Declaration – which envisions: "Indigenous education founded on the lifeways, traditions,worldview, culture and spirituality of the tribal community is abasic right of all indigenous people. It is a pathway of education that recognizes wisdom embedded in indigenous knowledge." (ACPC 2004) Since the Kalinga Declaration, ACPC facilitated teacher trainings, curriculumdevelopment workshops, tribal leaders' forum and other activities to prepare the communities and their indigenous teachers for the establishment of their Schools for Indigenous Knowledge and Traditions. According to Meneses (2004:2), the basic principles of SIKAT are: 1. Ownership - SIKAT is an idea that originated from the indigenous peoplethemselves, the concept and the results of its implementation are therefore also ownedby them. Important decisions are made by the SIKAT Council of Elders, consisting of 15 elected members of different tribes nationwide. 2. Emancipation – The SIKAT-programme is about indigenous people defining, developing and implementing their own education; content, inputs in curricula, lesson plans, and manuals come from the indigenous people involved in the

SIKAT-program. 3. Cultural Diversity – While globalisation brings along many positive consequencesand possibilities, it also brings the danger of cultural homogenisation. The SIKAT-program offers indigenous people a chance to revitalize their culture giving indigenous people the chance to contribute to society and suggest innovations based upon their perspectives. The cultural variety among indigenous communities offersindigenous people, from remote areas, to meet for an enriching inter-tribal interaction. 4. Environmental Sustainability – indigenous worldviews are in many ways holistic. For one thing, indigenous people have expressed their survival to be inherently connected to their natural environment not only on a material level, but also on aspiritual level. Indigenous communities' environment carries the soul of their ancestors, of their identity. The concept of ancestral domain and environmental sustainability urgently needed to safeguard this ancestral domain has a central place inthe SIKAT curriculum.5. Community-Centred – Local representatives who are immersed in trainings likedeveloping curriculum are the ones expected to eventually teach and sustain their respective community SIKAT school. 6. Rooted in Day to Day Reality – one reason for indigenous people to want to establish culturally responsive education is the experience that what children learn in mainstream schools is often not relevant in their day-to-day lives. Handbooks, curricula in mainstream education are highly westernised. Many indigenous children even become indifferent of their cultural background. The high drop out rate among indigenous students can be attributed to a school calendar that does not take into account the planting and harvesting season vital to many indigenous communities. SIKAT wants to develop a relevant curriculum to equip them with skills, knowledge and values to help contribute to society, and take pride in their indigenous identity, instead of being uncomfortable about it. 7. Recognition – SIKAT-participants often express aversion to be called para-teachers, or their education to be categorized as non-formal education. Through this they want to express that indigenous education should be recognized as quality basic education for their children, and not a form of additional education, just because it is different from mainstream education. Therefore advocacy and lobbying with the government, especially the Department of Education is an important point of attention. As can be observed, the SIKAT schools are implementing what UNESCO has only recently recognized: that the recognition of local and indigenous knowledge transforms the relationship of biodiversity managers to local communities. Ratherthan mere resource users whose practices must be managed, local people are recognized as knowledge holders in their own right with their own ecological understandings, conservation practices and visions of how resource management goals should be defined and attained (UNESCO 2003: 5). This is among the central tenets of indigenous education in the SIKAT schools. Sagu-Ilaw SIKAT The school was established by Datu Mandimati (Conrado Binayao) on February 28, 2002 in cooperation with ACPC via its SIKAT programme. The school was established for the Bukidnon Tribe of Manolo Fortich and was given the name Sagu-ilaw. Sagu-ilaw means "wisdom of the true, good and living story of Magbabaya - creator of the world, heaven and everything in it and the maker of man with his soul and spirit in man." The tribe decided to establish the school "top-down" – meaning that they designed Sagu-Ilaw SIKAT as a tertiary type school. The school's aim is to train para-teachers. The school's students attend class one day a week – only during Fridays. For theother days of the week, they are teaching kindergarten in their respective barangays (communities). The school currently has 25 students who teach in the following communities: Tankulan Kihari; Sankanan; Kibulawan, Kalumanan; Lingi-on; Katablaran, Guilang-guilang. The school uses 4 languages as mediums of instruction: English, Tagalog, Cebuano and Binukid. During the first year, Sagu-Ilaw oriented its students not only on Bukidnon-Higaonon cultural and language studies but also on the Philippine constitution and the IPRALaw. Students were also taught the principles and methods of teaching. Literacy and numeracy skills development went hand in hand with the teaching of traditional songs, dances and arts. Students were also introduced to community development. All of these were designed to equip the student to be effective teachers in theirrespective communities.

On the second year, students were taught the intricacies of the Bukidnon language – lexicon, grammar and usage. Bukidnon culture as well as migrant culture was likewise taught to promote understanding between the indigenous people and the lowlanders now in the province. The students were also introduced to the history, institutions and heroes of the tribe – things they would not have learned of in government schools. Ethnic songs, stories, dances as well as arts and crafts were also taught. The vocational, social and economic aspects of community development was tackled as well. By the third year, the students progressed in learning the different chants, stories, legends and customary laws of the tribe. Ethnic cultural practices, beliefs, rituals and ceremonies, as well as knowledge systems was then taught, incorporating community development and environmental conservation and protection. In order to protect thetribal members from exploitation from migrants and lowlanders, traditional political leadership and the Philippine justice system was taught. Students were also trained to teach Pilipino and English as a second language. Now in its fourth year, aside from teaching the students about Philippine and World history, vocational arts and crafts, Sagu-Ilaw is focusing on teaching its students aboutancestral domain. The school is also encouraging its students to conduct cultural research. All throughout the four years of their schooling, concern and care of the environment played a central role. This is not surprising since the tribe's stories, chants and songs highlight the interrelatedness of man and the environment. This philosophy, known to westerners as human ecology, is also a central tenet in the teachers' lessons in their communities. Problems Encountered The school is located in Manolo Fortich town proper, in the campus of Community Colleges. A modest building was set up using P200,000.00 (around $4,000.00) from ACPC. The school now runs solely out of the support of the tribe. Other than the initial support in establishing the building, there has been no funding support from any agency. Thus, the teachers work receiving no salaries, not even allowances. The ACPC continues to provide support in the means of continuous teacher training. Around two to three teachers of the tribe are trained; the trained teachers then trainothers in their school. Support from the local government has been minimal so far. Though the mayor has been supportive of the school, the current fiscal crisis in the Philippines has the government on a "belt-tightening" mode – thus, financial assistance has been hard to come by. The local government, fully supporting the idea that Sagu-Ilaw SIKAT should have its own premises, is currently trying to secure disposable government land for donation to the school. Occasional provision of funds for training (usually for snacks of the participants and honorarium of the trainor) is also provided by the local government. The establishment of the school, as stated in the IPRA Law, should have been through the NCIP. It is ironic, however, that the NCIP has provided very little support for the school. According to Datu Mandimati, the previous Provincial Officer of the NCIP was supportive of the idea of the school. But since his death, the NCIP has not responded to any of the proposals forwarded by the school. Most support the school now gets is through the private efforts of the tribe and the through the occasional trainings offered by the ACPC. The school has attempted linkages with established tertiary institutions to enhance its training capacities. Two schools in Davao City – the Ateneo de Davao and the University of the Philippines Mindanao - wanted to help. The tribe turned down the offer of the Ateneo for two main reasons: distance and control. The Ateneo, a Jesuit university, wanted control of the school, wishing to pattern it on its Jesuit foundations. The tribe refused, fearing the loss of the tribe's identity. The Ateneo then passed it to UP Mindanao, a state university. Unfortunately, politics reared its ugly head andnothing was concretised. Xavier University, in Cagayan de Oro City, also signified its interest in absorbing Sagu-Ilaw. The distance was closer compared to Davao City. But again, the tribe did not agree to the arrangements proposed by Xavier. Being a sister school of Ateneo, its Jesuit foundations would again lead to the loss of thetribe's identity. Last October 13, 2005 the University of Southeastern Philippines (USEP) launched the Pamulaan Center for Indigenous Peoples Education. This center offers degree programs such as BA Applied Anthropology and Participatory Development, BS Indigenous Peoples Education, BA Peace Building and Multi-Cultural Studies and BS Indigenous Agriculture (Calamba 2005). Although Pamulaan - which means "seedbed" - is a college education program designed for the IPs in the Philippines, these programs are under the USEP and those who will study under the Center are considered regular students of USEP and will follow the same rules and regulations of other degree programs of USEP. This model is one that Sagu-Ilaw fears would still lead to a loss of identity. According to UNESCO (2003: 7), while universal education programmes provide important tools for human development, they may also compromise indigenous language and knowledge transmission. Inadvertently, they may contribute to an erosion of cultural diversity, a loss of social cohesion and the alienation and disorientation of indigenous youth. This apprehension is mirrored by the tribal leaders who fear that with the Philippine school system patterned after western models, there is little hope of retaining tribal ways. Recently, the Department of Education (DepEd) released DepEd Order 42 series of 2004: "Permit to Operate Primary Schools for Indigenous Peoples and Cultural Communities". On the basis of this order, Sagu-Ilaw SIKAT established two primarylevel classes in their communities this year - in Sitio Consolacion, Guilang-guilang and Sitio Kibulawan, Kalugmanan (both in the Municipality of Manolo Fortich). According to this department order, indigenous schools are "encouraged to register with DepEd for mainstreaming in the educational system". The main problem faced by Sagu-Ilaw with the running of the indigenous school is that DepEd wanted control over the school – the tribe does not want this because, again, they fear that their identity would be lost.

To allay the fears of the indigenous people, the order encourages flexibility for three areas (DepEd 2004:1): "1. Curriculum – it should be flexible without undermining the balance between the attainment of the core learning competencies which every Filipino learner should master in the community and the indigenous culture. 2. Teachers – as much as possible, qualified teachers should teach the core subjects of the curriculum. However, in handling the concerns of the community, e.g. culture, traditions, songs, practices, para-teachers from the place or those who know the culture may be employed. They may not be holders of degrees in education but may be experienced or trained parents. 3. School Calendar –

while cultural/tribal idiosyncrasies are to be observed, the required calendar days of the school year should be adhered to as much as possible." Several problems are highlighted by the issuance of this order. As can be seen from the excerpt above, while indigenous schools are allowed to operate, it has to register with the department to make it a "valid school". By registering the indigenous school with the department, it will be obliged to modify its structure to fit in the government school structure, which is based on western models. Curriculum would be based on the Basic Education Curriculum (BEC), which would give emphasis on Math, Science, English, Filipino, and Social Studies. This would deviate from the purpose of the SIKAT schools where curriculum would be centred around the tribes' cultural traditions. Should indigenous schools register with the DepEd for "mainstreaming of the educational system", tribal ways would be relegated to supplementary subjects instead of it being the main focus of the school. If the schools are also registered, they would be obliged to have "qualified teachers to teach the core curriculum". This would refer to duly certified teachers who are often recipients of western-styled education. It has already been observed among SIKAT teachers the big challenge they are facing to outgrow their education in westernised schools and to rediscover their indigenous heritage. One example is the micro-curricula, which tends to become duplications of existing western ones. Though these concepts have been valuable for western society and western education, indigenous educators should challenge the concept and see if there's a more suitable one for theirsituation (Meneses 2004: 9). The labelling of indigenous teachers as "para-teachers" is again reflective of the lack of recognition by the government of the importance ofindigenous teachers. Even if these "para-teachers" do not meet the westernised criteria of teachers, they are teachers in their own right. The order to adhere to the Philippine school year is again a lack of recognizing the unique needs of the tribes vis a vis availability of children for harvests and other important cultural activities. Another section in the DepEd order also highlights some problems. Section 6 of the order states: "Children who finish studies in unrecognised schools but want to continue their studies in the regular schools may submit themselves to a Validating Test (Philippine Validity Test) to be administered by the National Education, Testing and Research Center (NETRC) to determine their competencies for proper grade placement." (DepEd O42 s.2004: 2) With this section, it states that for indigenous children to be admitted to government schools, they must pass the validating test. For the students to pass the test, they must have competency in the Basic Educational Curriculum (BEC) of the state. This section can be interpreted thus: 1) indigenous schools must register with the DepEd in order to allow their children to gain the necessary BEC knowledge and skills; or 2) indigenous schools who choose not to register should include BEC in their curriculum. The bottom line is that this section again does not allow for indigenous schools to develop a curriculum suited for their tribal traditions as identified by SIKAT. These problems have been foreseen by Sagu-Ilaw SIKAT and the tribe is working hard to meet these requirements of DepEd without sacrificing its identity and vision. This "tug-of-war", coupled by the financial difficulties of running a school, has led to some of the school's non-tribal partners to disappear. Datu Mandimati has observed that there is a "very weak commitment of individuals, government agencies and otherinstitutions in sustaining the project started". It is solely due to the determination ofthe tribe to have this school that has kept it going. Plans for the Future In November 4, 2004 the tribe established the Sagu-Ilaw Technical and Vocational School with the assistance of the several government agencies and from a grant from the German government. Equipment for wood working was donated by the Germans for the use of Sagu-Ilaw. The vocational school aims for imparting upon its memberscontinuous skills and vocational training in coordination with different governmentagencies. Another target is capability building for entrepreneurship through the fabrication of furniture crafts and housing components and also traditional art. The vocational school was designed in such a way that the products of the studentswould be sold and the funds earned would sustain the indigenous school. Theproblem they are currently facing is that the tribe cannot source wood because they cannot touch the trees in their ancestral domain along the slopes of Mt. Kitanglad. This is because Mt. Kitanglad is a nature reserve that is protected by the Department of Environment and Natural Resources. Datu Mandimati sadly says, "We cannot even use the wood in our own land". The only hope the tribe sees for the school to survive is for the tribe to utilize its ancestral domain. They believe that once they get this, they will no longer have problems in funding their activities. To address this situation, the tribe recently created the Non-Formal Education arm of Sagu-Ilaw which focuses on educating the adult members of the tribe on its rights on ancestral domain and land. The focus now of Sagu-Ilaw is on centering the education of the tribal members in the context of ancestral domain. As of the moment, the tribe is busy preparing their Ancestral Domain Sustainable Development and Protection Plan. What Now? Although the government has made strides in defending the rights of indigenous peoples and uplifting their state in society, it still has some ways to go in terms of indigenous education. The SIKAT programme is on the right track. What is needed would be government recognition and support. As of the present, most (if not all) indigenous schools are operating only with the support of the local tribal communities or of NGOs. The best the government can do as a start is to recognize SIKAT schools as legitimate schools different from government schools but equal in standing. The Department of Education could also provide more autonomy to its regional offices to collaborate with indigenous groups in curriculum formulation. As of the present, curriculum content and formulation is too centralized – it done in the capital of Manila and sent out to the regions. Autonomy could assist in the localization of content without veering away from the basic structure the central office wishes to achieve in the schools. Teacher-training institutions can also offer indigenous education as a programme to allow for future teachers to acquire skills needed to teach in indigenous schools. This programme should be patterned after the SIKAT curricula and veer away from the western model so often used in schools today. This could serve as a good bridge between the SIKAT curricula and the DepEd memo – since this programme would produce teachers that are equipped with cultural sensitivity and skills plus the Basic Education Curriculum content used in all Philippine schools. Exploratory talks are currently ongoing between Sagu-Ilaw and Bukidnon State College on plans for a course or programme about indigenous education based on Bukidnon culture. A collaboration is being proposed wherein

Sagu-Ilaw SIKAT would serve as a preparatory course and Bukidnon State College, through its School of Community Education and Industrial Technology, would serve as the finishing programme, awarding its graduates with diplomas. The graduates would then have the "legitimacy" that DepEd is looking for. Local and indigenous knowledge is a key action theme in the UN Decade for Education for Sustainable Development. It is an area that should not be limited to indigenous peoples alone, since we could all benefit from it. In the area of education, indigenous schools in the Philippines are still experiencing problems. The SIKAT project is a good template for empowering indigenous people through their own kind of education. If the government could assist in the SIKAT programme, and if teacher-training institutions would also offer these programmes, indigenous schools and local knowledge would finally gain the recognition is deserves.

21

Socio-Economic Aspect of Tribal Education : Issues and Prospects

—*Jyothi S. Shetty*

Abstract

Education refers to the method by which a society attempts to direct and accelerate the learning process of its individuals. In spite of efforts made by the constitution, the position of tribal education is still poor in India. The present paper examines the social and economic factors which lead to educational deprivation among the tribes. As most of their education is informal, the tribes find the formal type of education disinteresting. Poverty, the changing economy and lack of knowledge affect the educational development among the tribes. They are not aware of the educational facilities and the function and value of education. The attitude of teachers towards the tribal students is not healthy. The medium of instruction is not in their mother-tongues, the matter in the textbooks has no relevance to their culture and needs, as they have rich oral tradition they are sensitive to print. They are basically not interested in education so they have low motivation and aspirations. All these lead to educational deprivation among the tribes. Hence educational programmes could not make much progress due to their ignorance and illiteracy. So education among the tribes should be viewed against their background of economy and society.

Introduction

Education is a continuous process from birth to death. The real meaning of education is the harmonious development of the individual in the framework of the culture of the community to which he belongs. According to the Encyclopedia of Britannica (Vol. 7, 964) Education is "an attempt on the part of the adult members of a human society to shape the development of coming generation in accordance with its own ideals of life."

P.H. Prabhu (1954) defines education as : "In fact, real education has a value both in so far as it develops the individual personality as well as it 'socializes' the person and thus enabled him to keep in harmony with the material and moral framework of the group to which he belongs". The proper ideal of education must envisage a co-ordination of these two aims.

In the wider sense education is a universal phenomenon of socialization of the younger generation by the elder generation. It plays an important role in personality development in breaking social boundaries, raising the standard of life and in inculcating modern values in social, economic, political and cultural fields. Thus it is a cultural process in which inculcation of values, norms, morals and skills the members of a society, ensures continuity in each generation with regard to various aspects of society. Margaret Mead (1943) defines" education as the cultural process, the way in which each reborn human infant is transformed into a full member of a specific human society".

Tribal Education

India has the largest concentration of tribal population. Indian history reveals that historical general backwardness of the tribal along with isolation and subsistence economy has kept these tribal backward for many centuries. To improve their condition much attention has been given to their education, but it has made little progress among the tribal. In spite of efforts made by the constitution to equalize educational opportunities, more and more educational schemes are being implemented by the state and central Government for the educational development of tribal unfortunately the position of tribal position education is still poor in India.

The literacy rate among the scheduled tribe population recorded during 1961, 1971, 1981 and 1991 census was 18.53 per cent, 11.30 per cent, 16.35 per cent and 29.60 per cent respectively (Excluding population of age group 0-6). These figures are much lower than the corresponding figures for total population of India. It is observed that tribal literacy percentage in 1961 census was quite high than the succeeding censuses Since education has an inherent relation with culture, economy and society the need for an anthropological approach to education in tribal areas is needed. The scenario of education among the tribes who are considered backward needs to be examined.

National Scenario of tribal literacy during, 1991 census as compared to the general population is as follows:-

Literacy Rate among Scheduled Tribes during 1991 Census

Sr. No	*Name of States/UTS*	*General*	*Tribal*
1	*2*	*3*	*4*
1.	Andhra Pradesh	44.09	17.16
2.	Arunachal Pradesh	41.59	24.45
3.	Assam	52.89	49.16
4.	Bihar	38.48	26.78
5.	Goa	75.51	42.91
6.	Gujarat	61.29	36.45
7.	Haryana	55.85	—
8.	Himachal Pradesh	63.86	47.09
9.	Karnataka	56.04	36.01
10.	Kerala	89.81	57.22
11.	Madhya Prades	44.20	21.54
12.	Maharashtra	64.87	36.79
13.	Manipur	59.89	53.63
14.	Mizoram (Included in Assam)	49.10	46.71
15.	Nagaland	82.87	60.59
16.	Orissa	61.65	22.31
17.	Punjab	49.09	—
18.	Rajasthan	58.51	19.44
19.	Sikkim	38.58	59.01
20.	Tamil Nadu	56.94	27.89
21.	Tripura	62.66	40.37
22.	Uttar Pradesh	60.44	35.70
23.	West Bengal	57.70	35.70

1	*2*	*3*	*4*
Union Territories			
1.	Andaman & Nicobar Islands	73.02	56.62
2.	Dadra Nagar Haveli	40.71	28.21
3.	Lakshadweep	81.78	80.58
4.	Daman & Diu	71.20	52.91
	All India	52.21	29.60

Excluding population of age group 0-6
Source: Census of India 1991

The present paper focuses on socio-economic factors such as poverty, changing economy, desire, aspiration, motivation and attitude towards education, socio-economic aspects of the family, and awareness about educational facilities gender and education, which affect the educational development of the tribes.

Economic Aspect of Tribal Education

It is an accepted fact that the economic and socio-cultural aspects of a family affect the education of children in all societies in India. Education is essential as it enables one to take up their rightful place in the economic, social and cultural life of modern India and at the same time to keep respect of one's own culture. The culture and environment in which one is born and brought up shapes the personality of an individual to a large extent. This way education is related to culture.

After independence as the socio-economic conditions of the tribes was backward as compared to the general population the constitution makers and planners decided to allot money for development work in the tribal areas. Some were of the opinion that education was the only way to improve the condition of tribes while some believed that it was of no use educating the tribes when they didn't have enough to eat and that education would take care of itself once when the people's standard of living improved. But soon they came to realize that both education and economy are interdependent and complementary and the development of both could go on side by side. Economic development is a never-ending process and economic development without educational development does not have any sense because if people are not educated they cannot use the benefits of economic development in the best possible way. So adequate funds were released for education and economic development. In spite of facilities such as establishment of special schools, free schooling, scholarships etc the progress of tribal education has not been impressive.

The economic causes leading to educational deprivation among tribes are:

(1) Poverty:

Since most of tribal people are living under subsistence economy, life is very hard for them. Even the tribes who practice agriculture lead a hand to mouth existence. In agricultural families both male and female contribute to the economic activities of the house. Even among the non-agricultural tribes every member of the family goes to the forests to collect fruits, to dig roots and for hunting. Boys in the family take the cattle for grazing, help on the fields while girls are engaged in collecting firewood, helping the mother's in household activities, take care of the younger siblings. Thus sending children to schools means losing two healthy hands in the struggle for survival. Thus each child is an economic asset. If the child is sent to school, the parents have to feed him out of their meager income which puts a burden on the family economy. Save (1945) wrote "In case of people who hardly get bread twice a day, literacy is a tall talk". Verrier Elvin (1963) very appropriately sums up the situation in this way. "For a tribal family, to send it's grown up girl or boy to school, is essentially a matter of economies, and entails dislocation in the traditional pattern of division of labor. Many parents cannot just afford to send their children to school". Similarly Chitnis (1974) reported that a high proportion of ST students came from poor homes and belonged to rural occupations. Berdie (1954) observed that there is a very strong positive relationship between educational aspirations and income-levels. B.A. Deshmukh (2004) reported in his study that the Kokna tribe's school age boys and girls are engaged in agricultural and household work. He also found that economic cause as not only the factor for educational backwardness of Kokna tribe but social factors were also equally responsible.

Another important reason for their poverty is, they spend their earnings lavishly on rituals and ceremonies. They spend much on liquor which is a part of their socio-religious life.

(2) Low agricultural returns:

Their agricultural return is very low and hardly enough for their subsistence. R.S. Mann (1978) in his study on the tribes of Rajasthan observed that the low agricultural productivity is due to lack of irrigation facilities and also because the tribes do not use fertilizers and other modern techniques of agriculture. One can find a marked difference between the farmers of tribes and non-tribes. It is also seen that the tribes themselves are not enthusiastic towards increasing their agricultural production, they feel satisfied with whatever they get. In this connection R.S. Mann (1978; 76) has rightly said "Most of the Bhils still express that they are satisfied with whatever they practice. That means the hangover of traditionalism is not over. A Bhil will still not be ready to do any labour if he has food provision for a few days in his house. He shirks hard work and remains sitting idle".

Of late many industries have started working in the tribal areas but they do not employ the tribal youths as they do not have the desirable qualifications. So it would be worthwhile to open industrial training schools and give vocational guidance to the tribal students.

(3) Changing economy:

Changing economy affects the education and educational development affects the economic pattern. Due to the industrial growth in some places there is seasonal migration in search of labor which affects the education. There has been a sudden change in the economy and the corresponding change in education has not kept pace with it. Change in education is a slow process and therefore the tribals are not fully prepared to take the advantage of the sudden change in economy. Also the introduction of formal education has resulted in a change from agriculture and forest economy to service and wage earning economy. Many of the tribals are now working in the public and private sectors and government offices. This has created a fear in the minds of the traditional tribal that an educated boy will leave his family for he will be attracted to the city life in search of a job and would settle there. Ambasht (1970) observed in his study on the tribes of Ranchi district in Bihar that there are a good number of families who are losing grounds as farmers in tribal society and there is practically no one to look after the agriculture in the family and they fight over the the paternal property.

(4) Lack of Knowledge:

In tribal as well as other areas of the country various programmes have been taken up for economic development under the Community Development programme. But it is seen that these programmes have not succeeded as expected. Even to take advantage of these schemes, a certain degree of awareness, progress and education is necessary. N.K. Singhi (1979:4) says even to take advancement of these development schemes and obtaining modern jobs, education is necessary. Socio-economic development and expansion of education are thus closely interlinked and inter-dependent process. For e.g. the profit gained from the paddy crop, produced by the Japanese method of paddy cultivation was wasted on drinks and petty things. They didn't know that the income has to be used as revolving capital for the next season. Sometimes it so happens that the crop comes up very well but they get cheated of their money by crooks, money-lenders, Govt. employees and contractors. According to B.A. Deshmukh (2004) observed that the bulk of schemes in mixed tribal areas go to non-tribal people, the tribal people do not come forward to take up schemes as they have no trust in government agencies. This indifference is born out of ignorance and this is due to lack of education. Even if the economic programmes have succeeded, it is not seen in their standard of living as they have been cheated of their money by crooks.

(5) School timings:

The school timings are clashing with the agricultural hours. Ambasht (1970) noticed that during the agricultural season the attendance in the schools goes down while in the slack agricultural season the attendance goes up. This was seen in the tribal areas of Ranchi. Education suffers on account of the fact that the tribal boy or girl is an economic asset. Here too economy determines the number of pupils, the length of time of their stay at school. Here the form of education and the nature of schools do not conform to the economic circumstances. Education therefore should conform to agricultural season. Then only the economic need and educational activities could go together without clashing with each other.

Social aspect of Tribal Education

The social aspect of a community deals with the social customs, beliefs, attitudes and practices of man. It involves methods of grouping and grading people for the effective conduct of the various activities for common existence by sharing common activities under bonds of relationship. As the tribals form a small community they have their own structure, their own territory and their relations are direct and intimate. Some of the prevailing attitudes, customs, beliefs and practices among them lead to their educational deprivation.

As the tribe who practice hunting and are food-gatherers in India is very low the educational problems faced by them needs a special study. As most of the tribes are agricultural, artisan tribes, their lack of interest in education may be due to some other causes. Many studies have shown that economic cause is not only the factor for educational backwardness but social factors are also equally responsible.

The social factors leading to educational deprivation among the tribals are:

(1) Desire for education:

The urge for education has to be created among the tribal parents. They should be made aware and convinced that education will bring a change for their material well-being, and then only they will realize the value of education. For example Shaileshwar Prasad (1980) observed "In villages having Christian and non-Christian population, it has been noticed that most of the Christian parents send their children to school., whereas most of the non-Christian do not send their children to school because the utility of education has been well impressed on the minds of the Christian tribal parents". Among Christian tribes this awareness is so strong that the children are forced to go to school. B.A. Deshmukh (2004) reported that in Bihar Christian and Non-Christian tribesmen stay side by side. It is seen that one brother who is a Christian sends his children both male and female to school, while the other who is not a Christian is satisfied with his traditional way of life although both the brothers have same resources. An awareness of the importance of education has to be created by the social workers working in the tribal areas. Rathnaiah (1977), Shyamlal (1987), Das (1993), Shah (1992) and Patel (1984) studies indicate that the tribal parents themselves are not basically interested in the education of their children as they gave priority to economic pursuits over schooling Even if they are favorable towards education they do not actively participate in the process of education.

(2) Awareness about education and educational facilities:

It is found that fairly a large number of tribes are still unaware of the facilities and programmes for education. For example Shah and Patel's (1985) study covering 64 villages in Gujarat tribal areas shows that only about one-fourth of the respondents knew about industrial training institutes, about one-half of them know about colleges and hostels. Similarly about one-fourth of them know about preferences given to tribes for admission to educational institutions, reservation of seats in engineering and medical colleges, reservation of jobs in government and semi government organizations. It is seen that there is a positive and significant relationship between the level of awareness of the household heads, family's socio-economic status, the educational level of parents and family size on the educational attainment of their children. Rathnaiah (1977) study indicates that there is a strong and positive co-relation between adult literacy and child enrolment. Several studies like Ambasht (1970), Rathnaiah (1977), and Shah & Patel (1985) indicate that parental education assumes greater importance in schooling of their children and further continuance of the education from primary to secondary level. Regarding family size Shyamlal (1987), T.B. Naik (1969) observed that the enrolment of children increases as the size of the household increases as they may be able to spare a child for school as his job in the house could be taken over by some other member of the family. When asked why they were so selective they said "We have earmarked one child for education and the others to look after the cultivation" This indicates their typical attitude towards education. The aspects of tribal education will vary from area to area & nothing should be spared in understanding the problems which arise in different context as different tribal people are at varying stages of economic and cultural development.

(3) Low level of motivation

It has been also observed that limitations in the spread of education among the tribes are due to their low level of motivation and aspirations. It is seen that the gap between aspiration and achievement also restrict and is responsible for the success of any programme of social development. Shyamlal (1987) found that among the Bhils the parents had low motivation and low aspiration, but the students had high motivation for study to secure better employment. Rathnaiah (1977) also found in his study on the tribes of Adilabad district that the parents and children have low motivation and low educational aspirations, most would like to study up to matric level only and only a few wanted to go to college. The prime motive to study was to get 'some employment'. But as some tribal youths with moderate level of education could not secure paid employment and this is developing frustration among them. B.A. Deshmukh (2004) found that among the Koknas tribe in Maharashtra that the parents of the tribal children had low motivation which was seen from their low educational aspirations.

(4) Medium of instruction:

The basic drawback of the education system for the tribals is that the language that is being taught is alien to the tribal. Shyamlal (1987) reported that a major proportion of students felt problem in learning English and mathematics while a few students blamed the teacher for their low quality teaching. Basu (1993) has also discussed the importance of mother tongue as the medium of instruction. Singh (1997) found that "majority of the scheduled tribe students felt problems in learning English and Mathematics.

In brief, it can be said that all the findings emphasize that the best medium of educating them would be their own language at least up to primary level and then it can be changed over to the regional language.

The little spread of education among some of the tribes is mainly because of no provision has been made to teach them in their mother tongues.

(5) Content of textbooks:

Kundu (1980) points out that the 'textbook families' are urban upper middle class families whose customs, traditions, dress and food appear alien to the tribal learner. So they create a negative attitude towards their own culture. If the school and the curriculum are based on the culture of the learners, then they feel at home and then the school is just an extension of home for them. Education makes a person fit to face the problems of life with courage. Education in tribal areas therefore should have direct relevance to their needs.

(6) Oral tradition:

The influence of tradition on education is marked in all societies. Tribals have long oral tradition. Their history, myths and customs, folklore are orally handed down from generation to generation. This is well expressed through a santhan proverb "Purthi reak khon, thuti reak sorsa" (Memory is superior to books). Therefore they are sensitive to print and are poor in reading skills. So formal education for them is disinteresting. Moreover the tribes have rich history, literature, folk-lore, song, dance, music but the schools do not seem to have any provision to teach these aspects of tribal culture. So education for them should be made pleasurable by making use of the material of informal education like tribal plays, recitation, riddles, story-telling, fables, proverbs, etc. in their teaching.

(7) Existence of ethnic stereotypes:

A student's performance depends on the teacher's expectation which is often referred to as "Pygmalion Effect". If the teacher's expectation is low, the student tends to satisfy him by his poor performance. All these lead to culture conflict in the classroom. Kundu (1981) pointed out that negative stereotyping of tribals is very strong among non-tribals teachers. A survey of such stereotypes revealed that the non-tribal teachers have negative stereotypes of their non-tribal pupils such as 'they are genetically inferior in intelligence', their culture is inferior'. Desai and Patel (1981) reported that the attitude of teachers towards the tribal children was not healthy. Joshi (1981) also reported that the "heads of the tribal families expressed that the teachers did not show favorable attitude towards their children". Most of the teachers didn't have any training to work in backward areas. As they belonged to the upper castes they were prejudiced towards the tribal students. The tribal students are shy and submissive by nature and also due to the negative attitude of teachers they do not approach the teachers in case of difficulty resulting in poor results.

(8) Sex and enrolment:

It is seen that at the primary stage the girls are in large numbers, but in the middle standard the number is reduced. This is due to the differential conception of functional roles of girls in traditional societies. Early marriages are common among the tribals, so as soon as they attain the age of twelve or fourteen, they get married. In this context education is not considered necessary for girls.

K. Mann (1987) study on Bhil women of Rajasthan observed that the females are not allowed to attend school as the mother is deprived of her assistance in household & other works, school education is said by some, to spoil the girls, while some say sending females to schools is no use as they have to get married & it is a loss to the parents. This also explains the absenteeism & stagnation at schools.

Conclusion:

Education plays an effective role in bringing socio-economic development in all the types of society. A variety of measures were initiated and implemented in tribal areas to ameliorate their socio-economic condition and educational advancement. However these programmes could not make much progress due to the ignorance and illiteracy of the tribes.

Economic condition of tribals creates a bottleneck in the education of children. The tribal students come from poor families; many of them have to assist their parents in agricultural and other economic pursuits, so sending a child to school means an economic burden for parents. Also the attitude of giving priority to economic pursuits over education and lack of interest for education leads to educational backwardness.

Their agricultural return is low as they do not follow the modern methods of agriculture. Industries have started coming up in tribal areas but they do not have the qualifications to join them. Due to the industrial growth they migrate to towns in search of labor seasonally which affects their education. Due to their lack of knowledge they do not take advantage of the government schemes and are cheated by the contractors and moneylenders. The school timings clash with the economic activities so the attendance is low in the agricultural season.

Moreover the desire, motivation and aspiration for education are found to be low as the parents and guardians of the tribal students are generally illiterate and therefore cannot give proper guidance to their children. And therefore the level of aspiration is not much higher among the tribal students. A positive relationship is seen between the socio-economic aspects of the family, the literacy level of parents, family size and the enrolment and educational aspirations of children.

Little or no education is imparted through tribal mother tongues. Lack of education through tribal languages is partly responsible for the tribal's poor performance in education. The content in the textbooks is not based on their culture so it appears alien to them. As they are used to oral tradition they are sensitive to print and poor in reading skills. Also as the teachers are mostly non-tribes they are prejudiced towards the tribal students and being shy the students do not approach them for any problem leading to poor performance. Another factor dampening the zeal for education is the lack of general consciousness about the function of education and also the unawareness about the facilities available for education.

As per their social norm the marriageable age is quite low and they leave schools in the middle or in the latter part of secondary education. This is wastage in education. In case of girls due to their functional roles in the house, early marriages, the attitude that girls education is loss to parents all these are responsible for large number of drop-out among girls.

Thus education, economy and society are closely linked. Change in one is bound to affect the other two. So the educational problems of the tribes have to be viewed against the background of their economy and society. Only then will the educational efforts be successful. B.A. Deshmukh (2004) aptly quotes "of all the items in the development programme for the tribes, education is the most important as it is both the means and the end of real progress".

Suggestions

1. Considering the low literacy level of parents, social education containing awareness about the importance of formal education is to be created through Adult education classes.
2. The tribal children help their parents in agricultural activities. It is therefore better to run school in these areas during summer and non-agricultural season and close them in sowing and harvesting seasons.
3. Due to the poor financial condition the parents need their children help in household and agriculture work. Some schemes such as earn and learn can be introduced in the schools to encourage the tribal children to attend school.
4. The tribes have a deeply entrenched oral tradition, learning is a pleasurable thing for them. So oral reading, recitation, repetition, riddles, story-telling, role- playing can be applied in teaching the tribal students.
5. Attempts should be made to identify dominant non-cultural basis in existing textbooks and remove them as far as practicable.
6. The tribal students find English and Mathematic difficult so these subjects should be taught in an informal way by using examples of tribal life and culture. Teachers should be specially trained for this.
7. Lack of education through tribal language is partly responsible for the tribal poor reading ability. An important corrective against this would be the education of the tribal through their mother tongues.
8. To make the educational programmes successful there should be vigorous programs of social development. Social education will create in the tribal mind an awareness of their own surroundings, problems and needs with sense of national feeling. Instead of being only a literacy movement, it should include the whole canvas of the tribal life.

22

Issues Involved in Education Among Tribal Women: Review

—Marzieh Gorji Poshti

Whereas India has the greatest number of tribals, tribal studies suppose great significance. Majority of Indians tribal are illiterate and residing in rural. And most of them are dependent on traditional agriculture.

This paper focuses on tribal education in India in general and tries to find out problem of education among tribal women in particular. Women generally suffering from inequality in the society, but tribals' women face lots of problem because of their living condition. Majority of tribals people are illiterate and the literacy rate amongst children in predominately tribal areas has always been ruled by two major factors; initially the poor socio-economic conditions of tribal people and secondly the lack of political will and administrative commitment to provide adequate primary and secondary education in such remote tribal belts.

Tribal women participate in outdoor and indoor activities; girls have important role in family economic by working at home, farm and earn money to support family financial condition, so that it is not easy for the family to send their girls to school.

Introduction

Tribal studies assume great significance in India, which is home to a tribal population, spreads across its territory both in the hill areas and in the plains. According to Pariyarm M. Chacko (2005) said that; India has the largest number of tribes and perhaps the largest literature base on the subject.

Whereas India has the greatest number of tribals, tribal studies suppose great significance. Majority of Indians tribal are illiterate and dwell in rural. And most of them are dependent on traditional agriculture. Indian tribals constitute roughly 8 per cent of the nation's total population, nearly 68 million people according to the 1991 census of the total tribal population live there.

Pshah V., Patel T., (1984) stated that, education is concerned with learning. Learning is a life-long process. It refers to the method by which a society attempts to direct and accelerate the learning process of its members.

As Sah D.C. (2004) exposed that education in the tribal areas has always been a matter of great concern and the lack of it has always had a negative impact on the development of tribal people. The literacy rate amongst boys and girls in predominately tribal areas has always been governed by two major factors, viz., the poor socio-economic conditions of tribal people and secondly the lack of political will and administrative commitment to provide adequate primary and secondary education in such remote tribal belts.

The commitment of tribes to acquiring a formal education for their children varies considerably. Tribes differ in the extent to which they view education positively. Gonds and Pardhans, two groups in the central hill region, are a case in point. The Gonds are cultivators, and they frequently are reluctant to send their children to school, needing them, they say, to work in the fields. The Pardhans were traditionally bards and ritual specialists, and they have taken to education with enthusiasm. The effectiveness of education policy likewise varies by region. In those parts of the northeast where tribes have generally been spared the wholesale onslaught of outsiders, schooling has helped tribal people to secure political and economic benefits. Many tribal schools are plagued by high dropout rates. Children attend for the first three to four years of primary school and gain a smattering of knowledge, only to lapse into illiteracy later. Few who enter continue up to the tenth grade; of those who do, few manage to finish high school. Therefore, very few are eligible to attend institutions of higher education, where the high rate of attrition continues.

Sharma S. Ram. (1996) said that, education is considered to be the key to modernization and a catalyst to political and economic development of a society. There is a general agreement on the view that almost all the societies have been male dominated and the status of women has a direct relationship with the level of development of a society.

Also he added the significance of the education of girls cannot be over-emphasized. For full development of our human resources, the improvement of homes and for moulding the character of children during the most impressionable years of infancy, the education of women is of even greater importance than that of men. The education of women can assist greatly in reducing the fertility rate.

Deshmukh, B. A. (2004; 32) reveals that; 'Education To-day is not solving our economic problem. Formerly every youth used to participate in economic pursuits. Now only a part of them get good employment. The rest are unemployed or under-employed. To engage in agriculture is out of question for they have long ceased to be agriculturists mentally as their education had no such bias'.

To make education more attractive, it should hold a promise for conferment of economic benefit. It is urged that most of the tribal people would be reluctant to sacrifice the mere income which they derive from utilizing the services of their children for the uncertain future when the children will bring additional income to the family by getting employed outside.

People tend to respond more easily to stimuli, which have some continuity or analogy with their traditional values and forms, of organization. Continuity of cultural patterns is the main reason for the relative case of culture transfer. The system of education in tribal areas should have a tribal bias and the departure from their traditional values and attitudes should be minimum. Education makes a person fit to face the problems of life with courage. Tribal education, therefore, to be accepted by the people without much misgiving should have direct relevance to their basic needs and aspirations. The personality of the educator and that of the first few acceptor of the idea is important.

Education Tribal of Women

According to one article in Times of India, (1991), the women exhausted after the day's work that she is left with no energy to attend to any other programme, say education, meant for women welfare. Most of the girls are not spared for schooling because of more hands needed for the work. But due to outside contact people are now realizing the importance of education for girls. So, only the well-to do families, who can manage for extra working hands, can spare the girls for education and the poor girls are still kept busy with household or farm work. Hence to make use of the welfare and development programmes it is imperative to raise the economic status of the local people in general and women in particular. World Bank also emphasizes on the link of status of women to the poverty. In its report the World Bank recommends, "the surest and in fact the only way to lift India out of poverty is to educate and enhance The Status of Women".

The World Bank in its annual report further said that women in India, as a group, are more vulnerable than men in terms of education, employment ways, health care, and morality rates, and a range of other indicators. Hence need to improve their economy.

K. N. Dash (2004) said one of the most important aspects of backwardness of tribals is the lack of spread of education among them. In otherwise it may be said that all the base of the fallen state of tribal society is their widespread illiteracy. Education is a prerequisite for progress and development of any community. Acquisition of useful knowledge enables a person to attain the right objectives of life. Besides formal education in schools, education proceeds from birth to death. The process of socialization starts from the home. The child learns to adjust with surrounding from the family members and friends. But formal education on the schools helps the child to learn about outside world and equips him to adjust to the changing situation of the society. After independence special efforts have been made to improve upon the educational level of the tribal people of India. It's needless to improve their economic condition the tribals cannot improve their economic condition and take advantage of the various developments that are implemented for them.

The Following table shows tribal literacy rates in Maharashtra state.

Tribal literacy rates in Maharashtra state

No	*Year*	*Tribal M* /	*F*
1	1961	12.55	1.75
2	1971	19.06	4.21
3	1981	32.38	11.94
4	1991	49.08	24.08

Sources: India census.

Socio-economic problems in educating tribal girls

Economic Factors:

As Deshmukh (2004) quoted L. R. N. Srivastava's statement in the book *Tribal education* on the basis of his survey of educational situation among the tribal, he says that poor economic condition of the tribal societies is a great hindrance to successful education. Almost all the tribes-whether food gatherers, hunters, fishermen, shifting cultivators or settled agriculturist-lack enough food to maintain the family for the whole year. Education, therefore, is a luxury to them which they can hardly afford. Each school-going child in a tribal family is an economic unit and contributes to the family income. If the child is taken away from his normal economic work to attend school, the family is deprived of the little income, which he brings; instead, the parents have to feed the child out of their earnings which further reduces the economic stability of the family. According to the present system of education any economic benefit a tribal child can bring to his family will be only after 10 or 15 years of schooling. The parents have neither the patience nor the foresight to wait for such a long period. They can, however, be convinced easily it the education for them can be made productive right from the very beginning'.

Also in Economic condition, it is observed that the "tribal parents are not in a serious mood about the education of their children" Siggh 1981 reported that the 'majority of tribal students belonged to agricultural class, their family size varied from 5 to 8 members in large number of cases.

Poor financial condition is also one of the important reasons for children not attending the school. Srivastava, Dubey, Rath and Misra found that 'tribal students usually had poor family educational background' Joshi (1980) observed that '85% of the fathers (below 45 years of age) and 95% of the mothers had practically no education in schools.

Schools in tribal areas can directly become instruments for promoting economic development. In this connection the role of the teacher is significant. 'The text book' did not properly reflect the special needs of the tribal children.

Formal educational among the scheduled tribals has certain economic repercussions for a tribal family to sent their children to school is an economic proposition and entails dislocation in the traditional pattern of division of labour. The tribal boys help their parents in the agriculture field during busy agricultural season. The girl-child helps their mother in domestic work. Many parents just cannot afford to send their children to the school.

Social Factors: Just opening schools and allocating funds is not enough to provide education to tribal people. As social factors also play an important role in education. The tribes are not used to formal education as it not necessary to discharge their social obligations. Hence education should be presented to them in such a way so that it will suit their way of life and culture. One of the problems in tribal is cultural and for the tradition of culture is more respect for all especially for girls such as:

- Girls should helps to parents and care of home so no use of education.
- Early age at marriage of girls and boys. Girls marry between the age-group of 12 to 16 and boys between 15 – 20 years. The boys and girls do not like to attend schools after their marriage.
- The school is located at a far away place from the village and parent does not like their girls to send to the school.
- Girls are required to help in the house-held matters and sometimes required to earn by getting some minor employment in the village.
- The school has male teacher so parents doesn't like send girls for that school.

Malhotra O.P. (1998) stated, family plays a vital role in educating its young members being the first and important institution of education. "Education starts at birth with the primordial sharing," described by Werner and Kaplan. It continues as an interactional relation between more mature persons (mother, father, adults, as ever widening circle), who cares for the child and cannot escape his role as educator, and a less mature persons (infant, child, young person), who attaches himself to the more mature person and inevitably is educated (the one being educated).

Lack of Suitable Teacher

One of the major reasons for the slow growth of education in tribal areas is Lack of suitable teachers. The teachers employed in tribal schools do not appreciated the tribal way of life and their culture. They have sense of superiority and treat the tribals as savage and uncivilized so the students do not approach the teacher in case of difficulty.

Lack of Facilities

One of the major problems in tribal education is that of language. Most of the tribal languages and dialects are in the most rudimentary stage and there is hardly any written literature.

Attitude of Parents Toward Education

One of the important the issue of parental attitude towards education and educating the child, it is observed that the tribal parents are not in a serious mood about the education of their children. They do not like that their educated children should leave their family in search of jobs and leave agriculture as their profession.

Help in household work, agricultural work and looking after the babies was found main reason for not attending the school and drop out.

Modern Education

There are efforts where large numbers of schools have been started and modern education has been introduced. They had problem with modern education (1) Language of education (2) Content of education (3) They found it meaningless and could not relate to it. (4) They could not understand why child should be educated when he is economically viable modern education had very little to do with that. So in tribal context there was oral tradition. Thus no reading and writing. They did not learn through formal education.

Most of the tribal languages are only spoken language without having script of their own. The tribal education is usually imparted through the regional language which hinders the satisfactory educational development among the tribal people. Lack of script and absence of a literary tradition together stand as a constraint in the education of several tribal communities. The question of text books should be viewed from the point of view of script and also content. As the process of integration demands that the people of the state, the prescribed common text books should also include topics depicting the life of the tribals. This will enable both the tribals and non-tribals students to understand each other in a better way.

Conclusion

Education is an important tool of assisting tribal people in knowing their weaknesses and enables them to gain necessary knowledge in order to achieve progress in various spheres of their life in systematic or consistent manner. The needs of a tribal are ever changing. Every successive generation aims at making improvement in the existing pattern. Education helps in rebuilding and reorganising the experiences and needs of the tribal and thus eliminates the unworthy features of the society and builds up happier and better world.

Nowadays education in the tribal areas is a vital matter and lack of it is a harmful matter for the development of tribal people. The main problem among the tribal people is that parents are not aware about the advantage of higher education and they think education is not necessary for the boys and girls especially. They think that girls should marry and be as a good wife and good mother. When they have to choose between the education of their sons and girls they prefer to send their sons which they consider more important from economic point of view. The present study shows that economic reason is one of the problems in tribal and poor financial condition of the parents which needed boys and girls help in indoor and outdoor work was seen as an important factor to keep them away from the school.

Of course there are lots of facts about the problem of women education. But for improve the tribal education, needs to participate and cooperative of all governmental and domestic facilities. Actually the progressive of tribal depends on the increase of educated children. Thus without education a tribal cannot even dream to be modern.

23

Language and Schooling of Indigenous Children: Issues Related to Medium of Learning

—Nanjunda D.C.

Although research evidence has demonstrated the positive consequences of bilingual or multilingual schooling on cognitive development and social interaction processes, tribal children would require special programs to be able to cope. The Constitution of India allows the use of tribal dialect (mother tongue) as the medium of instruction if the population of the tribe is more than 100,000. Although the constitution on 1956 recognized the need for primary education in the mother tongue for linguistic minorities toady education still is being impaired primary in the 15 official languages and English. The denial of schooling in the mother tongue to children of tribal communities assumes significance in the context of their poor response to formal education and high attrition rates. An increasing number of researchers strongly advocate the use of the mother tongue or home language as medium of instruction in early stages of education. ST children face problems wherever teachers do not speak their dialect at all. Assam was the first state to prepare teacher training modules and separate teaching learning materials for the Bodo tribal language in 1995. A Growing body of research on language and education of ethnic minorities in western societies highlights at the crucial role played by home languages in early learning. This paper gives a platform to discuss some crucial issues relating to the instruction at the early state and reviews policy an practise relating to mother tongue education for tribal children in India.

Introduction

Scheduled Tribe in India are more like the "indigenous" or "tribal people" in other parts of the world. The population of Scheduled Tribes in India according to 2001 census is 8.43 crore. Education of Scheduled Tribe children is considered important, not only because of the constitutional obligation, but also a crucial input for total development of tribal communities. The literacy levels of the Scheduled Tribes according to the 2001 census is 47.10 per cent as compared to overall literacy rate of the total population i.e., 65.38 per cent, which shows a dismal picture of Scheduled Tribes education. So long as there is a gap between the literacy levels, the position of Scheduled Tribes will remain backward. Lack of education may lead to child exploitation, child labor, population explosion, etc., so the need of the hour is to bring quality education through 100 per cent school enrolment and retention with more emphasis on the girl child education. I have given some suggestions for imparting quality education among the Scheduled Tribes in order to uplift themselves and to overcome the socio-economic problems.

The spread of education among the weaker sections of our society is vital as education is a prime requisite for socio-economic development. The policy to promote educational interests of the weaker sections of the people, especially the Scheduled Castes and Scheduled Tribes, has been enshrined in our Constitution as a Directive Principle of State Policy. Therefore, the main thrust continues to be on education. The general level of literacy is very low and is lower still in the case of Backward Classes. To conclude in the words of Swami Vivekananda - "The Real India lives in the Villages. Unless we are able to uplift the Tribal and the backward classes, India faces to dark future. Along with their economic improvement they have to be raised culturally and spiritually."

Empowerment is about people - both women and men - taking control over their lives: becoming conscious of their own situation and position, setting their own agendas, creating space for themselves, gaining skills, building self-confidence, solving problems, and developing self-reliance. It is not only a social and political process, but an individual one as well - and it is not only a process but an outcome too. Realizing that Scheduled

Tribes are one of the most deprived and marginalized groups with respect to education, a host of programmes and measures were initiated ever since the Independence. Elementary education is a priority area in the Tribal sub-plans from the 5th Five Year Plan. Education of ST children is considered important, not only because of the Constitutional obligation but also as a crucial input for total development of tribal communities. One of the super goals of SSA is to "bridge all gender and social category gaps at primary stage by 2007 and at elementary stage by 2010". The issues and challenges in tribal education can be categorized as external, internal, socio-economic and psychological. The external constraints are related to issues at levels of policy, planning and implementation while internal constraints are with respect to school system, content, curriculum, pedagogy, medium of instruction etc. The third set of problems relates to social economic and cultural background of tribals and psychological aspects of first generation learners. The literacy level of Scheduled Castes and Scheduled Tribes is very low compared to the general literacy rate. Recognizing that education provides opportunities for a permanent change in the socio-economic status of these people, this Government gives top priority to education. Hence out of a sum of Rs. 448.91 crores provided in the Budget Estimate for 2004-2005 to this Department, more than 70 per cent is earmarked for schemes related to education. There is a need to evolve sensitive model of tribal education rooted in the psychological strengths of tribal children.

Traditionally referred to as adivasis, vanbasis, tribes, or tribals, Schduled Tribes constitute about 8 per cent of the population of India. There are about 573 Scheduled Tribes living in different parts of our country, having their own languages, which are varied from the one spoken in the State where they live. There are more than 270 such languages in India. According to the 2001census, the tribal population in India is 74.6 million. The largest number of tribals is in Madhya Pradesh (16.40 million), followed by Orissa (7 million) and Jharkhand (6.6 million). There were 16 million Scheduled Tribe children (10.87 million of 6-11 years and 5.12 million of 11-14 years) as of March 2001, out of the total child population in India of about 193 million in the age group of 6 to 14 years (Selected Educational

Statistics – 2000-01, Government of India). Education of Scheduled Tribe children is considered important, not only because of the Constitutional obligation but also as a crucial input for total development of tribal communities and also for the economic development of a country. One of the challenges in providing education to tribal children is to setting up school facilities in small, scattered and remote tribal habitations. The majority of the Scheduled Tribes live in sparsely populated habitations in the interior and in inaccessible hilly and forest areas of our country. So an attempt is made by the researchers to discuss and analyze the problems of tribal children's education in India since tribal children are neither culturally inferior nor cognitively less competent than the children of other groups.

Education has limited connotation. It is largely concerned with the existing formal structure of education and the institutionalized methodology of imparting knowledge to individuals. Within this very system exist many sub-groups of individuals with specific needs and tribals are one of them. In fact tribals form a large group of individuals in the Indian society. For several historical, economic and social reasons the scheduled groups have remained economically backward and socially retarded even to this day. The ST population accounts for 8.6 per cent of the total population of the country. There are many constitutional provisions and legislative support available for safeguarding the welfare and the interests of STs. In addition planned developmental efforts have also taken place through Five-Year plans. Despite the concern reflected inthe Indian Constitution and the developmental efforts initiated for the welfare and the development of STs, their socio-economic and political development is still far below the others and therefore much more needs to be done in this direction, including their empowerment – educational, social, economic and political – with due regard to their special identity – culturally, habitation ally, traditionally – and in terms of the tribals.

Education of Scheduled Tribe children is considered important, not only because of the constitutional obligation, but also a crucial input for total development of tribal communities. The spread of education among the weaker sections of our society is vital as education is a prime requisite for socio-economic development. The policy to promote educational interests of the weaker sections of the people, especially the Scheduled Castes and Scheduled Tribes, has been enshrined in our Constitution as a Directive Principle of State Policy. Therefore, the main thrust continues to be on education. The general level of literacy is very low and is lower still in the case of Backward Classes. There are 16 million ST children (10.87 million in 6-11 years and 5.12 million in 11-14 years) as on March 2001, out of the total child population of about 193 million in the age group of 6 to 14 years in the country (Selected Educational Statistics – 2000-01). Realizing that Scheduled Tribes are one of the most deprived and marginalized groups with respect to education a host of programmes and measures were initiated ever since the Independence. Elementary education is a priority area in the Tribal sub-plans from the 5th Five Year Plan. Education of ST children is considered important, not only because of the Constitutional obligation but also as a crucial input for total development of tribal communities. Another important development in the policy towards education of tribals is the National Policy on Education (NPE), 1986 which specified among other things the following;

* Priority will be accorded to opening primary schools in tribal areas.
* There is need to develop curricula and devise instructional material in tribal language at the initial stages with arrangements for switchover to regional languages.

The Sixth All India Educational Survey (1993) showed that 78 per cent of the tribal population and 56 per cent of tribal habitations have been provided primary schools within the habitation. In addition, 11 per cent of the tribal population and 20 per cent of tribal habitations have schools within less than 1 km radius. About 65 per cent of rural habitations covering 86 per cent of the total rural population have primary schools within the habitation or within a distance of half a kilometer, as against 56 per cent of tribal habitations with 79 per cent of tribal population. Mizoram and Gujarat have the highest percentage of population and habitations covered by primary schools within the habitations. Up to 95 per cent of the tribal population and 85 to 90 per cent of the tribal habitations in the states are provided with schooling facilities within the habitation.

Quality improvement: Development of culturally relevant materials in local languages. Most of the states recognize the need to address issues related to teachers' attitudes, medium of instruction, textbooks and materials, curriculum and pedagogy and teaching- learning process in tribal areas. An increasing number of researchers strongly advocate the use of the mother tongue or home language as medium of instruction in early stages of education. This assumes greater significance in the context of education of tribal children because their mother tongue is often quite distinct from the prominent languages in the state or regional languages. ST children face problems wherever teachers do not speak their dialect at all. From the perspective of language, it is desirable to have a local teacher from the same tribal community. Although research evidence has demonstrated the positive consequences of bilingual or multilingual schooling on cognitive development and social interaction processes, tribal children would require special programs to be able to cope. The Constitution of India allows the use of tribal dialect (mother tongue) as the medium of instruction if the population of the tribe is more than 100,000. Assam was the first state to prepare teacher training modules and separate teaching learning materials for the Bodo tribal language in 1995. Bodo is also a medium of instructions in some districts of Assam. The work on tribal language materials was undertaken through DIET staff and Block Resource Center / Cluster Resource Center coordinators who belonged to the tribal community. Resource material in Bodo language has been prepared and all workbooks at primary stage have been translated/adopted in Bodo language. In many districts, Garo medium workbook has been translated/adopted and distributed in the schools.

Most of the other States (Karnataka, Kerala, MP, UP, Bihar) have taken up activities for quality improvement of tribal area schools. One of the issues identified by the states was the problem faced by tribal children whose home language was very different from the regional language, which was the medium of instruction at the primary level. In Madhya Pradesh teachers' handbooks called Bridge Language Inventory (BLIs) have been prepared in 3 related tribal languages viz. Identified teachers were given training in using BLISs in their classrooms. The teaching-learning package called Dham Dhama Dham was translated into Gondi and supplementary reading material, Kopal, was developed for tribal children. The class I textbook Bharati has been translated into tribal languages. Supplementary TLM for tribal children has been developed in Jhabua district using local cultural form i.e. folk tales, songs, proverbs, riddles, to make the learning process interesting. In all, 450 teachers of 311 schools have been trained to use the supplementary materials. Researches have underlined the need to develop culturally sensitive programmes of school education that can ensure the dignity of tribal groups by providing them with economically viable options for life (Sinha & Mishra, 1997).

In many other states some attempts have been made for linking curriculum with the local needs of the communities. Such curriculum would make tribal children more sensitive to local contexts and sustain them in their respective environments instead of forcing them to move out in search of another life. In Karnataka a textbook for class I & II has been developed and introduced for Soliga language. A handbook has been developed for sensitization of teachers towards social and cultural specificities of tribal societies. In Maharashtra tribal language dictionaries have been developed. Language resource groups have been set up for Bhili, Pawara, Madia, Gondi, etc. Bridge material has been developed in Kerala has developed bilingual language materials at district level in Kasarkode, Waynad, Malappuram and Palakkad. Orissa took the initiative to develop a comprehensive strategy for education of tribal children as earlyas 1997. The state has initiated a number of activities for addressing the quality improvement of tribal education. Andhra Pradesh has developed bilingual dictionaries and teacher training has been organised in Warangal and Vizianegarem districts. Research studies have also been undertaken on the issue of language and maths learning by tribal children. It has been decided to use the multi-level kits developed for tribal areas in Vishakapatnam district and also in other tribal areas. Gujarat has developed dictionaries in Dangi and Bhili dialects. A local word glossary in Dangi has been prepared and distributed in schools for class I-IV in Dang district. Similarly a local word glossary in Adivasi dialect has been prepared for class I-IV in Banaskantha district and distributed in schools. The Vidyasahayaks were given training on the use of these dictionaries. Gujarat has also initiated extensive work for preparation of TLM in tribal languages. The TLM developed include flash cards for different languages and also cards for mathematics. These have been supplied to all schools in tribal areas. A Bridge Language Inventory has also been introduced in Ho and Mundari languages in Ranchi district of Bihar. Use of Local teachers The acceptance of teachers by the community as one of them is critical for increasing schooling participation in tribal areas.

An understanding of and respect for tribal cultures and practices and some amount of familiarity with the local language are important for teachers to gain this acceptance: The presence of tribal teachers, especially from the same community, has shown and improved school participation of ST children. Coming from the same community, it is believed that the teachers would understand and respect the culture and the ethos with much greater sensitivity. Studies suggest that teacher motivation contributes more to teaching – learning process than teacher competence (Vaidyanathan and Nair, 2001). Realising the importance of having teachers from the local community, many states have appointed community teachers or para teachers as they are popularly referred to. The deployment of community teachers was first experimented in the late Seventies in NFE and later in the formal school with the Volunteer Teacher Scheme of Himachal Pradesh (1984). Nineties saw spurt in the appointment of community teachers, who are from the local community and appointed by the gram panchayat or Village Education Committees. Different states have different schemes for appointing community teachers – Shiksha Karmi Scheme (Madhya Pradesh and Rajasthan), Shiksha Mitra Yojna (Uttar Pradesh), Lok Shikshak (Bihar), Andariki–Vidya Volunteer Scheme (Andhra Pradesh). Vidya Upasak Yojana (Himachal Pradesh), Shikshan Sevak (Maharashtra), Guruji (under EGS in Madhya Pradesh) Shikshak (under Basti Shala Scheme in Maharashtra) etc.

It is estimated that there are about 230,000 para teachers engaged in full time schools in the country (Ed.CIL, 2001). The issues relating to classroom transactions are difficult as they deal with well entrenched attitudes and prejudices of teachers as well as seemingly intractable problems of the huge difference between home and school languages. Attempts have been made to address the first issue through training programmes for teachers. However, more emphasis on attitudinal training of teachers on the lines of Orissa is required in most of the states. The second issue has been addressed mainly through the BLIs and primers in tribal languages. There may be a problem of acceptance of the tribal language as a medium of instruction in the tribal communities, therefore, adequate dialogue with tribal communities and their leaders is required to prepare them on this issue (Ganesh, 2003).

The constitution of India was framed in 1950 with an objective to guarantee social, political and economic Justice to all irrespective of caste, creed and religion. It was well visualized that development in education along with other allied sectors would play a vital role to bring about desirable changes in the country. That means that backward sections of Indian population i.e. Scheduled Castes and Scheduled Tribes and other backward section must be provided opportunity in education to develop critical thinking and self determination and contribute to the progress of the country. These promises laid the foundation for the attempt of Universalization of Primary Education in India. In 1950, target was set to universalize primary education among the entire eligible category of children within the age group of 6-14 years of age within a span of 10 years. During that period a great deal of expansion in education facilities was achieved. However, universalisation was still a distant dream. National Policy of Education (NPE),1986 and its subsequent modification in 1992 laid down clearly the following targets to achieve universalization of education at Primary stage. (i) Provision of universal Access to all eligible children by opening of formal or non-formal education Centers within a reasonable distance of one kilometer. (ii) Retention of all children in schooling centers and ensuring completion of 5 years of basic education.(iii) Provisions of Quality education where-by all children achieve minimum achievement level as per the standard. Karnataka is one of the 8th largest state in India, situated in the southern part. The total population of the State is 5.670 crores as per 2001 census (provisional). The scheduled castes and scheduled tribes comprise 22.21 and 16.20 percent respectively. The literacy percentage of the state is 63.61 per cent (excluding 0-6 population) in which male and female literacy stands as 75.95 per cent and 50.97 per cent respectively (Source census 2001, Provisional). If we consider the concentration of indigenous tribal communities, their highest concentration is found in the southern districts of Karnataka State. Chamaraja Nager (Karnataka) is one among these districts, which was formed carving out of earst- while district in 2000 in the process of expansion of districts in the State. The district lies between 29 degree to 80 degree in north latitude and 26 degree to 74 degree in the east longitude that occupies an area of 9580 square kilometers. The area is calculated to 7.9 per cent of the total area of the State. The district has a population of 923819 that is 3.24 percent of the total population of the State and rank 22nd in the State. The density of population is 143 as against 101 in 1991 per square kilometer. The district has recorded an increase of 15.27percent over the last enumeration in 1991.(Source Census, 2001, Provisional). The district has been the dwell of a number of indigenous tribal communities some very marginal and some quite significant as far as their population is concerned. The Tribal population of the district is 573379. The male and female constitute 233120 and 340259 respectively of the total population with a percentage of 58.51 in the district. As per 2001 Census (provisional) the literacy rate of both the sexes stands as 32.61percent. The literacy rate of male is 45.35 percent while that of female is 21.31 percent. They have their own mother tongue having no written script except one tribe, Nayaka who have got a written script. All the languages belong to the Austric Speech family (Jha & Jhingran, 2002).

Kannada Language, Textbook and Medium of Instruction

A lot of attempts have been made to mainstream the tribal children in education process. Most importantly by providing access, reading writing materials, free textbooks and empowering village community to participate in management of school. Achievements are also quite significant in areas of provision of access by opening of new schools, hostels, enrolment of children and empowerment of teachers through mass teachers training on child centered approach. However, there seem to be lack of achievement in retention and achievement of students (on the basis of completion rates) in schools. The dropout rate is still quite high and achievement scores in subjects need significant increase (Ganesh, 2006).

DPEP, Karnataka Study conducted on 1353 schools, 22535 students joined in 1998-99. There are many reasons why the system fails particularly in the case of indigenous tribals. This paper will discuss in detail the problems and issues limited to the area of language, textbook and medium of instruction and other issues directly or indirectly related to that. If we consider the case of tribal child and feature that motivate and de-motivate him in staying in school, we need to consider the background and inputs given to him as part of incentive to adopt the modern education successfully, some factors of importance maybe scrutinized. Language is a part parcel and vehicle of culture. It is the medium of expression. It can be symbolic or spoken. Language is learnt as part of the socialisation and enculturation process. It can not be taught in a sense that it is not merely sensible speech sounds rather typical cultural elements intrinsically linked and ingrained in it. Language can be learnt through interactions. The problem of providing free and compulsory education to all the children of the age group of 6-14 years by establishing sufficient numbers of schools in all areas in order to satisfy the directives of the constitution (article 45) poses many pertinent questions with at least one, for the education of indigenous tribal communities. Part-V of the constitution contains Directive Principles of State Policy contained in article 36-51. These principles are ideals which the State should strive for and some directions to the state executive and legislature as to how their powers be used. Besides these are few other directives addressed to the State in other parts of the constitutions, which like the Directive Principles are also non-justifiable. Article 350- A directs the State to take steps to provide adequate facilities for instructions in the mother tongue at the primary stage of education and particularly to the children belonging to the linguistic minorities mainly with a view to preserve their language and facilitate better understanding among such children. A tribal child is relatively less exposed to other languages at the age of his entry to the school, because of the tribals have their own Eco-zone where they inhabit in relative isolation and therefore have lesser exposure to the outside world. Jenu Kuruba the major tribal communities in Karnataka are least mobile. Their movement as observed is limited to a maximum of 20 kilometers i.e. from home to work sites and to weekly local market not far away from the village. That means they hardly migrate to other part of the district and State unlike Nayaka's who although migrate to other part of the country seasonally in negligible numbers for daily wage laboring. The tribal child entering school for the first time sees a completely different environment.

The building pattern with closed four walls, and sitting arrangement is alien to him. The teacher, his apparel and language - unseen and incomprehensive creates a sense of suspicion and fear in him initially. Subsequently the teachers' (mostly non-tribals) treatment makes impossible for him to continue in school. Here it's important to discuss the role of teacher in class room. It is often seen that teachers working in tribal areas have prejudices and biases towards tribal society and culture. They treat tribals as sub-human beings, who have a lot of blind beliefs and conservative ideas. To them the tribal language which has no written script does not qualify for a status of language and hence inferior. These senses of ethnocentrism are expressed in their dealings with tribal students in a classroom. He seldom inquires into the socio-cultural background of the tribal child. If one considers the case of a tribal child it is clear that he is no less competent even at a tender age. He acquires ability in learning songs at the age of 4-5 years. He learns beating of drums (Dhapa), dances memorising short stories, proverbs, and riddles and often creates new songs of his own in impromptu exchange with peers at the age of 10. He is so close to his things that he dares, dreams, fantasizes, plays and interacts with an infinite thing, words, jargons which no one can even teach him in post-primary education. If we consider the scope of learning language, we will see that a tribal child gets plenty of contexts at home, where every thing is informal and friendly and language learning is spontaneous. However, in school, there is dearth of context and every thing is formal and structured and the language of the book is considered as the highest kind of knowledge. The child has no scope to interact with friends while the teacher is taking a class on monologue basis. The child can not concentrate because of communication failure and monotonous classroom process and instead chastised, beaten by the teacher for not being attentive, responsive and not doing wee in studies. The hostile and in-conducive school atmosphere leads to dropping-out and discontinuation of most of the students from school. Above all the tribal children are the first generation academic learners and have least scope of support and help from parents and relatives who are illiterate. The psychologists, educationists and linguists are of the opinion that a child exposed to multilingual situations in initial years has faster cognitive and intellectual development. But this opinion does not hold well in tribal areas because in urban areas, the child gets its formal education through state language as the medium of instructions, which is his own mother tongue and gradually exposed to other languages. But in tribal society, the child is directly introduced to the State language used in schools rather than his own mother tongue. Another reason is that in urban areas the child has relatively plenty of opportunity to interact with people coming from different linguistic areas. He is exposed to electronic media, Radio and T.V., which not only are the medium of entertainment but also are scope of learning and adopting traits and ideas. The tribal child has absolutely no scope where he gets exposed to other languages. There are many tribal language which has no script. Hence, preparation of suitable textbooks for such category children is a challenging task. In Karnataka, the textbooks are supplied free of cost to tribal and other categories of children.

The language of the textbooks is in standard state language for school students all over the state. It is believed that experts knowing tribal culture and language prepare these books. However, it is found that the books have contents of subjects which are reflective of dominant society. The books have few local specific contents and some time specters and description of animals, birds, trees, etc. alien to the tribal child which poses problem to comprehend. The colour of pictures is not realistic and lacks brightness. All the pictures are often bi-coloured. Overall the cover page, contents and contexts are not local specific and relate to the real life situations of the tribals for which the text book is not appreciated and adopted by the tribal children. The Paradox Considering the constitutional directives and actual implementation of educational scheme one would certainly find a gap or mis-match between what should have been done and what has been done so far. A country like India, where diverse linguistic groups are found, some quite significant and some negligible in number pose a great problem as to how to streamline them in the education process.

As per the constitutional directives the basic education may be provided free of cost to indigenous tribal in their own mother tongue which seems to be a Herculean task for any state government. The indigenous tribal although have a definite territory, they have a number of sub-groups within it. Therefore, language varies in a limited geographical area and within a particular tribe. It also varies from sub-tribe to sub-tribe. Language of one sub-tribe is quite different from another within the limited geographical area due to impact of bordering community and their exposure to outside world. Such examples are innumerable in this district. One such example is that in Kollegal (as administrative division of the district) which has a sizeable number of Jenu Kuruba population and sub-sections like Soliga and Nayaka (relatively assimilated) who live close to each other. Although there are certain similarities in language and culture they differ a lot linguistically. Any textbook on either language could not solve the problem. Secondly, in case of multi-lingual situations in a classroom, whereby students come from different tribal or sub-tribal groups, the problem for the teachers is as to what should be the standard medium of instruction for all the children. This has been a feature of all residential schools running in the district by Schedule Caste and Schedule Tribe Department. The teacher knowing one tribal language finds it impossible to teach students coming from different ethnic and language background. Thirdly, the teachers, mostly non-tribals, do not have adequate knowledge of tribal language. There are tribal teachers (mostly Betta Kuruba and Jenu Kurubas), who can be useful for children. But there is no consideration of the above fact and a Soliga teacher posted in a Jenu Kuruba dominated village or school is as good as non-tribal teachers as they do not know the language of Jenu Kurubas. In the second case some of the non-tribal teachers who have been working reasonably for a long time at a particular tribal area have experience of tribal language where all the students belong to a particular tribal group. However due to a number of reasons, like health hazards (endemic malaria proneregion), lack of basic human facilities like shelter, market place and postal facilities, they get themselves transferred to other parts paving way for posting of a new teacher in his place. Fourthly, the problem could have been subsided with the engagement of sufficient number of local teachers from the community. But unfortunately there is dearth of qualified tribals who can be appointed as teachers in schools. The problems and issues in language, textbook and medium of instruction are very typical to the tribals of Karnataka as to any other region of the country where multi-ethnic and multi-lingual indigenous tribal groups are existing. Development in the education sphere can only be possible when the key issues are addressed properly. These are the issues and problems, which can fail the entire education system even before it is actually implemented unless addressed through strategic planning. Any generalized planning across the board for all category of children not only create an environment of education among tribals but also will delay and break the pace of spontaneous educational development. Therefore, careful and calculative measures must be taken keeping in view the educational need vis-a-vis the cultural orientation of the tribals (Nanjunda , 2007).

Some indicative, if not exhaustive suggestions are given below. 1. Linguistic mapping should be done to assess the incidence and category of tribals before planning for their education. 2. The medium of instruction should be in the mother tongue by way of using bi-lingual primers prepared in a decentralized manner. That means it is not the state or district, it is the block where the teachers (tribal) with educated (although a few) tribal persons will prepare the text book for their own category of children. 3. The school environment should be attractive with gardens, plantations, and children friendly elements with cost effective locally available raw materials. The school must have play materials and self-learning materials for the children to create interest in them to attend school regularly. 4. The teacher working in a tribal dominated school should be rightly informed about his role. He should be oriented on the richness of heritage and culture of the tribals. He should have enough patience to bear the tribal child in a classroom and act as a friend and facilitator rather than a master. 5. The non-tribal teachers working for longtime inspite of various health hazards by knowing the tribal language should be identified and compensated with incentives and rewards as a token of commendations for their valuable services towards the education of tribals so that other non-tribal teachers will be interested to join the force. 6. Tribal teachers should be identified by their category and be posted to schools where he can serve his community children better. 7. The village community although illiterate, they are great assets as far as education onart and craft is concerned. Their resources should be used while topics related to agriculture horticulture and material culture are transacted in the classroom. 8. Innovation through research on various aspects of education must be conducted so as to identify problems and their solutions. The problems and issues identified at this juncture may seriously affect the future developments in the district. Hence, it is high time that appropriate strategies must be built up to find out ways and means not to subside but to mitigate the problems for the future.

Conclusion

The discussion presented above gives us two important lessons. One is that the cognitive qualities of tribal children have to be viewed and evaluated taking into consideration their ecological and cultural contexts that place very different demands on day-to-day life. Because of differences in the demands of tribal ecology, the patterning of their cognitive abilities shows considerable variation from those of other groups. A related and more important lesson is that tribal children are neither culturally inferior nor cognitively less competent than the children of other groups. Instead many of their skills and abilities are highly developed and extremely sophisticated. The implications of these findings for schooling of tribal children are clear. A programme of schooling, which does not pay attention to the ecological, cultural and psychological characteristics of tribal children is highly unlikely to make any significant impact. The educational system of the dominant non-tribal population is of very limited value in the tribal cultural milieu because it does not match with the lifestyle of individuals and the needs of the tribal community. Linking school education with life in general and the needs of the tribal communities in particular is a most important step that requires serious attention. The evidences suggests that tribal children do possess the basic cognitive abilities and psychological dispositions necessary for successful participation in school. Yet tribal children have very low levels of participation and success in school education programmes. This points to our failure to develop a sensitive model of education that is rooted in the psychological strengths of tribal children. Studies indicate that, in comparison to other groups, hunters and gatherers possess a high level of visual and tactual differentiation; they demonstrate capacity for fine judgment of shape and size of stimuli as well as spatial relations and they produce fine categorization of an array of objects (Mishra et. al. 1996). These abilities are required for success in science, art, music, dance, athletic activities, and vocations like carpentry, tailoring, wood and stone crafts.

These skills need to be utilized not only for education of tribal children in schools, but also in the broader economic spheres of tribal life. Such attempts will be helpful in generating and promoting the sense of competence, self-efficacy, self-respect and positive self-image among tribal children in general. Such attempts are also highly likely to provide tribal children with a culturally meaningful, ecologically valid and economically viable altertribal to life by reinforcing the dignity of their culture and identity. Ever increasing contact of tribals with the outside world over the years has introduced several changes in their culture and life. These changes are reflected in their psychological characteristics also. Studies (e.g. Mishra et. al. 1996) indicate that their ways of perceiving the world, categorizing objects, interpreting pictures, and strategies of learning and memory become more similar to those with whom they interact and negotiate their life in these changed circumstances. This suggests that tribal children can acquire all those skills that the members of other groups of the society possess. What is important on our part is to develop a positive frame of mind about tribal children. This is possible only through sensitivity to tribal culture and life, recognition of the cognitive strengths of tribal children, and appreciation of their personality qualities. Efforts in these directions will be very helpful in organizing the programme of tribal education as well as promoting economic and other aspects of tribal development.

Similarly a clear policy for language use in schools has to be developed. Research evidence suggests that significantly fewer students drop out of schools in which the language of tribal groups is used for instruction at the primary level. Development of primers in the tribal dialect involving content from the local context will go a long way in ensuring children's active participation in the learning process in school. While there is a general need for improvement in physical facilities in all schools in remote tribal regions, change in perceptions and outlooks of teachers about tribal children are equally important. Teachers must be sensitized to the cultural and behavioral strengths of tribal children and motivated to do their best for them in schools. Incentives should be initiated to attract effective teachers to work in tribal schools and to retain them there. Only such motivated teachers are likely to generate interest among tribal children towards schools education by attempting to link the contents of the curriculum with the existing realities of tribal communities through the use of innovative technologies.

24

An Experiment in Tribal Education : Where is the End?

—*Sharad Kulkarni*

Tribal communities lead a secluded life and keep minimum contacts with the non-tribal communities. Their main characteristics are simple life style and shyness of contact with others. They do not consciously and openly discuss their main problems of poverty, exploitation and unfair treatment by non-tribal. They have developed what Paulo Freire calls a culture of silence.

Conscious efforts were made to make them discuss their problems of demeaning treatment by others and their silent acceptance of low status to inculcate and assert their self respect. A well trained anitator also made a group of tribal youths to analyze the problems of indebtedness and consequent bondage. This also helped to find out solutions.

The problem of all pervading poverty was also discussed in the specific conditions in their hamlets. The lively dialogue pointed out the need to discuss the problems of land alienation and lack of education and highlighted the need to organize to make the community aware of these and other problems through strengthening their organization.The paper describes the contents of the dialogues and illustrates the use of new pedagogy in the educational experiment.

Introduction

Tribal communities in India, like their counterparts in other countries, are not a homogenous group. They are a significant minority and constitute about 9 percent of the Indian population. Most of the members of these communities still practice subsistence agriculture live in small hamlets somewhat away from the towns and villages inhabited by non tribal. Many of them are illiterate or have only primary education. Majority of them also lead a very poor life and are treated as living below the poverty line. Two major characteristics are simple life style and shyness of contact with others. They mainly live in their own hamlets inhabited by members of the same tribe. Tribal dialects have a very limited vocabulary. They have a limited contact with the non tribal world. All the tribes are endogamous and marry with members living in the nearby area. Even the literate and somewhat educated members of the tribe do not read much except newspapers. Books are rare commodity in the isolated hamlets nor are they felt necessary in the daily life. In some areas many members of the tribe do move to towns and cities for wage labor in lean seasons but even there they prefer to live in groups and keep only the minimum necessary contacts with non-tribal.

Culture of Silence

In the process of rapid development, industrialization and urbanization tribal communities have to face the problems of abject poverty, displacement and consequent erosion of their culture. So long as they were living in isolated areas, they had a distinct cultural life with their own dances, songs and rituals. Away from the currents of modernization and the complexities it created, the tribes led a somewhat protected simple life based on co-operation instead of competition, aloof from the highly raised and sometimes unreachable aspirations of luxurious life. This has kept them away from the stress, frustrations and consequent psycho-somatic ailments of the members of the developed non-tribal communities. However, this has also made them victims of cheating and oppression at the hands of the police, forest guards, other village level Government functionaries and last but not the least money lenders, traders and powerful non-tribal farmers. Till recently many of them were bonded laborers deprived of minimum wages and prescribed hours of work. They suffered in silence and developed what Paulo Freire calls a culture of silence.[1] 'In the culture of silence the masses are 'mute' that is, they are prohibited from creatively taking part in the transformations of their society and therefore prohibited from being. Even if they can occasionally read and write because they were 'taught' in humanitarian – but not humanist – literacy campaigns, they are nevertheless alienated from the power responsible for their silence.

Illiterates know they are concrete men. They know that they do things. What they do not know in the culture of silence – in which they are ambiguous, dual beings – is that men's actions as such are transforming, creative, and re-creative. Overcome by the myths of this culture, including the myth of their own 'natural inferiority', they do not know that their action upon the world is also transforming. Prevented from having a 'structural perception' of the facts involving them, they do not know that they cannot 'have a voice', that is, that they cannot exercise the right to participate consciously in the socio-historical transformation of their society, because their work does not belong to them'.

In such situations the role of education is to create critical consciousness that includes knowledge and creates an urge to act to change the situation. 'The act of knowing involves a dialectical movement which goes from action to reflection and from reflection upon action to a new action'. Tribal communities do face severe and several problems. They are all the time aware of their poverty, exploitation and helplessness. But in their culture of silence there is no problematisation, no knowledge of the conditions that create problems and dehumanize them. Education for them is to attain freedom from oppression and freedom from fatalistic passive attitude of helplessness. 'Problematization, which means both asking questions and calling into question and is therefore a challenging attitude, is, at one and the same time, the beginning of an authentic act of knowing and the beginning of an act of subversion of 'over determination', that is, subversion of praxis inverted upon man'.

Experiment

There are social action groups and community based organizations that are trying to change this oppressive situation. The first task is to make the members of the tribe aware and critically conscious of their oppression by developing praxis which is a chain of action, reflection and action. 'Man's vocation realizes itself in his praxis, which transforms and expresses the world. In its turn, this praxis, which is action and language, turns back upon man and 'over determines' him; that is to say, it conditions him and defines the horizon of meanings within which his further action is to take place. Education – like all other processes of socialization – tends to reinforce this 'over determination'. From the inherent ambivalence of education, namely, its capacity to bring out what is least determined in man as well as to program and determine him'.

One activist working with a community based organization and with vast experience of formal teaching and knowledge of Freire method of pedagogy began his conscientisation work in a small tribe living in an area not far from Mumbai in Maharashtra. Some of his dialogues with a group of tribal youth illustrate a novel method of tribal education. Unfortunately no records were kept of all the proceeding of this three day workshop. The camp was organized by the organization and there were about 20 participants. All of them were literate and hence literacy was not on the agenda. Main object was to create awareness among the cadres of tribal problems and the need to organize community on certain pressing issues.

The camp began with self-introduction by the participants. One introduced himself as Ramya the other as Babya. Others also told their names. The animator asked them to tell their full names and pointed out that the names they were telling were in fact the derogatory abbreviations of their real names. The participants were surprised as they were accustomed to be addressed by these names. Ramya was a derogatory abbreviation of Ram, the name of a Hindu god. Babya was a derogatory abbreviation of Baban. The animator then asked them to tell the name of the trader in the village. They told that his name was Laluseth. Lalu is an abbreviation of Lalaji while Seth is a respectable suffix. The animator asked them why the Seth is not called Lalya, a derogatory abbreviation. They had never thought of this. The discussion reveled that while the tribal persons were known by derogatory names which they themselves have accepted, the non-tribal were not called by such derogatory names. It was agreed that this was an insulting practice applied only to tribal persons. The tragedy was that they themselves have accepted this insulting practice. The animator asked if anything could be done to curb the practice. The only answer was that they must in future tell and write their full names and correct others calling them in derogatory form. The animator told them that self respect begins with oneself. Belief in once self respect and asserting it in transactions with others is the first step towards asserting one's humanity. He pointed out that one of their slogans was that adivasi is a man and not an animal. (Adivasi is a general terms used for the tribe and its members) They were shouting this slogan in processions and public meetings, but at the same time they were not only accepting derogatory names but were also using them.

There was a discussion on the bonded labor system in the area. Moneylender lends some money for ceremonies like marriage. Major part of the loan is in kind. The man for whose marriage the money is given agrees to repay it by working on the farm of the lender or his relative. Both the man and his wife work for years as bonded laborers and are paid only limited food grains per day. The food grains are for their own consumption. In addition some clothes are given on common festivals. Interest is added to the loan every year and the accounts are kept by the lender. The debt is never repaid and the lender always shows a positive balance. This goes on for years and even for generations, if he takes loan for his son's marriage. Luckily the Government of India abolished the system by the Bonded Labor System (Abolition) Act of 1976.

The animator asked the group if any one amongst them was recently married. One of the participants said that his marriage took place before six months. The animator asked him to give details of the amount his father has spent on the occasion. The participant told that his father spent about 15,000 rupees he borrowed from his master in addition to his own small amount. The father approached the master who readily agreed to loan the amount provided his son and wife agreed to work on the farm of his relative till the amount was repaid from his and her wages. The father agreed and asked for some advance to buy clothes for the bride, the groom and their near relations. The master told him that his cousin had a cloth shop in the tehsil town. He would give him a letter to allow them to purchase what they wanted. He assured that he would pay the shop owner. In this tribe buying clothes for marriage is a big event. The participant with his father and uncle and the father, mother and uncle of the bride went to the tehsil town and visited the shop. On reading the letter the shop owner welcomed them and offered tea to all. The group was very impressed with this unusual courtesy. The owner assured them that he would give the best available cloth at cheap price. They were not to pay the bill as his cousin has assured to pay the amount. He also said that marriage is a sole man occasion that comes only once in life and honor was more important than money. He also told them that the tailor in his shop would stitch the pant and the shirt for the groom. The group purchased cloth for the groom's clothes and also two saris for the bride, in addition to some blouse pieces and towels for the relations. (It is customary to give a towel to close relations in return for their gifts.) He was not ready to disclose the total bill and promised that it would be around Rs. 500/- inc uding tailoring charges. Expenses amounting to Rs. 100/- on travel were met from the father's personal cash. In a marriage in the tribe everyone is called for the feast. The usual dish is crushed wheat boiled and mixed with Jaggery. The wheat and the Jaggery was given by the money lender from his own shop. Most of the money lenders in the area have shops that sell food grains, jaggery and other commodities. He also gave Rs. 500/- in cash to meet the payments for bride price (dej) and payment to the priest, band players and others. The participant told that the marriage was a grand event and all appreciated it. He also told that three days after the marriage he and his wife have began to work on the farm of the lender's relative. They are paid 5 kilos of paddy every day. He does not know what amount has been recovered from neither their wages nor the balance. The animator wrote the account on the board and asked who the main beneficiary of the whole affair was. All unanimously said that it was the lender. One participant humorously remarked that it was really a lenders marriage.

The next question was to find out a solution. Some participants suggested that the bride price should be nominal. The purchases should not be made on credit and an activist from the organization should be present when the purchases are made. All the expenses should be met from the fathers or groom's money and if necessary from borrowing from the relatives and friends. Some participants pointed out that the parents of the bride would not accept such conditions. Usually the boys from the tribe do not marry a girl from the same hamlet. The participants from different hamlets said that they would persuade the girls and their parents from their hamlet to accept these conditions that would avoid the bondage of the girl and her husband. It was also agreed to organize group marriages at one place and on the same day to reduce expenses on food, musical bands etc. The system of group marriages started and continues to this day. It has also been widely followed by other organizations in tribal areas.

On the second day it was decided to discuss the issue of poverty. This was a big challenge. Because of very simple life style and shyness of contact with non tribal, members of the tribes have not developed ability to grasp abstract ideas. They know corruption and oppression by the police, forest guard and others but are not able to grasp the bureaucratic system. To them cheating by shop keepers, money lenders and others is a known fact of life but they do not understand capitalism, profit motive and other abstract ideas. Poverty is their main problem and it has to be discussed to make them aware of it. The animator asked who among the participants were poor. Everybody said that he was poor. Then the question was who is not poor and the answer was that a household that can have two meals a day all the year is not poor. (Surprisingly this concept of poverty is similar to the definition of poverty based on calorie consumption). The question was whether bigger tribal farmers were poor or not. The answer was that they were also poor as they had to go without food for some days in an year. The only families that would afford two meals a day throughout the year were of a primary school teacher and the local shop keeper. The teacher was getting monthly salary and the shop keeper was selling goods and getting money every day.

The question arose why they were poor and the discussion brought out the problems of small land holdings, unemployment for many days in an year, low wages and so on. It was agreed that they should pursue education of their younger siblings to enable them to find out jobs out of agriculture. It turned out that some households had earlier larger land holdings but these were taken over by the moneylenders. This led to the discussion of the alienation of tribal lands. It was found out that many participants were not aware of the laws that prohibited alienation of their lands and also of laws that were made to restore their alienated lands. They were also not aware of the laws restricting money lending. It was agreed to organize a special camp to discuss this laws. It was agreed that they should form a Tarun Mandal (youth club) to discuss these and other issues affecting tribal communities. It was also agreed to strengthen their organization to check exploitation at the hands of the government officials and others.

It is unfortunate that no records of the discussion at these camps have been kept. However, all these point out that it is necessary to adopt a new method of pedagogy to generate awareness among the tribes. The method should be based on participatory dialogue instead of a one way discourse. Awareness generation can take place effectively through such dialogues. This needs patience and takes time but this is the only effective way to change the centuries old silence of tribal culture.

25

A Study on Responsiveness of Welfare Programmes Among Tribal Communities in Thirumoorthi Hills Udumalpet (Taluk), Coimbatore

—Mr. A. Jayaraman, M. and A. Arockia Maria Michealraja

The study titled "Responsiveness of welfare programmes among tribal communities in Thirumoorthi hills" Commenced on 2007. The study has been conducted by administering a structured interview schedule in accordance with the core objectives (Kindly refer proposal) with the proposed methodology. The entire study is exploratory in nature, hence simple random sampling technique has been adopted to categorize the sample, which included 60 households out of a hamlet consisting 90 households, constituting the definite universe under the study area that is Thirumoorthi hills of Udumalpet Taluk with in Coimbatore district. The general findings pertaining to the present research study includes with the Socio – Economic background, revealed that a vast majority of the respondents were male lying within nuclear family type and all of them were Tamil – Hindus, (In addition to these findings vast majority of them were Illiterates, daily wage earners and having income below Rs.1000/-per month,) The were equi – distributed in terms of marital status (Married and Unmarried) and head ship dependencies (male and female) respectively. The tribal were well aware and very good response about the programme implemented by the Government and NGOs (Non Governmental Organizations) in respectively. Two NGOs namely Nesakkarangal and CITTA were into operator towards tribal development (SHGs (Self Half Groups), Vocational

Training and Educational Development) at Thirumoorthi Hills. All the respondents were satisfied with the Self – Employment activities of the NGO also Government have envisaged into Socio-economic, educational, Health, Savings and Cultural development schemes exclusively for Tribal population. The formulation of Self Half Group among the respondents and one fourth of the respondent's awareness on self-employment were mainly through NGOs. But they possess poor awareness level on the ways functions and safeguard measures of welfare schemes and the programme devised by Government and NGOs. Majority of the tribal community were not aware about vital schemes vize; Movalur Ramamirtham Ammayar Marriage Fund, Dr.Dharmambal widow Remarriage Fund, TamilNadu Government Intercaste Marriage Fund, Old age and Handicapped Reservation for public place, Young Widow's children educational Fund and Employment Reservation, Village Library Facilities, Dr. Ambathkar educational loan, Free Coaching for Higher Education, Bio – Gas, Land Renovation Work, Hill Area Development Programme, Family Income Generation, Women Employment, First Aid Training, Diseases Awareness, TamilNadu Culture and Recreational Development, Five years Postal Savings, Post Office Old Age Pension, Mother Theresa Orphan Marriage, EVR Mamiyammal Widow's Children Marriage Fund, Sathiyavani Muthulackshmi Maternity welfare schemes respectively. A vast majority of the tribal community were aware of the social welfare schemes viz, Free Tailoring Machine Distribution, Two Female Children Fixed Deposit, Old Age Pension, Handicapped Assistance Fund, Death Cremation Fund, Dr. Muthulackshmi Maternity Benefit Fund, Two Female Children Welfare Fund, Educational Institution Reservation, Free Education, Free Book, Educational Scholarship, Mid – day Meals, Free Uniform, Free Buss Pass, Free Land Distribution, Rations Card, House Renovation Work, Free Electricity, Free Drinking Water, Bovine Growth, Self Employment, SHG, Individual Income Generation, Family Income Generation, Family Economic Development, Post Office Savings, Free Television and Free Gas Distribution schemes respectively Major portion of the respondent's awareness on welfare schemes were due to Exclusive ways such as; Media like radio and newspaper, Government department that is, Social Welfare Department:

NGOs through SHGs, Village President respectively. The researcher found there is a sheer necessity for ample promotional measures based on majority of the responses by the respondents, Inches: education, self –employment and self – awareness. Inorder to alleviate the project scenario. In the light of the present research study some of the suggestive measures were identified viz. Decentralized separate tribal welfare department, direct contact with collectorate officiable and direct approach by appointing trustworthy governmental functionaries, Abolition of corruption and tribal welfare programmes through SHGs frame work.

Introduction

Our country has been unique for the culture diversities. It had contained peacefully for centuries. People of all areas and religions had come and settled intermingling within these hospitable shares to make the people of this subcontinent. The tribal 'adivasis' being the earliest tribals of this country, can certainly make the minimum claim of doing no less Indian then the rest of us. The tries are no longer left isolated. The modern world with its industries and highways, markets and trades has inexorable moved closer to the tribes and they too, have came closer to it, discarding their tribal dresses for more com forming near and covering their semi-nudity wherever it prevailed metal and plastic pots and pans have now arrived in their households, replacing the ground- shells and hand crafted earth ensnare.

Etimological Orign

The English term "tribe" is derived from the Latin word "tribus"- The term "tribus" was used to refer to the ancient 'Indo-European Institutions". Literally, it denoted the socio-political structure prevailed in the society. The Latin term 'tribus' embraced the greek words like 'genos' and 'phratra' and even the Latin terms like 'gens' and 'curia' in its annotation.Among these terms, except 'curia', other terms like 'genos' phratia' and 'gens' high lightened the concepts of kingship and political annotations on its terminology. Hence from these we can deduce the hypothesis that there existed some sort of relationship between kingship organizations and political organizations. By 'adivasis' we mean early inhabitants as those who lived in the primitive periods'. Once they were they were the real owners of the land. They were rich in their culture and tradition. Hunting and hardworking became their focus for livelihood.

Tribal Welfare Schemes in Tamil Nadu

The need of the hour for Tribal Development is to reduce the gap between the Tribal and Non-Tribal population with respect to economic, educational and social status. The objective is to integrate the Tribal into the main stream of economic and social development. A separate Directorate has been functioning for the Welfare of the Tribals since 1.4.2000. The Directorate of Tribal Welfare pays special attention to 14 Districts where Scheduled Tribes concentration is more. Out of the 36 Scheduled Tribe communities in the State, 6 Tribal Communities (i.e.) have been identified as Primitive Tribal Groups. The other Tribals living in scattered areas are classified as Dispersed Tribes. The area where the population of Scheduled Tribes exceeds 50% of the total population is declared as Integrated Tribal Development programme area. The Integrated Tribal Development Programme area exists in 7 districts. The Government of Tamil Nadu has adopted the Tribal Sub Plan concept to improve their socio economic conditions. Tribal Sub Plan is being implemented since 1976-77. Accordingly, all the Departments while allocating the Annual Plan Outlay, for the Tribal Sub Plan would ensure that Tribals are benefited by their welfare and development programmes, at least to the level of their population in the State. As per 2001 census, Scheduled Tribe population in Tamil Nadu is 6.51 lakhs. The Tribal Sub Plan is getting facelift during 2006-07 in Tamil Nadu. During the year 2006-07, the State Annual Plan outlay is Rs. 12500/- core. Out of which, as per sub head 796, meant for Tribals in the Plan Budget Link Book, an amount of Rs. 23.68 crores has been allocated under Divisible Scheme, which is higher than the allocation made during the previous years. Further Rs. 139.47 crores under indivisible scheme will be allotted to Tribal Sub Plan. The total flow to Tribal Sub Plan for the year 2006-07 is Rs.163.15 crores.

Housing Scheme

Housing Schemes are implemented by the Government in order to improve the standard of living of the Tribals, living in hill areas as well as in plains. Based on this, every year houses are constructed at the rate of Rs. 34,000/- per house in plain area and Rs. 36,500/- per house in hill area. The entire cost of this scheme is borne by the Government. During the year 2006-07 a sum of Rs.16.80 lakhs has been allocated for this scheme.

Provision of Drinking Water Supply

The Tribal areas where there is need for drinking water are identified and necessary provision is made. Every year funds are being allocated for this purpose. This scheme will be continued during 2006-07 with a sum of Rs. 32.00 lakhs.

Economic Development

LAMP Co-operative Societies have been formed not only to market the produce of the Tribal people by eliminating middlemen but also to provide short and medium term credits and to supply essential consumer articles to the Tribals at fair prices. There are 19 such societies functioning in Tamil Nadu. Four Vocational guidance centers in the hill area of Uthagamandalam, Sankarapuram, Kollimalai and Javvadumalai and one Industrial Training Institute at Sankarapuram in Villupuram District are functioning for providing job to the Tribals. 25 Primary Health Centres, 76 Health Sub Centres, 7 Siddha hospitals, 5 Government Dispensaries and one Siddha Mobile Units are functioning in the Tribal area for the benefit of the Tribals.

Family-oriented Income Generating Schemes

Family - oriented programmes for the economic development of Primitive and Dispersed Tribes have been charted out and Sheep units are being supplied. A sum of Rs.10.14 lakhs has been allocated during the year 2006-07 for this scheme.

Financial Assistance for Partner in Inter Caste Marriage

Assistance given up to a limit of Rs. 40,000 those who are getting marriage. For this one of the partners should belong to scheduled tribe. Application can be submitted after one year from the date of marriage.

Rational Financial Assistance

At time of exceptional urgency financial assistance is given for expenditure connected with death, medical treatment and rites performed after a death.

Financial Assistance for Marriage of Poor Scheduled Tribe Girls

Financial assistance not exceeding Rs. 10,000 in each case is made available to poor scheduled tribe. People with annual income of Rs. 12000 only are eligible for this assistance.

Central Sector Scheme for Development of Primitive Tribal Groups

During the year 2005-06, under Central Sector Scheme for development of Primitive Tribal Groups, the Government of India have sanctioned a sum of Rs.79.55 lakhs for the construction of 225 houses and training / awareness camp for 400 trainees in 8 districts. During the year 2006-07, a sum of Rs. 255.00 lakhs have been allocated tentatively by Government of India under this scheme.

Tribal Self Help Groups

Emphasis is laid on Self Help Groups to empower Tribal women. 3,410 Self Help Groups consisting of 51,544 Tribal Women have been formed and are functioning successfully in the State.

Hill Area Development Programme

For the Welfare of Tribals residing in Nilgiris District, the Hill Area Development Programme is being implemented by the Collector of Nilgiris. In the year 2006-07, a sum of Rs. 566.84 lakhs is earmarked for this scheme.

Tamil Nadu Adi Dravidar Housing and Development Corporation (TAHDCO)

Tamil Nadu Adi Dravidar Housing and Development Corporation was formed for the exclusive development of Scheduled Caste and Scheduled Tribe. It is functioning since 1974 and it is implementing various economic development schemes for the upliftment of the socio economic status of Scheduled Caste and Scheduled Tribes. The Corporation has two distinct wings viz. Technical Wing and Development Wing. The Technical Wing is executing the construction works such as hostels, school buildings, teacher's quarters, class-rooms etc. The Development Wing of the Corporation is implementing welfare schemes by formulating need-based economic development schemes for the economic development of Scheduled Caste and Scheduled Tribes.

Economic Development Programmes for Women

The focus of schemes has been shifted from benefiting only individual beneficiaries to largely for women's Self Help Groups (SHG by allocating 75% of allocation of the District Action Plan to A Dravidar and Tribal Self Help Groups.

Land Purchase Scheme

The empowerment of women would enhance the family status as a whole and the society at large. The Land Purchase Scheme is meant only for women from Scheduled Caste and Scheduled Tribe community. Under this scheme, financial assistance to 8000 Scheduled Caste and Scheduled Tribe women in the pattern of 50% subsidy and 50% bank loan is given for purchase of land, land development, minor irrigation facilities and animal husbandry activities.

Financial Assistance to Individual Beneficiaries

Under the individual beneficiaries programme, individuals will be given financial assistance for self-employment ventures, as per their choice.

Employment Oriented Training Programmes

To provide more employment opportunities to Scheduled Caste / Scheduled Tribe youth, various training programmes are given to them. Vocational training programmes for Scheduled Caste and Scheduled Tribe youth have been streamlined by forming District Vocational Training Selection Committee under the Chairmanship of District Collector. These training programmes are conducted by Central and State Government.

Self Employment Programme for Youth

A scheme called "Self Employment Programme for Youth" (SEPY) is being implemented in which, specific viable activities are identified and selected youth are trained and escorted by an agency to start micro enterprises on a sustainable basis. This will benefit 4,000 Scheduled Caste, Scheduled Tribe youths with an assistance of Rs. 11.25 crores.

Hostel Facilities

One hundred and eleven parametric hostels and 3G. RIB schools are being run to help the education of scheduled tribes students. It is those students who do not stay within reasonable distance from the school are the beneficiaries. 30 students are given accommodation in each hostel. On the basis of available space, more students are admitted to hostels. In the hostels 10% of accommodation is being reserved for students of other communities.

Financial Assistance for Board

The scheduled tribes students who seek admission in Boarding are being paid Rs. 200 per month apart from free uniform clothes.

Promotional Prize to Students

Students who get either 45% or higher marks in the 8th and the 9th class are given Rs. 50 and those who get 45% or more mark in the 10th class examination, are given Rs.200 as encouragement grant. Students who pass the 10th Plus two, Degree examination in the first class are offered Rs. 2,500, 3000, 3500 respectively.

Assistance for Study at Tutorials

Students who fall in the 10th examinations are given assistance in the following manner lump sum grant Rs. 100 Monthly stipend Rs. 600 (60x10) Tuition fees Rs. 450 Assistance is being made available to students who fall in Predegree examinations also.

Enhanced Assistance to Capable Students

50- Students selected from among those to 4th class on the basis of the marks scored by them and they are sent to eminent residential schools. Under this scheme the total expenditure on account of tuition fee, residential facilities, boarding dress and educational aids is met by the Government.

Educational Recreation Centers

Educational recreation centers are being run in the scheduled tribes residential centers. These centers are being provided with furniture, books, newspapers and recreational aids.

Provision for Clothing

Every year 2 pairs of uniform is given to each students belonging to lower primary classes of the tribal schools.

Financial Assistance for Appearing for Interview

Traveling allowance will be given to the candidates who appear for interviews conducted against vacancies in the central and state government services. They are paid either the exact bus fare or second class train charges.

Pre – Examination Training Centre

For training candidates for appointment to the vacancies notified by the Tamil Nadu Public Service Commission, Union Public service commission, Banks and other institutions of public sector; 3 pre- Examination training centers are functioning in many districts. The candidates are given monthly stipend for this training.

THIRUMOORTHI HILLS TRIBAL

The Thirumoorthi Hills is located 20 km away from Udumalapet, Coimbatore District. The specialty of Thirumoorthy Hill is the famous, three Hindu Goddess (Brahma, Vishnu and Siva) are locating at a same place. Thirumoorthi hills tribal lying near by Thirumoorthi Dam, it known as Thirumoorthi mala Tribal settlement. Around the place, there are kulipetti, Mavadappu, Talinji Tribal settlement. These settlements are inside the forest. The Thirumoorthi mala tribal were located at Jallimuthanpara before 50 years, they were Hunting, Forest resource collection, agriculture and land owners. Aforestation purpose the government set out the people to Thirumoorthi tribal settlement. Thirumoorthi hills tribal community previously called as Malai Kadar but now this name changed to Malai Pulayan. And also the community name was changed the government records. we cannot say the tribal communities are non civilized, like other people, their kingdom is modernized on their way of dressing, communication, rituals but they practicing old traditions, norms, folks and culture of their community. Infrastructure, communication, road facilities, health provisions, economic condition is very poor and Illiteracy, poverty, unemployment also playing a significant role. In future due to Government Programmes, role and functions only their community overall develop in future.

Statement of the Problem

Today in India tribals are facing so many socio, economic, culture problems; tribal people are considered one of the depressed classes in India they are living in forest or hilly area for away from the civilized people. They are socially, economically exploited by others. According to our constitution they have so many privileges and rights but they don't know how to utilize this, there government formulating number of policies and implementing number of programme but they don't know about it, the reason is not so much, it is simple because of their illiteracy, lack of awareness, and exploitation. After independence government implementing number of welfare Programmes for the tribals, but in practical now also tribal are in poor condition, cannot see that much of development through this varies Programmes. Because due to some reason, or lack of responses. In this study researchers study to find out the responsiveness to welfare programme among tribals. Result of this study can utilize for other officials and the authorities to find out the reasons and to take appropriate solution for their problems and they have to take new steps to the development of tribals.

Pilot Study

The pilot study is a preliminary study of the concerned. It gives the researcher a clear idea about the different variables involved, nature of the problem, possible difficulties in data collection availability of the respondents etc.

Objectives of the Study

- To identify various welfare Programmes implemented by the government departments in Tirumoorthi hills.
- To study the role and functions of government in promotion of welfare programme.
- To bring awareness among the tribal populations towards various welfare programmes.
- To highlight extent of responsiveness among the tribal community.

- To offer suggestion for promotion and better implementation of welfare programme.

Research Design

A research design is the logical and systematic planning in directing the research. It is not a highly specific plan to be followed without deviations but rather a series of guide post to keep one headed in the right directions. It is a tentative strategy of research processes which is most likely to be modified by new aspects, new conditions, new responsiveness of the social welfare programmes in government role and functions etc., the researcher has used exploratory research design for their study.

Tools for Data Collection

For the study researcher used interview schedule for having valuable and reliable data. Researcher used interview schedule because of most of the tribals were illiterate, and also researcher used observation, case study, communication with popular persons etc.

Sample Size

Sample size of this study consists of 60 respondents from the total universe.

Data Collection

Primary data are those, which are collected fresh and for the first time and thus happened to be original in character. Secondary data are those which have already been collected by someone and which have already been passed through the statistical process. Secondary data are collected from various books, journals, magazines, Internet etc., the secondary data helped to frame theoretical background for the study.

Sample Method

The researcher adopted Simple random sampling method for the study.

Pre-test

To find out relevance of the various items in the Interview Schedule a pre–test was conducted by distributing it to 5 tribal people this facilitated the researcher to find out the relevance of the items in the interview schedule. Few questions were rephrased in the interview schedule; the questions were modified.

Table 1. Distribution of the respondents by their personal details:

S.No	Variable	Classification	No .of respondents	%	Total 1%
1.	Sex	Male	44	73.33	100
		Female	16	26.66	
2.	Age	Below 30	10	16.66	
		30 -50	34	56.66	
		Above 50	16	26.66	
3.	Marital Status	Married	50	83.33	100
		Unmarried	1	1.6	
		Widow/Widower	9	15	
4.	Education	Illiterate	41	68.33	100
		1 – 5	16	26.66	
		5 – 10	3	5	
5.	Occupation	Daily Wages	46	76.6	100
		Old age Pension	6	10	
		Forest Resource Collection	7	11.66	
		Water Man& Balwadi Ayya	2	3.33	
6.	Income	Bellow 1000	55	91.66	100
		1000 – 2000	4	6.66	
		Above 2000	1	1.66	

Above the table shows that the personal details of the respondents, sex wise nearly ¾(73.33%) the respondents were male and above ¼ (26.66%) of the respondents were female, Age wise respondents distribution are above half (56.66%) of the respondents age between 30-50 years, 26.66% of the respondents age above 50 and 16.66% of the respondents age below 30 years. marital status wise the respondents distribution as the vast majority (83.33%) of the respondents were married and 15% of the respondents were widow and widower, educational wise respondents distribution majority (68.33%)of the respondents were illiterates, above ¼ (26.66%) of the respondents were up to elementary level and only 5% of the respondents were entered the education up to middle school level. occupation wise majority (76.66) of the respondents dependence on daily wages, 11.66% of the respondents dependence on forest resource collection, 10 person of the respondents getting old age pension and 3.33% of the respondents working as a government departments. Income wise respondents distribution as vast majority (91.66%) of the respondents monthly income below Rs. 1000, 6.66% of the respondents monthly income in-between Rs. 1000 – Rs. 2000 and 1.66 % of the respondents monthly income above Rs. 2000.

Hence the table clearly shows the majority of the respondents are Illitrates, daily wages and their income level is so poor and also the respondents mortality rate is high because the number of the respondents are widow/widower and nil respondents who are crossing above 70 years.

Table 3. Distribution of the Respondents by their Awareness and Responsiveness of Welfare Schemes

S.No.	*Schemes*	*Aware*	*Partially Aware*	*Not Aware*	*No. Respondents %*
1.	Muvalur Ramamirtham Ammaiar Memorial Marriage Scheme	25 (41.66)	4 (6.66)	31 (51.66)	60 (100)
2.	Widow remarriage Scheme	30 (50)	- (50)	30	60 (100)
3.	Inter Caste Marriage Scheme	30 (50)	8 (13.33)	22 (36.66)	60 (100)
4.	Widow Remarriage Scheme	18 (30)	6 (10)	36 (60)	60 (100)
5.	Orphan Children's Marriage Scheme	14 (23.33)	3 (5)	43 (71.66)	60 (100)
6.	Free Tailoring machine Distribution Scheme	43 (71.66)	3 (5)	14 (23.33)	60 (100)
7.	Two Children time Deposit Scheme	46 (76.66)	4 (6.66)	10 (16.66)	60 (100)
8.	Old Age Pension Scheme	58 (96.66)	1 (1.66)	1 (1.66)	60 (100)

S.No.	Schemes	Aware	Partially Aware	Not Aware	No. Respondents %
9.	Handicapped Pension Scheme	35 (58.33)	2 (3.33)	23 (38.33)	60 (100)
10.	Burial Ceremony Scheme	55 (91.66)	3 (5)	2 (3.33)	60 (100)
11.	Maternity Benefit Scheme	38 (63.33)	5 (8.33)	17 (28.33)	60 (100)
12.	Reservation for Public place scheme	8 (13.33)	2 (3.33)	50 (83.33)	60 (100)
13.	Young Widow's Children Educational Fund	25 (41.66)	8 (13.33)	27 (45)	60 (100)
14.	Two Female Children Educational welfare Fund	35 (58.33)	5 (8.33)	20 (33.33)	60 (100)
15.	Village Library Scheme	2 (3.33)	5 (8.33)	53 (58.33)	60 (100)
16.	Reservation Scheme for Educational Institution	28 (46.66)	8 (13.33)	24 (40)	60 (100)
17.	Free Education	50 (83.33)	5 (8.33)	5 (8.33)	60 (100)
18.	Debt Scheme For Educational	3 (5)	2 (3.33)	55 (91.66)	60 (100)
19.	Free Books Scheme	50 (83.33)	5 (8.33)	5 (8.33)	60 (100)
20.	Scholarship Scheme	40 (66.66)	5 (8.33)	15 (25)	60 (100)
21.	Mid day Meals Scheme	60 (100)	-	-	60 (100)
22.	Free Bus Pass Scheme	60 (100)	-	-	60 (100)
23.	Free Uniform Scheme	60 (100)	-	-	60 (100)
24.	Reservation For Employment	5 (8.33)	29 (48.33)	26 (43.33)	60 (100)
25.	Age Relaxation	5 (8.33)	7 (11.66)	48 (80)	60 (100)

S.No.	*Schemes*	*Aware*	*Partially Aware*	*Not Aware*	*No. Respon dents %*
26.	Providing DA/TA for Attending Interview	-	3 (5)	57 (95)	60 (100)
27.	Fees relaxation for their Application	-	-	60 (100)	60 (100)
28.	Agriculture Free Land Distribution Scheme	29 (48.33)	10 (16.66)	21 (35)	60 (100)
29.	Agricultural Land Reconstruction Scheme	14 (23.33)	10 (16.63)	36 (60)	60 (100)
30.	Agricultural Free Electricity Scheme	60 (100)	-	-	60 (100)
31.	Agricultural Free Water Scheme	53 (88.33)	4 (6.66)	3 (5)	60 (100)
32.	Cattle Breeding Scheme	60 (100)	-	-	60 (100)
33.	Forest Area Development Scheme	17 (28.33)	9 (15)	34 (56.66)	60 (100)
34.	Family income generation Scheme	11 (15.33)	8 (13.33)	41 (68.33)	60 (100)
35.	Self –Employment Scheme	31 (51.66)	6 (18.33)	23 (11.66)	60 (100)
36.	Women Development Scheme	11 (18.33)	7 (11.66)	42 (70)	60 (100)
37.	Self Help Group Scheme	60 (100)	-	-	60 (100)
38.	Individual Economic Development Scheme.	7 60	9 (15)	44 (73.33)	60 (100)
39.	Free Housing Scheme	48 (80)	3 (5)	9 (15)	60 (100)
40.	Free Electricity Scheme	35 (58.33)	3 (5)	22 (36.66)	60 (100)
41.	Free Drinking Water Scheme	36 (60)	2 (3.33)	22 (36.66)	60 (100)
42.	Civil Supply Scheme	38 (63.33)	17 (28.33)	8 (13.33)	60 (100)
43.	House Reconstruction Scheme	46 (76.66)	3 (5)	11 18.33)	60 (100)

S.No. Schemes	Aware	Partially Aware	Not Aware	No. Respondents %
44. Free Patta Distribution Scheme	60 (100)	-	-	60 (100)
45. Bio Gas Scheme	12 (20)	15 (25)	33 (55)	60 (100)
46. Free Gas Scheme	60 (100)	-	-	60 (100)
47. Free TV Distribution Scheme	60 (100)	-	-	60 (100)
48. Free Cloth Distribution Scheme	60 (100)	-	-	60 (100)
49. Post Office Time Deposit Scheme	18 (30)	14 (23.33)	28 (46.66)	60 (100)
50. Post Office SB Account	10 (16.66)	10 (16.66)	40 (66.33)	60 (100)
51. Post Office DC Account	2 (3.33)	11 (18.33)	47 (78.33)	60 (100)
52. Post Office Five Year Savings Scheme	9 (15)	15 (25)	36 (60)	60 (100)
53. Post Office Old Age Pension Scheme	7 (11.66)	3 (5)	50 (83.33)	60 (100)
54. First Aid Training Scheme	-	-	60 (100)	60 (100)

The table no. 2 shows that distribution of the respondents by their awareness of the welfare schemes. Social welfare scheme wise respondents distribution, Majority of the respondents were well aware and good response given by the following schemes namely Widow remarriage Scheme (50 per cent), Inter Caste Marriage Scheme (50 per cent), Free Tailoring machine Distribution Scheme (71.66 per cent), Two Children time Deposit Scheme (76.66 per cent), Old Age Pension Scheme (96.66 per cent), Handicapped Pension Scheme (58.33 per cent), Burial Ceremony Scheme (91.66 per cent), Maternity Benefit Scheme (63.33 per cent). And Muvalur Ramamirtham Ammaiar Memorial Marriage Scheme (57.66 per cent), Widow Remarriage Scheme (60 per cent), Orphan Children's Marriage Scheme

(71.66 per cent), Reservation for Public place scheme (83.33 per cent), of the respondents were Not aware and poorly responded. Few of the respondents were partially aware all the social welfare programmes.

Educational welfare schemes wise respondents distribution: Majority of the respondents were aware and well responded to the following schemes; these are Two Female Children Educational welfare Fund.(58.33) , Reservation Scheme for Educational Institution (46.66 per cent), Free Education (83.33), Free Books Scheme (83.33), Scholarship Scheme (66.66), Mid day Meals Scheme (100), Free Bus Pass Scheme(100), Free Uniform Scheme (100), and Young Widow's Children Educational Fund (45 per cent), Village Library Scheme (58.33 per cent), Reservation Scheme for Educational Institution, Debt Scheme For Educational (91.66 per cent), Scheme for Free Couching and Training of All Competitive Examinations (100 per cent) and few per cent of the respondents were partially aware the welfare schemes.

The employment schemes wise respondents distribution; Majority (48.33 per cent) of the respondents are partially aware and 43.33 per cent of the respondent are not aware and poorly responded the reservation for the employment scheme and 8.33 per cent of the respondents well aware and good responses given by the respondents. Age relaxation scheme wise the respondents distribution as a vast majority (80 per cent) of the respondents not aware and poor responses given by the respondents, 11.66 per cent of the respondents are partially aware and poor responses given by the respondents and 8.33 per cent of the respondents are aware the scheme and well responded. Providing DA/TA for attending interview scheme wise the respondents distribution as 95 per cent of the respondents not aware the scheme and 5 per cent of the respondents are partially aware the scheme in overall all the respondents are poorly responded the scheme. All respondents not aware and poorly responded the fees relaxations for the application for jobs.

Agricultural schemes wise respondents distribution ; majority (48.33 per cent) of the respondents were well aware and highly responded the Agriculture Free Land Distribution Scheme 35 per cent of the respondents were not aware and poorly responded, and rest of the 16.66 per cent of the respondent partially aware and poorly responded the scheme.

60 per cent of the respondents were not aware and poorly responded Agricultural Land Reconstruction Scheme, 23.33 per cent of the respondents were aware and well responded and few (16.63 per cent) of the respondent were partially aware the scheme, All the respondents were well aware and responded the Agricultural Free Electricity Scheme, Agricultural Free Water Scheme wise the respondents distribution as, 88.33 per cent of the respondents were well aware and responded, 6.66 per cent of the respondents were partially aware, and 5 per cent of the respondents were not aware the scheme and poorly responded. All the respondents were well aware the Cattle Breeding Scheme and good responses given by the respondents,Forest Area Development Scheme wise respondent's distribution as, 56.66 per cent of the respondents not aware, 15 per cent of the respondents were partially aware and poorly responded and 28.33 per cent of the respondents were well aware and responded.

Economic development schemes wise the respondents distribution; Family income generation scheme wise among the total respondents 68.33 per cent of the respondents were not aware, 13.33 per cent of the respondents were partially aware the scheme and poorly responded rest of 15.33 per cent of the respondents were well aware and responded the scheme. Self – Employment Scheme wise the respondents distribution as, 51.66 per cent of the respondents were well aware and responded, 18.33 per cent of the respondents were partially aware and 11.66 per cent or the respondents were not aware the schemed and poorly responded. Women Development Scheme wise respondents distribution as,70 per cent of the respondents were not aware, 11.66 per cent of the respondents were partially aware and poorly responded the scheme remaining 18.33 per cent of the respondents were well aware and responded the scheme. All the respondents were well aware and very good responses given by Self Help Group Scheme. Individual Economic Development Scheme wise respondents distribution as 73.23 per cent of the respondents were not aware, 15 per cent of the respondents were partially aware and responded poorly remaining 11.66 per cent of the respondents were well aware and responded the scheme.

Housing and housing related schemes wise the respondents distribution; Free Housing Scheme wise among the total respondents 80 per cent of the respondents were aware, and well responded 15 per cent of the respondents were not aware, 5 per cent partially aware the scheme and poorly responded Free Electricity Scheme wise the respondents distribution as, 58.33 per cent of the respondents were well aware and responded, 36.66 per cent of the respondents were not aware and 5 per cent or the respondents were partially aware and poorly responded.Free Drinking Water Scheme wise the respondents distribution as, 60 per cent of the respondents were well aware and responded, 36.66 per cent of the respondents were not aware, 3.33 per cent of the respondents were partially aware the scheme and responded poorly. Civil Supply Scheme wise respondents distribution as, 63.33 per cent of the respondents were well aware and responded, 13.33 per cent of the respondents were not aware, 28.33 were partially aware and poorly responded the scheme. House Reconstruction Scheme wise respondents distribution as, 76.60 per cent of the respondents were well aware and responded, 18.33 per cent of the respondents were not aware, 5 per cent of the respondent were partially aware and poorly responded the scheme. All the respondents were well aware and responded the scheme. Bio Gas Scheme wise respondents distribution as, 55 per cent of the respondents were not aware, 25 per cent of the respondents were partially aware and poorly responded the scheme remaining 20 per cent of the respondents were well aware and responded the scheme.All the respondents were well aware and responded the following schemes as, Free Gas Scheme, Free TV Distribution Scheme, Free Cloth Distribution Scheme.

Saving schemes wise the respondent's distribution as; Post Office Time Deposit Scheme wise the respondents distributions as, 46.66 per cent of the respondents were not aware, 23.33 per cent of the respondents were partially aware and poorly responded rest (30 per cent) of the respondents were well aware and responded the scheme. Post Office SB Account scheme wise the respondents distribution as, 66.33 per cent of the respondents were not aware, 16.66 per cent of the respondents were partially aware and poorly responded remaining 16.66 per cent oaf the respondents were aware and well responded the scheme. Post Office DC Account scheme wise the respondents distribution as, 78.33 per cent of the respondents were not aware Scheme, 18.33 per cent of the respondents were partially aware remaining 3.33 per cent of the respondents were aware and well responded the scheme. Post Office Five Year Savings Scheme wise the respondents distribution as, 60 per cent of the respondents were not aware, 25 per cent of the respondents were partially aware and poorly responded and 15 per cent of the respondents were well aware and responded the scheme. Post Office Old Age Pension Scheme wise the respondent distribution as, 83.33 per cent of the respondents were not aware, 5 per cent of the responded were partially aware and poorly responded the scheme rest of (11.66 per cent) of the respondents were aware and well responded.

Health scheme wise the respondents distribution, all the respondents were not aware and poorly responded the First Aid Training Scheme and Diseases Awareness Scheme.

Table 3. Respondents Distribution by Way of Aware the Welfare Schemes

S.No	*Items*	*Media*	*NGOs*	*Government Departments*	*Political party*	*No. of respon-dents %*
1.	Radio & News paper	6(10)	-	-	-	6(10)
2.	Collector office	-	-	1(1.66)	-	1(1.66)
3.	Social welfare department	-	-	2(3.33)	-	2(3.33)
4.	NGO People (SHG)	-	42(70)	-		42(70)
5.	Village President	-	-	-	2(3.33)	2(3.33)
6.	More than 2 Items	-	7(11.66)	-	-	7(11.66)
	Total	6(10)	49(81.66)	3(5)	2(3.33)	60(100)

Above the table no. 3 explain the respondents distribution by way of aware the welfare schemes. 70 per cent of the respondents were aware the welfare schemes through SHGs, 10 per cent of the respondents were aware through radio and News

Papers, Each 3.33 per cent of the respondents were aware through social welfare department and village president, 1.66 per cent of the respondents were aware through the collector office and 11.66 per cent of the respondents were aware more than two media.

Table 4. Role of Government and Government Department to Improve their Community.

S.No	*Roles*	*No of Respondents*	*Percentage*
1.	Introducing Welfare Scheme	5	8.33
2.	Awareness	20	33.33
3.	Coordination	7	11.66
4.	Guide	5	8.33
5.	Help/ protection	2	3.33
6.	Not responded	21	35
	Total	60	100

The above table no 4 shows that distribution of the respondents by the awareness about the role of government and government department to improve their community 35 per cent of the respondent not responding about the role of Government and NGO, 33.33 per cent opinioned that awareness is the main role of Government and NGO 11.66 per cent opinioned that coordination is the main role of Government and NGO 8.33 per cent opinioned that introducing welfare programme is the main role of Government and NGO 8.33 per cent opinioned that guidance is the main role of Government and NGO 3.33 w per cent opinioned that help and protection is the main role of Government and NGO.

Table 5. Respondents Distribution on the Reason for not Develop their Community.

S.No	*Roles*	*No of Respondents*	*Percentage*
1.	Lack of Awareness	20	33.33
2.	Lack of Education	18	30
3.	Lack of quality leader	2	3.33
4.	Poor economic Condition	5	8.33
5.	Exploitation	15	25
	Total	60	100

Hence the table no: 5 indicates that the Respondents distribution of reason for not develop their community 33.33 per cent of the respondents were said that lack of awareness, 30 per cent of the respondents were said that lack of education, 25 per cent of the respondents were said that exploitation by others, 8.33 per cent of the respondents said that poor economic condition and 3.33 per cent of the respondent said that lack of qualified leaders.

Table 6. Respondents Expectation from the Government.

S.No	*Fields*	*Respondents*	*Percentage*
1.	Education	17	28.33
2.	Economic	14	23.33
3.	Self employment	11	18.33
4.	Welfare Awareness	5	8.33
5.	Medical	10	16.66
6.	All of the above	3	5
	Total	60	100

Table 7. Distribution of the Respondents by their Suggestions for their Own Development.

S.No	*Suggestions*	*Respondents*	*Percentage*
1.	Direct contact with government and government departments	8	13.33
2.	Tribal welfare departments near by their village	4	6.66
3.	Flexible approach	5	8.33
4.	Awareness	16	26.66
5.	Abolition of corruption	7	11.66
6.	Government welfare programme come through SHGs	4	6.66
7.	Appoint honest persons	16	26.66
	Total	60	100

The above table no 4(28) indicates that distribution of the respondents expectation from the government. It indicates that

28.33 per cent of the respondents are expecting education, 23.33 per cent of the respondents are expecting economic development, 16.66 per cent of the respondents expecting medical care, 18.33 per cent of the respondents expecting self employment, 8.33 per cent of the respondents are expecting Welfare Awareness, and 5 per cent of the respondents are expecting above all fields for their development.

The above table no. 4(28) indicates that distribution of the respondents the based on the suggestions for their own development. It shows that each of (26.66 per cent) of the respondents suggestion is awareness and appointment of honest person for their development, 11.66 per cent of the respondents suggestion is abolition of curuption, 13.33 per cent of the respondent suggestion is Direct contact with government and government departments, 8.33 per cent of the respondent suggestion is flexible approach by the government, and remaining each of the 6.66 per cent of the respondent suggestion is Tribal welfare departments near by their village and Government welfare programme come through SHGs.

Major findings of the study:

- Majorities (73.33 per cent) of the respondents are male.
- Above one third (36.66 per cent) of the respondents were comes under the age group of 30-40years,
- Majority (83.37 per cent)of the respondents of the were married,
- Majority (68.33 per cent) of the respondents were illiterate
- Majority (76.66 per cent) of the respondents are daily wages,
- Majority(63.33 per cent) of the respondents monthly income is below Rs.1000/-
- Majority (50 pre cent)of the respondents well aware and good response given to Widow remarriage Scheme
- Majority (50 pre cent)of the respondents well aware and good response given to Inter Caste Marriage Scheme
- Majority (71.66 per cent) of the respondents well aware and good response given to Free Tailoring machine Distribution Scheme

- Majority (76.66 per cent) of the respondents well aware and good response given to Two Children time Deposit Scheme
- Vast Majority (96.66 per cent) of the respondents well aware and good response given to Old Age Pension Scheme
- Majority (58.33 per cent) of the respondents well aware and good response given to Handicapped Pension Scheme
- Vast majority (91.66 per cent) of the respondents well aware and good response given to Burial Ceremony Scheme
- Majority (63.33 per cent) of the respondents well aware and good response given to Maternity Benefit Scheme
- Majority (58.33 per cent) of the respondents well aware and good response given to Two Female Children Educational welfare Fund
- Majority (46.66percen) of the respondents well aware and good response given to Reservation Scheme for Educational Institution.
- Majority (63.33) of the respondents well aware and good response given to Free Books Scheme.
- Majority (66.66) of the respondents well aware and good response given to Scholarship Scheme.
- Vast majority (100) of the respondent were aware mid day Meals Scheme, Free Bus Pass Scheme, Free Uniform Scheme
- Majority (80 per cent) of the respondents were not aware and poor responses given for the age relaxation scheme
- Majority (95 per cent) of the respondent were not aware about providing DA/TA for attending interview
- All respondents not aware and poorly responded the fees relaxations for the application for jobs.
- Majority (48.33 per cent) of the respondent were well aware and highly responded Agriculture Free Land Distribution Scheme

- All the respondents were well aware and responded the Agricultural Free Electricity Scheme
- Majority (88.33 per cent) of the respondent were well aware and responded Agricultural Free Water Supply Scheme
- All the respondents were well aware about the Cattle Breeding Scheme and good responses given by the respondents
- Above half (56.66 per cent)of the respondent were not aware and poorly responded Forest Area Development Scheme
- Above half (68.33 per cent) of the respondent not aware about the Family income generation scheme
- Above half (51.66 per cent) of the respondent of the respondents were well aware and responded Self – Employment Scheme
- Majority (70 per cent) of the respondents were not aware regarding Women Development Scheme
- All the respondents were well aware and very good responses given by Self Help Group Scheme.
- Majority (73.23 per cent) of the respondent were not aware, Individual Economic Development Scheme
- Majority (80 per cent) of the respondents were aware, and well responded Free Housing Scheme
- More than half (58.33 per cent) of the respondents were well aware and responded to Free Electricity Scheme
- Above half (60 per cent) of the respondent were well aware and responded Free Drinking Water Scheme
- All the respondents were well aware and responded the following schemes as, Free Gas Scheme, Free TV Distribution Scheme, Free Cloth Distribution Scheme
- Above half (60 per cent) of the respondent were not aware Post Office Five Year Savings Scheme
- Majority (83.33 per cent) of the respondent were not aware Post Office Old Age Pension Scheme
- Majority (70 per cent) of the respondent aware that the welfare schemes reaching through SHGs

- One third (33.33 per cent) of the respondent opinioned that awareness is the main role of Government and NGO
- One third (36.66 per cent) of the respondent said that there is no protection from government
- One third (33.33 per cent) of the respondent were said that lack of awareness, is the reason for not develop their community. 30 per cent of the respondents were said that lack of education is the reason for not develop their community
- Above half (58.33 per cent) of the respondent said that education is the most prefers welfare area for them
- One third (35 per cent) of the respondent says economic development is the area were government Not preferring importance for their community
- One third (28.33 per cent) of the respondent expecting special attention on educational improvement
- Majority (26.66 per cent) of the respondent each of suggest that awareness and appointment of honest person for their development.

Conclusion

A study on the responsiveness to welfare programme among the tribal community in Thirumoorthy hills, it shows that the awareness and responsiveness to the welfare programme among the tribal is poor. The main reason is they are not aware about the Programmes, majority of them are illiterate and also they are exploited by government and other officials. They expecting educational, economic development guidance and proper awareness. In most of the awareness programme, there is only a poor response but in some cases they are well aware and good response. The problem revealed that Government and Non Governmental Organization should provide more care and special concentration on awareness and guidance to these tribals, for good response from the tribal community. In spite of all their efforts made by the government majority of ST are still in the lower strata in Thirumoorthi hills. These people are not properly utilizing the schemes made for them, because of the lake of awareness, lack of education and exploitation of their community. But now a day they know about the exploitation by others, in future we can see an Empowerment of tribal communities.

26

Education of the Marginalized People: Survival of the Fittest

—John S. Gaikwad

Tribal are the weakest of the weaker sections. During British period most of the pre-literate communities were kept away from literacy as well as formal education. After independence, measures were taken to Integrate and develop the tribal and bring them in the mainstream. The various program for Tribal Development included the component of education. Literacy and level of education are two basic indicators of development achieved by a society. The literacy rate among the tribal population in Maharashtra State is less than the overall literacy rate for the general population. Similar trend is observed for the literacy rates of male and female tribal population. The data related to educational level indicates that the drop out rate is conspicuous after the primary level and again after matric / secondary levels among majority of the Scheduled Tribes. At present there are about 1000 Ashram Schools in Maharashtra State.

Enrolment in Government Ashram Schools is preferred most because the admission makes the student eligible for free food and clothing, apart from free education. The parents do not prefer to admit their children in the nearby primary schools (day schools). The total number of female students enrolled is much less for all the standards. It is observed that the enrolment decreases from standard I to standard X. The dropouts at early stage can be attributed to the feeling of 'alienation' imposed by Marathi as the medium of instruction. Responsibilities of contribution in the income generation activities or helping the family are major reasons for drop-outs. Early marriages contributed to the drop-out of girls. Many of the first generation learners are not capable of adjusting themselves with the structured set up of formal education. Educated children are considered to be a loss to the family.

The network of ashram schools should became effective, efficient and yield optimum results in terms of academic excellence and quality.

Awareness among the tribal about the importance and relevance of education would replace the apathy with pro-active enthusiasm for education of the children.

Introduction

Tribal are the weakest of the weaker sections. One of the most distinct features of the tribal is their 'Habitat' which usually is in deep interior forest with difficult terrain, in hilly or non hilly region. Taking into consideration their distinct culture and habitation, the British preferred to conveniently keep the tribal in isolation, on the pretext of protection of the tribal and preserving their culture. Unfortunately these factors kept these pre-literate communities away from literacy as well as formal Education (However, there a very few exceptions to this). With this, the tribal were kept away from the main stream.

After independence, it was decided to bring the tribal in the main stream. In order to bring the tribal in the main stream, two different approaches were advocated:-

(*i*) Assimilation and Development of Tribal.

(*ii*) Integration and Development of Tribal.

Preference has been given to an Integrated Approach for Tribal development.

Prior to 1950, the Government of India had no direct program for the education of the tribal. With the adoption of the Constitution, the promotion of education of Scheduled tribes has become a special responsibility of the Central as well as of the State Government. Like all other sectors of socio-economic life, educationally the tribal are at different levels of development (Ratha S.M. – 1986).

Attempts were made to give a desired shape to the objectives of the development of the 'Scheduled Areas' by various administrative measures ranging from Block Development Programs, Multipurpose Community Development Blocks and Integrated Tribal Development Projects under Tribal Sub Plan. The various development programs implemented for Tribal Development included the equally important component of Education.

Education has the potential for –

- human resource development;
- improvement of quality of life; and
- Contribution in the process of planned social change.

Pandit Jawaharlal Nehru has delineated the goals/five fundamental principles (Panchashel) for tribal development, [which have been mentioned by Pandit Nehru, in his 'Foreword' to the second edition (1959) of 'A Philosophy for NEFA', by Verrier Elwin].

These five fundamental principles (Panchasheel) of tribal development are:

1. People should develop along the lines of their own genius and we should avoid imposing anything on them. We should try to encourage in every way their own traditional arts and culture.
2. Tribal rights in land and forests should be respected.
3. We should try to train and build up a team of their own people to do the work of administration and development. Some technical personnel from outside will, no doubt, are needed, especially in the beginning. But we should avoid introducing too many outsiders into tribal territory.
4. We should not over-administer these areas or overwhelm them with a multiplicity of schemes. We should rather work through, and not in rivalry to, their own social and cultural institutions.
5. We should judge results, not by statistics or the amount of money spent, but by the quality of human character that is evolved.

Pandit Jawaharlal Nehru advocated the need for 'psychological approach' for achieving psychological integration (A New Deal for Tribal India – Report of the Scheduled Areas and Scheduled Tribes Commissions 1963) – (Quoted in Mathur H.M.-1977:489-90).

In NEFA, Pandit Jawaharlal Nehru gave 'priority' to roads and schools and was of the opinion that "given these communication and schools, they would advance rapidly and give a credit to the country in many ways" (1952-A).

Pandit Jawaharlal Nehru's love for the tribals found expression in his efforts to mix with them as frequently as possible, to show friendly and familiar gesture...and safeguard their interests (Vidyarthi – 1968). Addressing an All India Conference of the tribals held at Jagdalpur, in March 1955, he advised his tribal brethren in the following words:

"Wherever you live, you should live in your own way. This is what I want you to decide yourselves, how you would like to live. Your old customs and habits are good. We want that they should survive but at the same time we want that you should be educated and should do your part in welfare of our country" (1955:16).

In spite of his anxiety to see the tribal educationally and economically advanced, he always hoped that there would be no attempt made to impose others ways of life on them in a hurry. "..Let the change come gradually and be worked out by the tribal themselves" (Nehru-1957).

Observations, Analysis & Discussion

Literacy and level of education are two basic indicators of the level of development achieved by a group/society. The Literacy results in more awareness besides contributing to the overall improvement of health, hygiene and other social conditions.

Literacy and Educational level – Among Scheduled Tribes in Maharashtra State.

According to the 2001 census, the overall literacy rate among the tribal population in Maharashtra State is 55.20. This is less than the overall literacy rate for the general population in Maharashtra State, even during the 1991 census.

Table 1. Literacy among Scheduled Tribes.

Year	*Literacy (Maharashtra State)*					
	General Population			*Tribal Population*		
	Male	*Female*	*Total*	*Male*	*Female*	*Total*
1961	42.04	16.76	29.82	12.55	1.75	7.21
1971	51.04	26.43	39.13	19.06	4.21	11.74
1981	58.65	34.63	47.02	32.38	11.94	22.29
1991	76.56	52.30	64.87	49.08	24.08	36.77
2001	86.27	67.00	76.90	68.42	43.10	55.20

Source: Census of India 19961, 1971, 1981, 1991 and 2001.

The literacy rate among the male population among the tribal in Maharashtra, as per 2001 census is 68.42. This is less than the literacy rate among the male population the general population in Maharashtra State, even during 1991 census.

The literacy rate among the female population among the tribal in Maharashtra, as per 2001 Census is 43.10. This is less than the literacy rate among the female population among the general population in Maharashtra State, even during 1991 census.

This table indicates that the rate of literacy among the female population among the tribal in Maharashtra is less than –

(*i*) the literacy rate of the male population among the tribal in Maharashtra ; and

(*ii*) The literacy rate of the female population among the general population in Maharashtra.

A low rate of female literacy in India has always been a matter of concern. Female literacy in India can be attributed to several economic and social compulsions.

(Mahatma Jotirao Phule a social reformer in Maharashtra did a pioneering work in the field of educating the girls and women from down trodden classes of the society. He did this work with the help of his wife Savitribai, many years before getting independence. In the city of Pune, he started a school for girls, when the girls were not allowed to take education. Both

Jotiba and Savitribai were harassed by the orthodox people in the society. In recognition of this Pioneering work, the building in which the school for girls was located, has been declared to be preserved as a National Monument).

This trend of female literacy reflects gender inequality and discrimination.

Moreover, indicators of socio-economic development and the physical quality of life index in several sociological / anthropological studies have clearly brought out the relevance of literacy and education of girls and women. The National Policy of Education (1986) has assigned an emphatic, interventionist role to educate the girls for bringing about changes in the status of women, leading to empowerment of women.

Once women perceive the relevance of education, they will willingly send their children, especially girls to school. If women are educated, then –

- child marriages are prevented;
- they have an awareness about maternal and child health;
- knowledge and awareness about health and family welfare programmes;
- acceptance of small size norm;
- there is a strong depressant effect on child bearing;
- knowledge and awareness about health, hygiene and sanitation;
- (National Literacy Mission – 1992).

Table 2. Literacy in Maharashtra – Scheduled Tribes Population and General Population*

Population	*Literacy*		
	Male	*Female*	*Total*
Scheduled Tribes	68.42	43.10	55.20
General Population	86.27	67.00	76.90

*(*Source :* Census of India 2001).

According to 2001 Census, percentage of literate persons (those who can read and write with understanding) aged 7 years and above, among ST population of Maharashtra is 55.2 percent, which is lower than 76.9 percent reported for the state population as a whole. The literacy data shows that the ST population of the state has made significant improvement in literacy during the decade 1991-2001. The literacy rate, which was 36.8 percent in 1991, has increased by 18.4 percentage points in 2001. Though the literacy rate has improved substantially among ST population 'it is still much below the literacy rate of the state population. The female literacy rate of 43.1 percent among ST population is lower as compared to 67.0 percent among the total female population of the state.

Table 3. Educational level attained by Scheduled Tribes in Maharashtra*

Educational Level	*Percentage of literates*
- Literate without educational level	3.3
- Below Primary	41.7
- Primary	25.7
- Middle	13.6
- Matric/Secondary/Higher Secondary/ Intermediate etc.	13.4
- Technical and Non-technical Diploma	0.2
- Graduate and above	2.1

*(*Source :* Census of India – 2001).

Out of the total literates, 45 percent are literates without any educational level, or have attained educational level below Primary level. The literates, who have attained education upto Primary and Middle levels constitute 25.7 percent and 13.6 percent respectively. 13.4 percent are having educational level up to Matric/Higher Secondary etc. levels, implying that about every 7th Scheduled Tribe literate is a Matriculate. Literates with educational level of Graduation and above are 2.1 percent.

The educational level table shows that the drop-out is conspicuous after the Primary level and again after Matric / Secondary levels among the majority of the Scheduled Tribes.

Population in the age 5 – 14 years are the potential students. Two third (66.2 percent) of the Scheduled Tribe population in this age group is attending various educational institutions.

Literacy and Educational level reflect the Network of Schools and Enrolment. Educational level has reflected the problem of Drop-out to be conspicuous after the primary level and after the secondary school level.

[The state of Maharashtra has been witnessing the phenomena of non-tribal 'posing' as belonging to tribal community – by virtue of partial/complete similarity in nomenclature. This phenomenon is reflected in the census data also. Hence, as far as the scheduled tribes' population is concerned, the different demographic indices are inflated at least to a considerable extent (Gaikwad John S. – 1986). This is true in case of the indices related to literacy also. Hence this fact needs to be kept in mind while considering the census data related to scheduled tribes in Maharashtra]

Ashram Schools: Scenario in Maharashtra

Prior to 1972, there were a few Ashram schools in tribal areas of Maharashtra State. Most of these Ashram Schools were managed by Voluntary Organizations. During 1972, Government of India encouraged the State Governments to implement the ambitious scheme of Ashram School Complex in the Tribal Sub Plan areas in different states. Accordingly the Government of Maharashtra launched the scheme of Ashram School Complex in the State. To begin with, about 31 Ashram School Complex were established by the Government of Maharashtra during 1972-73. During 1972-73, there were about 20 Ashram schools managed by Voluntary / Non-Government organizations. At present there are about 550 Government Ashram Schools in Maharashtra. In addition to the Ashram Schools managed by Government, there are about 500 Ashram Schools managed by voluntary / non government organizations. As per the Government policy, the voluntary organizations get 100% Salary grant, in addition to the grants required for the day to day needs of the resident students.

Apart from Ashram Schools, the tribal areas in Maharashtra also have Primary Schools (day Schools) managed by the Zilla Parishads.

Enrolment in Ashram Schools

Despite the growing network of Ashram Schools in the Tribal areas, and the increasing awareness about importance of education among the tribals, there are many children who are never enrolled in Ashram Schools nor in the nearby Primary Schools (day Schools).

Enrolment in Government Ashram Schools is preferred most because the admission makes the student eligible for free food & clothing, apart from free education. It is a fact that even if the parents are willing, some children do not get admission in Ist std. In the Ashram Schools (managed either by Government or by a voluntary organization). It is also observed that the parents do not prefer to admit their children in the nearby Primary Schools (day schools).

It is observed that the total number of female students enrolled is much less for all the standards (Bhanu & Kulkarni 1995). Further they observe that only 50.00% of the eligible children (6 to 14 years) attend the schools. There are a few villages where more than 80.00% of the eligible children never attended the school" (1995:47).

Retention / Dropouts

Retention needs to be looked as an important index of success of the program and not merely as "Education Wastage."

The following table illustrates the trend of average number of students enrolled in the Tribal Sub Plan Area in Maharashtra State.

Table 4. Average Number of Students enrolled.

Standard / Stage	*Boys**	*Girls**	*Total**
I	108602	91372	199000
V	56000	39600	95600
VIII	35500	20400	55900
X	25300	13000	38370

*(Number of students rounded to nearest hundred).

(*Source:* Table 8 – from 'Adiwasinche Shikshan' by Dr. Govind Gare)

It is observed that while the average enrolment in standard I in the Tribal Sub Plan Area in Maharashtra State is about

2 lakh children, the average number of students enrolled in standard VIII is about 55,000. This number further comes down to about 40,000 students at standard Xth level. Hence, it is observed that the enrolment decreases from standard I to standard X.

As far as the enrolment of girls is concerned, it is observed to be apparently in tune with the sex ratio, only during the enrolment in standard I. Thereafter the average number of enrolment for girls is observed to be declining rapidly. The enrolment of girls at Xth standard level is about 50% of the enrolment of boys. (Gaikwad John S –1984, 1989).

Drop-out at an early stage

In a study regarding Ashram Schools, Ghode M. (1995) observes that "the Ashram School children complained about the language used by their teachers, which was not easily grasped by them as it was different from their dialect." (1995:181).

One more factor which may be considered to be responsible for drop-outs at primary stage itself is the feeling of 'alienation' imposed by Marathi – as the medium of instruction. The dialects spoken by Bhil, Pawara, Korku, Kolam, Gond, Pardhi, Halba are entirely different from Marathi. Hence this situation demands that the teachers should feel comfortable to communicate with the students (at least in lower classes), in their own dialect.

Pandit Jawaharlal Nehru gave considerable thought on the language problem which he considered exceedingly important from the psychological point of view. He made it perfectly and absolutely clear that "Government would encourage the tribal languages". He stood not only for allowing the tribal languages to continue but made it his policy "to encourage and help them to flourish" (Vidyarthi L.P. – 1968). In this matter, he was greatly influenced by Lenin and others who won the goodwill of the tribal people of the Soviet Republic by encouraging their language, by going out of their way in helping hundreds of dialects, by preparing dictionaries and vocabularies and even by evolving new scripts where there were none (Vidyarthi L.P.- 1968).

Pandit Jawaharlal Nehru was convinced that it was a wise policy of Lenin of winning over illiteracy and above all to create an impression on them that they could live their own lives and in the light of this lesson, he advised all of us "to go out of our way to do so in context with Indian Tribal population" (1952).

The problem of medium of instruction has been posing a great irritant partly because we have not understood the tribal sentiment for his own language and partly because disintegrative Socio-Political forces misguide the tribal.

An UNESCO report on the medium of instruction, emphatically recommends that even where leaders of the tribal people do not want their language to be the medium of instruction, an attempt should be made to persuade them to change their mind. Article 350 A expects every local authority to provide adequate facilities for instruction in the mother-tongue at the primary stage (Ratha S.N., 1986).

Apart from the dialect problem faced by the tribal students at an earlier stage, equally important is the 'impact of the contents of the text books, at least at an earlier state. The contents of the text books certainly play an important role in shaping the attitudes and outlook of the children. Hence there is a need to consider this vital fact and design the text books for tribal children at least in lower classes. Text books containing familiar context is likely to have the potential of binding force that can prevent the dropout at an earlier state. Verrier Elwin (1963) observes that –

> In the successful formulation of the policy for the tribal education, text books assume great importance. They should include lessons depicting the life of tribal, their folklore, songs, history and the lives of their cultural heroes. These subjects should be woven into ordinary text books as well to enable the non tribal and tribal people to understand each other and give them added confidence that their way of life, history and culture are getting adequate support from other members of the society.

Taking into consideration, the conditions and special needs of the tribal, the Dhebar commission had suggested a separate cadre of teachers for tribal areas (Vidyarthi L.P., 1986).

Ghode M. (1995) further observes that recreational facilities are not available for the Ashram School children, during their leisure time. Further it can be stated that in case of young children, the feeling of home sickness, loneliness and shyness are yet another important factors which contribute to the phenomena of dropouts at an earlier stage. It is obvious that the small children would more frequently remember their home, parents and others in the new environment.

At this point it needs to be elaborated that the earlier Scheme of Ashram School Complex was more comprehensive. The educational program and the hostel were considered to be a single unit. With the provision of teachers' quarters, teachers were always expected to be 'near' the students even after the school hours. The teachers in the Ashram Schools had an opportunity to play the role of parents of the students in Ashram Schools.

After facing many hurdles, all the activities other than formal education were completely discontinued. The educational program and the hostel became independent of one another. The teachers are almost dissociated from the students, after the school hours. The Hotel Superintendent is expected to look after the School children after the School hours. However, the Hostel Superintendent concentrates only upon his/her responsibility of providing food to the Ashram school Children.

Another major reason for drop-outs has been observed to be the responsibility of contribution in the income generation activities or helping and supporting the family.

These responsibilities include:

- Participation in the agricultural activities;
- Participation in the operations in the forests;
- Participation in the activities related to food gathering;
- Participation in household activities;
- Looking after siblings;
- Cooking;
- Early marriage is an important factor responsible for drop-out of girls.

Regarding the apathy shown by the tribal for sending their children in schools – Elwin observes that:

"For a tribal family, to send its grown up girl to boy to school is essentially a matter of economics; and entails dislocation in the traditional pattern of division of labor,....many parents cannot just afford to send their children to school" (Elwin 1963:84).

Lack of motivation, enthusiasm and interest in studies among some of the first generation learners, leads to failure which further leads to inferiority complex that ultimately leads to abandoning the stream of formal education. It is apparent that being first generation learners, many of the tribal children are not capable of adjusting themselves with the structured set up of formal education.

The author had an opportunity to interview drop-out students and their parents in the tribal areas of Nandurbar, Nashik, Gadchiroli, Thane and Amravati Districts. Some of the parents indicated the awareness that if their children are educated they can get jobs. Despite such awareness, they were not at all keen to educate their children. Some of the illiterate tribal felt that – "educated children are a loss to the family".

This feeling is deep-rooted in their experience that – after exposure to the mainstream of formal education, many individuals partially dissociate from the traditions of the community. Some individuals develop a disliking for activities related to agriculture. This disliking result in an avoidance of activities related to agriculture. In such cases the activities related to agriculture are considered to be below dignity. Such individuals aspire for white-collared jobs in Government offices. In the quest for a Government job, some of them make a compromise with the situation and are satisfied to accept even class IV jobs.

Thus it is observed that ignorance, illiteracy and lack of awareness, motivation and enthusiasm lead to apathy for education. The tribal parents do not understand the relevance and importance of education. They are not aware that education has the potential to change the future of their children. Hence they do not feel like compromising with the present situation and motivate their children to complete their education properly. Though the comprehensive package of free education along with free food and clothing is apparently attractive. It is a fact that this package does not have the potential binding force, which can prevent the drop-outs.

It is observed that the drop out rate among the day scholars is considerably higher in comparison to the drop out rate among the students in the Ashram Schools. It is a fact that if the parents are educated then they themselves try their level best to prevent their children from getting off the tract of formal education.

While doing research on Tribal Health, the author observed that the tribal consider the entire Health services set up and health programs as 'something imposed from outside world' (Gaikwad John S – 1995). It is apparent that the preliterate tribal look at the formal education system as 'something imposed from outside world and which is not relevant and important in the frame work of their traditional culture'.

Conclusion

Considering the network of about 1000 Ashram Schools in the Tribal Sub Plan areas of Maharashtra State, there is a need to ponder upon how best this network of Ashram Schools can be utilized to improve the quality of education. The network of Ashram Schools should become effective, efficient and yield optimum results in term of academic excellence and quality. Apart from the present network there is a need to establish more Ashram Schools. Moreover attaining these objectives and goals is not dependant merely upon availability of funds and infrastructure.

In order to achieve these goals, there is a need of a judicious combination of political will, effective administrative, Academic aptitude, rationality, efficiency, motivation, Zeal, Dedication, sincerity etc. on the part of the administrators and teachers (Gaikwad John & Gare G.M 1986). Moreover, psychological approach is necessary for a result oriented outcome.

The illiterate and semi-literate tribal need to be made aware about the importance and relevance of educating their children. Their apathy needs to be replaced with enthusiasm for education of the children.

Apart from academic excellence and quality there is a need to tackle the problem of dropouts. The students should become aware about the need, relevance and importance of formal education for their development. Such an awareness and enthusiasm would change their attitude and outlook that will motivate them to remain in the mainstream of formal education. The first generation learners need to be equipped with the techniques of adapting and adjusting to the new environment of formal education. Special efforts are necessary to prevent the girls from going away from the main stream of formal education. The parents and the girls both need to be aware that in a changing scenario, new employment opportunities for girls are opening up in all fields. The National policy of Education (1986), has assigned an emphatic interventionist role to educate girls for bringing about changes in the Status of women, leading to empowerment of women. Empowerment of Tribal Women would certainly contribute to increase in literacy and educational level, along with associated developments.

Further this would facilitate overall development and thus contribute in the improvement of 'quality of life' of tribal.

27

Tribal Education in Rayagada : A Review of Language, Textbook and Medium of Instruction

—Akshaya K. Kanungo and Hrushikesh Mahapatra

India attained Independence in the year of 1947 and the country was at an impoverished state. Majority of Indians; illiterate and ruralities were dependent on traditional agriculture. Industrialization was not taken shape and majority of the people lived below poverty live. The constitution of India was framed in 1950 with an objective to guarantee social, political and economic Justice to all irrespective of caste, creed and religion. It was well visualized that development in education along with other allied sectors would play a vital role to bring about desirable changes in the country. That means that backward sections of Indian population i.e. Scheduled Castes and Scheduled Tribes and other backward section must be provided opportunity in education to develop critical thinking and self determination and contribute to the progress of the country. These promises laid the foundation for the attempt of Universalization of Primary Education in India. In 1950, target was set to universalize primary education among the entire eligible category of children within the age group of 6-14 years of age within a span of 10 years. During that period a great deal of expansion in education facilities was achieved. However, universalisation was still a distant dream. National Policy of Education (NPE), 1986 and its subsequent modification in 1992 laid down clearly the following targets to achieve universalization of education at Primary stage. (i) Provision of universal Access to all eligible children by opening of formal or non-formal education Centres within a reasonable distance of one kilometer. (ii) Retention of all children in schooling centres and ensuring completion of 5 years of basic education. (iii) Provisions of Quality education where-by all children achieve minimum achievement level as per the standard. Orissa is one of the 30 states in India, situated in the eastern part along the coast of Bay of Bengal. The total population of the State is 3.670 crores as per 2001 census (provisional). The scheduled castes and scheduled tribes comprise 22.21 and 16.20 percent respectively. The literacy percentage of the state is 63.61% (excluding 0-6 population) in which male and female literacy stands as 75.95% and 50.97% respectively (Source census 2001, Provisional). If we consider the concentration of indigenous tribal communities, their highest concentration is found in the southern districts of Orissa State. Rayagada is one among these districts, which was formed carving out of east- while Koraput district.

The district lies between 19 degree to 20 degree in north latitude and 23 degree to 84 degree in the east longitude that occupies an area of 7580 square kilometers. The area is calculated to 4.9 percent of the total area of the State. The district has a population of 823019 that is 2.24 percent of the total population of the State and rank 22nd in the State. The density of population is 116 as against 101 in 1991 per square kilometer. Out of the total population, 405631 are male and 417388 are female. The sex ratio stands as 1029 females per 1000 males. The district has recorded an increase of 15.27 percent over the last enumeration in 1991. (Source Census, 2001, Provisional). The district has been the dwell of a number of indigenous tribal communities some very marginal and some quite significant as far as their population is concerned. The Tribal population of the district is 473379. The male and female constitute 233120 and 240259 respectively of the total population with a percentage of 57.51 in the district. As per 2001 Census (provisional) the literacy rate of both the sexes stands as 16.20 percent The literacy rate of male is 47.35 percent while that of female is 24.31 percent. They have their own mother tongue having no written script except one tribe, soura, who have got a written script. All the languages belong to the Austric Speech family. The table here reflects an idea about the block-wise concentration of indigenous tribals with their mother tongue. SL.

A lot of attempts have been made to mainstream the tribal children in education process. Most importantly by providing access, reading writing materials, free textbooks and empowering village community to participate in management of school. Achievements are also quite significant in areas of provision of access by opening of new schools, hostels, enrolment of children and empowerment of teachers through mass teachers training on child centered approach. However, there seem to be lack of achievement in retention and achievement of students (on the basis of completion rates) in schools. The dropout rate is still quite high and achievement scores in subjects need significant increase.

There are many reasons why the system fails particularly in the case of indigenous tribals. This paper will discuss in detail the problems and issues limited to the area of an gauge, textbook and medium of instruction and other issues directly or indirectly related to that. If we consider the case of tribal child and feature that motivate and de-motivate him in staying in school, we need to consider the background and inputs given to him as part of incentive to adopt the modern education successfully, some factors of importance maybe scrutinized. Language is a part parcel and vehicle of culture. It is the medium of expression. It can be symbolic or spoken. Language is learn as part of the socialisation and enculturation process. It can not be taught in a sense that it is not merely sensible speech sounds rather typical cultural elements intrinsically linked and ingrained in it. Language can be learnt through interactions. The problem of providing free and compulsory education to all the children of the age group of 6-14 years by establishing sufficient numbers of schools in all areas in order to satisfy the directives of the constitution (article 45) poses many pertinent questions with at least one, for the education of indigenous tribal communities.

Part-V of the constitution contains Directive Principles of State Policy contained in article 36-51. These principles are ideals which the State should strive for and some directions to the state executive and legislature as to how their powers be used. Besides these are few other directives addressed to the

State in other parts of the constitutions, which like the Directive Principles are also non-justifiable. Article 350- A directs the State to take steps to provide adequate facilities for instructions in the mother tongue at the primary stage of education and particularly to the children belonging to the linguistic minorities mainly with a view to preserve their language and facilitate better understanding among such children. A tribal child is relatively less exposed to other languages at the age of his entry to the school, because of the tribals have their own Eco-zone where they inhabit inrelative isolation and therefore have lesser exposure to the outside world. Kondh the major tribal communities in Rayagada are least mobile. Their movement as observed is limited to a maximum of 20 kilometers i.e. from home to work sites and to weekly local market not far away from the village. That means they hardly migrate to other part of the district and State unlike Souras who although migrate to other part of the country seasonally in negligible numbers for daily wage laboring. The tribal child entering school for the first time sees a completely different environment. The building pattern with closed four walls, and sitting arrangement is alien to him. The teacher, his apparel and language - unseen and incomprehensive creates a sense of suspicion and fear in him initially. Subsequently the teachers' (mostly non-tribals) treatment makes impossible for him to continue in school. Here it's important to discuss the role of teacher in classroom. It is often seen that teachers working in tribal areas have prejudices and biases towards tribal society and culture. They treat tribals as sub-human beings, who have a lot of blind beliefs and conservative ideas. To them the tribal language which has no written streptose not qualify for a status of language and hence inferior. These senses of ethnocentrismare expressed in their dealings with tribal students in a classroom. He seldom inquires into the socio-cultural background of the tribal child. If one considers the case of a tribal child it is clear that he is no less competent even at a tender age. He acquires ability in learning songs at the age of 4-5 years. He learns beating of drums (Dhapa), dances memorising short stories, proverbs, and riddles and often creates new songs of his own in impromptu exchange with peers at the age of 10. He is so close to his things that he dares, dreams, fantasizes, plays and interacts with an infinite thing, words, jargons which no one can even teach him in post-primary education. If we consider the scope of learning language, we will see that a tribal child gets plenty of contexts at home, where every thing is informal and friendly and language learning is spontaneous. However, in school, there is dearth of context and every thing is formal and structured and the language of the book is considered as the highest kind of knowledge. The child has no scope to interact with friends while the teacher is taking a class on monologue basis. The child can not concentrate because of communication failure and monotonous classroom process and instead chastised, beaten by the teacher for not being attentive, responsive and not doing wee in studies. The hostile and in-conducive school atmosphere leads to dropping-out and discontinuation of most of the students from school. Above all the tribal children are the first generation academic learners and have least scope of support and help from parents and relatives who are illiterate. The psychologists, educationists and linguists are of the opinion that a child exposed to multilingual situations in initial years has faster cognitive and intellectual development. But this opinion does not hold well in tribal areas because in urban areas, the child gets its formal education through state language as the medium of instructions, which is his own mother tongue and gradually exposed to other languages. But in tribal society, the child is directly introduced to the State language used in schools rather than his own mother tongue. Another reason is that in urban areas the child has relatively plenty of opportunity to interact with people coming from different linguistic areas. He is exposed to electronic media, Radio and T.V., which not only are the medium of entertainment but also are scope of learning and adopting traits and ideas. The tribal child has absolutely no scope where he gets exposed to other languages. There are many tribal language which has no script. Hence, preparation of suitable textbooks for such category children is a challenging task. In Orissa, the textbooks are supplied free of cost to tribal and other categories of children. The language of the textbooks is in standard state language for school students all over the state. It is believed that experts knowing tribal culture and language prepare these books. However, it is found that the books have contents of subjects which are reflective of dominant society. The books have few local specific contents and some times pictures and description of animals, birds, trees, etc. alien to the tribal child which poses problem to comprehend. The colour of pictures is not realistic and lacks brightness. All the pictures are often bi-coloured. Overall the cover page, contents and contexts are not local specific and relate to the real life situations of the tribals for which the text book is not appreciated and adopted by the tribal children. The Paradox Considering the constitutional directives and actual implementation of educational scheme one would certainly find a gap or mis-match between what should have been done and what has been done so far. A country like India, where diverse linguistic groups are found, some quite significant and some negligible in number pose a great problem as to how to streamline them in the education process. As per the constitutional directives the basic education may be provided free of cost to indigenous tribal in their own mother tongue which seems to be a Herculean task for any state government. The indigenous tribal though have a definite territory, they have a number of sub-groups within it. Therefore, language varies in a limited geographical area and within a particular tribe. It also varies from sub-tribe to sub-tribe. Language of one sub-tribe is quite different from another within the limited geographical area due to impact of bordering community and their exposure to outside world. Such examples are innumerable in this district. One such example is that in Kashipur (as administrative division of the district) which has a sizeable number of Kondh population and sub-sections like Pengo, (relatively primitive) and Desia (relatively assimilated) who live close to each other. Although there are certain similarities in language and culture they differ a lot linguistically. Any textbook on either language could not solve the problem. Secondly, in case of multi-lingualsituations in a classroom, whereby students come from different tribal or sub-tribal groups, the problem for the teachers is as to what should be the standard medium of instruction for all the children. This has been a feature of all residential schools running in the district by Schedule Caste and Schedule Tribe Department. The teacher knowing one tribal language finds it impossible to teach students coming from different ethnic and language background. Thirdly, the teachers, mostly non-tribals, do not have adequate knowledge of tribal language. There are tribal teachers (mostly Souras and Kondhs), who can be useful for children. But there is no consideration of the above fact and a Soura teacher posted in a Kondh dominated village or school is as good as non-tribal teachers as they do not know the language of Kondhs. In the second case some of the non-tribal teachers who have been working reasonably for a long time at a particular tribal area have experience of tribal language where all the students belong to a particular tribal group. However due to a number of reasons, like health hazards (Rayagada is an endemic malaria proneregion), lack of basic human facilities like shelter, market place and postal facilities, they get themselves transferred to other parts paving way for posting of a new teacher in his place. Fourthly, the problem could have been subsided with the engagement of sufficient number of local teachers from the community. But unfortunately there is dearth of qualified tribals who can be appointed as teachers in schools. The problems and issues in language, textbook and medium of instruction are very typical to the tribals of Rayagada as to any other region of the country where multi-ethnic and Multi-lingual indigenous tribal groups are existing. Development in the education sphere can only be possible when the key issues are addressed properly. These are the issues and problems, which can fail the entire education system even before it is actually implement edunless addressed through strategic planning. Any generalized planning across the board for all category of children not only create an environment of education among tribals but also will delay and break the pace of spontaneous educational development. Therefore, careful and calculative measures must be taken keeping in view the educational need vis-a-vis the cultural orientation of the tribals. Some indicative, if not exhaustive suggestions are given below. 1. Linguistic mapping should be done to assess the incidence and category of tribals before planning for their education. 2. The medium of instruction should be in the mother tongue by way of using bi-lingual primers prepared in a decentralized manner. That means it is not the state or district, it is the block where the teachers (tribal) with educated (although a few) tribal persons will prepare the text book for their own category of children. 3. The school environment should be attractive with gardens, plantations, and children friendly elements with cost effective locally available raw materials. The school must have play materials and self-learning materials for the children to create interest in them to attend school regularly. 4. The teacher working in a tribal dominated school should be rightly informed about his role. He should be oriented on the richness of heritage and culture of the tribals. He should have enough patience to bear the tribal child in a classroom and act as a friend and facilitator rather than a master. 5. The non-tribal teachers working for longtime inspite of various health hazards by knowing the tribal language should be identified and compensated with incentives and rewards as a token of commendations for their valuable services towards the education of tribals so that other non-tribal teachers will be interested to join the force. 6. Tribal teachers should be identified by their category and be posted to schools where he can serve his community children better. 7. The village community although illiterate, they are great assets as far as education on art and craft is concerned. Their resources should be used while topics related to agriculture, horticulture and material culture are transacted in the classroom. 8. Innovation through research on various aspects of education must be conducted so as to identify problems and their solutions. The problems and issues identified at this juncture may seriously affect the future developments in the district. Hence, it is high time that appropriate strategies must be buildup to find out ways and means not to substituted to mitigate the problems for the future.

India attained Independence in the year of 1947 and the country was at an impoverished state. Majority of Indians; illiterate and ruralities were dependent on traditional agriculture. Industrialization was not taken shape and majority of the people lived below poverty live. The constitution of India was framed in 1950 with an objective to guarantee social, political and economic Justice to all irrespective of caste, creed and religion. It was well visualized that development in education along with other allied sectors would play a vital role to bring about desirable changes in the country. That means that backward sections of Indian population i.e. Scheduled Castes and Scheduled Tribes and other backward section must be provided opportunity in education to develop critical thinking and self determination and contribute to the progress of the country. These promises laid the foundation for the attempt of Universalization of Primary Education in India. In 1950, target was set to universalize primary education among the entire eligible category of children within the age group of 6-14 years of age within a span of 10 years. During that period a great deal of expansion in education facilities was achieved. However, universalisation was still a distant dream. National Policy of Education (NPE), 1986 and its subsequent modification in 1992 laid down clearly the following targets to achieve universalization of education at Primary stage. (*i*) Provision of universal Access to alleligible children by opening of formal or non-formal education Centres within a reasonable distance of one kilometer. (*ii*) Retention of all children in schooling centres and ensuring completion of 5 years of basic education. (*iii*) Provisions of Quality education where-by all children achieve minimum achievement level as per the standard. Orissa is one of the 30 states in India, situated in the eastern part along the coast of Bay of Bengal. The total population of the State is 3.670 crores as per 2001 census (provisional). The scheduled castes and Scheduled tribes comprise 22.21 and 16.20 percent respectively. The literacy percentage of the state is 63.61% (excluding 0-6 population) in which male and female literacy stands as 75.95% and 50.97% respectively (Source census 2001, Provisional). If we consider the concentration of indigenous tribal communities, their highest concentration is found in the southern districts of Orissa State. Rayagada is one among these districts, which was formed carving out of earst- while Koraput district (one of the 13 Tribal Education in Rayagada : A Review of Language, Textbook and Medium of Instruction Akshaya K. Kanungo Hrushikesh Mahapatra 30 Orissa Review* September - 2004 old districts) in 1992 in the process of expansion of districts in the State. The districtlies between 19 degree to 20 degree in north latitude and 23 degree to 84 degree in the east longitude that occupies an area of 7580 square kilometers. The area is calculated to 4.9 percent of the total area of the State. The district has a population of 823019 that is 2.24 percent of the total population of the State and rank 22nd in the State. The density of population is 116 as against 101 in 1991 per square kilometer. Out of the total population, 405631 are male and

417388 are female. The sex ratio stands as 1029 females per 1000 males. The district has recorded an increase of 15.27 per cent over the last enumeration in 1991. (Source Census, 2001, Provisional). The district has been the dwell of a number of indigenous tribal communities some very marginal and some quite significant as far as their population is concerned. The Tribal population of the district is 473379. The male and female constitute 233120 and 240259 respectively of the total population with a percentage of 57.51 in the district. As per 2001 Census (provisional) the literacy rate of both the sexes stands as 35.61 per cent. The literacy rate of male is 47.35 per cent while that of female is 24.31 per cent. They have their own mother tongue having no written script except one tribe, soura, who have got a written script. All the languages belong to the Austric Speech family. The table here reflects an idea about the block-wise concentration of indigenous tribals with their mother tongue.

A lot of attempts have been made to mainstream the tribal children in education process. Most importantly by providing access, reading writing materials, free textbooks and empowering village community to participation management of school. Achievements are also quite significant in areas of provision of access by opening of new schools, hostels, enrolment of children and empowerment of teachers through mass teachers training on child centered approach. However, there seem to be lack of achievement in retention and achievement of students (on the basis of completion rates) in schools. The dropout rate is still quite high and achievement scores in subjects need significant increase.

There are many reasons why the system fails particularly in the case of indigenous tribals. This paper will discuss in detail the problems and issues limited to the area of language, textbook and medium of instruction and other issues directly or indirectly related to that. If we consider the case of tribal child and feature that motivate and de-motivate him in staying in school, we need to consider the background and inputs given to him as part of incentive to adopt the modern education successfully, some factors of importance maybe scrutinized. Language is a part parcel and vehicle of culture. It is the medium of expression. It can be symbolic or spoken. Language is learnt as part of the socialisation and enculturation process. It can not be taught in a sense that it is not merely sensible speech sounds rather typical cultural elements intrinsically linked and ingrained in it. Language can be learnt through interactions. The problem of providing free and compulsory education to all the children of the age group of 6-14 years by establishing sufficient numbers of schools in all areas in order to satisfy the directives of the constitution (article 45) poses many pertinent questions with at least one, for the education of indigenous tribal communities. Part-V of the constitution contains Directive Principles of State Policy contained in article 36-51. These principles are ideals which the State should strive for and some directions to the state executive and legislature as to how their powers be used. Besides these are few other directives addressed to the State in other parts of the constitutions, which like the Directive Principles are also non-justifiable. Article 350- A directs the State to take steps to provide adequate facilities for instructions in the mother tongue at the primary stage of education and particularly to the children belonging to the linguistic minorities mainly with a view to preserve their language and facilitate better understanding among such children. A tribal child is relatively less exposed to other languages at the age of his entry to the school, because of the tribals have their own Eco-zone where they inhabit inrelative isolation and therefore have lesser exposure to the outside world. Kondh the major tribal communities in Rayagada are least mobile. Their movement as observed is limited to a maximum of 20 kilometers i.e. from home to work sites and to weekly local market not far away from the village. That means they hardly migrate to other part of the district and State unlike Souras who although migrate to other part of the country seasonally in negligible numbers for daily wage laboring. The tribal child entering school for the first time sees a completely different environment. The building pattern with closed four walls, and sitting arrangement is alien to him. The teacher, his apparel and language - unseen and in comprehensive creates a sense of suspicion and fear in him initially. Subsequently the teachers' (mostly non-tribals) treatment makes impossible for him to continue in school. Hereit's important to discuss the role of teacher in classroom.

It is often seen that teachers working in tribal areas have prejudices and biases towards tribal society and culture. They treat tribals as sub-human beings, who have a lot of blind beliefs and conservative ideas. To them the tribal language which has no written script does not qualify for a status of language and hence inferior. These senses of ethnocentrism are expressed in their dealings with tribal students in a classroom. He seldom inquires into the socio-cultural background of the tribal child. If one considers the case of a tribal child it is clear that he is no less competent even at a tender age. He acquires ability in learning songs at the age of 4-5 years. He learns beating of drums (Dhapa), dances memorising short stories, proverbs, and riddles and often creates new songs of his own in impromptu exchange with peers at the age of 10. He is so close to his things that he dares, dreams, fantasizes, plays and interacts with an infinite thing, words, jargons which no one can even teach him in post-primary education. If we consider the scope of learning language, we will see that a tribal child gets plenty of contexts at home, where every thing is informal and friendly and language learning is spontaneous. However, in school, there is dearth of context and every thing is formal and structured and the language of the book is considered as the highest kind of knowledge. The child has no scope to interact with friends while the teacher is taking a class on monologue basis. The child can not concentrate because of communication failure and monotonous classroom process and instead chastised, beaten by the teacher for not being attentive, responsive and not doing we in studies. The hostile and in-conducive school atmosphere leads to dropping-out and discontinuation of most of the students from school. Above all the tribal children are the first generation academic learners and have least scope of support and help from parents and relatives who are illiterate. The psychologists, educationists and linguists are of the opinion that a child exposed to multilingual situations in initial years has faster cognitive and intellectual development. But this opinion does not hold well in tribal areas because in urban areas, the child gets its formal education through state language as the medium of instructions, which is his own mother tongue and gradually exposed to other languages. But in tribal society, the child is directly introduced to the State language used in schools rather than his own mother tongue. Another reason is that in urban areas the child has relatively plenty of opportunity to interact with people coming from different linguisticare as. He is exposed to electronic media, Radio and T.V., which not only are the medium of entertainment but also are scope of learning and adopting traits and ideas. The tribal child has absolutely no scope where he gets exposed to other languages. There are many tribal language which has no script. Hence, preparation of suitable textbooks for such category children is a challenging task. In Orissa, the textbooks are supplied free of cost to tribal and other categories of children. The language of the textbooks is in standard state language for school students all over the state. It is believed that experts knowing tribal culture and language prepare these books. However, it is found that the books have contents of subjects which are reflective of dominant society. The books have few local specific contents and some times pictures and description of animals, birds, trees, etc. alien to the tribal child which poses problem to comprehend. The colour of pictures is not realistic and lacks brightness. All the pictures are often bi-coloured. Overall the cover page, contents and contexts are not local specific and relate to the real life situations of the tribals for which the text book is not appreciated and adopted by the tribal children. The Paradox Considering the constitutional directives and actual implementation of educational scheme one would certainly find a gap or mis-match between what should have been done and what has been done so far. A country like India, where diverse linguistic groups are found, some quite significant and some negligible in number pose a great problem as to how to streamline them in the education process. As per the constitutional directives the basic education may be provided free of cost to indigenous tribal in their own mother tongue which seems to be a Herculean task for any state government. The indigenous tribal although have a definite territory, they have a number of sub-groups within it. Therefore, language varies in a limited geographical area and within a particular tribe. It also varies from sub-tribe to sub-tribe. Language of one sub-tribe is quite different from another within the limited geographical area due to impact of bordering community and their exposure to outside world. Such examples are in numerable in this district. One such example is that in Kashipur (as administrative division of the district) which has a sizeable number of Kondh population and sub-sections like Pengo, (relatively primitive) and Desia (relatively assimilated) who live close to each other. Although there are certain similarities in language and culture they differ a lot linguistically. Any textbook on either language could not solve the problem. Secondly, in case of multi-lingualsituations in a classroom, whereby students come from different tribal or sub-tribal groups, the problem for the teachers is as to what should be the standard medium of instruction for all the children. This has been a feature of all residential schools running in the district by Schedule Caste and Schedule Tribe Department. The teacher knowing one tribal language finds it impossible to teach students coming from different ethnic and language background. Thirdly, the teachers, mostly non-tribals, do not have adequate knowledge of tribal language. There are tribal teachers (mostly Souras and Kondhs), who can be useful for children. But there is no consideration of the above fact and a Soura teacher posted in a Kondh dominated village or school is as good as non-tribal teachers as they do not know the language of Kondhs. In the second case some of the non-tribal teachers who have been working reasonably for a long time at a particular tribal area have experience of tribal language where all the students belong to a particular tribal group. However due to a number of reasons, like health hazards (Rayagada is an endemic malaria proneregion), lack of basic human facilities like shelter, market place and postal facilities, they get themselves transferred to other parts paving way for posting of a new teacher in his place. Fourthly, the problem could have been subsided with the engagement of sufficient number of local teachers from the community. But unfortunately there is dearth of qualified tribals who can be appointed as teachers in schools. The problems and issues in language, textbook and medium of instruction are very typical to the tribals of Rayagada as to any other region of the country where multi-ethnic and multi-lingual indigenous tribal groups are existing. Development in the education sphere can only be possible when the key issues are addressed properly. These are the issues and problems, which can fail the entire education system even before it is actually implemented unless addressed through strategic planning. Any generalized planning across the board for all category of children not only create an environment of education among tribals but also will delay and break the pace of spontaneous educational development. Therefore, careful and calculative measures must be taken keeping in view the educational need vis-a-vis the cultural orientation of the tribals. Some indicative, if not exhaustive suggestions are given below. 1. Linguistic mapping should be done to assess the incidence and category of tribals before planning for their education. 2. The medium of instruction should be in the mother tongue by way of using bi-lingual primers prepared in a decentralized manner. That means it is not the state or district, it is the block where the teachers (tribal) with educated (although a few) tribal persons will prepare the text book for their own category of children. 3. The school environment should be attractive with gardens, plantations, and children friendly elements with cost effective locally available raw materials. The school must have play materials and self-learning materials for the children to create interest in them to attend school regularly. 4. The teacher working in a tribal dominated school should be rightly informed about his role. He should be oriented on the richness of heritage and culture of the tribals. He should have enough patience to bear the tribal child in a classroom and act as a friend and facilit at or rather than a master. 5. The non-tribal teachers working for longtime inspite of various health hazards by knowing the tribal language should be identified and compensated with incentives and rewards as a token of commendations for their valuable services towards the education of tribals so that other non-tribal teachers will be interested to join the force. 6. Tribal teachers should be identified by their category and be posted to schools where he can serve his community children better. 7. The village community although illiterate, they are great assets as far as education on art and craft is concerned. Their resources should be used while topics related to agriculture, horticulture and material culture are transacted in the classroom. 8. Innovation through research on various aspects of education must be conducted so as to identify problems and their solutions. The problems and issues identified at this juncture may seriously affect the future developments in the district. Hence, it is high time that appropriate strategies must be built up to find out ways and means not to substituted to mitigate the problems for the future.

28

Ashram Schools in Action : A Case Study of Karnataka

—Nanjunda D.C., Midatala Rani and Annapurna, M.

Unity in diversity is our main strength. Our land is cradle for various traditions, religious, ethnic, cultural, customs and linguistic groups. We can say it is more or less a plural society. Hence the researchers can get plenty of data to study cross-cultural aspects of the country. Even though India has diverse groups only few percentage has eating fruit of main stream development and a larger section of the under privileged of the society has remained near the periphery or long away from the so-called development. The greatest challenge that the Government of India has been facing since independence is the proper provision of social justice to the scheduled tribe people, by ameliorating their socio-economic conditions. Scheduled Tribes, constitute the weakest section of India's population, from the ecological, economic and educational angles. They are practically deprived of many civic facilities and isolated from modern and civilized way of living since so many centuries. The British rulers really did something in providing certain facilities in villages and towns such as, education, transport, communication, medical etc. though inadequate and mainly with self-interest. But it did nothing for ameliorating the socio-economic conditions of tribal people, except to the people in North-East region of the country, because of certain reasons. Firstly, the British administrators thought it expedient generally to leave the tribals alone, as the task of administration in the hill areas was difficult and costly. Secondly, Tribal Development in India -A Study in Human Development Kulamani Padhiit was considered desirable to keep away the tribals from possible political influence from the world outside world. Thirdly, some of the British officers genuinely felt that left to themselves, the tribal people would remain a happier lot. The Scheduled District Act of 1984 had therefore kept most of these areas administratively separate, the same situation was allowed to continue under the Govt. of India Acts of 1919 and 1935. However, after independence this policy was abandoned and new policy of tribal development and integration was initiated. The Constitution of India has made definite provisions for the welfare and uplift of the tribal people throughout the country.

Tribal Population: There are approximately two hundred million tribal people in the entire globe, which means, about 4% of the global population. They are found in many regions of the world and majority of them is the poorest amongst poor. According to 1981 census, the population of Scheduled Tribes in the country was 5.16 crores, consisting about 7.76% of total Indian population, which means one tribesman for every 13 Indians. Literacy rate of Scheduled Tribes is very low compared to the general literacy rate. Recognizing that education provides opportunities for a permanent change in the socio-economic status of these people, this Government gives top priority to education. Hence out of a sum of Rs. 448.91 crores provided in the Budget Estimate for 2004-2005 to this Department, more than70% is earmarked for schemes related to education. There is a need to evolve sensitive model of tribal education rooted in the psychological strengths of tribal children.

Indian Tribals

Scheduled Tribe in India are more like the "indigeneous" or"tribal people" in other parts of the world. The population of Scheduled Tribes in India according to 2001 census is 8.43 crore. There is no definition of a tribe in the Constitution but one may distinguish some characteristics that are generally accepted: self-identification, language, distinctive social and cultural organisation, economic under-development, geographic location and initially, isolation, which has been steadily, and in some cases, traumatically, eroded. Many tribes still live in hilly and/ or forested areas, somewhat remote from settlements. Indian tribes constitute roughly 8 percent of the nation's total population, nearly 68 million people according to the 1991 census. One concentration lives in a belt along the Himalayas stretching through Jammu and Kashmir, Himachal Pradesh, and Uttar Pradesh in the west, to Assam, Meghalaya, Tripura, Arunachal Pradesh, Mizoram, Manipur, and Nagaland in the northeast. Another concentration lives in the hilly areas of central India (Madhya Pradesh, Orissa, and, to a lesser extent, Andhra Pradesh); in this belt, which is bounded by the Narmada River to the north and the Godavari River to the southeast, tribal peoples occupy the slopes of the region's mountains. Other tribals, the Santals, live in Bihar and West Bengal. There are smaller numbers of tribal people in Karnataka, Tamil Nadu, and Kerala, in western India in Gujarat and Rajasthan, and in the union territories of Lakshadweep and the Andaman and Nicobar Islands. The extent to which a state's population is tribal varies considerably. In the northeastern states of Arunachal Pradesh, Meghalaya, Mizoram, and Nagaland, upward of 90 percent of the population is tribal.

However, in the remaining northeast states of Assam, Manipur, Sikkim, and Tripura, tribal peoples form between 20 and 30 percent of the population. The largest tribes are found in central India, although the tribal population there accounts for only around 10 per cent of the region's total population. Major concentrations of tribal people live in Maharashtra, Orissa, and West Bengal. In the south, about 1 percent of the populations of Kerala and Tamil Nadu are tribal, whereas about 6 per cent in Andhra Pradesh and Karnataka are members of tribes. There are some 573 communities recognized by the government as Scheduled Tribes and therefore eligible to receive special benefits and to compete for reserved seats in legislatures and schools. They range in size from the Gonds (roughly 7.4 million) and the Santals (approximately 4.2 million) to only eighteen Chaimals in the Andaman Islands. Central Indian states have the country's largest tribes, and, taken as a whole, roughly 75 per cent of the total tribal population live there.

Apart from the use of strictly legal criteria, however, the problem of determining which groups and individuals are tribal is both subtle and complex. Because it concerns economic interests and the size and location of voting blocs, the question of who are members of Scheduled Tribes rather than Backward

Classes (see Glossary) or Scheduled Castes (see Glossary) is often controversial. The apparently wide fluctuation in estimates of South Asia's tribal population through the twentieth century gives a sense of how unclear the distinction between tribal and non tribal can be. India's 1931 census enumerated 22 million tribal people, in 1941 only 10 million were counted, but by 1961 some 30 million and in 1991 nearly 68 million tribal members were included. The differences among the figures reflect changing census criteria and the economic incentives individuals have to maintain or reject classification as a tribal member.

Tribal Education in Karnataka

The total population of Karnataka, as per 2001 Census is 52,850,562. Of this, 3,463,986 are Scheduled Tribes (STs). The ST population constitutes 6.6 percent of the state population and 4.1 percent of the country's ST population. Forty-nine STs have been notified in Karnataka by the Scheduled Castes and Scheduled Tribes Order (Amendment) Act, 1976 and by the Act 39 of 1991. This is the second highest number, next to Orissa (64) if compared with the number of STs notified in any other states/Uts of the Country. Five STs namely, Kammara, Kaniyan, Kuruba, Maratha and Marati have been notified with area restriction. Kuruba and Maratha have been notified only in Kodagu district, where as Marati in Dakshina Kannada, Kaniyan in Kollegal taluk of Chamarajanagar and Kammara in Dakshina Kannada and Kollegal taluk of Chmarajanagar districts of Karnataka.

Of the STs, two namely, Jenu Kuruba and Koraga are among the Primitive Tribal groups (PTGs) of India having population of 29,828 and 16,071 respectively in 2001 Census Jenu Kuruba are mainly distributed in Mysore, Kodagu and Bangalore districts, and Koraga in Dakshina Kannada and Dharward districts. In the present census, a low growth rate of 1.6 percent and a negative growth rate of 1.5 percent have been reported for the Jenu Kuruba and Koraga respectively.

Out of total literates, 39.2 percent are literates without any educational level or have attained below Primary level. The literates who have attained education up to Primary level and Middle level, constitute 29.3 percent and 11.8 percent respectively. 15.8 percent of the literates are having educational level up to Matric/Higher Secondary etc. Levels, implying that every 6th ST literate is a Matriculate. Literates with educational level of Graduation and above are 3.1 percent. Individually, Gond (3.6 percent) have the highest percentage of Graduation and above educational level.

There were 16 million ST children [10.87 million of 6-11 years and 5.12 million of11-14 years) as of March 2001, out of the total child population in India of about 193 million in the age group of 6 to 14 years. [Selected Educational Statistics – 2001Government of India] – Education of ST children to considered important, not only because of the constitutional obligation but also as a crucial input for total development of tribal communities. Most tribal children do not understand the textbooks, which are generally in the regional language. The appointment of non-tribal teachers in tribal children's schools is another problem. The teachers do not know the language the children speak and children do not understand the teacher's language. An attempt has been made in this present research study to analysis educational status and working nature of Ashram schools of the tribal children in Karnataka. Data on completion rate, repetition rate, dropouts rate, attendance rate, transition rate and enrolment rate for primary schoolchildren have been collected based on both content analysis and filed work during the year 2006 July to 2008 January. Education is considered to be an important mechanism for economic development in India, especially for those who have been exploited viz. The scheduled castes (SCs) and scheduled tribes (STs). As these sections of our society were traditionally and historically deprived of their basic rights, education was far away from their reach. However the literacy rates for the STs is increasing at a very high rate after independence due to protective discrimination. The rate of literacy has gone up substantially for all social groups in 2001 as compared to 1991 in Karnataka. The rate of literacy was high among non-ST as compared to STs in Karnataka. There was a fluctuation in the rate of literacy by districts in Karnataka. The education status of urban population was high as compared to rural population. Further, the educational status of males was high as compared to females. The educational status has gone up for all social groups in 2001 as compared to 1991. The education status of Scheduled Tribes was low as compared to that of other social groups in KarnatakThe tribal ST population of Karnataka increased to 34.64 lakh in 2001 from 19.16 lakh in 1991.The decadal growth rate during this period is a high 80.8 per cent, caused not by a spurt in fertility rates but by the addition of several new tribes to the Scheduled Tribes (ST) category. The decadal growth rate is higher for females (81.9 per cent) than for males (79.8 per cent).The highest decadal growth rate occurred in Mysore district (around 328.0 per cent), Bagalkot (261.6 per cent), Dharwad (201.1 per cent) and Belgaum (193.0 per cent).The decadal growth rate is negative in Dakshina Kannada (-2.9 per cent). Raichur (18.1 per cent) has the highest percentage of ST population followed by Bellary (18.0 per cent), while Chitradurga (17.5 per cent), which had the highest percentage of ST population in 1991 came down to third place in 2001 on account of its bifurcation. The reverse is true of Raichur. Bellary has the highest population of Scheduled Tribes as a percentage of the ST population in the state (10.6). The tribal population of Karnataka increased to 34.64 lakh in 2001 from 19.16 lakh in 1991.The decadal growth rate during this period is a high 80.8 per cent, caused not by a spurt in fertility rates but by the addition of several new tribes to the list of existing group of Scheduled Tribes.

Sex ratio

The sex ratio for Karnatka Scheduled Tribes (972) is higher than the all-India average (964) for STs as well as the state average (965) according to the 2001 census. There has been a perceptible improvement in the sex ratio of STs since 1991 when it was 9 Among the southern states, Kerala performs well with 1,021 followed by Tamil Nadu (980). Andhra Pradesh is below Karnataka with 971. The child sex ratio for the 0–6 age group is also higher (960) than the state average of 946. Culturally, there is greater gender equity among the Scheduled Tribes compared with the general population, which is largely shaped and driven by a male-dominated discourse that prioritises son preference. Across districts, one impressive finding is that Udupi (1023) has a sex ratio higher than Kerala's followed by Kodagu and Bagalkot (996) while Bangalore Urban, typically, has the lowest sex ratio (913) followed by Haveri (941), Dharwad and Bijapur (944) and Bidar (950).

Literacy Rate

The literacy rate of STs in Karnataka is a cause for concern, as it has consistently been lower than that of the total population. The literacy rate among Scheduled Tribes, which was 36.0 per cent in 1991, increased to 48.3 per cent in 2001,while the state average moved up from 56.04 to 66.64 per cent. The gap between the literacy rate of the total population and the ST population is very wide, although there has been a marginal decline of about 1.6 percentage points in the last decade. The decennial literacy rate of the ST population has increased at a faster pace (12.3 per cent) than the rate for the total population (10.6 per cent). The literacy rate of urban STs (64.6 per cent) is higher than the overall literacy rate of STs and compares quite favorably with the state average. The female literacy rate among STs in 1991 was 23.6 per cent and it increased to 36.6 per cent in 2001.While it has increased at a faster pace than the male literacy rate (the increase during the decade was 13.0 percentage points for females and 11.8 percentage points for males) the gap between the ST male and female literacy rate declined only marginally, from 24.3 in 1991 to 23.1 in 2001, which is slightly higher than the gap between the male and female literacy rates for the total population (22.92 in 1991 and 19.22 in 2001).The literacy rate for ST women is the lowest in the state in comparison with all women as well as Scheduled Caste women. The literacy rate for rural ST women is a low 33.3 per cent compared with 56.9 per cent for men (Table 10.1).Overall, the Scheduled Tribes in the state have markedly lower literacy rates than other groups. The fact that they are above the all-India average in respect of men and women is, of course, an indicator that Karnataka has performed better than many other states in this respect. However, the literacy status of the STs in Karnataka, which is in marked contrast to the improvements in literacy of other social groups, is a matter of concern and needs strong policy initiatives to push up literacy levels significantly. Dakshina Kannada district (72.95 per cent) has the highest literacy rate followed by Bangalore Urban (72.83

per cent), Udupi (69.62 per cent), Uttara Kannada (62.74 per cent), Shimoga (62.11 per cent), Tumkur (59.69 per cent) and Chikmaglur (58.84 per cent). The literacy rate is the lowest in Raichur (29.01 per cent), followed by Gulbarga (32.40 per cent) and Kodagu (40.37 per cent).While the literacy rate of Scheduled Tribes has improved in the decade 1991-2001, they still have a long way to go before they catch up with the rest of the population. The ST literacy rate in The literacy rate of STs in Karnataka is a cause for concern, as it has consistently been lower than that of the total population.

Though the literacy rate for women has increased at a faster pace than for males, it is still problematic because it is so much lower than the literacy rate for all women in 2001. Districts that have high literacy rates have also done well with regard to STs with the exception of Kodagu. This is clear when we look at the statistics of districts with low literacy rates, such as Raichur (48.81) and Gulbarga (50.01), where the literacy for STs is also poor (29.01 and 32.40 respectively).The low literacy level suggests that the programmes of the Education Department have not had the desired effect on this very vulnerable sub-population. More concerted efforts are required to bring STs' literacy on par with the state average, at the very least. Culture-specific curricula would be a step in the right direction. Since illiteracy and poverty are factors that play off one another to create a cycle of deprivation, ensuring greater cohesion at the gram panchayat level between anti-poverty programmes and school enrolment/retention drives would provide the poor with viable ways to access education. Education Low literacy rates are matched by less than satisfactory educational attainments across all levels of primary, secondary and tertiary education. Many schools in tribal areas suffer from high dropout rates. Children either never enrol or attend for the first three to four years of primary school, only to lapse into illiteracy later. The attrition rate is quite strong at various levels of the educational system thereafter. The first step in the education ladder is enrolment, where performance is high for most social groups, except STs. For instance, the gross enrolment ratio (GER) in 2001, for STs for Classes I–VIII (90.12) was significantly lower than the GER for all students (98.81) and SCs (104.57).This inequality is heightened even more by the gap between the GER for south Karnataka (110.62) and north Karnataka (74.21). The GER for girls (103.64) is also much better in the southern districts than in north Karnataka (70.22). In that respect, the GER of the Scheduled Tribes in south Karnataka more closely approximates the overall GER of other social groups. The northern districts are caught up in a cycle of deprivation: they have the highest levels of ST population and also have poor human development indicators. Among districts, Bangalore Urban (319.10) and Bijapur (270.65) had high GERs, but then, the proportion of ST population in these districts is not significantly high. Districts with high ST populations did not perform well: Bellary (76.47), Raichur (58.21) and Bidar (48.76) are well below the state average. Kodagu has the lowest (73.41) GER in south Karnataka, followed by Davangere (76.23), Chamarajnagar (86.02) and Chitradurga (87.03). It is noteworthy that the ST population of Chitradurga and Davangere forms a significant percentage of the state's total ST population.

Scheduled Tribe children have the lowest levels of achievement (4.166 years) compared with SC (4.235 years) and non-SC/ST (4.458 years) children in case of karnataka. Not surprisingly, in this context, then, ST children also constitute the highest percentage of out-of-school children (2.42), compared with the state average of 1.54 per cent. The percentage of out-of-school ST girls (2.67) is the highest across all categories. The Sample Survey of ST households conducted by the Department of Economics and Statistics in 2004,which elicited responses from persons in the age group 9–35 years, found that the principal reasons for females dropping out of school were (i) to work at home and (ii) their parents could not afford to pay for their education. The reasons are identical to the ones adduced to SC girls and indicate that the poor cannot afford the high opportunity costs of education. Girls are the first to be pulled out of school to work at home and take care of siblings to enable their mothers to work. In such cases, families do not find the many incentives offered by the government such as free uniforms, text books and even scholarships, an adequate compensation for lost wages. For boys, family work is the main reason for dropping out. Akshara Dasoha, the recently introduced midday meals programme for school children, will have a more sustained impact on ensuring enrolment and retention hereafter. Enrolment in secondary education is lower than in primary education.This is part of a pattern of attrition, which increases with levels of education and occurs across all social groups.The GER, in Classes I–X, in 2000-01, was 81.17, which was considerably lower than the GER for SCs (94.31) and all students (89.95). The differential between boys (85.59) and girls (76.51) was also higher than for SCs and all students. As with primary education, there is a marked disparity between the GER for south Karnataka (100.10) and north Karnataka (66.03).While a similar regional trend exists for all students and SCs, the disparity is not as high as it is with STs; Gulbarga (32.86), Bidar (43.06) and Chitradurga (77.93) were all below the state average. GER for Bellary and Raichur (61.89 and 43.89), which have the highest proportion of ST population, is very poor. What are the outcomes for students who overcome the barriers of poverty and gender and stay the course? Surprisingly good, if performance in school examinations is taken as an indicator of educational attainment. Scheduled Tribe students performed well in the Class VII examinations in 2002, with a pass percentage of 88.25, which was higher than the pass percentage of all students (87.31) and SC students (87.87). Girls (89.41) had an edge over boys (87.39) as in all social groups. The inference is that girls will perform well academically, if they are enabled to overcome the socio-economic constraints that keep them out of school. This is apparent when we look at the percentage of students who passed the S.S.L.C examinations from 2001–2005 where ST girls have out performed ST boys, SC boys and SC girls (Table 10.3). In 2005, ST girls had a pass percentage of 55.18,which is higher than the percentage of ST and SC boys and SC girls. This outcome only serves to support the earlier finding that the performance of girl students in general, and ST girl students in particular, is exemplary, once they make it past the roadblocks. It is found that, the dropout rate increased with levels of education. In the sample surveyed, there were only 0.18

per cent women graduates and 1.40 per cent male graduates, and only 0.02 per cent ST women were post-graduates. Scheduled Tribe students, in general tertiary education, cluster primarily in government.

Unequal access to schooling is further exacerbated by the fact that ST children stay in school for the least amount of time, as indicated by the mean years of schooling. In 2003-04, STs constituted 4.46 per cent of students in government colleges and 2.80 per cent in private aided colleges. There is a marked disparity in the enrolment of boys (3,209) and girls (1,652). This gap in male and female enrolment in general degree courses is uniform across government and private aided colleges. The percentage of ST students in engineering colleges averaged 0.1 per cent from 1996 to 2000 and went up to 1.7 per cent in 2002-03. Scheduled Tribes enrolment in engineering diploma courses is a minimal 0.2 per cent (Annual Reports, DTE; Annual Report VTU 2002-03).This places young ST graduates in a disadvantageous position when they seek jobs in a market that wants trained technical professionals. They are ill-equipped to take advantage of the IT-fuelled boom in jobs in Karnataka. Economic status Historically, the tribal economy was based on subsistence agriculture and/or hunting and gathering. However, since the tribal people treated land as a common resource, they rarely had land titles, and thus, lost their lands to outsiders when exploitation of forest resources began to take place on a significant scale. This ensured that a majority ended up as small and marginal landholders. The 2001 Census data reveals that around half the ST population is in the workforce. Women constitute about 41.7 per cent of the workforce. More than 85 per cent of the working population is in rural areas. The distribution of main workers (76.4 per cent) is concentrated in the rural parts of the state where a high 51.5 per cent work. Bellary has the highest percentage of main workers (11.5 per cent) followed byRaichur (7.8 per cent).The highest percentage of ST marginal workers lives in Raichur (11.7), which also has the highest proportion of the ST population to the total population, clearly indicating their highly precarious livelihood status. Land holdings.

Table 1. Enrolment of ST Students during 2006-2007.

Sl.No.	*Schools*	*Scheduled Tribes (numbers in lakh)*			*% of STs to General Enrollment*		
		Boys	*Girls*	*Total*	*Boys*	*Girls*	*Total*
1.	Primary School	0.47	0.41	0.88	2.68	1.56	4.24
2.	Middle School	0.21	0.11	0.29	2.01	1.26	3.27
3.	High School	0.11	0.06	0.17	1.45	0.44	1,89
4.	Higher secondary	0.08	0.02	0.10	0.89	0.18	1.07
	Total	0.74	0.50	1.24	7.03	3,44	10.47

Source: Department of Education, Bangalore.

Table 2. Enrollment in Ashram Schools (2006-2007)

	Schools	*No. of Schools*	*Total no enrollment*
1	Primary Schools	97	33506
2	Middle Schools	18	14466
3	High Schools	08	4674
4	Higher Secondary Schools	03	3846
		126	56,492

(*Source:* SC/ST Development Corporation.

Table 3. Standard wise Enrollment of ST Children

Dist	*1*	*2*	*3*	*4*	*5*
Mysore	56.23	44.77	44,67	52.45	47.55
Kodagu	56.71	44.29	34.78	54.45	45.52
CH Nager	55.54	45.46	54.7	56.23	43.77
Bangalore	54.29	44.71	57.9	59.76	40.34
Bangalore Rural	55.67	58.9	54.9	58.89	41.21
Hassan	43.6	44.87	55,78	57.87	45.9
Mandya	46.7	49.9	44.9	44.4	54.9

Tumkur

Table 4. Synopsis of Nature of Ashram Schools

S.No.	*Name of the district*	*Total no. of Ashram school visited*	*Total no. of students (2007)*	*Boys*	*Girls*	*Total no. of teachers*	*Total no. of regular teachers*	*Drop outs*	*Funda mental facilities provided*
1	2	3	4	5	6	7	8	9	*10*
1.	Mysore	20	732	465	267	61	16	204	Only for 11schools
2.	Kodagu	12	452	254	198	45	11	125	Only for 4
3..	Chickmangaore	11	411	328	183	47	9	117	Only for 5schools
4.	Dakshin Kannda	11	398	302	96	41	1	98	Only 7 for schools
5.	Udupi	7	328	216	112	23	5	87	Only for 5 schools
6.	Chitradurga	2	93	54	39	6	1	12	Only for 1 schools
7.	Belgam	4	187	109	78	5	1	56	Only 2 for schools
8.	Raichur	2	46	29	17			34	——
9.	CH Nager	19	662	485	177	58	16	143	Only 13 for schools
10.	Bellary	3	121	69	52	9	2	24	Only 1for schools
11.	Davangeri	2	72	55	17	5	1	12	——

1	2	3	4	5	6	7	8	9	10
12.	Bangalore	6	296	119	76	13	4	35	Only 4 for schools
13.	Bidar	1	56	29	27	3	—	9	Moderate
14.	Bijapur	1	51	32	19	5	—	12	—
15.	Dharwad	1	58	31	27	3	—	6	—
16.	Gadag	1	63	29	32	3	—	9	—
17.	Gulberga	1	89	41	38	3	—	11	N0
18.	Hassan	1	38	21	17	2	—	7	No
19.	Haveri-	2	88	53	35	8	2	18	Satisfactory
20.	Kolar	3	118	87	31	5	1	21	Only for 1 schools
21.	Koppal	2	125	78		6	1	24	Only 1 for schools
22.	Mandaya	1	53	13		4	1	8	—
23.	Shimogga	3	214	112		7	1	41	Only for 1 schools
24.	Tumkur	3	113	65		9	1	37	Only for 1 schools
25.	Karwar-	1	28	17		5	1	2	—
26.	U kannda	—							—

Table 5. Dropout Rates of Scheduled Tribes (Class I-V) in Various Districts of Karnataka 2006-2007

Districts	*Boys*	*Girls*	*Total*
Mysore	64.23	73.95	68.64
Kodagu	60.16	81.81	71.26
Chickmangaore	53.18	66.11	59.39
Dakshin Kannda	31.30	52.27	38.59
Udupi	56.04	63.78	59.38
Chitradurga	78.03	74.24	76.81
Belgam	73.01	84.20	75.72
Raichur	62.27	69.78	65.17
CH Nager	62.21	58.19	60.71
Bellary	65.13	67.10	66.00
Davangeri	68.00	67.95	67.99
Bangalore	57.91	58.37	58.13
Bidar	45.83	49.23	47.42
Bijapur	46.67	49.0	47,9
Dharwad	39.78	30,87	33,78
Gadag	N/A	N/A	
Gulberga	54.67	58.9	56,8
Hassan	59.7	61,7	59.0
Haveri-	56.8	59.0	58.8
Kolar	34,6	37,7	36.7
Mandaya	43,12	48,90	47.89
Shimogga	56,71	59.11	58.00
Tumkur	64,23	66.80	66.91
Karwar-	N/A	N/A	
U. Kannda	N/A	N/A	

Mentioned in percentage

Table 6. Achievement Levels (Class-I-V) of Scheduled Tribe Students in Districts Studied so for Consolidated

Districts	*Subjects*		
	Mathematics	*Language*	*Environmental Sciences*
Mysore	4.55	6.18	4.12
Kodagu	4.08	5.58	8.51
CH Nager	4.44	5.35	5.04
Bangalore	3.23	7.70	7.12
Bangalore Rural	3.19	6.15	4.29
Hassan	2.87	4.60	4.84
Mandya	5.11	5.24	7.35
Tumkur	3.09	5,7 2	3.02

Mid-Term Assessment Survey

Table 7. Co-curricular activities among the Studied Ashram Schools

S.No.	*Districts*	*School parlia-ment*	*Debate*	*Drama*	*Essay*	*Cultural prog.*	*School*	*All national festival*	*Social service*
1.	Mysore	7%	—	13%	11%	—	65%	78%	—
2.	Kodagu	2%	23%	—	—	—	56%	67%	2%
3.	CH Nager	4%	18%	44%	—	27%	77%	89%	—
4.	Bangalore	—	—	^7%	—	21%	85%	91%	—
5.	Bangalore Rural	—	—	65%	2%	—	44%	89%	—
6.	Hassan	—	11%	31%	—	—	—	56%	—
7.	Mandya	—	3%	38%	—	—	—	66%	2%
8.	Tumkur	—	9%	—	—	24%	—	87%	—

Mentioned in percentage

Table 8. Successful outcomes of Ex Students of Ashram Schools (2000-2007)

S.No.	*Dist.*	*Gradua-tion*	*PG*	*Ph.D.*	*IAS/ IPS*	*Class I*	*Other Govt. Job*	*Private Job*	*Own Business*
1.	Mysore	118	33	9	1	14	19	14	9
2.	Kodagu	56	9	—	—	7	11	7	4
3.	CH Nager	102	17	7	1	4	21	14	11
4.	Bangalore	63	21	3	—	8	17	4	3
5.	Bangalore Rural	11	6	—	—	3	2	11	3
6.	Hassan	18	9	3	—	—	1	8	—
7.	Mandya	25	7	1	—	—	1	4	2
8.	Tumkur	33	5	2	—	2	7	6	—

Result and Discusion

(a) Disparity in the existence of the schools

Compared to the other major tribals of the state these primitive tribal groups are a more disadvantaged population. As for as non-existing facility within a habitation is concerned, one can find that other major tribes of the State are placed in a favorable situation relative to their total population. Looking at the disparity condition in terms of deprivation, more children of primitive tribal group school age children are deprived of a primary school within their habitations. Children belonging to the other major tribes like *Soligas, Betta kuruba* and *Male kudiya* are in a better position than the PTGs thay have atlest one Ashram or Jeneral school within their habitations (Shukla, 1998). However so for as the number of habitations without a school is a concerned PTGs child are highly in a disadvantaged position. In general primitive tribal children should have to commute more than 3-km distance to attend a school. In some case it is even more. Distance is also one of the major drawbacks in case of providing education to the people who are still away from modern world. Many of the parents don't like to send their children especially of their girl children to school, which is quite for away from their original habitation. Finally while a large population of the country school age children still face the disadvantage of distance between their own habitation and the location of a primary school, the more disturbing situation is this disadvantage is high in case of PTGs habitations in the tribe belt of Karnataka.

Language-A Medium of Instruction

The tribal situation in India presents a varied and complex picture and poses peculiar problems of social and economic developemnt. Demographically speaking, there are more than 244 scheduled tribes with many sub-groups speaking some 100 languages /dialects. Most unfortunate thing is that major portion of government's resources is diverted to concessconal provisions and little is left for the development of tribal education, language and culture of these two PTGs. The striking aspect that emerges from the scanty data on languages in primary education is the almost total absence of tribal language in schools. The attitude of our policy planners towards these tribal people appears to be one of assimilation. Little is being done to preserve their culture. Our policy scientists have almost all-major and minor tribes suffer with this kind of negligence. Not much work has been done to find out minimum and maximum resistance into their culture. Linguistic experts have made no attempt to standardize tribal languages by developing scripts, elaborating lexis and writing grammars and dictionaries in tribal languages. Till today there has not been any serious efforts to provide basic education in their respective mother tongues. No proper curriculums have also been framed based on tribal culture and tradition. Present education system does not orient the tribal children towards perusing their own mode of life. In phonology and syntax, the tribal languages are quite different from the medium of instruction like Kannada except in certain mutually borrowed lexical items due to their close contacts over a long period of time. This is one of the vital reason responsible for these PTGs poor literacy and dropout problem among tribal children (Pasayat, 1995).

Attitude of non-tribal teachers towards tribal children and, tribal language is stereotyped. The social distance in high. Teachers impose their own culture is indifferent. Teachers from tribal comminutes have de triblised ot the extent that they don't understand the role of mother tongue in teaching in primary stage. No teacher either from tribal or non trial comminutes have raised this issue that how the tribal children face difficulties in understanding the school issue that now the tribal children face difficulties in understand in school language and how the language gap hampers the construction of knowledge.

Primary Schools According to Different Language Used as Medium of Instruction-1986

(c) Urban Biased

The success of one's education largely depends on the motivation. Basically tribals are living with low socio -economic status. Obviously the level of motivation and self-esteem will be comparatively low among tribal children. The main reason for this problem is current education system is more or less urban based non-tribal and absence of culture specific. Even though these tribals are emotionally attached to their local cultural norms Govt. has no interest in providing education which is more suited to the tribal children. Modern teaching methodologies, content of the text, appointment of non-tribal teachers and parameters for evaluations have become *Grains of Iron* to the low motivated tribal children. Implementation of uniform textbooks both for urban and tribal children are one more hit to them. The theory, concepts, values alien to tribal people is generally contained in the textbooks which generates negative attitude and a big blow to the learners' self-confidence. There is no attempt to take stock of the existing situation regarding instructional materials in tribal languages. Education policy documents also have not dwelt on the magnitude of tasks that are involved in the preparation of primers and textbooks for tribal children and have not outlined the concrete steps that have to taken in this direction. The increasing tendency for tribal people to retain the regional language as their mother tongue is only one indicator of their growing vulnerability in the face of these larger social processes (Verma, 1995).

The problem of dropout persists among all categories of children in both urban and rural India. However, in the context of children studying in Classes 1-10 the gap between the ST and total population of dropouts has widened from 1990-91 to 1998-99. The reduction in the dropout rates could because of various incentive shames run by the State Govt. for edition of ST children such as providing free textbooks, uniforms and scholarships in Govt. schools. But schemes such as those providing for hostels for ST boys adngirls are not implemented fully by the State owing to lack of financial resources and therefor fewer ST children pursue high school education and very few up to the college level. The policy of reserving seats for ST students at higher education levels is no widely availed since a ledge number of ST students do not even reach those levels and dropout at lower levels of school education. Even the Ashram shools run by both Govt. and NGO are poory minted and sometime lack Venn thebasic facilities. Given the low level of literacy among the ST population, several chidden from these comminutes happen to be 'first generation learns' and in the absence of State support for heaping them to cope with studies, many children drop out of the schools. This disproportionately low representation of ST children at higher level of education compounds the existing disparities among Indian society. Lack of proactive government in favor of the STs is not linked only to lack of resources. Govt. in difference and lack of political will are largely responsible for the state of affair (Mahendale, 2001).

(d) Inaction of teachers

Teachers are the real directors of every tribal school. There was a time in India where teachers were equal to the God. The major problem is that Govt. is recruiting teachers from the urban area to teach tribal children. A report say that only 0.56% of teachers is basically from either Anthropology or Sociology discipline. Majority of the teacher are from non-tribal community. Many of them have studied only in English medium schools and they even don't know the regional language properly. In this situation how one can expect to teach the relatively disadvantaged tribal children down to their level. More unfortunate thing is that many schools don't have teachers for all the subjects. Even though many NGOs are hiring teachers to teach at tribal schools many of them even don't have any basic degrees in education like BEd/ TCH. Some of the teachers are prejudious about the performance of the tribal children. As they are the only literate persons having some political connections in the tribal areas, they neither fulfil their duties properly nor the concerned higher officers dare to take any action against them for dereliction of their duties.

(e) What teacher says?

Many of the teachers are of the opinion that tribal children cannot understand the modern Kannada language. Content of the text is too standard to their level. Few of them will complain about the ignorance of the parents. More over teachers are facing many problems in the tribal areas. Proper residential and medicinal facilities are a nightmare. Higher education for their children some time will not possible. Since many primitive tribal hamlets live deep in to the forest some time it will be humanely impossible to reach the school due to the lack of appropriate transport. More over feed back from the students is completely absent. No proper laboratory facilities to teach Science effectively. Teachers raised and brought up in a more sophisticated urbanized society would find it difficult to adjust themselves to the cultural shock that generates communication gap.

(f) Parents' apathy

Tribal community feels childhood or adulthood largely depends not on the physical age but on the degree of responsibility that children could successfully fulfill. Apart from that children's responsibilities towards the family and the contributions they make are significant and much important while conceptualizing the above mentioned terms. In tribal society children from the early age will be engaged in cooking food, fetching water, siblings care, support in the field, collection minor forest food, grazing etc. Decision to give a chance to a child to spend happy childhood is not isolated from other aspects of household decision making nor are they purely household based. They reflect the norms and values of the wider community within which the tribal household is located and the social and economic possibilities which local contexts offer to different categorized of households. Hence, parents may think sending child to school means dislocation of traditional pattern of earning livelihood and of division of labour in their societies. Most vital problems of low literacy among tribal children is that children are considered by parents as economic assets to the family.

He education of tribal girl children is more neglected because of deep-rooted beliefs, traditions and mid-sets. Educationalist philosophers use the concept of false consciousness to refer to the existence of beliefs and values that individuals socialize into and operate upon. It can be argued from that the universalist perspective that the parents believe that girls need to be socialized into their adult roles as children nd the formal education has no meaning for them.

Universal Primary Education

The question of how elementary education can and be made universal has not received the attention it deserves. We think that issues should be highlighted. Recent study has shown that an alarmingly large number of children do not become literate even after four years of primary education especially in both rural and tribal areas (Sharma, 2002). Hence, total school effectiveness and actual learning have to be the central theme rather than secondary concern for universal education. Further, more important is that how effective schools are and successive learning basically depend not only on school level inputs but also on many vital factors outside the school. Basic infrastructures of Ashram Schools in tribal areas are worst than any thing in many southern districts of Karnataka. Many schools even don't have hard roofs. Hostels are ruining. Unavailability of play ground, lab and library and separate toilets are most common in many tribal schools where children of these two PTGs are learning. Absence of extra curricular activities makes children learning as a kind of unavoidable burden. Since tribal children are completely different from urban children or atleast from rural children learning should be a joyful experience for them other wise simply they may be dropouts. For genuine universal elementary education the impact of the wider context on schooling has to be understood in a better way.

Absence of Central Monitoring Unit

Absence of effective monitoring unit on the tribal schools is one of the major drawbacks in case of development of tribal education. Concerned inspecting staffs hardly visit to the tribal schools. Some time even only one time in a year. This makes teacher to lack commitment to their profession. Some people reported that teacher' visit one or two times in a weak to the schools only. This is also due to low level of motivation, inspiration and commitment among the inspecting staff, which are again matched, by the low level of motivation and interest among the teachers. This is the high time that Govt. should think to strengthen or establish Centralized Monitoring Unit especially for Tribal School and better unit chief from either Anthropology or Sociology background.

In the light of above discussion we may conclude that on one hand, economic backwardness is responsible for the low percentage of literacy in the younger generation and on the other social backwardness and lack of social consciousness are responsible for low percentage of children attending schools. When the school going children are few it can be well understood that higher education will be a rare phenomena in these PTGs.

Hence, along with other development it is also necessary that we should create some awareness about significance of education among tribles the facilities available to them for education and the role of education in their upliftment of socially economically and politically condition of the tribal community.

The internal problems of tribal education refer to the quality of school provision, suitable teachers, relevance of content and curriculum, medium of instruction, pedagogy and special supervision. A majority of schools in tribal areas are without basic infrastructure facilities. Normally, the school buildings in tribal areas are with thatched roofs, dilapidated walls and non-plastered floors. Research evidences shows that a large number of tribal schools do not have teaching learning materials and even blackboards. In tribal areas the opening of a school is equated with the posting of a teacher and same is the case with the ashram schools. It is found that in most of the ashram schools which are residential in nature there is not enough space for the children to sleep. Consequently, the classroom turns into the dormitory and vice-versa. Due to lack of minimum sanitary provisions it is not uncommon to find that many children studying in ashram schools are afflicted by contagious diseases like scabies, diarrhea etc. leading to high dropout rate. The schools in tribal areas just function within a bare minimum facility.

Policy Suggestions

1. There are many basic difference can be seen between major tribals and primitive tribals in case of India. Hence, the Govt. should bring a new educational policy especially for primitive tribals. It must be culturally and geographically specific. Moreover educational experts should be very sensitive while framing the policies which should not destroy the social solidarity of the tribes and kill their zest for life.

2. It is well revealed fact that modern education cannot cater to the basic needs of the tribes. Modern education system cannot deem to have held much relevance for them since they are from the outer world. During our fieldwork it has been revealed that tribals consider 'culture as their first educator'. Hence there is a need

to identify the areas of minimum and maximum resistance to innovations in their culture and vital linkage to their cultural fabric. Once we identify enough space we can imbibe education in to their culture.

3. It is the high time to have special education programme made for tribal children in consonance with the privileged cultural pattern and also in keeping with the needs and resources of the area concerned in order to secure the maximum amount of tribal children participation. Moreover new education programme should be in a the position to assert the existing perception, behaviour and action in education seeking process and culturally determined attitude towards use of different system of education.

4. The state Govt. should construct a Textbook Commission especially for tribal education developemnt. While framing the textbooks experts should focus on three-impordent prospectvies1 Linguistic 2 Instrumental 3 and the Culture. From the primary level itself all text materials should be in their respective mothertongue. There is need to evolve scripts, grammar, and as well as appropriate vocabulary to communicate 'school knowledge'. Proper training should be given in tribal language, culture and society to the non-tribal teachers working in the tribal areas.

5. Lack of good quality teachers in sufficient numbers resulting in high pupil teacher ratio may be an important factor in explaining the variations of educational status in these two PTGs in education. Given the inaccuracies in enrolments and the attendance/absence of teachers, probably pupil teacher ratio may not be efficient and meaningful variable representing the quality of tribal education.

6. Ashram Schools should have a multi-purpose complex. If, possible there should be a provision for selling and buying of consumer goods and minor forest products. Further Ashram Schools initially must emphasis on the

service rendered to the primitive tribals than on costly building. 'In the initial stage provision should be made for a Kacha thatched Ashram type building rather than a pucca building' (Monthy, 2003).

7. The socio economic context, along with the development dimension is an integral part of school effectiveness. On the other hand it is difficult to ensure good school quality in less developed tribal areas. On the other hand, it is found that area type affects learning directly by influencing poverty levels and also opportunities and motivation for learning. The impact of the area type on schools and learning is such that no description or analysis of schools can be meaningfull with out a parallel understanding of the area type (rural, hamlet of major tribals or primitive tribals)

Conclusion

Education cannot change in any fundamental way unless we change our basic patterns of thinking and interacting so that learning can become a way of life. Teachers, parents, administrators, district resource and community people are coming together throughout hundreds of school communities to learn how to revitalize their schools with a process known as "Tribes." Evaluation of Tribes Learning Community Schools has examined the impact of the Tribes process on student behavior, academic performance, school culture, and teacher collegiality. Studies have shown that: Tribes TLC has a positive impact on classroom environment, teachers report spending less time managing student behavior, students are significantly less likely to be referred for disciplinary problems, the Tribes process helps teachers address performance and content standards, students in well-implemented classrooms score significantly higher on standardized tests than students from comparison groups, teachers report increased staff collegiality and planning. "Responsive Education" is an essential pedagogy for academic achievement and school reform. It is the synthesis of artful teaching practices. It is based on understanding the critical developmental needs of a student age and cultural group. The

Goal is to engage all teachers, administrators, students and families in working together as a learning community that is dedicated to caring and support, active participation and positive expectations for all students.In spite of sixty years of independence and more than fifty five years of planned development and social provision for accelerated socio economic development of weaker sections, the gap in literacy levels among the general population and the socially disadvantaged sections is persisting and in some cases this gap is further widening.

29

Educational Profiles of Three Tribes in Maharashtra; (Media, Laman & Thakar)

—Devendra Babanrao Mohite

Indian population consists of largest concentration of tribal communities in the world. Tribal population is about 8 % of the total population in India. According to World Bank and the Indian Council of Indigenous and Tribal People, the tribes of India are indigenous people.

This is the account of ethnographic studies on education among Madias of Gadchiroli, Lamanis from Pune and Thakars of Raigarh district of Maharashtra. From these Lamani is nomadic tribe. Madias and Thakars are scheduled tribe people. The studies were done in different periods during 1997 to 2007.

All of the three tribes show very poor literacy level. An Ashram school among Madias in Perimili village of Gadchiroli provided adequate facilities for schooling and boarding for the students in the surrounding area. The number of the Madia students enrolled in the school was 78.64 % of the total enrollment. Considering the efforts done by the teachers and the facilities provided only few students scored satisfactory results in the particular year.

In case of Lamanis in Pune city literacy level was still low and the number of school going students was negligible. The seasonal migrants among these people had many problems in getting an education. The problems they faced were related to their lifestyle of wandering here and there and their bondage with the labour work.

The Thakars in Mograj village of Karjat having severe poverty *were* surveyed for their educational status. The literacy among Thakars according to this study was less than 40%. The education up to higher levels is rare in this community. The literacy up to primary or secondary level yields nothing in daily lives according to these people. The illiteracy among elder generation and / or lower literacy level show the failure in literacy programmes run by the various agencies since long time.

The tribal education is an important issue as it affects directly the development of these communities. The lack of education leads to marginalization of them and the other kinds of exploitation to the poverty.

Introduction

In the ancient India the access of knowledge was limited to Brahmins, one of the five varnas of Vedic society. All the people from rest of four varnas and the aboriginal people remained deprived and exploited by the stratification system operated through caste hierarchy. Many social and religious revolutionary movements have long histories.

Until the nineteenth century Indian Society was suffering from casteism, poverty, illiteracy and many social problems at their higher intensities because of duel slavery in Hindu caste system and that of British rule. Although in this period Christian missionaries started schools all over the country. In this period many socio- political movements came up. The great social reformers Mahatma Phule and Savitribai Phule started the first school for girls of all castes in Pune in 1848. Where Savitribai became the first female teacher of India. They started one more school for adult learners in the same year. In the year 1849, eighteen more schools were started for girls, Shudras and Ati-shudras. Other significant social reformers in this period were Raja Ram Mohan Roy, Chhatrapati Shahu Maharaj and Maharshi Karve. In his regime Chhatrapati Shahu Maharaj declared the Compulsion of Primary Education for all tribes and castes in June 1913. On 8th September 1917. He issued the law of Free Primary Education compulsory for all. And opened primary school in every village populated 500 to 1000 persons. He enhanced women's education also.

In the British rule the government formulated special administrative arrangements and special programmes for Dalits and for the tribal people and for the development of tribel dominated areas. Scheduled District act 1874 offered special status for the tribal dominated areas of old Madras Presidency. According to Behura NK, Panigrahi N. 2006, "It formulated the concept of 'Scheduled Districts' with special civil and Judicial administration." In 1882, Indian Education Commission suggested to grant free education for tribal children.

Dr. B. R. Ambedkar having foresight of development of depressed classes argued for separate electorate for these people. The then British Prime Minister R. McDonald declared the communal Award on 17th August 1932, under which the depressed classes were recognised as minority community and were assured representation with separate electorate for twenty years duration. But Gandhiji, the father of nation opposed this decision by fasting unto death. Dr. Ambedkar had to accept compromise upon the principle of proportionate representation of 147 seats in the provincial legislatures and 18% seats in central legislature of India. This agreement known as Pune Pact (came in action on 24th September 1932) has some of the roots of failure in development programmes for backward communities.

After independence the Constitution of India issued special provisions for development of weaker section of people. Under various policies, different strategies have been developed for overall development of weaker sections. There are special provisions to endeavour education in tribal communities.

Tribes in India

The Indian population has the largest concentration of tribal communities in the world next to Africa. There are more than five hundred different tribal groups, which are further subdivided into several subgroups. Their population constitutes about 8% of the total population of the country. Among these some major tribal groups are Bhil, Gond, Ho, Mina, Khond, Naga, Munda, etc. are scattered all over the Indian subcontinent. Bhils and Gonds along with their subgroups together are more than 25% of the whole tribal population of India.

There are some debates on which term should be used for these people; either tribals or forest-dwellers, or adivasis meaning aboriginals. According to Singh K. S. (2006), "the question whether the tribes of India are an indigenous people is widely debated, the scheduled tribes of India were recognized as indigenous people by the World Bank in 1991, and the Indian Council of Indigenous and Tribal People treats adivasis as indigenous people. The government of India has however disagreed. The question is not yet resolved academically and charged with emotion."

Indigenous people, the adivasis are scheduled mainly under STs, NTs, DTNTs, etc. by the constitution of India. These people have their own socio-cultural identities. They are isolated, different from Hindu varna-ashram and caste societies. They inhabit in remote forests, hilly regions or deserts. They still use the primitive techniques of farming and means of production, and practice their own political organizations.

The Present Study

This article deals with the studies of three tribal groups focused on their educational profiles, viz. Madias of Gadchiroli, Lamans from Pune and Thakars of Raigarh. The studies were done in different time periods. For the purpose the samples selected were as follows:

- **1997:** Madia students of Government Post Basic Ashram School at Perimili village in Aheri tahesil of Gadchiroli.
- **1999:** 500 families from Laman Tanda (settlement) at Pashan, 7 nomadic families of the same tribe at Chatushringi in Pune city and 13 families of the same tribe from Saswad block at Dive village of Pune District.
- **Dec. 2007:** A third study was done on Thakars at Magraj village and its hamlets, Situated in Karjat tahesil of Raigarh District.

Here by I am trying to co-relate the educational situations among different tribal groups in different locations and periods.

1: Functioning of Ashram School Among Madias of Gadchiroli:

The first Ashram school was established in 1960s in Adilabad District of Madhya Pradesh. Ashram school provides free lodging and boarding to the tribal students in their own area. In the beginning period Ashram schools were associated with farm lands and they provided for agricultural studies in their curricula.

The Ashram School at Perimili was developed on 5 acres of land. It offered all kinds of schooling and hostel facilities for students from 1st to 10th Standard. It included teachers and servant quarters. Water was available from bore well. The toilets for students were nonfunctional and the students used to go outside in forest for nature calls. Ashram school had its own flour mill, kitchen and dining hall and many such facilities. No farm land is there for school. Eleven teachers and three non teaching workers were employed in this Ashram School. The Ashram School at Perimili provides adequate schooling and hostel facilities so that considerable number of students from the surrounding villages come here to get an education.

In the year 1997-98 total number of students from 1st to 10th standard enrolled was 375 being boys 253 and girls 122. Out of these, number of Madia students was 295; boys 208 and girls 87. Percentage number of Madia students to the total number of students enrolled was 78.64%. The distances from the native places of the students to the Ashram School ranged from 0 to 110 km.

The detailed distribution of the distances and the percentage of Madia students:

Percentage no of Students	44.5%	50%	2%	0%	2%	1.5%
Distance from their native place to Asharam School (km)	0	10	10-50	50-80	80-100	100-110

In the ashram school majority of the students are Madias. They are 78.64% of the total enrollment.

Class and category wise enrolment of students in Post Basic Ashram School at Perimili In 1997-98 gives information about girls and boys studying in 1st to 10th standard

	Boys	*Girls*	*Total*
Hostel	181	62	243
Day scholar*	18	30	48
Non facility*	54	30	84
Total students, all categories	253	122	375
Number of Madia students	208	87	295
Percentage of Madia students to the total students			78.64%

*Day-scholar: having boarding facility once a day.

*Non facility: No hostel facility.

Although the teachers of the Ashram school endeavour for the students' development through education, the results in final examination show the poor performance of the students, which may affect their future progress in the education. The promotion to the upper class through examination may cause difficulties in studies in higher classes. Besides the adequate facilities provided to the students, why do the teachers need to promote many (65%) students to the higher standards?

Madia students' performance in the examination commenced in 1996-1997 (Ashram School Perimili) all classes:

Result	*Percentage of Madia Students*
Passed	31%
Promoted	65%
Failed	4%
Total	100%

2. Educational status of Lamanis at Laman Tanda pashan of Pune City and some seasonal migrants:

An ethnographic research was done on "Socio-cultural and economic changes among Lamanis at Pune. These people are settled in urban area of Pune since more than 30 years. They have migrated from Rajasthan and Hyderabad. They mainly work as construction labourers and brewers and traders of illicit liquor. They observe Holi, Diwali and fair of Sewalal with their indigenous rituals and traditions. They sacrifice black goats on various occaissions. The head of this tanda was a woman.

500 families were studied from this location. The extent of school going students was very less not exceeding more than 3%. The schools run by Corporation of Pune were available for this settlement. The number of children was reported decreasing from first to tenth standard. Thus the problem of drop out was severe in this settlement. Some social workers among the same tribe run the pre-schools and adult literacy classes. One of them was also engaged in tuitions for school going children. Although very less students reached up to 12th or beyond that and stopped

their education. (only 2-3 cases were observed). The school going and dropped out children were observed baiting for earning money in the Tanda they used this money for their own expenditure and leisure. Non of the parents had any contention against this.

Extent of schooling children observed at Laman tanda, Pune (1999)

No of families	*Family size*	*No. of Schooling children all classes*	
		Boys	*Girls*
500	5 to 6	40	20*

* All the girls were studying below fifth standard.

Besides this 20 families were studied which were found as seasonal migrants and made their livelihoods on digging for telephone lines and water pipelines, and to some extent on farm labouring. These people were studied in Pune city as well as Saswad tahesil of this district.

These peasants and wanderers among Lamanis who are migrated from Karnataka especially keep on changing the places for labor and can not send the children to schools. Many of the adolescents report that they had got education in Kannada medium and could not get any job in Maharashtra or else where on the basis of literacy. From 20 families only 5 persons were reported to have some education in Kannada medium which is shown in the following table.

Literacy (Kannada medium):

Place	*No of families*	*Education*	*Male*	*Female*	*Age (years)*	*Occupation*
Chatushringi	7	5th	1	0	30	Labourer
Ganesh khind						
Pune		7th	0	1	24	Labourer
Dive, Saswad	13	5th	0	1	13	Labourer
Tahesil, Dist.						
Pune		6th	0	1	15	Labourer
Total	20	—	2	3	—	—

These children educated in Kannada medium cannot continue their education in Maharashtra because of the instruction medium offered here is Marathi in government schools which lead them leave the education in between. On the other side they had to help their parents waging for livelihood.

3. Education among Thakars of Karjat in Raigarh District

Thakar is the primitive tribe. Thakars inhibit in hilly forests of Sahyadri ranges in Maharashtra. They have their separate, isolated villages. The neighbouring communities are Katkaries, Aagrees and Mahadeo Kolies. Thakar and Katkari are forest dependent tribes. Thakars of Raigarh District were studied in Mograj village of Karjat tahesil They are shifting cultivators. Because of restrictions of forest department and the government land record authorities the practice of shifting cultivation is not possible today and they are changing to settled agriculturists. They keep local varieties of cows, oxen, buffalos, goats, wild rabbits and foul. They grow paddy in rainy season and pulses in winter in very less extent. They are hunters and gatherers. In winter after harvest they start to collect forest produce viz. resin, leaves, wild fruits etc. and hunt for wild bores, hares etc, but it is just a hardship because of poor flora and fauna. They are economically deprived people. Woman has equal status in Thakar family. Majority of women claim that they are heads of their families. They have their own deities. Intervention of Hindus lead them observe Hindu festivals. The traditional political organization is on the way of extinction. The dress patterns and many traditions are still observed. The changes are observed in men's dress patterns and behaviours, as they are prone to accept any change at first. Women still obey many traditions. The houses are constructed by wattle and daub on square plinths, pyramidal roofs, thatched by hay. The government housing schemes like "Indira Aawas Yojna" introduced the brick and cement houses in the same traditional pattern. The material culture exhibits the lifestyle of the community.

Thakar Population of Mograj village:

The population of Thakars of Mograj is 948 as shown in the following table. The sex ratio is 947 women per thousand men. Men and women share equally in the economical matters and both work for their livelihood. Almost in all the occupational categories men and women are involved equally. Women do the house work besides their main occupations. Thus the household work especially cooking, fetching the water, cleaning and maintaining the house are their additional work. Men and women both collect the firewood from the forest.

Thakar Population of Mograj village:

Name of the village	*Name of Pada / Hamlet*	*Number of the families*	*Pupulation*		
			Male	*Female*	*Total*
	Mograj & Anandwadi	102	249	244	493
Mograj	Malegaon	70	167	158	325
	Pimpalpada	26	71	59	130
Total		198	487	461	948

The details of sample selected for the study of educational achievement, and occupations amongst Thakars:

From this population 53 households were studied consisting of 320 people.The figures of literacy show the number of persons who had ever been enrolled in the school. Although the people who are so called literate hardly read or write in practice who leave the school in between. Excluding these students and children the elder generation is studied here for their educational achievement, age, gender, and the various occupations.

The table given below shows the extent of literacy in the four hamlets among males and females.

Table showing population and literacy in mograj village, thakar people.

Sample Selected					*Family Size*	*Literacy*			*Illiteracy*		
Pada or Hamlet	*No. of households*	*Population*				*M*	*F*	*T*	*M*	*F*	*T*
		M	F	T							
Mograj	25	71	65	136	5.44	46	25	71	25	40	65

Anadwadi	15	43	34	77	5.13	27	14	41	16	20	36
Malegaon	9	35	35	70	7.78	19	9	28	16	26	42
Pimpalpada	4	19	18	37	9.25	6	3	9	13	15	28
Total	53	168	152	320	7	98	51	149	70	101	171

Table showing number of school-going students and the children under 5 years of age or those not enrolled to school.

School Going students				*Infants (should be enrolled to school in feature)*		
Pada or Hamlet	*M*	*F*	*T*	*M*	*F*	*T*
Mograj	17	13	30	2	6	8
Anandwadi	14	6	20	4	1	5
Malegaon	7	2	9	3	6	9
Pimpalpada	3	2	5	2	4	6
Total	41	23	64	11	17	28

The literacy Status Among Thakars

Government of India provides for infrastructure and all kind of facilities to run the educational programmes. Although Thakars are severely lagging behind all kind of benefits. The literacy level is very low in this population.

In case of Thakars here, only one male was found who was studying in the final year of graduation from the sample population.

Educational Achievements in Various Age Groups:

Considering the part of sample population from which the individuals who are not engaged in schooling or education consisting of literate as well as illiterate were studied focusing on their age, occupation, sex and economy. The educational achievement is almost less than 40%. The maximum educational attainment is up to H.S.C. level. Only three males were reported to achieve this level. The figures of illiteracy in elder generation indicates the failure in literacy programmes run by government and non government agencies. Likewise the literacy level in this generation focuses on wastage in education at their time. The economic and socio-cultural factors are mainly responsible for the situation. The education is not yet perceived as a mean of development by the Adivasis. They have many problems in their daily lives. In the present situation they can not get much income or food from the forest because of continuously decreasing flora and fauna. The spreading cities and their burden on forests for timber and other products result in many problems. Because of uncontrolled deforestation and various environmental problems the biodiversity is disturbed. These all factors along with socio-political issues affect lives of these people.

Table showing age groups and the educational achievements among Thakars:

Age of person	*Education* *Illiterate*	*Prime School*	*Achievement* *Middle School*	*High School/ SSC*		*Total HSC*
10 to 19	12	11	5	4	1	33
	36.4%	33.3%	15.2%	12.1%	3.0%	100.0%
20 to 35	47	19	10	8	2	86
	54.7%	22.1%	11.6	9.3%	2.3%	100.0%
36 to 50	14	1	3	2	0	20
	70.0%	5.0%	15.0%	10.0%	.0%	100.0%
51. to 60	11	0	0	0	0	11
	100.0%	.0%	.0%	.0%	.0%	100.0%
61 to 70	13	0	1	0	0	14
	92.9%	.0%	7.1%	.0%	.0%	100.0%
71 and more	2	0	0	0	0	2
	10.0%	.0%	.0%	.0%	.0%	100.0%
Total	99	31	19	14	3	166
	59.6%	18.7%	11.4%	8.4%	1.8%	100.0%

Livelihood Patterns

The occupational categories mainly observed are farming, farm labourer and wage labourer respectively 28.3%, 24.1% and 18.1% respectively. Extent of petty business is very low. There is only one small shop run by a woman in Anandwadi earning up to 50 rupees a day. Because of the low literacy level they have to work on labouring jobs for livelihood or traditional patterns as shown in the table below.

Table showing occupations and educational achievements among Thakars.

	Education	*Achievement*				
Occupation	*Illiterate*	*Prime School*	*Middle School*	*High School/ SSC*		*Total HSC*
Farming	27	8	5	6	1	47
	57.4%	17.4%	10.6%	12.8%	2.1%	100.0%
Farm labourer	23	10	3	3	1	40
	57.5%	25.0%	7.5%	7.5%	2.5%	100.0%
Wage labourer	20	4	4	2	0	30
	66.7%	13.3%	13.3%	6.7%	.0%	100.0%
Selling of forest produce and hunting	0	1	0	0	0	1
	.0%	100.0%	.0%	.0%	.0%	100.0%
Service	2	2	2	0	1	7
	28.6%	28.6%	28.6%	.0%	14.3%	100.0%
Farming and labouring	6	4	0	0	0	10
	60.0%	40.0%	.0%	.0%	.0%	100.0%
Not known	3	0	0	0	0	3
	100.0%	.0%	.0%	.0%	.0%	100.0%
All kind of seasonal works	1	0	0	0	0	1
	100.0%	.0%	.0%	.0%	.0%	100.0%
Unemployed	5	2	4	3	0	14
	35.7%	14.3%	28.6%	21.4%	.0%	100.0%
Not applicable Retired	12	0	0	0	0	12
	100.0%	.0%	.0%	.0%	.0%	100.0%
Petty business	0	0	1	0	0	1
	.0%	.0%	100.0%	.0%	.0%	100.0%
Total	99	31	19	14	3	166
	55.6%	18.7%	11.4%	8.4%	1.8%	100.0%

The people are dependant on their traditional occupations. They have no hopes of job opportunities if they get any education. More than 95% of the people are dependant on farming and the forest where they live. Besides educational safeguards they must be assured removal of all kinds of exploitation. For example, Thakars gather the precious material from the forest viz. resin, honey, medicines etc. and they get hardly 30% of the market rate or even low rates for the forest produce because there in the market they have not any power. One of the respondent told that she collected 5 kg. of resin during last year and sold it at Bheemashankar at the rate of 70 Rs / kg. In the retail market it costs 200 Rs / kg. There is not any food process is done. The same situation is faced by farming Adivasis. Our agricultural market policies and practices are the most exploiting Machineries for farmers of all communities. Thus they can not prosper by selling the farm produces.

Gender and Education

Female education among Thakars is very low. Only 25.6% of female are reported to be educated as per the table given below. The extent of leaving the school gradually increases from primary level to the higher ones. Among 78 women studied only 20 women had ever got some education in their lifetime.

Table showing Gender and educational Achievement among Thakars

Gender of person	*Education Achievement*					*Total*
	Illiterat	*Prime School*	*Middle School*	*High school/SSC*	*HSC*	
Male	41 46.6%	20 22.7%	14 15.9%	10 11.4%	3 3.4%	88 100.0%
Female	58 74.4%	11 14.1%	5 6.4%	4 5.1%	0 .0%	78 100.0%
Total	99 59.6%	31 18.7%	19 11.4%	14 8.4%	3 1.8%	166 100.0%

Conclusion

From the studies done on the above three tribes the following conclusions can be drown:

Functioning of Ashram School among Madias

The Government Post Basic Ashram School at Perimili in Gadchiroli provides for schooling and hostel facilities from first to tenth standard students. The total enrollment of this Ashram School was 375 students in 1997-98. From Which Madia students were 295 being 78.64% of the total students. The students from the surrounding area up to 110 km come here to get an education. Considering the Ashram School facilities and the Madia students' performance in the examination commenced in the year 1996-97. Only 31% of the Madia students passed examination with desirable merrit and 65% needed to be promoted to the upper classes. The Ashram School education and the facilities provided consist of certain shortcomings. Or the education schedules and syllabi are not easy for the students from such a primitive community. Functioning of this school among Madias is not satisfactory.

Education among Lamanis

Lamanis at Pashan in Pune city are migrants from Rajasthan and settled here since more than 30 years. The data shows only 60 children from 500 families enrolled the in school. The number of drop out students was observed increasing from primary level to the higher ones. Other seasonal migrants also showed very low literacy. In Pune 7 such families were studied from which 2 youths were found literate; other 13 families consisted 3 only. These 20 families were seasonal labourers and they had been educated up to primary level in Kannada medium. These people working in Maharashtra had not any application of their education in Kannada medium nor they could continue their education here, because the medium of instruction offered is Marathi in Maharashtra. This can be considered as wastage in education. These people have only the way of labourering for their subsistence.

Education among Thakars of Karjat

Thakars of Mograj in Karjat have population of 948 persons. 53 households consisting of 320 people were studied. The educational achievement is less than 40 % among elder population which is further studied for various parameters viz. age-group, occupation etc. The average level of educational attainment fall upto 4th standard or even below. In Mograj village of Karjat from the population around about 948, only one person was reported to achieve the education up to B. A. who is studying his final (III) year. Since the education among most of the thakars is up to primary level or below H.S.C. yields not any job opportunity almost all of these people are either hunters and gatherers or agricultural labourers.

Comments

From the figures of literacy it is difficult to guess the real extent of educational status or literacy. The policy of government seems to literate people just to enable them reading different advertisement like Coka - Cola or Colgate. The present situation of tribal education in not satisfactory and needs many improvements conclusion. In day to day life the person who can sign is considered as literate. There is a large mass of people who can sign but can't read or write. This is so because plenty of students leave the school in primary stages of education. Afterwards they hardly practice reading or writing but they can sign any kind of document. Many times in adult education programmes people leave the classes after learning to write their own names only or after they can sign. In case of adult education they cant expect any benefit of such education and they just attend the campaign neutrally but in practice they have to sign many Govt. documents like property sell deeds agreements etc. and without any matter they sign many such documents. These people who can make signature and attended few standards of schools are literate as per Govt. surveys. When the literacy for all campaign started many officials used to refuse thumb impressions of peoples and suggested any other person from the family or other one who could sign. Thus the Govt. documents were prepared in such a way that they could depict the success of such campaign.

Not only the tribal students but all should be given some vocational trainings in the course of education. They should be encouraged to get higher education. But the situation is like that, the educated students have to suffer unemployment is the usual practice. On the other hand the parents cannot afford the expenses of growing children. They hardly make money because of seasonal unemployment on one side and gradually vanishing flora and founa of their territory and the students have to plunge into the play of struggle for existence.

The orthodox, antirevolutionary movement by certain organizations, like R.S.S. are in progress in the remote tribal pockets. These people are spreading blind faiths in tribal areas They make these people worship Hindu gods, and the tribal people are gradually forgetting their own cultural traits.

In their bulletin Satyashoddhak Vidyarthi Sanghatana states that Dr. S. Radhakrishnan made it compulsory that every educational institution will start its daily routine with religious prayers. He also imposed Hinduist philosophical studies compulsory in curricula. This kind of things badly affect the real ways of socio-cultural development.

30

Non-Government Organizations v/s Rural and Tribal India : Some Highlights

—A. Arjibefunn and Nanjujda D.C. & Lancy D' Souza

India is pre-dominantly an agricultural country. About 70 percent of her population depend directly or indirectly on agriculture. Moreover, agriculture is the major source of national income and exports. Therefore, the prosperity of agriculture is the prosperity of the country. In other words, agriculture is the backbone of the Indian agriculture. The activities of agriculture are carried out in the villages and village is the soul of India. Gandhiji also remarked that the real development of India lies in the development of rural areas. Therefore, the development of rural areas is, in fact, the development of the country. This present paper deals about the vital role of NGOs in rural development.

Rural development as part of social change is defined here as a process of expanding the decision-making horizon and extending the time frame for appraising investment and consumption choices by rural disadvantaged people collectively, and not necessarily at the village level but at even higher levels of aggregation. By supporting only NGOs, agencies reduce pressure on public and market agencies for reform and self-renewal. NGOs led by managers or leaders who are often from an urban context, by their own creativity, suppress or fail to nurture the creativity of the local disadvantaged. Social change thus becomes more and more dependent on external leaders. Sustainable processes will require correspondence between people's *access* to resources, *ability* to convert access into investments (that is, skills for using resources), and *assurance* of future returns from present investment (vertical assurance) and about others' behaviour vis-à-vis one's own (horizontal assurance or collective rationality). The changes in the network of access, ability, and assurance for DVs and the people have to be achieved simultaneously. Voluntarism may affect any one or more subsets of the developmental triangle of access, assurance, and ability of the people and thus may remain restricted in its impact. The propositions that follow deal with the way that voluntarism has been related to the process of social change in India. Given the range of experiences, it is indeed a synoptic account (Guptha, 2001).

Process of Voluntarism

Several church-based NGOs came into existence when international aid agencies offered relief at the time of the Bihar famine in the 1960s. Most of the relief was in the form of consumables such as foodstuffs, clothes, and medicine. The organizational structure for the distribution of this aid was different from the structure for managing durable assets such as rigs for drilling wells, transportation, and buildings. The move from relief to reconstruction attracted many young people. Instead of going back to pursue their professional careers, they remained behind to organize people, manage food for work programs, drill wells, or provide health and education facilities.

Many aid agencies sought legitimacy through relief but subsequently indulged in other interventions. The reaction of state agencies was to incorporate such volunteers or voluntary organizations as appendages of public relief and development programs. Such incorporation also took place in many NGOs, which came into the picture much later. An interesting feature of these organizations was that having begun with a community approach (relief was needed by all), they continued to use an eclectic approach to development.

Social conflicts were merely noted by some and participated in by others. The institutionalization of voluntarism in intermediary support or funding organizations or grass-roots organizations gave a techno managerial start to the intervention strategies. A negative feature of such aid was that in regions prone to frequent natural calamities, people started losing their self-help initiative. State relief in the form of employment or food was not linked with a mobilization of voluntarism among the people. Dependency so created made the task of many radical NGOs even more difficult. People could not understand why mobilization around a radical ideology should be a reason for forging immediate material benefits.

Ravi Rajan (1988), while analyzing rehabilitation and voluntarism, observed four distinct styles: (1) intervening organization took on the provision of relief and rehabilitation as its primary task, became dependent on the government, and with the diminution in the governments' own commitment to the cause, soon collapsed; (2) volunteers served as "conscience keepers," pursuing change through systematic research reports; (3) trade union activists demanded charge of the industrial plant to provide employment through altertribal use of plant and machinery; and (4) perhaps the most significant strategy by volunteers was to reject the idea of voluntarism as propounded by the state. Rather, voluntarism was redefined to include sustained mobilization, the struggle for better relief, access to medical data, questioning the scretiveness of the part of the government, legal activism, and questioning the right of the government to give such a low priority to the life of the poor. Voluntarism of this nature is difficult to mobilize in backward rural areas given the dispersed nature of settlements and weak social articulation, low media attention, and poor networking among interventionists.

Radical groups using violent means of social change have sought support essentially from Maoist philosophy. After the Chinese aggression in 1962, covert support to these groups increased, and income disparities intensified after the first phase of the green revolution. Technological change had provided the spur for a large number of young people, particularly from West Bengal and Andhra Pradesh, to plunge into the field of violent social change. The attempt was to annihilate rich farmers and other symbols of perceived oppressive classes or those considered class enemies. Another stream of volunteers who entered the field of rural development came with innovative ideas for providing relief during the 1964-1966 drought in different parts of the country. These volunteers became crucial instruments of social dynamics. The war in 1965 with a neighboring country led to a slowing down of U.S. aid to India. The search for indigenous altertribals became intense, and the legitimacy of voluntarism increased (Khare,2003). The period between 1966 and 1972 was full of economic crises. The economic environment in the preceding decade had been aimed at the closure of the Indian economy through import substitution. Droughts, wars (1965, 1971), devaluation of currency, and inflationary pressure created an environment of social unrest in the organized and unorganized sectors. Death from starvation was supposed to have been eliminated (almost) after the drought of 1965-1967. Maharashtra started an employment guarantee scheme during the drought of 1972. In the wake of large-scale violence in 1966 and 1967 by left-wing radical groups, the report of a confidential inquiry committee by a committed civil servant (Appu) set up by the Home Ministry argued for an immediate thrust toward target group oriented programs of rural development suited to location or ecology and class-specific need.

The Small and Marginal Farmer and Agricultural Labourer Development agencies, the Drought-Prone Area Programme, and the Tribal Development and Hill Area Development plans followed. Decentralized development in the policy was accompanied by greater political centralization from 1970 to 1977. A movement based on Gandhian values that called for total social revolution was spearheaded by Jaya Prakash Narayan in 1973 and 1974. It attracted a large number of young people, particularly in Gujarat, Bihar, and Maharashtra, and many of these young people continued with voluntary work.

The government declared a state of emergency from 1975 until 1977, after a prolonged railway strike, and even urban people realized for the first time the implications of a non-democratic coercive state. Voluntarism was also sought out as a sign of despicable deviance. People has the option of being incorporated into the repressive state structure or being jailed or victimized. The post-1977 phase of change in political continuity through the single-party rule brought many Gandhians committed to decentralized development into the mainstream. Tax concessions for voluntary initiatives by commercial companies were introduced for the first time by the

Janata government in 1978, and many innovative organizations came into being. A number of developmental volunteers who worked in commercial organizations found this an opportunity for exploring new organizational space. Some misused this option but many did not.

For the first time, professionals and young activists were offered competitive salaries in addition to autonomy for work unheard of in mainstream organization by and large. These events were also accompanied by a change in the policy of international aid agencies, which started shifting from funding better implementation of government programs bureaucratically to better implementation by NGOs. It was unfortunate that creative avenues in the NGOs. It was unfortunate that creative avenues in the NGOs got generally fossilized because of their proximity to the state and their participation in implementing standardized programs(Green, 1998).

A change of government in 1980 and the restoration of rule by the Congress party led to the expected withdrawal of tax concessions; the centralization of voluntarism (companies could contribute to the Prime Minister's fund for rural development and seek fresh grants from it for action programmes); the halting of the direct transfer of funds from a commercial balance sheet to the social (less easy to account) balance sheet; the standardization of developmental programs such as the Integrated Rural Development Programme (IRDP); the withdrawal of higher allocations to the IRDP for backward areas and putting them on par with other areas; and the merger of earlier adaptive or responsive programs into a standardized IRDP, with credit-linked subsidy as the dominant mode of relationship. Another interesting development was the return of naxalite (radical Maoist leftists) underground workers to the mainstream was non-violent but articulate strategists of social change. For the first time, several ex-naxalites sought election in 1977 and some were elected.

The social space for altertribal development was filled by volunteers with vlarying backgrounds; ex-radicals; liberal or social democrats who were dissatisfied with the workings of the state and wanted to influence the distribution of resources; enthusiastic urban activists who after looking for a career, failed to get one and returned to a mainstream profession rather quickly; young professionals with technical or other disciplinary backgrounds who launched action-research projects or supported other professional groups; retired civil servants, ex-Gandhians, lawyers, and so on, who formed independently or with the support of aid agencies large NGOs; and quasi-state organizations promoted to provide technical, financial, marketing, or other support to NGOs, artisans, and other beneficiaries of state-sponsored developmental programs.

At the time when social space for volunteers was widening, opportunities for career growth in mainstream organizations also began to increase. The first phase involved the growth of the banking sector after nationalization in 1969. A large number of bright young men and women with backgrounds in science, the humanities, or engineering joined banks, insurance corporations, and other such systems. "Brain drift" as opposed to "brain drain" took a heavy toll by depriving academic disciplines of bright students and luring some professionals on the margin away from other direct social development systems. The post-1980 boom in the consumer goods industry and the continued growth of banking and other public and private ventures further increased the flow of young people toward such careers. The opportunity cost of those who chose to work in NGOs did indeed increase. The question we want to address next is "What are the processes by which voluntarism in mainstream organizations can complement the efforts of NGOs not merely in bringing about social change on the micro-level but also in influencing public policy in favor of the disadvantaged?" (www.aisid.org)

Implications for Action and Research

Generating extra-organizational space for developmental volunteers within mainstream organizations is a necessary condition for sustainable social development. One study on bank and NGO cooperation for poverty alleviation in backward regions noted that there was no NGO working in the fifty most backward sub-regions of Gujarat. State organizations like the National Bank could not gain credibility in supporting NGOs if they did not provide the opportunity for exploration and experimentation to volunteers within their system. NGOs often did not recover even the operating costs of many services from people. In the process, such NGOs remained perpetually dependent upon aid agencies. Moreover, accountability of the NGOs in regard to the poor was so low that most NGOs did not aim at inducting poor people into their own management structures. One nationalized bank invited its clerks to volunteer for two years in a village development program in an area of their choice without any loss of seniority upon their return. This triggered numerous innovative experiments by DVs.

The hands of DVs in technology generation, adaptation, and diffusion system working on unpopular problems of larger social concern needed just as much attention. How can professionals who disregard professional rewards and devote attention to such problems but cannot put pressure for reform on their own organizations be sustained? Empowering them will require recognition of their voluntarism by a body of concerned scholars and activists. No national award has been given to date to any bank officer for initiating innovative schemes. So much so that about ten million rupees for new innovative schemes for rural development provided at the national level remained unspent because no system existed for identifying and recognizing DVs within the mainstream system.

Can the capacity of urban people to manage their own affairs be provided by urban volunteers who come from very different cultures? The poor do not cooperate with developmental organizations because they are not recognized as possessing any *richness* in terms of their cultural and moral fiber. The findings of our research are seldom shared with those from whom we collect data. Involving the rural poor as co-researchers of social phenomena, building upon cultural roots of voluntarism, and showing respect for common property institutions can change this situation. Acknowledging local initiatives can spur their transformation into innovations. Documenting people's knowledge and identifying the scientific merit of some sustainable resource management altertribals can rekindle people's experimental ethic. Institution building requires the dispensability of external leadership, the recognition of an inverse relationship between status and skills, and the discrediting of values that generate helplessness. "Lateral learning" among developmental volunteers and NGOs can be triggered to provide empirical basis for building a "theory in and of" action (www.rud. ac.in)

Conclusion

Voluntarism in rural development in India has not been accompanied by pressure for policy change except in regard to environmental issues. Often action at the local level has not been linked with lobbying at the macro level. Recognizing that the state and markets perform better if kept under constant check, developmental volunteers within the organizations will have to serve a sort of "insurgent" function so as to align, anonymously, with grass-root activists, NGOs, and professionals. International agencies can strengthen local social change by broadening local ideas and innovations into global thinking and by providing global space for developmental volunteers to validate their hypotheses.. Right Livelihood awards constitute one such source of international recognition. If the rural poor of India could communicate with the homeless in America, surely the cultures of deprivation would provide the basis for collection action. Social innovators and DVs around the world are struggling for similar space in a society where one does not have to go through a phase of unbridled accumulation followed by guilt, charity, and benevolence for the have-nots. Sustainability in nature and society requires players, whistle blowers, spectator rules, and creative chaos. DVs are arguing that the losers in a game should not lose the right to play on the same field again. Asking them to play only on separate fields (in the form of volags) will eventually rob the game of the chaotic waves of sorrow and joy. Should we let it convert the spectators into warriors?

31

Human Development of Nomadic and Denotified Tribals : A Search for Proximate Determinate

—Srivatsa S. and Sharma W.S.

Nomadic communities constitute approximately 7% of India's population. Marginalization continues to characterize the nomadic experience, and phenomena such as urbanization and environmental conservation schemes have contributed to the increasing impoverishment of these communities. In turn, the growing poverty has contributed to high rates of malnutrition, illiteracy and landlessness amongst these communities. Land continues to be the primary source of livelihood, social and financial security in rural India. Consequently, many of these communities view settlement as the solution to their current difficulties. Although exercising the right to self-determination is essential to the identity of a community, the movement to settle raises many concerns. Impact analyses have to be conducted to determine how settlement will affect the cultural identity of the community, how the dynamic relationship between the community and the land will be altered, and how community custom scan be preserved in light of the change in lifestyle. The needs of the community have to be identified and articulated in order to design programs that facilitate lifestyle adaptation. Ecological impacts of displacement must also be examined since nomadic communities have helped to preserve eco-diversity through their sustainable hunting, farming, herding and for aging practices.

Primitive Traits

A majority of the Nomadic tribes exhibit the primitive traits even today. They still live in tribal groups moving from place to place in caravans in search of livelihood. The various practices like worship of nature in different forms, animal sacrifices during religious ceremonies, adorning head with horn (Banjara woman), not wearing a blouse (Wadar woman) are only a few of them to demonstrate this fact. Their social life is still governed by *Jat Panchayats*, a primitive form of social organization. Every year they assemble at Madhi a village in Nagar district of Maharashtra state, in annual fair where the sessions held by the *Jat Panchayats* of each tribe sort out various issues pertaining to individual and social problems.

Geographical Isolation

From generation after generation, these tribes have had wandering traditions and they have hardly been integrated in the society. In fact, the society has always looked at them with mistrust and suspicion due to the stigma of criminality attached with them. In that sense they have been living a life of isolation from the rest of the society. Some of these tribes still prefer to stay near jungle, away from the villages. Their temporary settlements are known as *pal* or *pada*.

Social Backwardness

The Nomadic and Denotified tribals have no means of production and livelihood as a result of which they have to move from village to village in the form of a caravan. Also, the children are deprived of education. They cannot take education through regular school systems in a settled society due to this unstable life style. They are left away from the mainstream of life and their life is fossilized in poverty, superstition and ignorance. They have remained backward economically and socially. Apart from the criteria mentioned above there are two other criteria which make these tribes eligible for having constitutional safeguards which are enjoyed by the Scheduled Tribes.

Nomadic Way of Life

As already mentioned these tribes have wandering traditions. In absence of any means of survival and lack of education to fit into the settled society they are forced to continue with this tradition for bare survival in the most degrading and sub human conditions. Thousands of families belonging to these tribes wander from place to place and stay in temporary structures rarely fit for humans beings to stay. Unless they settle at one place or another, unless they are provided with opportunities of education and employment they will never be in a position to integrate themselves in the society and avail of the benefits of modern civil life.

Stigma and Criminality

Though Criminal Tribes Act was repealed in 1952 the stigma of criminality is still attached with them. Due to this stigma they are the victims of persecution and torture at the hands of the British and the state machinery. Anywhere an act of theft or robbery takes place persons belonging to these tribes in the surrounding area are arrested and subjected to various forms of torture. In the eyes of the society they are still criminals, and a wide gulf exists between them and the rest of the society.

Historical Perspective of the Problem

In the year 1950, the list of Scheduled Castes and Scheduled Tribes was released. The Criminal Tribes Act was repealed in 1952. Though the Criminal Tribes Act Enquiry committee had categorically made the recommendations to the Central Government regarding these tribes they were deprived of the Constitutional safeguards due to both the acts of commission and omission. Thereafter the issue was swept aside due to the conflicts of the state formation on the linguistic pattern and these tribes in Maharashtra became victims in the process.

Following the linguistic pattern of state formation the territory of the early Nizam state was shared by Andhra Pradesh, Maharashtra and Karnataka. While the tribes in the territory included in Andhra Pradesh and Karnataka enjoy the constitutional status and privileges, the same tribes in the territory of Marathwada region included in Maharashtra are deprived of it for no fault of theirs. Similarly, it is ironical that tribes like the Kaikadi and Pardhi in Vidarbha, which was previously a part of Madhya Pradesh, enjoy the constitutional status, in the rest of Maharashtra they are deprived of it.

Since the Nomadic and the Denotified tribes which form the lowest rungs of the society fulfill all the criteria applicable to the ST they enjoy the constitutional status in most other states. Unfortunately, their counterparts in Maharashtra, though they share the same dialect, life style, cultural practices, social customs and blood relations they are deprived of the status of the Schedule Tribes. Instead of doing away with the injustice, the government went on including more and more castes and tribes in the Schedule of the NT's and DNT's pushing the original tribe against the wall.

The Nomadic and Denotified tribes constitute about five million of population in Maharashtra and about 60 million all over India. There are 313 Nomadic Tribes and 198 Denotified Tribes. Due to the wandering traditions over hundreds of years without any ostensible means of livelihood under the influence of the caste system, they are forced to live under sub human conditions. The large section of these tribes is known as "Vimukta jaatis" or the Ex-Criminal Tribes because they were branded as criminals by birth under the "Criminal Tribes Act 1871", enacted by the British Government. In spite of the repeal of the act in 1952, they are still treated as Criminals by birth and subjected to harassment and persecution at the hands of the police and the state machinery. However, they have been deprived of the status of Scheduled Tribes provided by the constitution due to certain historical circumstances and the acts of omission and commission on part of the Government and the society.

Criteria for Constitutional Safeguards

After Independence, under Article 366 (25) of the Constitution of India certain tribes were classified as Scheduled Tribes and have been provided with constitutional safeguards under Article 342 (2) on a national basis. The classification was made on the basis of the following criteria, which are fulfilled by the NT's and the DNT's being the most depressed sections of society.

Our study has revealed that, among other factors, State failure to provide the legal infrastructure to facilitate land holding and protect tenure has exacerbated the vulnerability of the nomads. In many cases, landless families are forced to move into unoccupied land. Their lack of legalstat us however, leaves them vulnerable to evictions. Further, the communities' inadequate access to basic amenities such as water, grazing land

and roads are violations of human rights, pursuant to the Indian Constitution and international law. A review of India's international and domestic commitments regarding land and housing rights has also shown that the right to adequate housing must be adapted to the community's needs. Thus, regardless of a community's choice of lifestyle, the universal standards of adequate housing must be met.

Executive Summary

The grassroots demand to formally articulate and advocate for the rights of the nomadic communities has yielded a pilot study conducted by Habitat International Coalition's Housing and Land Rights Network (hereinafter HIC-HLRN) in collaboration with Muktidara Sansthan, a community based organization. For the purpose of the study, six nomadic communities were visited in the Alwar district ofthe state of Rajasthan, namely the Bhopas, Bawarias, Gadhiar Lohars, Kalbelias, Nats andBanjaras. The methodology of the inquiry included: observing the living conditions in the communities and recording instances of State failure to provide basic living amenities, reporting how land allotment schemes are implemented and retrieving testimonial evidence of human rights violations such as forced evictions, police brutality and racial harassment. Visits and investigations were facilitated by the local organization, Muktidara Sanstan. The primary objective of the study was to identify the substantive concerns of the communities and to articulate these concerns within the paradigm of fundamental human rights, in particular, the right to land and adequate housing. It is hoped that by broadening the discussion to the universal language of rights, the report will: 1. Provide the communities with tools to assert their rights more effectively; 2. Emphasize the need for further, in-depth studies to be conducted, in light of the absence of information about nomadic tribes in India; 3. Identify problems that may arise during the adaptation to sedentary life; 4. Raise public awareness about the issues confronting nomadic tribes; 5. Initiate the creation of ties with other nomadic communities within India; 6. Pave the way towards a network with the Roma communities of Europe to strengthen the advocacy for nomadic rights on the international level.

Observations and Findings: While HIC-HLRN recognizes that not all nomadic communities wish to alter their nomadic lifestyle, the research team observed that many communities are choosing to pursue sedentary lifestyles because traditional livelihoods have become unsustainable. All the communities studied live well below the poverty line. Finding food is a daily challenge as urbanization has encroached upon common lands used for agriculture and conservation laws limit access to the forest produce that is critical to survival. The movement to settle is in part, a response to narrowing livelihood options as communities work toward the ultimate goals of self-reliance and the preservation of their culture:11. Through the classification of Scheduled Castes and Scheduled Tribes, the Indian Constitution provides legal benefits to communities that have been historically marginalized. The exclusion of some nomadic communities from the constitutional categories denies them these legislative safeguards and benefits.2. The failure of the government to implement land reforms that recognize the customary rights of nomadic communities is a denial of the right to legal security of tenure, a fundamental component of the human right to adequate housing.3. On a normative level, the nomads continue to suffer social isolation, ostracism and suspiciondespite the constitutional guarantee to promote and protect the cultural and economicconcerns of Scheduled Castes, Scheduled Tribes and Other Backward Classes.2Pursuant to both international and national legal obligations in matters of housing policy, the State must remain accountable in ensuring access to adequate housing and monitoring the impact oftheir housing policies. Presently, no formal scheme exists to address the housing needs of nomadic communities.

Recommendations

The State must comply with all its commitments in accordance with the Constitution of Indiaand the various international treaties it has ratified. Development and resettlement measures mustbe established with the consent and collaboration of the nomadic communities. The right toadequate housing can only be realized if various international criteria are fulfilled including: theright to secure tenure, availability of services, materials, facilities and infrastructure, habitability;

accessibility for disadvantaged groups, affordability; location that allows access to schools andjobs, and housing policies that respect the cultural identities of the inhabitants.3Presently, theseminimum core obligations are not realized.

Citizenship Rights. Recognize the citizenship rights of such communities by implementing participatory processes that encourage the voice and visibility of nomadic community members in all levels of decision-making. In this light, voter identity cards should be issued.2. Sensitize law enforcement officials through training and awareness programs. Ensure that strong punitive action is taken in cases of police brutality. Training programs should be established involving national, state and civil society human rights institutions3. Develop public awareness campaigns to promote better understanding about nomadiccommunities.4. Repeal of the Habitual Offenders Act, taking into consideration the historical stigma suffered by nomadic communities as social outcasts prone to crime.5. Community-based groups are key players in reacting and responding to the needs of affected communities and lobbying for policy reform. The State must recognize their roles as intermediaries and collaborate with them when designing policies for livelihood training and land reform. Land Entitlements and the Right to Adequate Housing1. Ensure transparency and administrative efficiency in all state transactions with the affected communities. Application for title deeds should be dealt with as a priority. Written explanations should be given to claimants for any delays in the application process.2. Update land records to include the customary rights of access and use of nomadic communities. For example, migration routes should be mapped out and access to these lands should be facilitated.3. Ensure that nomadic communities are given time and the forum to voice their needs and to discuss land allotment and encroachment issues, especially during public hearings held at the panchayat, or village, level.4. Improve accessibility to records for verifying title deeds and other associated informationt for encourage transparency.5. Perpetrators of forced eviction are punished to the full extent of the law and a schedule of sanctions for such offences should be published. Right to Livelihood1. Initiate dialogue and a policy of public participation with the Department of Forestry with regards to environmental conservation schemes. In that regard, the Indian Forest Act and Wild Life Protection Act should be amended to include provisions that enjoin public consultation with communities affected by conservation measures. It is crucial that future establishment of protected areas should begin with the consent and the cooperation of the indigenous communities.

Historical and Legal Overview of Nomadic Communities in India

The ghumantoos, or nomads, of India are mobile tribes, each characterized by a distinct culture that is reflected in their beliefs, customs and traditional practices. Each jati practices a hereditary occupation and often speaks a specialized dialect. The exact number of the nomadic population is unknown because a formal census has never been conducted of these nomadic communities in India. However, informal studies indicate that about five hundred endogamous groups make their home in India, two dozen of which can be found in Rajasthan. Nomadic communities constitute about 7% of the Indian population.4At present, nomadic communities are found in the states of Andhra Pradesh, Maharashtra, Gujarat, Karnataka, Tamil Nadu, Haryana and Punjab. Pastoral nomadic communities also live in the Himalayan region in India. In general, nomadic tribes are organized into sub bands of five to fifteen families, each headed by an elder who wields the authority to settle disputes. A panchayat, or village council often governs inter-jati affairs. Family size may range from five to twenty five people, since the family group commonly includes extended family members. The sub band might travel on independent routes and maintains a self-contained existence and governance for most of the year. However, bands belonging to the same ethnic group return annually to the tribe's customary camping ground in order to regroup. During these reunions, marriages are performed, cattle are traded and communal bonds are reformed. 5 Non-pastoral nomads traditionally depend on sedentary communities for their subsistence by providing services or goods to the communities they frequented during their travels. Each jati practices a particular craft such as basket weaving, blacksmithing and acrobating. In the past, because of the varied lifestyles and occupations of the tribes, livelihoods could be sustained and inter-tribe competition for jobs was minimal. Today, nomadic communities in India are confronted with barriers of discrimination and exclusion. Colonial laws that declared these tribes to be "criminal" and caste segregation have contributed to this marginalization. Despite the repeal of such laws and constitutional guarantees of equality, hierarchical social norms and historical prejudices continue to color the treatment of nomads today. For example, nomadic children are excluded from attending schools and families are banned from water wells and houses of worship. Physical contact with members of upper caste communities is forbidden because members of the nomadic community are considered impure. Thus, they are made to eat from different utensils and restricted from the facilities frequented by members of the upper castes. Caste based violence is a prevalent concern. Nomadic communities are commonly blamed for high incidents of crime and soaring unemployment rates in the villages. Nomads that attempt to settle have had their houses burnt by members of settled communities unwilling to live in close proximity with nomadic families. The nomads continue to be targeted as objects of physical abuse: members of the community are physically threatened, stoned and mobbed by villagers intent one radicating the social problems allegedly caused by the nomads. These incidents are largely unreported because caste bias often extends to local law enforcement agencies and the media. Exclusion from schools contributes to high rates of illiteracy and unemployment. These social problems have, in turn, caused widespread poverty and high mortality rates. Lacking the academic requirements, most nomadic community members do not qualify for basic jobs. Legislative and constitutional guarantees have not translated into work opportunities, training, health care and schools.

Nomadism v. Settlement

The livelihoods of nomadic communities have been affected by various phenomena. Pastoral nomads and nomadic hunters and gatherers have been particularly affected by privatization, degradation in the quality and quantity of natural resources and restrictions on their access to these resources. For non-pastoral nomads, mechanization, industrialization, and advances in modern entertainment technologies have also had adverse implications on livelihoods. Diminishing sources of income is the principle cause of the growing numbers of nomadic tribes shifting to sedentary lifestyles. This change in lifestyle often requires occupational change as well. For example, nomadic tribe members are increasingly resorting to wage labor.6It must be emphasized that the choice to pursue a nomadic or settled lifestyle rests solely with the individual or the community. However, the question of settlement raises several critical issues: 1. How will settlement affect the cultural identity of the communities? 2. Will engaging in new professions and livelihoods result in the erosion of cultural identity and stifle the heritage connected with the freedom to travel? 3. What will adaptation entail, considering that many of these communities have known no other way of life and are not trained to perform tasks relevant to sedentary life? 4. What are the ecological impacts of resettlement?. How will settlement policies affect other communities that want to continue the nomadic way of life?

Criminality: Notification and Denotification

The prevailing social and economic impoverishment of the nomadic communities must be understood within its historical framework. Marginalisation of nomadic communities began with the British assumption of sovereignty in 1858. Sovereign laws replaced tribal customary laws and contributed to the dissolution of the traditional fabric of Indian society. Through the enactment of a succession of land and criminal legislation, nomadic communities were divested of usufructuary and hunting rights to the land, forests and animals from which they derive their livelihoods. Prior to the 19th century, the nomads of India fulfilled specialized roles, connecting distant villages by making available goods and know-how from regions that were otherwise inaccessible. Even though excluded by caste, nomadic communities had a defined place within the social structure as they provided a variety of distinct services ranging from blacksmithing to entertainment. 7 The Criminal Tribes Act In 1871, the colonial government enacted the Criminal Tribes Act with the objective of gaining greater control over rebel rural regions that resisted British annexation of land. In effect, tribes listed in the Act were declared "criminal." Law enforcement officials were granted wide discretion regarding the management and governing of such enlisted communities, enabling them to carry out summary convictions and imprisonment without trial. Pursuant to the Act, the listed communities were subjected to mandatory daily registration that severely curtailed their movement. Rehabilitation camps were established in which criminal tribe members were "chained, shackled, caned and flogged while being surrounded by high walls ... in the name of the homegrown science of "curocriminlogy", it was declared they would be cured of their criminal propensities if they were given work." 8 In 1952, the Criminal Tribes Act was repealed and replaced by the Habitual Offenders Act. The listed tribes were officially de-notified. However, the stigma of criminality still remains and the nomads continue to be perceived as social outcasts. Nor did de-notification affect the cycle of derivation. De-notified tribes are not an enumerated class under the constitutional schedules and because of this, lack the constitutional safeguards and benefits enjoyed by the Scheduled Castes and Tribes. Although some tribes have been included in recent amended lists, many impoverished tribes meriting specialized concessions remain unscheduled. 9 The National Human Rights Commission (NHRC), in a historic meeting held in February 2000, recommended repeal of the Habitual Offenders Act. 10 The NHRC pledged to monitor the atrocities suffered by de-notified communities, reorient police training systems and to sensitize State machinery. The Commission recommends that each state work out an Action Plan addressing the requirements and special problems of these groups. However, to date such recommendations have yet to be implemented and the State of Rajasthan has not repealed the Habitual Offender's Act.

Exclusion from Reservations

The Constitution makes provisions for the protection and "uplifting" of Scheduled Castes and Scheduled Tribes. To implement the constitutionally mandated welfare schemes, the tribes were identified and schedules were drawn up in 1950. However, orders for de-notification for "criminal tribes" were not passed until 1952. As a result, the de-notified tribes were excluded from the constitutional schedules. This exclusion has numerous implications: 1. The Scheduled Caste and Scheduled Tribes (Prevention of Atrocities) Act 1989, prohibiting the violation of the civil and political rights of enumerated castes and tribes, does not apply to de-notified tribes. As such, violations of human rights cannot be addressed under its provisions. 2. De-notified tribes do not qualify for reservations and concessions. This contributes to the lack of representation in government and exclusion from employment opportunities. Some de-notified tribes have been categorized as scheduled tribes in state lists but there has been no uniformity in the implementation of classification policies. The stigma of criminality and nomadism hinders the integration envisioned by government policies. Because their history, experiences and circumstances differ from that of other intermediate castes, a distinct framework of entitlements for ex-criminal tribes must be created. In a submission to the National Commission to Review the Working of the Constitution of India, jati representatives requested the creation of a separate schedule, particularly reflecting the needs of de-notified tribes. 11 However, the government has yet to respond to this submission. Protection for Scheduled Castes and Scheduled Tribes Today, although legally denounced, caste segregation prevails. As an illustration, in 1991, only 29% of Scheduled Castes and 36% of Scheduled tribes were literate. 12 The Constitution of India designates special provisions for the improvement of the so-called "backward" classes, or Scheduled Tribes and Castes. In addition to the prohibition of discrimination guaranteed to everycitizen, the constitution includes safeguards to ensure that social and economic disabilities arealleviated. 13 The Constitution also stipulates that a National Commission be appointed toinvestigate the conditions of these classes and identify the sectors and classes of society that should qualify for aid. These identified classes are subsequently listed and granted constitutional protection. 14 In addition, the Constitution guarantees the implementation of welfare schemes and provides for special reservation of seats in the Legislature for Scheduled Castes and Tribes. 15 Toprotect the civil and political rights of Scheduled Castes and Tribes, the Scheduled Castes and Scheduled Tribes (Prevention of Atrocities) Act was enacted in

1989.1611 See All India Banjara Seva Sangh's Report to the National Commission to Review the Working Constitution of India, 2000.12UNDP India, UNDP India Reports, citing 1991 Census India, online: <http: www.undp.org.in> (date assessed: 10 November 2003). The Registrar General of India has not released literacy rates for SC/STs from the 2001 Census. 13 Article 15. 14 Article 340. 15 Article 275(1), Article 330. 16 Scheduled Castes and Scheduled Tribes (Prevention of Atrocities) Act 1989 (33 of 1989), 11 September 1989.

Implications of Conservation and Eco Diversity Schemes

Various legislative enactment's aimed at ecological preservation have eroded the customary rights of hunting, foraging and trapping of nomadic communities. Pastoral nomadic tribes that are restricted from reserved land are unable to graze their herds and non-pastoral nomads that depend on the forests for resources are similarly deprived of the main source of their livelihoods. The establishment of protected areas has not only alienated communities from their cultural heritage, but has also contributed to the growing poverty amongst nomadic communities. Government initiatives to promote biodiversity have either failed to recognize the right of affected nomadic communities to participate in eco management policies or have not made suchparticipation mandatory. Forest officials often penalize pastoral nomads for their efforts to protect the forest, not understanding the relationship of mutual dependence and respect nomadic communities share with the environment. 17 Nomadic communities have long lived in harmony with their natural surroundings, respecting and protecting the integrity of the lands. Their sustainable hunting, collecting, pastoral and farming practices have helped to preserve eco diversity. For example, by raising their animals in conditions close to what is found in the wild, the rearing practices of pastoral nomads have contributed to the maintenance of tribal breeds of animals. 18 Land management policies can therefore best rengthened by incorporating their insight, know how and traditional practices. Despite this, nomadic communities continue to be excluded from resource management decisions. The Wildlife (Protection) Act 19 Enacted in 1972 with a view towards ecological conservation, the Act prohibits:1. The hunting or capture of wild animals without a permit and authorizes state appropriation of any wild animal bred in captivity. 20 Permits are only granted for an exhaustive list of purposes, including education, scientific research and scientific management. 21 Provisions addressing the needs of communities that practice hunting indigenously are not included within the Act. Pursuant to the Act, tribes are prohibited from capturing the animals that have been their only means of income. 2. The collecting of plants from forest lands. 22 Tribes who sustain themselves with forest products and the sale of medicines made from plants must seek a permit in order to legally maintain their everyday activities.3. The Act also enables the state government to declare tracts of forest reserved for conservation purposes.

Individuals with prior claims to the lands must tender an application to assert their rights. 24 Such stringent bureaucratic requirements substantively discriminate against the nomadic communities as many lack there sources to undertake land claims.4. The Act prescribes for the constitution of a Wild Life Advisory Board. The Board exercises an advisory role when the state formulates conservation policies. Although the provision allows for tribal representation on the Board, it does not explicitly impose mandatory participation. Ultimately, the State wields the discretion to determine the Board's constitution and thus has the capacity to veto tribal representation.

Indian Forest Act: The Indian Forest Act empowers the state government to declare any forest land and forest produce "reserved." After a declaration of reservation, the state government has full management control over the land and its resources, including the power to levy duties on timber or forest produce collected and harvested within reserved forests. The Act also prohibits grazing, clearing, trapping or hunting within reserved forests. In effect, the Act grants the government wide regulatory ambit to restrict access to reserved lands, but this power is not circumscribed by a corresponding state obligation to consider particular needs of the nomadic populations that depend on the forests for their livelihoods. Although shifting cultivation is allowed, the state government heavily regulates the practice. 28 This right is deemed by the courts to be a privilege subject to the discretion of the government. 29 The court's interpretation invalidates the customary rights of pastoral nomads. Claimants must submit to the jurisdiction of the state government who demarcates the amount of land suitable for the needs of the applicant. The Land Acquisition Act: The land rights of the nomads are also diminished by the enactment of legislation related to land. The Land Acquisition Act 1894 describes the circumstances and reasons for which private land can be acquired by the State. There are three salient characteristics of the acquisition process: First, the government must declare its intent to acquire. Second, any person "interested" in filing anobjection to the intention to acquire has 30 days to do so after declaration of intention. 30 Third, any claim for compensation requires the production of entitlement documents. This requirementexcludes nomadic communities from compensation since nomadic lifestyles preclude the finding of permanent occupation and "ownership" as envisioned within the Act.

Confronting Discrimination

India's northwest state of Rajasthan is home to 24 nomadic tribes with an estimated population of nearly four million people. In recent years, phenomena such as industrialization, urbanization, and the enactment of various land and forest policies have decimated their traditional livelihoods. In the past, nomadic communities were viewed with fear and distrust because of their distinct social norms but growing poverty has widened the social gap between settled and nomadic communities, contributing to their increased isolation. 31 In Rajasthan, relationships with settled communities have deteriorated and hostility against the nomadic existence has intensified. Because traditional livelihoods are no longer sustainable, many nomadic communities, including the six studied in this report, seek to settle permanently. These six communities have settled mainly in so-called "wastelands" or uncultivated, unoccupied government land under state jurisdiction. Hostile resistance from settled communities hinders adaptation to sedentary lifestyle. This hostility manifests in many different ways: homes are burnt, children are denied entry in schools, families are prohibited from using village wells or pumps and community members are subjected to harassment from local law enforcement.I ntroduction to the six studied communities: Banjaras, Gadiya Lohars, Nats, Bhopas, Kalbelias and Bawarias. Banjaras Known as the traders of salt and cattle, the Banjaras are, according to folklore, descendants of the Charan people who were bards to the Rajputs. Their nomadic lifestyle began during the Mughal dynasty, when they became carriers in the Mughal army. Their nomadism continued throughout the colonial period when they became transporters of food grain and followed transport routes through Gujarat, Rajasthan and Kabul. Also known as the ghumantoos, or people of the cattle, the tribe is known for their distinct religion that is a blend of Hindu, Sikh and Muslim rites and beliefs.

Government of India is obliged to respect and protect the human right to adequate housing. The human rights paradigm engenders State accountability and offers the perspective, the standards and the mechanisms to ensure that entitlements are effectively realized. This framework also ensures that the overarching themes of equality and indivisibility of rights inform the discussion of land and housing entitlements. In the case of the Rajasthani nomads, the fight for land and housing rights must also be understood in the context of discrimination and exclusion. Caste bias and anti-nomadic sentiments profoundly affect access to land, education and employment opportunities. The systemic discrimination suffered by members of nomadic communities is a flagrant breach of human rights norms. The Indian Constitution: The Indian Constitution enumerates the fundamental rights and duties of the State, and protects individual liberty by guaranteeing economic, social and political justice for all. The overarching philosophy of the Constitution is promulgated in a preamble that delineates the objects the Stateis obliged to promote and the spirit in which the constitutional provisions should interpreted, namely, the ideals of justice, liberty and equality. Although the right to property has been omitted from the set of fundamental rights protected by the Constitution, the right to adequate housing is recognized and protected as a subset of other fundamental rights. 36 Article 21 provides that no person be deprived of his or her life and personal liberty.

The courts have held that the right to life encompasses the right to live with human dignity. The Supreme Court affirms that living with dignity necessarily entails that the core amenities of life are readily accessible. Thus, the right to shelter is a constitutional guarantee. The Legal Framework: The Right to Land and Adequate Housing 35 Re Berubari Union, A. 1960 S.C. 846.364 4th Amendment Act, 1978. Because the right to property is not a fundamental right, any person deprived of property as a result of governmental policy has fewer means of redress against the government including restricted access to compensation.

Not only is the State obliged to recognize the right to an adequate standard of living including food, clothing and housing, the provision also requires State intervention to take the appropriate measures to ensure the effective realization of the right. The Committee on Economic, Social and Cultural Rights has reiterated in General Comment 4 that the right to housing is not restricted to shelter but encompasses the right to live in security, peace and dignity. The Committee also notes that realization of other rights such as the right to participate in decision-making is indispensable to the full enjoyment of the right to adequate housing. Several international instruments address the specialized housing needs of women and children. Article 14 ensures that "women enjoy adequate living conditions, particularly in relation to housing, sanitation, electricity and water supply, transport and sanitation." For children, CR C Article 27 calls on State Parties to assist parents and guardians in providing the child with proper food, clothing and housing. The Maastricht Guidelines make it incumbent for State Parties to ensure the progressive realization of enumerated economic, social and cultural rights, irrespective of resource scarcity and level of economic development. These guidelines set the international norms for monitoring and adjudicating economic, social and cultural rights. Progressive realization therefore requires immediate State action, demonstrating that measurable progress and specific targets are set and satisfied. The Indigenous Question-Quest for Recognition In recent years, much international attention has been devoted to issues affecting indigenouspeoples. 52 Aboriginal communities have made enormous strides in ensuring that their rights are protected in international instruments. The ICERD and ICCPR both guarantee self-determination for indigenous communities and General Recommendation XXIII of the CERD Committee directs State Parties to parties to recognize and protect the rights of indigenous peoples to own, develop, control and use their common lands, territories. 53 Limburg Principle 14 qualifies that special measures are required to protect the rights of indigenous peoples. 54 Currently, there is no consensus on whether the term indigenous applies to the tribal groups of India. The Government of India has not recognized the adivasis as indigenous peoples of 51 Maastricht Guidelines on Violations of Economic, Social and Cultural Rights, Maastricht, January 22-26, 1997. 52 See, for example, Douglas Sanders "Indigenous People on the International Stage," in The Indigenous Question: Search for Identity ed.Walter Fernandes, Indian Social Institute, New Delhi: 1993. 53The relevant articles in the ICCPR are Article 1 and Article 27. See also ICERD, Articles 2.2 and 5(c). 54 See Annex 4 for the text of Article 14.

General Observations 1. Many of the challenges that confront nomadic communities today can be attributed to continued caste based discrimination and alienation from settled communities. 2. The combination of modern technology and legislation aimed at eco-conservation has caused the diminishment of traditional livelihoods, leading to widespread impoverishment. Regional and national governments have not taken measures to address the problem of narrowing livelihoods or provided support for these communities. As a result:• Families are denied their rights to adequate housing.• Communities fall further into the cycle of deprivation.• Historic patterns of marginalization and exclusion are repeated. 3. Denial of the right to housing and land has adverse implications on other aspects of life. For example, without having a permanent address, children cannot to be registered in schools and communities lose their political voice because they are not included on voter lists.4. Lack of information and knowledge about the lifestyles, needs, customs and traditions of nomadic communities contribute their marginalization.

Observations Regarding Land Entitlements and the Right to Adequate Housing 1. Many nomadic communities have expressed the desire to pursue sedentary lifestyles. Often, settlement efforts are hindered by public antipathy towards nomadic communities. • Government housing policies have not addressed the particular obstacles that nomadic communities face regarding settlement such as the existence of caste hostility.• Land allotment processes are carried out on a municipal level and often reflect the local caste segregationist attitudes. Applications for title deeds filed by nomadic families are not processed, reportedly due to pressure exerted by members of settled communities on local land allotment authorities.

Recommendations:

The Road Ahead

In many instances, nomadic settlements have been destroyed and the inhabitants, forcibly evicted by members of non-nomadic communities.• It has been reported that caste bias extends to local law enforcement authorities. As a result, civil atrocities committed against nomadic communities, including incidents of forced evictions and intimidation, are not pursued.• In many cases, First Information Reports filed against perpetrators are not been followed through with formal investigations. 3. Access to adequate accommodation is the immediate concern amongst many nomadic tribes. Typically, housing and living conditions in the settlements are inhabitable:• Civic amenities such as piped water and electricity are non-existent. One hand pump is commonly installed for each settlement and overuse has affected the quality of water pressure.• Types of shelter vary according to the lifestyles of the tribes, ranging from make- shift tents to thatched huts. However, most shelters do not provide adequate protection to the elements.• Conditions within the settlements are squalid due to lack of sanitation facilities.• Access to health care, schools and public distribution shops is severely limited by poor road connections. 4. Nomadic communities are often denied their rights to due process, information and rights to participate when dealing with district authorities.• Tribes are not informed about community meetings where land allotment is planned and discussed.• District land allotment authorities allegedly refuse to provide information when nomadic tribe members inquire into the status of their title deed applications.• Contrary to constitutional guarantees, customary (caste) laws bar nomadic families from ownership of land in some villages. For these arrangements, a percentage of in comederived from the harvest is taxed for rent.

Observations Regarding the Denial of Human Rights1. A vast majority of nomadic communities subsist below the poverty line but ration cardsare not distributed in the settlements to facilitate access to more affordable food and fuel. 2. The Forestry Act and Wildlife Conservation Act continue to deny customary rights of hunting and foraging, foreclosing significant livelihood options.3. Incidents of harassment, intimidation or violence due to caste hostility are under-reported because law enforcement authorities have exhibited caste based bias.

Law enforcement authorities commonly raid and search settlements without warrants under the guise of nuisance control or crime prevention.5. Inadequate access to schools contributes to the high illiteracy rates amongst the nomadic communities. Many families are unable to register their children in schools without permanent addresses or identity cards. Often, children are subjected to harassment in the village schools.

Policy Suggestions

To the Government of India:1. Establish constitutional safeguards for de-notified tribes that have been excluded from constitutional schedules. Recognize that these tribes face a specific form of marginalization due to the stigma caused by enactment of the Criminal Tribes Act. 2. In the development of legislation and policies to protect the rights of nomadic communities, ensure compliance with India's obligations under the international human rights instruments, in particular its obligations to protect these communities from all forms of discrimination. Guarantee the meaningful participation of nomadic communities in all levels of decision making by initiating dialogue with the communities and reserving positions for them in the government. 4. Drafting of a national habitation policy for nomadic communities that seek to settle, with the caveat that settlement policies can only be implemented with the consent and consultation of the communities. Drafting should take place in consultation with, inter alia, the nomadic communities, civil society organizations, ecologists and economists. 5. Provisions should be made to ensure women's right to property. A system of subsidized loans and grants or cooperative schemes should be established to ensure that land and adequate housing are accessible and affordable. 6. Nomadic communities must be included in the National Census. Organized and in-depth social- economic studies have to be conducted to forecast the potential problems communities may face in their adaptation to sedentary life.7. Recognize and respect the citizenship rights of nomadic communities. The Census and Election Commissions should work concurrently to ensure that voter identity and ration cards are issued and distributed in the settlements. Regularized birth registration should be enforced. 8 The Indian Forest Act and the Wildlife Conservation Act should be amended to include a provisionthat enjoins prior consultation with communities affected by conservation measures. 9 In relation to the state obligations arising out of international commitments on the right to adequate housing and non-discriminationsee the draft guidelines prepared by the Special Rapporteur on Adequate Housing in his 2002 report to the UN Commission onHuman Rights.

Initiate livelihood training in cooperation with the community that is designed to address their particular needs.10. Facilitate access to education, including more vigilant monitoring of the quality of instruction in informal schools.11. Promote public awareness and re-education by advocating against caste segregation.12. Establish halting sites for nomadic communities who maintain the traditional nomadic or semi-nomadic lifestyle. This will enable families to provide addresses when registering children in school or applying for social benefits.13. Implement the recommendations of the National Biodiversity Action Plan. This includes giving effect to co-management policies and recognition of customary rights of access and use of natural resources. To the Government of the State of Rajasthan:1. Amend the Land Revenue Act 1956 to lower entitlement criteria for nomadic communities. 2. Repeal the Habitual Offenders Act as recommended by the National Human Rights Commission in February 2000.3. Monitor land allotment processes on the district level to ensure transparency andaccountability.4. All records should be computerized to ensure easy access to land records, information on title deed applications and information on land availability. Timely and reasonable explanations in writing should be provided for any delays in the application process for title deeds. 5. Training programs should be carried out to sensitize law enforcement authorities, state and local authorities, civil society and the general public about nomadic issues. A zero tolerance policy for the use of excessive or unjustified force must be institutionalized. 6. Forcible evictions carried out by members of settled communities must be dealt with swiftly, to the full extent of the law. 7. An organized monitoring system should be implemented to ensure that the living conditions in nomadic settlements are adequate and that families are accorded access toelectricity and water. To NGOs and CBOs:1. NGOs and CBOs should collaborate their efforts in a nation wide and international campaign to advocate and raise public awareness about the issues of land entitlements for nomadic communities. A national alliance should be established, bringing together NGOs working for nomadic rights, in order to design a coordinated strategy to place the plight of nomadic communities in the forefront.

The Nomadic and Denotified Tribes are National tribes. They have no place of their own. Hitherto, their life is a long tale of suffering and persecution due to the absence of a means of livelihood and the stigma of criminality attached to them by the sedentary society. While it may take years and years to remove this stigma, the injustice meted out to them due to the act of omission and neglect could well be corrected without any further delay. It will be impossible for these tribes to enjoy human rights or the civil rights available to the citizens of India unless there is a positive intervention of the government in the form of Constitutional safeguards.

More human rights education should be conducted within communities. 3. NGOs should utilize international human rights instruments and mechanisms to strengthen the arguments for land entitlement and to ensure more vigilant monitoring of government implementation of international law obligations.4. Funding and technical expertise should be provided to local CBOs engaged in livelihood training and adaptation programs for communities that wish to settle.5. Strengthen alliances with Roma lobby groups in Europe in order to exchange and learn from their experiences in national and international advocacy as well as benefit from theirnetworks.6. Explore means to advocate and raise awareness about nomadic issues on the international agenda in the way that indigenous and dalit rights groups have done in recent years.

32

Addressing the Marginalized Tribal Children : Multilingual Education in Orissa

—Deoranjan Kumar Singh, Mahendra Kumar Mishra

Multilingualism, which is constitutive of the identity of a child and a typical feature of the Indian linguistic landscape, must be used as a resource, classroom strategy and a goal by a creative language teacher. This is not only the best use of a resource readily available, but also a way of ensuring that every child feels secure and accepted and that no one is left behind on account of his / her linguistic background.

Education is the outcome of experiential learning of human society. It is ingrained in the life and culture of the people. The concept of formal schooling is a modern phenomenon in which the life experiences of the students are fragmented into different subjects and disciplines in order to understand the world in a systematic manner. The land, language and culture determine the learning of the people and through socialization the whole society learns (transmits knowledge, skills and attitudes) from one generation to the other across time and space. The globe has many human societies and many cultures. Some of them have facilities of modern education and some have not. So even in the twenty first century, some have the facilities of information technology and some are still non-literate. Even after centuries of co-existence, privileged and marginalized societies have maintained the inequities existing between them. Therefore rights and equity in education are still a dream in human society where half of the population is struggling for survival. At this juncture, the challenge for human kind is to bring a transformation in social order where the most underprivileged have a voice.

Geography determines the life style of the people. This leads to a culture of difference in human life and society. Culture is shaped and created with the adaptation of nature. People try to understand and interact with nature and their life is shaped accordingly. They survive by struggling in many situations, thereby learning to live. Their personality and identity is shaped accordingly.

The cultural symbols are created to signify the differences of one social group from the other. Some are considered civilized whereas some are not. Of course this distinction is the creation of the people who consider themselves superior to others in terms of achieving power, knowledge, property and service. They formulate the standard set of rules of development through which they measure the standard of living of others. The disparity along with the dichotomy of cultural values puts some people in mainstream and some in the group of the marginalized.

The marginalized have their own set of standard rules and practices that is created by themselves. Albeit, people of mainstream culture try to impose their cultural values and try to mainstream marginalized peoples. Being fascinated with the mainstream culture, people of marginalized group also some times acculturate with them, forgeting their social values. This results in irreparable cultural loss. This happens when cultural hegemony is operative in the government and in the institutions that should be serving all people equally, and when it invades the thinking of the marginalized because of their desire to become like the mainstream culture.

Tribal people in the world have made substantial contributions in shaping human culture, more particularly in shaping the concepts and worldviews of man-nature relationship and interdependence of natural with supernatural. They believe in an integrated worldview that has the scope for survival. Their life is their experience. Their collective memory and expression is their learning. Their work is their education. Every action is associated with creative memory embedded with purpose and meaning. Their learning is not isolated from their lives.

The concept of education among the tribal/indigenous society is different from the formal education system. The reading and writing of letters is not found in the indigenous educational system. Writing was existent in wall painting; complex creation was in the craft, weaving, and invention of ethnic-technology. But these have not been thought of as formal education. The learning of all these aspects was in the practice of the people, and was highly active, productive, expressive and generative all as part of informal learning.

But the gap is that schools in tribal areas are provided with the curriculum and instructional materials uniformly made in the state headquarters without proper representation of indigenous teachers. The medium of instruction is also the state language. Thus the content and language of the indigenous children is not represented in the curriculum and textbooks. Teachers, tribal or nontribal, have to use the same materials in the schools without considering the cultural context of the children of divergent cultural environments.

Indigenous knowledge is still not a part of formal learning systems. Therefore the designers of school programs coming from a different world have not tried to initiate an understanding of the needs of indigenous children's learning; rather a uniform curriculum tries to meet the need of all children irrespective of cultural and linguistic variations in the state.

The creator of indigenous knowledge is the community. This knowledge is shared in their society. Many communities are multicultural and they don't feel threatened by living in a village with a multiplicity of ethnic groups, languages and cultures. Diversity of culture has enriched society. Diversity is not a threat to National Integration, but promotes cultural harmony and peaceful co-existence. People from different cultures and different languages live together in communal harmony. The right to freedom of expression and co-existence of culture is a healthy practice for a democratic government. Interestingly, while this has not been a problem in the village, it has been a problem in schools. This means that schools are not ready to cater to the needs of the context specific issues of divergent social groups.

The aim of this paper is to understand the indigenous education of Orissa and to explore how the indigenous peoples have been marginalised across time and space.

Prior to 1994 it was almost a dream to think of imparting education of marginalized children in their mother tongue or to recognize the tribal culture in education. Language of the tribal children was not considered important assuming that all children have the ability to learn in the state language as the state curriculum was uniform for all children irrespective of race, gender and language. Some of the points to consider are:

- Orissa has provided a uniform education to all the children irrespective of linguistic/ethnic and cultural variations.
- The dominant culture and language groups of the state have developed curriculum and textbooks without involvement from indigenous teachers.
- Cultural content, mother tongue of the children and cultural context of the indigenous children are ignored, thereby providing a curriculum of the dominant culture group
- Teacher training in the state has not addressed the context specific issues nor the learning difficulties of indigenous children and teaching difficulties of tribal area teachers

The state has not had an institution to address the education of indigenous children because of the following reasons.

1. The global movement of indigenous education has still to reach the state and to sensitize the state on adopting the bottom up approach of indigenous learning system.
2. Some people believe in mainstreaming the indigenous children, ignoring the mother tongue of indigenous children.

The net result leads to disintegrate the cultural diversities and create a culture of dominance. Indigenous people lose their identity and self-confidence. This also leads to language disadvantage of indigenous children. Denial of language results in denial of culture. This affects the cognitive development of

teachers, gradually this conception began to be removed and a new dimension of equity education was initiated in the state. The platform for this dimension was the District Primary Education Programme (DPEP). This new initiative was to take care of the disadvantaged groups as special focus groups. A substantial spade work was taken up in DPEP in eight of Orissa's tribal districts. This work included attitudinal training for teachers, preparation of bilingual primers along with supporting educational materials, linguistic mapping and survey, community mobilisation, and the use of folklore in primary education etc. Though it was limited, it was a major breakthrough in Orissa to understand that education of tribal children needed special attention, or else the literacy of tribal learners would not be achieved.

Having a platform with a national initiative to address the constitutional obligations, SSA took a second look at the education of tribal children in a more intensive manner. It was the Orissa Child Census 2005 and Child Tracking system which brought understanding to the system about the gamut of problems and issues recurrent in the field of tribal education, from different perspectives. This led to planning for area specific/ cluster specific intervention.

Literacy in Orissa

Literacy in Orissa, according to the Census of India 2001, is 63.61 % whereas the percentage of tribal literacy is 37. 37%. The gap between overall literacy and tribal literacy is 26 %. While literacy rates of tribals in Orissa was 9. 46 % in 1971, it was 13.96 % in 1981. It rose to 27.10 % in 1991 and in 2001 it was 37.37 %. This indicates the slow progress in literacy of tribal people in Orissa over the last three decades.

The literacy profile of Scheduled Tribes as per the Census of India 2001 reveals the literacy situation and status of the district. While the highest literacy of Jagatsingpur is 79.8%, the lowest literacy district is Malkangiri having 30.53%.

Tribal Female Literacy

The female literacy rate in the state is 50.97% whereas the tribal female literacy rate is 23.37% (as per the census of India 2001) and the gap is 27%. In the case of low female literacy, seven districts of Orissa have below 30% women's literacy. These districts are Kalahandi (29.56%), Nuapada (26.01%), Gajapati (28.91%), Koraput (24.81%), and Rayagada (24.31%) Nawarangpur (21.02 %) and Malkangiri (21.28%).

The following table compares literacy rates between the general population with tribals in seven districts of Orissa which have literacy rates below 30%.

Name of the district	*Total female literacy*	*Tribal female literacy*	*Tribal male literacy*	*Total Tribal literacy*
Gajapati	28.42	14.83	17.69	27.77
Kalahandi	29.28	17.15	51.70	34.17
Koraput	24.26	8.38	29.25	18.68
Malkangiri	20.67	7.50	23.01	14.69
Nuapada	25.79	16.18	50.69	13.12
Rayagada	24.56	10.07	31.16	20.29

Census of India, 2001.

The above Table indicates the challenges of literacy in the highly tribal populated districts.

The Linguistic Minority districts in tribal context of Orissa:

Name of the district	*Number of Schools*	*Tribal Children (6-14) enrolled*	*Major language spoken*	
Nabarangpur	1095	69437	Bhatra, Paraja, Gondi, Kondh	
Mayurbhanj	1493	64500	Santal, Munda, Kol, Bhumij, Ho, Mundari, bathudi	43148 Santali
Koraput	1202	60909	Kondh, Jodia paraja, Gadaba, Bhumia,	Desia as link language is closer to Oriya
Sundargarh	1104	60829	Munda, Oram, Kishan, Santali, Gond	
Rayagada	1241	51552	Kondh, Saora, paraja	
Malkangiri	808	33988	Koya, Gadaba, Bhumia, Bonda, paraja	
Gajapati	649	23764	Saura, Kondh	
Kandhmal	449	21351	Kondh	

Name of the district	*Number of Schools*	*Tribal Children (6-14) enrolled*	*Major language spoken*	
keonjjhar	486	14477	Juang, Munda, Bhuiyan	
Balesore	438	12939	Santali, Kol, Munda, Ho, Bhumij,	6047 Santali
Kalahandi	232	8721	Kondh,	
Jajpur	267	4846	Munda, Juang, Santal, Ho, Kol	
Sambalpur	140	4372	Kishan, Munda, Oram	
Total		396767		

The rest of the districts have very small tribal populations and they have assimilated into the mainstream Oriya language.

Tribal Children's Profile in Orissa

The total population of ST children in the state between ages 6-14 is 1744281, out of which 1343538 are enrolled, and 205742 are out of school ST children (CTS 2006, OPEPA). While the total ST children of 6-14 age group constitute 25.87 % of the total child population of the state, their enrolment rate is 88.92% in the school and the out-of-school ST children in the state is 11.08%. The enrolment of ST children in primary schools is 1153574 and the enrolment of ST children in upper primary stage is 189,964.

Table. Class wise Number of ST Children in the State.

Class	*Boys*	*Girls*	*Total*
Class-I	164864	153775	318639
Class-II	131350	120904	252254
Class-III	124284	114147	238431
Class-IV	99770	84855	184625
Class-V	86999	72626	159625
Class-VI	62366	45474	107840
Class-VII	47803	34321	82124
Total	717436	626102	1343538

School Type	*Boys*	*Girls*	*Total*
Primary (I-V)	607267	546307	1153574
Upper Primary (VI-VII)	110169	79795	189964
Total	717436	626102	1343538

Source: Orissa Child Census 2005.

Out of the total tribal children enrolled in primary stage it is found from the study that tribal children up to Class V fail to read sentences fluently.[1] They also fail to understand the content of the textbook written in the state language.

Dropouts

During 2002-03 to 2004-05 it was revealed that the dropout of ST children is about 20% higher than the general dropout rate. In 2004-05 the over all dropout of children was 32% and dropout of ST children was 52 percent. In the case of ST girls it was 56% and the gap was 23%.

The dropout of children in elementary stage is higher than the primary stage. While over all dropout of all children at elementary stage was 49.2%, the dropout of ST children was 69% and in the case of ST girls it was 72%. The gap of dropout is above 20% the normal dropout rate.

(Child Census 2005 and CTS 2006, OPEPA: www.opepa.in)

SCHOOLS WITH LINGUISTIC MINORITY:

'Language is not everything in education but without language everything is nothing in education' (Wolff 2006). ADEA Report, 2006 South Africa)

The Orissa Child Census 2005 conducted by OPEPA reveals that out of 30 districts in the state, 11 districts contribute towards nearly 80% of the total out-of-school ST children. The numbers of out-of-school ST children in these districts are Mayurbhanj (40708), Nabarangpur (28217), Keonjhar (21797), Koraput (21517) followed by Rayagada (18719), Malkangiri (17161), Kalahandi(13608), Sundargarh (11177), Balesore (10700), Gajapati (10037), and Kondhmal (9244). This indicates that the districts with high tribal population coupled with lack of access because of language are at a disadvantage.

According to Orissa Child Census 2005 there are 11479 schools in the state having 20 + students from linguistic minority groups. The total number of such students in these schools is 6, 73 622. Nearly 2/3 of them belong to Santali (58287); and other tribal language group (396,104). (Child Census, 2005 and CTS 2006, OPEPA)

Ten districts of Orissa have a concentration of 90% tribal children with linguistic variations. One thing that is clear from this information is that the out-of-school children in the districts also have a high gap between home language and school language.

We can infer with the above information, that language is a major factor which affects the education of children. Should we infer that the reason for out-of-school children in these ten districts is due to the unattractive school atmosphere where the tribal children fail to get proper education? The answer is yes. But the issues are manifold, coupled with language, parental awareness, teacher's attitude, unattractive school atmosphere and mismatching curriculum and instructional materials. Why are tribal children pushed out from the school and why does the school fail to attract the child?

The result is that when the child is denied access to her own language her education is blocked and her language and culture are neglected. (King, 2005) This means that education is not child centered, but teacher centered. Teacher centered education continues for the children who speak the state language, ignoring the diversities of culture. The picture shown below portrays the weak foundation in bridging the gap of home language and school language.

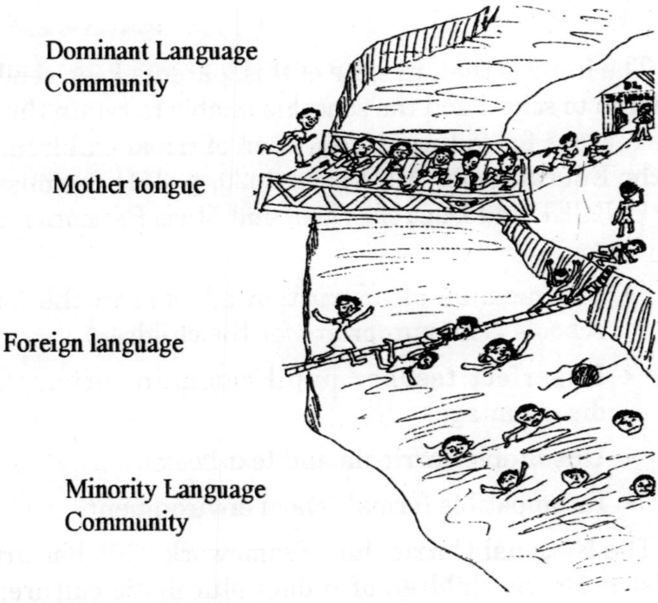

Source : Susan Malone, SIL, Bangkok.

Tribal parents send their children to schools, but many parents are not concerned with their schooling. They understand that education changes the value of life. Even the poorest person also likes to educate her children. But why the school is not able to attract the children is a matter of concern for all those who work for the education of tribal children.

Situation I : - Oriya School with tribal children

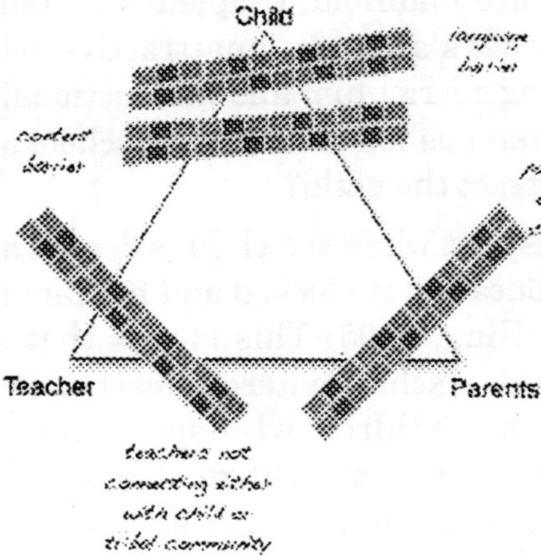

©Mahendra K Mishra, 2007

The irony is that, in spite of this, parents keep sending their children to school and the school is unable to retain the children. The reasons for failure in education of tribal children, as noted by the Education for All (Vision 2020, p. 311) commissioned by the UNICEF and Dept of School and Mass Education are given as follows:

- The medium of instruction adopted in the tribal area schools is inappropriate for the children
- Imperfect teacher pupil communication (language disadvantage)
- Unsuitable curricula and text books
- Incompatible formal school environment

The National Curriculum Framework 2005 has articulated a vision for the children of India's pluralistic culture; a vision that seeks to ensure that children would learn and construct their own knowledge and connect their own experiential learning with that of the school based on its guidelines, and irrespective of rural, urban or tribal. Children's expression is possible when a child has the right to think and speak in her own language.

At present, schools, in the light of NCF 2005, are so common in terms of maintaining the uniformity of language, content and curriculum that the children of cultural diversities and linguistic minority have no other choice than to adopt the content and language of the majority. This results in the predominance of cultural hegemony.

Non-tribal teachers face big challenges in non-tribal schools in Orissa. The following table indicate the types of schools that are available in Orissa.

Schools with 100 % ST children	3421
Schools with 99-90 % ST children	2499
Schools with 89-80 % ST children :	2184
Schools with 79-70 % ST children	1993
Schools with 69-60 % ST children	2009
Schools with 59-50% St children	2012
Total Schools :	

Coming to the classroom situation it is found that in Class I to Class III there are 8,03000 ST children in the state. It is seen that tribal children in Class I to Class III fail to achieve the content knowledge due to two reasons:

1. The language of the text book and the language of instruction by the teacher in the classroom is not intelligible to them and
2. The content of the curriculum and instructional materials used in the classroom is not contextualized.

Besides, the teachers have little knowledge about addressing the multilingual and multicultural needs in the classroom. In some countries multi-lingualism and multi-culturalism have been considered as an opportunity to widen the horizon of human language and culture in the classroom. In our situation it is considered to be a problem. While co existence of diverse cultures and languages in a village has never been a problem to the children or the parents in the social context, when the same children are in school, the question of conflict arises. This indicates that the school curriculum is not able to meet the learning needs of the children of such a culturally diversified society. This leads to serious learning disadvantages.

Multilingual education across the globe has established that children from minority languages do not pose a problem to the system if their languages are used in the classroom. Rather, an opportunity exists to explore the strength of linguistic diversities. According to language pedagogists, children are more multilingual before they come to school. Language maintenance in the classroom creates a cultural harmony and tolerance among the children.

What is Multi-Lingual Education?

Multi-lingual education is a programme of learning through mother tongue where the children explore their experiential knowledge, supported by the community knowledge to provide learning from their own cultural context, and then to connect their knowledge with new knowledge of the wider world. The principles for the adoption of MLE depends on:

- a strong educational foundation in the first language
- successful bridging to one or more additional languages
- enabling the use of both/all languages for life-long learning.

The purpose of a multi-lingual education programme is to develop appropriate cognitive and reasoning skills enabling children to operate equally in their native, state and national languages, starting in mother tongue with transition to second (Oriya) and third languages (English). The curriculum is based in the culture of the local community, using local knowledge and customs through which a child can develop common concepts in all areas of learning.

It provides a strong foundation and a good bridge for the children to transition from one language to the other within a span of five years or more and acquire competency in all languages. Research shows that a child who is strong in her mother tongue is also strong in other languages.[2]

A very important aspect of MLE is the curriculum and instructional materials. These materials come from the cultural context of the community in which the world of the child is reflected. This enables the child to develop a strong cognitive ability to expand her understanding of the world around her.

In the MLE programme the teachers must be from the tribal community. The teacher and the community develop the curriculum and textbooks. This is done by using a village or community cultural calendar where significant cultural events such as festivals, major agricultural activities, hunting, fishing, and seasons are mapped against the 12 months of the year. This process suggests the likely significant or generative themes, and a possible sequencing of the themes for designing a curriculum and based on that they prepare the instructional materials.

Children come to the classroom with knowledge. They have knowledge about their language. They certainly have basic interpersonal skill (BICS). They have acquired knowledge about their environment, their customs, and some skills. Provided with a curriculum that builds on what they already know they acquire cognitive academic language proficiency (CALP)[3] . Hence local knowledge in which the child develops her cognitive ability is important in shaping her learning.

The community plays a major role in school management and developing curriculum. The local knowledge of the community is shared and discussed and the community shares the knowledge used in the classroom. Teachers from the tribal areas tap their community resources which then shape the curriculum.

Situation 2 : Tribal teachers with tribal children

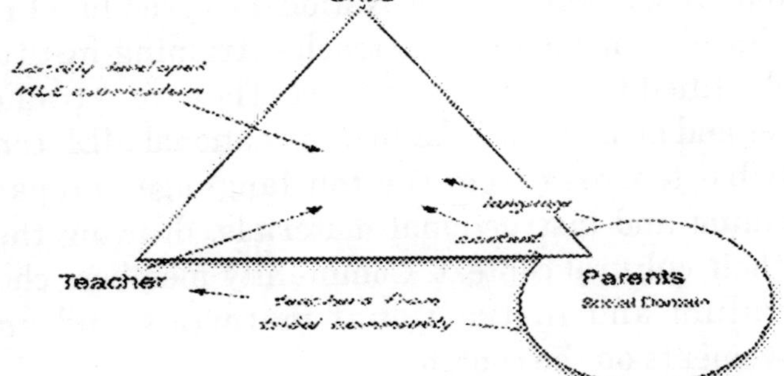

©Mahendra K Mishra 2007

Multi-lingual Education in Orissa

Orissa as a state with varied linguistic situation has adopted Multi-lingual Education in principle. In 2006-07, the state Tribal Advisory Committee decided to begin with ten tribal languages to be used as the medium of instruction. The selection of languages was based on educational need, social demand, and gap of home and school language. Endangered languages like Bonda and Juang were also taken into consideration while selecting the schools.

The languages chosen were from two groups:

1. Major eight languages:

   Santali, Saura, Koya, Munda, Kui, Kuvi,Oram, Kishan,

2. Endangered languages: Bonda and Juang.

Initiation

The year of preparation is 2006-2007. Two hundred schools in the ten languages were identified for the beginning of the project. One criterion for school selection was the homogeneity of the population it served. These schools had to be 100% monolingual. This was to ensure transition of 100% tribal language in Class I to 100% Oriya language in Class V over a period of five years.

Teachers and language resource persons were selected from each of the ten tribal communities. They were given training in the construction of a local curriculum based on a thematic approach and in the use of child-centred approaches in the use of these curriculum materials. The local curriculums developed followed the guidelines of the National Curriculum Framework 2005. Faculty members from teacher training institutes were also identified for academic support. They were trained on the theories and methods of MLE by International MLE consultants. The tribal teachers from the ten languages prepared their curriculum and instructional materials, drawing the content from their cultural context. Community members checked the curriculum and instructional materials and suggested improvements on the content.

MLE resource persons collected cultural materials from their own community. The reason for the tribal resource persons in combination with tribal teachers was that a teacher may be a tribal, but it can't be assumed that she knows her own culture.

Process of Theme Selection using a Village Calendar

The regular calendar year was divided in to three main seasons: Summer season, rainy season and winter season. Themes for each season were selected for language and mathematics. Environmental education was integrated with language and mathematics in Class I and Class II.

Construction of Curriculum:

The curriculum is based on the village calendar of the tribe. The environment, culture, society, flora and fauna, nature and the universe of the visible world of the child is reflected in the construction of the curriculum. The space and time, and the process of tribal life in their socio-cultural cultural context are manifested in the curriculum. The circle of the cultural calendar is divided into three main terms, based on the seasons. Theme webs were prepared based on the principles of NCF-2005 with reference to the basic skills of Language, Mathematics, Environmental Studies, Physical Education, Health Education and Moral Education.

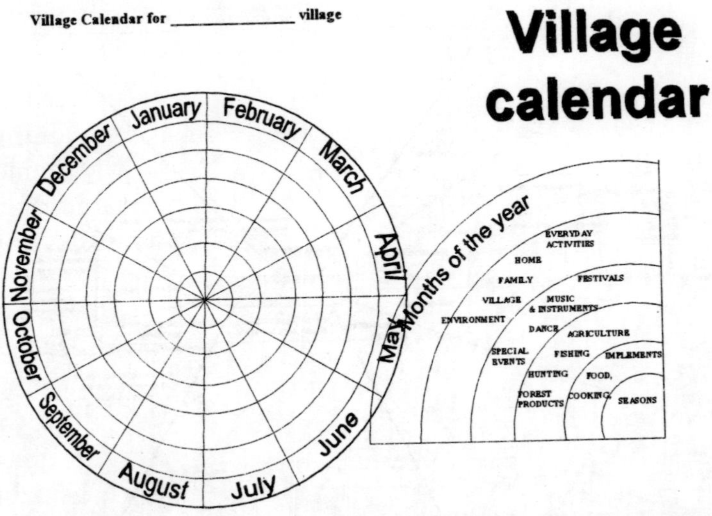

(*Source:* Pamela Mackenzie and Steve Simpson, SIL, Hyderabad,India)

An academic year is divided in to three terms:

Term –I April to July

Term –II August to November

Term –III December to March

Each term is divided in to ten weeks. Each week represents one theme. Each theme includes language and mathematics. Theme web are prepared for language and mathematic independently.

For language learning, theme web is prepared on reading and writing using the cultural themes. Environmental Science is ingrained in language theme for Class I curriculum.

What is a Theme Web

A theme web is a diagram, which looks like a spider's web or a wheel. Various activities related to the teaching theme on which it is based can be filled in on the diagram. The teaching theme, a word, is placed at the center or hub of the diagram. Around that are the various areas or subjects that can be integrated through the connection between the subjects and the theme. A theme web is useful as a framework for constructing a curriculum. Following are examples of a general theme web for any topic, a theme web for one topic or theme, and the math theme web that goes with it and fits into the cultural maths part of the larger theme web.

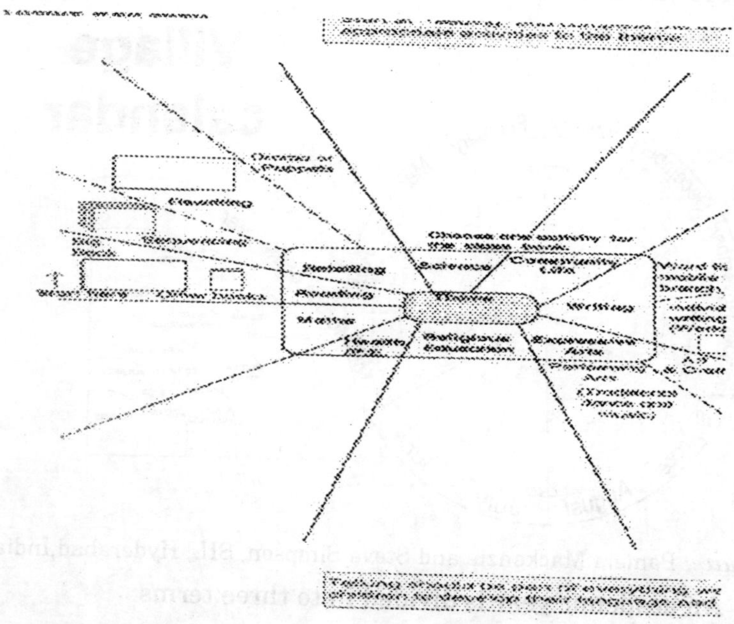

Source : Dr. Dennis Malone, SIL Int'l, Bangkok.

The theme web is divided into two roads. Road I stand for accuracy and correctness or skill development. Road II focuses on meaning and communication, including the experiences of the child with content drawn from her cultural environment. While Road II represents the experience of the child from the socio-cultural context, which is basic interpersonal communicative skill (BICS) Road I stands for cognitive academic language proficiency (CALP) skill.

An example of how these two approaches are used is as follows:

Road I Accuracy and Correctness	Road II Meaning and Communication
The morning is for skill-based development, which is to develop confidence and competence through practice with engagement through games.	The afternoon is to learn meaning based conceptualised learning rooted in learner's background and culture, and with an emphasis on encouraging the creativity of the child.

Development of Instructional materials

Based on the above conceptual framework, development of instructional materials in language has been made as follows.

Road I - Accuracy and Correctness:	Road – II – Meaning and Communication
• Alphabet Chart • Alphabet Book	• Big Book (stories)- 30 • Small Book (stories) -60 • Listening Stories – 60 • Chart Stories for Shared Reading (e.g. Experience Stories told by the children and written down by the teacher exactly as expressed by the children - 60 Story book, Folktales, Riddles, Folk songs etc. (to be collected by the children, teachers in the village and the community members)

The development of instructional materials as defined in the syllabus of National Curriculum Framework 2005 for language, mathematics and EVS were followed while preparing it. It is interesting to note that the cognitive aspect of tribal culture is manifested in the instructional materials and the purpose of using an item of culture in the materials is meaningful in the context of learning and teaching. In this way it is a rediscovery of local knowledge in classroom.

Time Table

The school year is divided into thirty weeks, each week representing a weekly theme.The weekly theme is again divided in to daily lesson plan. And the Road I and Road II activities are distributed for learning and teaching. Weekly and daily lesson plans are prepared in the orientation programme of the MLE teachers.

Implementation

For Class I, twenty schools for eight language groups were identified and for the endangered languages, ten schools for the Juang language and five schools for the Bonda tribes. Teachers from tribal communities have been engaged in the Pilot MLE Schools. Community involvement has been ensured in the field of using the language of the child in the classroom. Training of teachers is imparted and monitoring group to MLE schools have also been trained. The schools are operational and outcomes between these seven months are:

- Irregularity of the student in the classroom is decreased
- Creation of child friendly atmosphere in the classroom.
- Able to communicate freely in the classroom
- Active participation in the learning process
- Fear and Shyness reduced

Community involvement in MLE School is encouraging. Some of the responses are:

- Community members and Parents Shows their keen interest in the teaching process and involved in the teaching learning process.
- The establishment of school museum in the MLE classroom involves the community in a meaningful way.
- Reflection of culture in the School curriculum

- MLE provides a very good platform for documentation and storage of community resources.

Impact of MLE in other teachers are also revealing. Some of them are being

- In the opinion of others teachers MLE classroom transaction is more result oriented.
- The presence of Mother tongue teacher able to reduce the irregularity of students particularly in class-1.
- Inclusion of traditional game, song, dance and story in the school curriculum able to create child friendly atmosphere inside the classroom.
- Small children are no more shy and can freely express their feelings inside the classroom

Capacity Building Through District Institutes of Educational Training DIETs

State Council of Educational Research and Training (SCERT) Orissa has taken adequate steps to translate the MLE.DIETs are the district level academic support institutions under SCERT. Seven DIET staff has been actively involved in the training process at the state level and also in the field level activities. Interestingly, because of their new awareness, many of the DIET staff has changed their beliefs after MLE training was imparted to them and after understanding the education of tribal children from their socio-cultural context.

Monitoring and Supervision

The existing establishment challenges any new innovation or creativity. Education of equity for the disadvantaged children does not escape this reality. Some key stakeholders' reactions to teaching the tribal children in their mother tongue is well known to those who have struggled for multi-lingual education. One gap is the misconception of field functionaries due to non availability of training and orientation on new theories and methods that are being implemented. Another is their traditional make belief that do not allow them to adopt the new concepts and programmes. Therefore many noble ideas fail in the field.

The Zakir Hussain Center for Educational Studies, Jawaharlal Nehru University, New Delhi under the leadership of Prof. Ajit Kumar Mohanty, has agreed to provide academic support and community based monitoring support to MLE in Orissa in two languages, i.e. Saora in Gajapati district and Kui in Kondhmal district. The Center will help the pilot MLE schools in the following ways:

- By providing field support through training of the community on language and curriculum,
- School management and
- Preparation of some young people and community leaders for school monitoring for the coming three years.

Eight schools (four from Saora and four from Kui) have been identified and considerable engagement of the community is being sought for support and staff from the community has been engaged for monitoring. This should help in community ownership of the project, as well as to understand the importance of the community's own language and culture in education.

In order to address the implementation of MLE in the field, field functionaries need to be briefed about the project and their assistance in monitoring will be necessary. Therefore the District Level functionaries like BRCCs and CRCCs and the concerned headmasters of the MLE pilot schools have been trained on MLE concepts and the process of implementation.

MLE in Orissa is a new area of intervention addressing the issues related to education of tribal children where the teachers and the community are brought together. An important by-product of this intervention hoped for in tribal communities is the maintenance of their cultural identity and an improvement in the literacy rate. This would be the contribution of education—to improve literacy as well as enriching the cultural plurality of Orissa.

A series of workshops have been conducted in Bhubaneswar, Orissa for preparation of Curriculum and Instructional materials during 2006-07. These have been based on an understanding of the cultural themes of the tribal community. They have resulted in the preparation of a locally based curriculum as per the National Curriculum Framework 2005 syllabus.

Monthly resource day meetings will be held every fourth Saturday among the MLE pilot school teachers. Feed back and monitoring will take place during the implementation of MLE in the field.

Other Initiatives

In addition to the MLE as a pilot initiative, other initiatives have been taken up in Orissa. One is SRUJAN and another is RUPANTAR.

What is SRUJAN?

Srujan is a cluster approach to community-based, child friendly and culturally appropriate intervention for tribal education.

This programme envisions the following:

- Ensured access by identifying the out of school children/dropout children and by mobilizing their parents;
- Ensured regular attendance of enrolled children in the school by activating the VEC/MTA and parents;
- Creating a child friendly atmosphere in the school through adopting child centred activities which are familiar to the children (games, music, art, craft, tales, songs);
- Bridging the gap of home language and school language in the school /classroom for better learning of tribal children;
- Tapping community resources (oral and material resources) for curricular support;
- Developing school-community interaction and responsibility by PRIs and traditional tribal leaders;
- Creating a local resource pool in the CRC for tribal education;

The Cluster approach to tribal education involves the following activities displayed in the following table.

No	School type	Issues	Interventions
1.	Schools with 100%-90% tribal children.	*Gap of home language and school language *Community awareness	Teaching in language of the children (L1)
2.	Weak VECS/passive PRIs/non-involvement traditional leaders	Role clarity and responsibility of community and PRIs is not assessed	Orientation of VECs on MLE Training of PRIs Jati Mahasabha
3.	High Dropouts	Lack of follow up in schools	Parental counseling
	Low achievement	Lack of proper subject competency	Analysis of LATS result: identifying the groups with low achievements, grouping them subject wise and remedial coaching
4.	Teacher absenteeism	Weak VEC	VEC empowerment
5.	Teachers skill/ attitude	Lack of training on MLE/language	Training on MLE Attitudinal training
6.	Child unfriendly atmosphere	Lack of child friendly atmosphere	Activities: Story telling festival Art, drawing and craft mela Traditional games/ sports Singing, dance and music (All day Saturday)
7.		Lack of tapping local resources (materials and oral)	Engagement of tribal youth as Educator/ Community mobilisers/ language resource teacher for MLE Preparation of village wise resource persons

Rupantar

Rupantar is a comprehensive teacher training programme to help bring a transformation in the mind of the teachers serving in tribal areas, so that increased responsibility results for tribal children and tribal area schools. This activity was introduced in eight DPEP districts of Orissa during 1997- 2001 and teachers from 55 tribal Blocks were trained. The initiation was witnessed with a lot of questions, but in the course of time, teachers of tribal areas started rethinking their role in the classroom and society in the context of tribal education. Language played a major role in understanding the education of tribal children and their connection to society. Prior to the training a teacher was asking "what shall I do? The tribal children don't understand my language." But the after effect of the training was meaningful when a teacher said, "What shall I do if I don't understand the language of the children?"

Why Attitudinal Training?

Attitudinal Training (AT) is a necessary component of any teachers training (TT). Why is attitudinal training (AT) of teachers important? When attitude is referred to, it usually means a particular idea or assumption, which forms the basis of one's behaviours and actions. How we think or act is largely determined by our beliefs or ideas about certain things. Attitudes therefore are an important determinant of behaviour.

If behaviour is to be changed or modified, it comes from a change in attitudes. However changing of attitudes is not an easy task because they have been formed over the years and are often taken for granted. Though some attitudes are positive and promote healthy growth of the mind, the attitudes detrimental to growth and development of the mind have to be done away with.

With regard to teacher training, the attitude of teachers towards tribal children, their culture, text books, transactional methods, curriculums etc, have to be first understood. Wherever a particular attitude comes in the way of healthy development of the mind and fosters negative thinking it has to be removed. Therefore the aim of Attitudinal Training (AT) is to question the underlying values and belief systems, which determine behaviors and removes from the mind those beliefs and assumptions which are contrary to healthy thinking.

Attitudinal Training (AT) is different from Teachers Training in many ways. Teachers Training usually equips the teachers with a knowledge base on:

- The importance of activity based teaching
- How to teach Language, Mathematics and EVS
- How to handle multigrade classroom situations
- How to handle multilevel grades inside the classroom
- How to improve transactional strategies inside the classroom.

Though Teachers Training is useful in making the teachers aware of newer and better methods of making learning more meaningful and enjoyable, it does not address many more crucial issues. There is little attempt to help the teachers understand the psychology of tribal children and to study the world through their eyes. No emphasis is laid on making the teacher's sensitive to the socio-cultural milieu of tribal children and understands their emotions and sentiments. The psychological factors leading to fear and apprehensions in the minds of tribal children, failures in class, the increasing rate of dropouts and consistent poor performance is often neglected. Also, the ethnic stereotypes of teachers towards the tribal society, tribal children and tribal culture have not been broken through to develop a healthy educational milieu.

However a closer look at all these problems reveals that a teacher plays a major role in the life of the child. The reasons for failure or better performance can be attributed to the role played by a teacher inside the classroom. The positive attitude of teachers toward children will go a long way in creating an environment of mutual love, cooperation and trust, thereby encouraging children to come to school regularly and also to perform better.

Attitudinal Training (AT) therefore aims at making the teachers rethink their traditional teaching practices and styles, question their personal beliefs and assumptions which they initially took for granted, remove some of these prejudices and think of ways of making themselves more endearing to the tribal children and their culture. This automatically reflects in enrolment, retention and greater achievement.

To summarize the difference between Teachers Training and Attitudinal Training (AT)

1. Concept	Teachers Training aims at bettering pedagogic skills, class room transactions.	Attitudinal Training makes the teachers sensitive to issues concerning the psychology of tribal children. Analyse and reflect on their emotions and actions, which could have affected children psychologically.
2. Methodology :	Discussion and analysis in a straightforward manner.	Indirect attempt to discover the inherent values, beliefs, practices, assumptions, biases and prejudices with a view to change them.
3. Implications :	Improved teaching methods, better classroom transactions	Change in attitude. Moving beyond the boundaries of the textbook and understanding the child. Linking the background of the child with the textbooks teaching methods, thereby leading to better teacher community interaction and pupil-pupil interaction.

OBJECTIVES OF ATTITUDINAL TRAINING

- Identification and sensitization of teachers on attitudinal issues and to develop training strategies and the skill to do the session planning.
- To assess the attitude of teachers towards tribal children as learners and also as a cultural group. The attitudinal training topics are language, culture, children, and parents, teaching methods.

- Identify the current social bias, which stands against tribal education and its reflection in the textbook and transactional strategies.
- Examine the beliefs, assumptions and stereotypes of the teachers about tribal children and their culture
- To acknowledge that it is not the tribal child, rather the school and the class room transactions that create problem in the growth of the tribal children and their learning outcomes.
- To make the teacher non-judgmental, less ethnocentric and dismissive.
- To tune the school and the teacher towards identifying the potentials of tribal children so as to know how the tribal children learn in their social atmosphere.
- To understand and make use of the tribal language, culture, and customs in the learning processes of the children.
- Identify strategies to link the language resources of tribal children with the medium of instruction at school and to know the process in which a child learns language.
- Develop basic approaches towards language, arithmetic, EVS, using the knowledge base from the natural and cultural environment of tribal children.
- To make use of tribal folklore in the learning process to make the classroom contextualized (in language, EVS and arithmetic).
- Identify the concepts, skills, information, and attitudes required by the teachers to understand and make the school suitable to tribal children.

Targets

At present, Orissa SSA has adopted three major programmes.

1. MLE in 200 monolingual schools of 10 tribal languages in 26 Blocks of 8 districts
2. Srujan: (Cluster approach to tribal education) in 141 Blocks over a period of 2 – 3 years. At present in 2007-08 only 35 Blocks have been adopted on pilot basis.
3. Rupantar: Additional attitudinal training will be imparted in 141 tribal Blocks where more than 60 % teachers are non tribals, needing an understanding of tribal language, culture and education of indigenous children in their tribal context.

Conclusion

The MLE curriculum, community involvement, teachers who speak the indigenous child's language, work together with the Srujan and Rupantar programs to overcome the problems encountered by Tribal children.

Future activities include extending the MLE program up to Class Seven, as well as introducing mother tongue education into early childhood education within the Anganwadi system.

Orissa is part of a growing movement in India at the forefront of educational change. Three other states—Andhra Pradesh, Jharkand and Chhattisgarh, are also embarking on similar programs. Orissa's program is unique in its emphasis on community involvement through its Srujan and Rupantar programs.

RESOURCE SUPPORT:

International Resource persons:

Prof. Debiprasanna Pattanayak, Ex Director, Central Institute of Indian Languages, Mysore at present in Bhubaneswar.

Prof. Khageswar Mohapatra,Viswa Bharati, Shantiniketan, and Ex Director, Academy of Tribal Dialects and Culture, Bhubaneswar.

Dr Ajit Kumar Mohanty, Prof. Psychology in JNU, New Delhi.

Mr Steve Simpson, International Consultant of Literacy, Summer Institute of Linguistics, Canada.

Mrs Vicky Simpson, International Consultant, Linguist, SIL, Canada

Contact for information

spd@opepa.in

Contact: mkmfolk@ gmail.com

URL : www.opepa.in

1 Jhingran, D, language Disadvantaged, 2005 pp.

2 Tove Skutnab kangas,

3 Cummins Jim, BICS and CALP, in web site : www.jimcummins.com

4 Mackenzie P, 2004, A Master Trainers Manual on MLE in Andhra Pradesh, (2004)

33

Educating Tribal Children : A Suggestive Framework for the NGOs

—Nanjunda D.C., Parvathy D.C. and Chinnappa D.E.

The work of NGOs in the fields of primary education, micro-financing and alternative income generation programmes have also made important contribution in the effort to spreading education among tribal and rural India. However, unless NGOs make significant improvement in their performance in promoting sustainable livelihood for the poor their best efforts may not prove sufficient for empowerment through education.

Despite the formation of specific policies and projects for dealing with improvement of educational status of the tribals, and the implementation of a large number of programmes by the government and NGOs in pursuance of these policies, the impact on tribal education in the country is minimal. The basic reason for the failure of many programmes is that they are simply not designed to do so. All programmes, which will be implemented by the NGOs, should be geographically and culturally specific.

Experts are of the opinion that as long as prejudice continues to exist regarding value of education it would be difficult to reform them. Simple legislation is not enough. Since along with prejudice, acute economic crisis is the prime reason behind non-accepting of reforms through education the only method of convening parents is by compensating the family adequately for the loss of income. In this corner point, all NGOs must and should think rather than to provide some alternative income generation programme to assisting producers organizations. If NGOs seriously wants to be in this field and, if so, necessarily specialize and they should think much larger scale programmes and projects. Not only this, they should have high quality of human resource to mange themselves as organizations and their operations in a more

Since tribal education has some socio-economic touch NGOs should requires long term multi-pronged strategy to be carried out on a continuous basis. Although at policy level NGOs have been perceived as developmental agents, yet the scene at the grassroots level is not always in consonance with this subjectivity. It is so because base level Government functionaries some time see NGOs workers as outside encroaching/ occupying their space. (Baland and Robinson, 2001). And on other side few NGOs thinks different Governament agencice are the main hurdles in their way. This may be the major weakness of many NGOs Their mutual interactions and even collaboration makes the effort more effective.

Here both Government and voluntary agencies should change their attitude and should be complimentary to each other and must take confidence in each other. The NGOs should make a lot of homework in making people's participation in educating and training to improve their of professional skills, overcoming behavior and cultural resistance of tribal communities may be preferably involved in tackling the problem of educational development and always they should try to became closer to the tribal people. Many NGOs believe economic compulsion is not only the reason why parents are not sending their children to school. The recent survey shows that more than 29.27% of tribal working children is the need to supplement the family income while only 7.56% of child worker were required to gain employment to earn a minimum living for their families. Only 1.56% are working part time, to finance their own education besides contributing to the inadequate family income. So all NGOs must think in the way of giving more and more low cost job oriented education and their by encouraging more women joining the work force besides empowerment of tribal women would go a long way in elimination prejudieous about education.

Apart from parents disinterest in education, the second main reason is the present pattern of education system in our country.

Many tribal children are not attending schools because their parents want them to work for the reasons other than economic crises. For example child might lost his interest in the education, failed in the same class many times, corporal punishment by the teachers, parents might wanted to continue their family occupations in the early age, hanging with bad friends, threat of probable unemployment in the future, earn additional income to the family, etc. Hence NGOs should think about present education scenario and better concentrate on these topics.

Since many parents do not under stand the significance of the education, NGOs have to work to create awareness about the value of the education. As soon as possible NGOs should open *Home work centers* where any school going child can come and get help to complete his home work under the guidance of a trained teacher, and *Community play centers* where all children come and can play any games like carum, chess and volleyball-etc. if so few problems related to the educational aspects of can be solved. All children would have certain inherent skills. It is necessary to equip with certain skills suited their aptitude, NGOs should conduct most advanced type vocational training courses and must be more suitable to the dropout children because these dropout children are potential child laborers. These courses should be suited for child worker in general and in vocations for those working children who combine their work with studies. Also in order to provide opportunity to working girls for supplementing the family income NGOs should take some step to develop co-operative societies. Through this, young working girls having responsibility for organizing training, making raw materials, available and selling the products goods to the market.

Learning from others

Organizations like DEED, ROAD, CROSS and Cultural Survive are some of the important NGOs working on tribal education Issues and have valuable lesson from the field to others. In Karnataka especially Rural Organization For Appropriate Development (ROAD) a Mysore-(Karnataka) based NGOs has successfully implemented all above mentioned programmes in its working area. But before learn any thing from others they have to concede that the work being done by agencies is addressing the same education relaed issues as the NGOs are trying to grapple with. But it is impordent to note that, each NGOs will have different ideas regarding poverty focus, community acceptance, beneficiary owner ship, funds, human resource, planing strategies-etc.

Resources from the Mainstream

1. Finances

Since almost all NGO's is totally depend on either foreign or Indian grants for their activities, it is necessary to rise capital from mainstream sources, such as the development financial institutions and the bank. If so it will have two benefits; first it will make NGO's more accountable in terms of effective use of money ad also it opens much larger sources of funds that foreign and Indian grants. Almost all-financial institutions like SIDBI, ICICI, NABARD, IDIBI have by accumulated years of experience in funding NGOs through grants for experimental projects NGOs can approach these institutes to get fund as loans with longer than normal repayment and moratorium periods and lower interest rate or they can rise money from the corporal sectors.

2. Human resources

NGOs are known to have highly experienced and committed individuals. Many NGOs have good grassroots worker but not at middle levels. If so, the grassroots worker may not get any guidance and support. So NGOs should hire more experienced persons in education, Anthropologists and experts in other related field. If NGOs would like to move from direct implementing agencies to supporting producers organization, they need to have higher caliber of people at all levels is accentuate. Those in support roles have to be more versatile, having broad-based knowledge of various cultural factors which are hindering the tribal education programmes successfully (Basu and Van, 1998).

3. Technology

As another step towards effectiveness in implementation educational related programmes NGOs need to have link with various technology generation institutions blessed with a very large scientific and technological research infrastructure in

India. For example ICAR, IVTC (Institute of Vocational Training Center), etc. in addition to state level research and training institutes. Since education issue is related to more than one field NGOs should get a lot of technical support from these institutions. The presence of professionally trained staff in NGOs greatly facilitates this process of acquiring technology and adaptation to the local situation and to the poor triabl families.

Training should be relative to the ground situation and executed by the professionals only. Training techniques have to be related to the experience of the participants and must simultaneously appeal to their thinking and emotions. Behavioral games, stimulation's and case study basses discussions are some useful techniques and visit to other organizations will be also be useful.

4. Expertise

NGOs should have a vast pool of technical experts and professionals specialized in project finance, socio-economic analysis, training and capacity building, technical aspects, computing, tribal infrastructure, tribal financial institutions, planning, monitoring and evaluation, etc.

5. Knowledge

As education is a complex phenomenon all NGOs should have certain useful concepts which have a bearing on successful educational related programmes like.

1 NGOs should understand social structure, caste and class problem, dynamic of social changes, political economy of resources and policy analysis of tribals (Verma, 1998).

2 communication theory; diffusion of innovation; group dynamics and collective action; training and organization development; and any appropriate educational technology

6 Skills tribal education related specialist NGOs should have certain.

Following Skills

— Wining, confidence of tribal people

— Building them to try out new ideas

— Conducting detailed feasibility studies

— Identifying and tying up with source of in puts

— Acquiring and adaptation of new educational technology

— Professional training to the staff and policy makers (Mahajan 1993).

Conclusion

In this paper a strong argument has been made that tribal education related NGOs should re-examine their approaches in this field due to it's inherent complexity and difference rather than relief and welfare programmes. They should exclusively focus on educated related issues only. If these kinds of NGOs could succeed in promoting sustainable livelihood for the poor, so that they can develop requisite level of expertise in tribal development related sub sectors. And NGOs must think of much larger scale projects and draw financial and human resource from the mainstream. Policies and projects should adopt a holistic approach, taking in to the consideration socio economic set-up of working area. They should also enter into collaborative relation ships with Governament agencies and other NGOs. NGOs try hard to solve grass-root level of problem and they should think in upgradtion of living standards and education status more particularly of the tribal women and children. More than this, NGOs should learn in employment generation in non-agricultural sectors will increase demand for quality education from the parents.

References

Ambasht, 1970 'A Critical Study of Tribal Education', New Delhi: Chand & Co.

Anjali Kurane 2005 Socio-economic development among the Warlis of Maharashtra in Dimensions of research in Anthropology Vol. 2 Serial Publication Delhi.

Basu, Ashok Ranjan and Nijhawan Satish. (1995) *Tribal Development Administration in India.* New Delhi: Mittal Publications.

Chatterjee, 2000 Educational Development of Scheduled Castes: Looking Ahead, Gyan Publishing House, New Delhi.

Chacko, M. Pariyaram (2005) *Tribal Communities and Social Change.* New Delhi. Saga Publications.

Chaudhri, D.P. (1997), 'Female Tribals and Gender Bias in Tribal Education in Indian States: 1961-1991.' The Indian Journal of Labour Economics, Volume 40, no. 3, pp. 493-505

Dash, K. N. (2004) *Invitation to social and cultural Anthropology*: New Delhi, Atlantic Publisher and Distributors.

Dash, K. N. (2004) Invitation to social and cultural Anthropology: New Delhi, Atlantic Publisher and Distributors.

Deshmukh, B. A. (2004) *Tribal Education. New Delhi*: Sonali Publications.

Deshmukh 2004 Tribal Education, Sonali Publication, New Delhi.

Gupta, Danda, 1984, *Tribal Education in India,* Anthr ical Survey of India, Calcutta

Kailash, G 1993 'Tribal Education and Occupation: Dynamics of Impact and Change', New Delhi: Nank Publication

Kumar A. 2002 Tribal Development in India, Sarup and Sons, New Delhi.

Kamlesh Mann. (1996) *Tribal women: on the Threshold of twenty-first century*. New Delhi, M.D. Publication PVT. LTd.

Kothari, B, Vijaya, P G, Chand S & Sharma, R (2000): *A Review of Primary Education Packages in Madhya Pradesh,* Indian Institute of Management, Ahmedabad.

Kumar, K, Priyam, M & Saxena, S (2001): *Looking Beyond the Smokescreen: DPEP and Primary Education in India,* Economic and Political Weekly, Vol. 36 No. 7

Kailash, G 1993 'Tribal Education and Occupation: Dynamics of Impact and Change', New Delhi: Nank Publication

Lieten, G.K., A.K. Karan & A.K. Satpathy (2005), Children, School and Work: Glimpses from India. New Delhi

Leclercq, F (2003): *Education Guarantee Scheme and Primary Schooling in Madhya Pradesh,* Economic and Political Weekly, Vol. 38 N0. 19

Mathur, H.M., 1996 'Anthropology and Development in Traditional Societies', New Delhi: Vikas Publishing.

Malhotra, O.P. (1998) *Tribal Education: Impact of Education on Tribal Life and Adjustment,* New Delhi. Cosmo Publications.

Mishra, S 1998 'Education of Tribal Children in Inida' (Internet)

Mathur, H.M., 1996 'Anthropology and Development in Traditional Societies', New Delhi: Vikas Publishing.

Mohanty, P.K 2002. *"Development of Primitive Tribal Groups in India,"* Kalpaz Publication: New Delhi

Manmatha Kundu 1994 Tribal Education: New Perspectives, Gyan Publishing House, New Delhi

Malhotra, O.P. (1998) *Tribal Education: Impact of Education on Tribal Life and Adjustment,* New Delhi. Cosmo Publications.

Meenakshi 2004 Policies and Strategies for Tribal development. Rawat Publications, Jaipur and New Delhi.

Makhan jha, 1995, *"An Introduction to Indian Anthropology,"* Vikas Publishng House, New Delhi

Prakash 2006 Development of Indian Tribes. Discovery Publishing House. New Delhi.

Patel, Tara. (1984) *Development of education Among Tribal Women.* Delhi: Mittal Publications.

Patel, M. L. 1994. *"Development and Dualism of Primitive Tribes"*, M.D Publications: New Delhi

Rao and Vaidehi Status of tribal education in TN, *Kurukshetra* 2004

Rajarshi Roy 2007 Ethno – Pedagogy, Education of tribes, teacher's training, and juxtaposition of status, Shipra Publications, Delhi.

Rajarshi Roy 2007 Ethno – Pedagogy, Education of tribes, teacher's training, and juxtaposition of status, Shipra Publications, Delhi.

Rao and Vaidehi Status of tribal education in TN, *Kurukshetra* 2004

Raina, V (2002): *Point by point response by Vinod Raina to the Note circulated by R.Gopalakrishnan, Secretary to the Chief Minister, Government of Madhya Pradesh, detailing the Government's case for closing down HSTP,* at url http://www.cisl.columbia.edu/grads/presi/EKLAVYA/HSTPreportResp.html posted in 2002, accessed on 2nd February 2006.

Raina, B (2006): *Anti-Reservation Protest: Shoring up Privilege,* Economic and Political Weekly, Vol. 41 No. 20

Rammurthy, A (1990): *Shiksha, Sanskriti Aur Samaj (Education, Culture and Society)*, (in Hindi) Shrambharati, Munger.

Sen, K M (2000): *Bharater Shanshkriti (The Culture of India)*, in Bengali, Viswabharati Publications, Santiniketan.

—————— (2000): *In the Wonderland of Primary Education* in *From Your School to Our School*, Rajiv Gandhi Shiksha Mission, Government of Madhya Pradesh.

Sujatha, 1994 'Quality education Educational Development among Tribes,' New Delhi: South Asian Publishers.

Sujatha, 1994 'Quality education Educational Development among Tribes,' New Delhi: South Asian Publishers.

Sharma, S. (2002). "Tribal Welfare and Development" Sarup and New Delhi: Sons Publications.

Singh, B. (1977). "Tribal Development at Cross Road" *Man in India*. 57(3): 229-247.

Shama, S. Ram. (1996) *Women's Education: A Conceptual Framework*. New Delhi: Discovery Publishing House.

Shah, P. Vimal and Patel Tara (1985). *Social Contexts of Tribal Education*. New Delhi: Concept Publishing Company.

Sharma S. Ram. (1996) *Education of Women of Scheduled Castes and Scheduled Tribes*. New Delhi: Discovery Publishing House.

Singh Bhupinder and Mahanti Neeti. (1995) *Tribal Education in India*. New Delhi: Inter- India Publications.

Sah 2004 Tribal Issues in India, Rawat Publication, Jaipur and Yatindra Singh Sisodia New Delhi.

Singh 1982 Economics of the tribes and their transformation, Concept publication.

Shah, P. Vimal and Patel Tara (1985). *Social Contexts of Tribal Education*. New Delhi: Concept Publishing Company.

Sharma S. Ram. (1996) *Education of Women of Scheduled Castes and Scheduled Tribes*. New Delhi: Discovery Publishing House,.

Singh Bhupinder and Mahanti Neeti. (1995) *Tribal Education in India*. New Delhi: Inter- India Publications

Shukala, 1998. 'Education of Indigenous People', www.google search.

Shama, S. Ram. (1996) *Women's Education: A Conceptual Framework*. New Delhi: Discovery Publishing House.

Saxena, *Draft National Policy on Tribals: Suggestions for Improvement*

Von Fürer-Haimendorf, Christoph. *Tribes of India: The Struggle for Survival*. Berkeley: University of California Press

Verma, R.1995. *"Indian Tribes Through the Ages,"* Publication Division, Ministry of I and B, Governament of India.

Vidut Joshi 1998 Tribal situation in India: Issues in Development, Rawat Publication, New Delhi.

Vinoba Gautam, 2003, Education of tribal children in India and the issue of Medium of Instruction: A Janshala experience

Vargheses, 1993 'Quality in Primary Education' New Delhi: BR Publishing House

Wazir, Rekha (ed.) (2000), The Gender Gap in Basic Education. NGOs as Change Agents. New Delhi: Sage Publications

Weiner, Myron (1991), The Child and the State in India. New Delhi: Oxford University Press

Index

D

M

T

GY/56